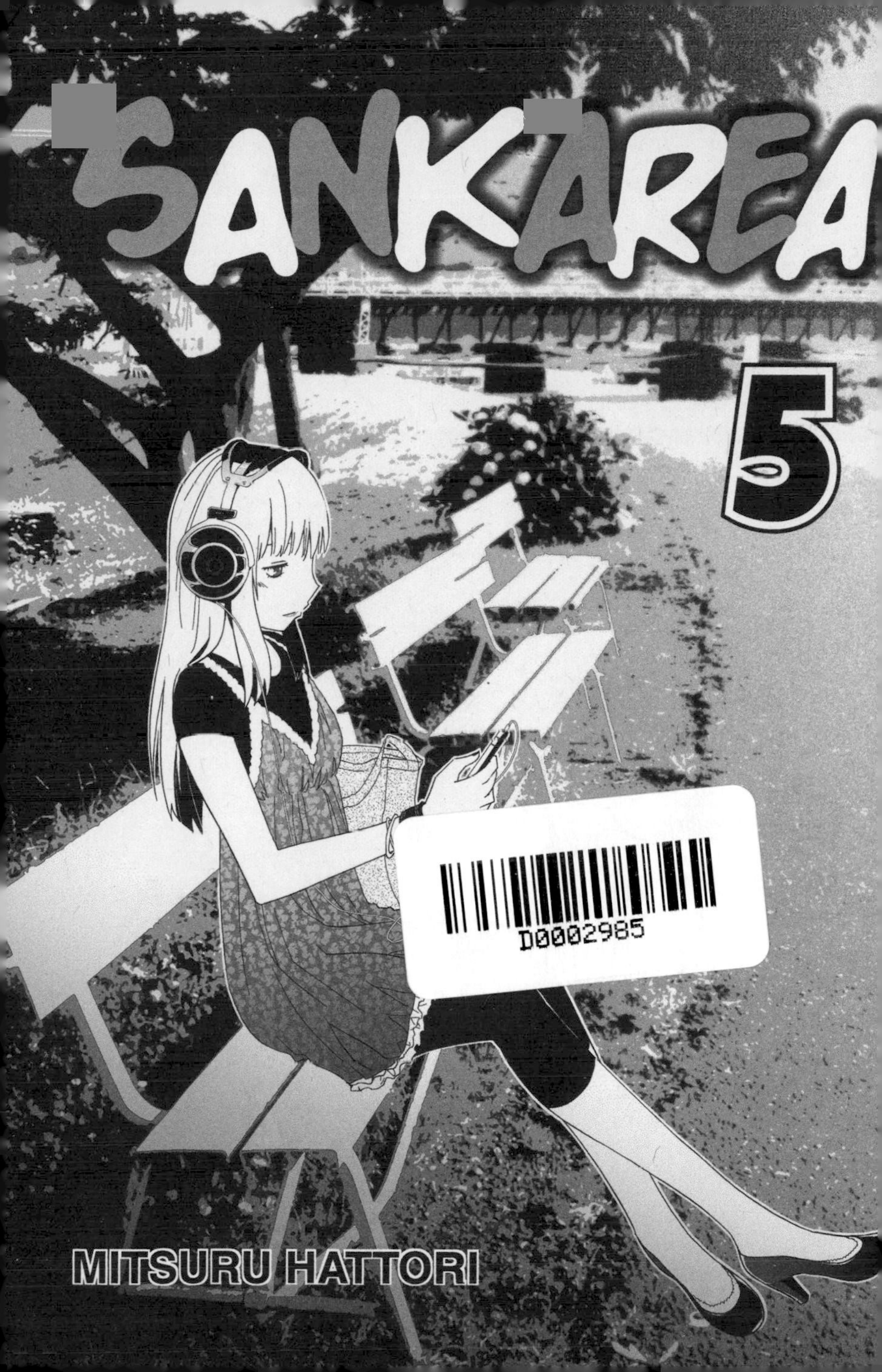
SANKAREA
5
MITSURU HATTORI

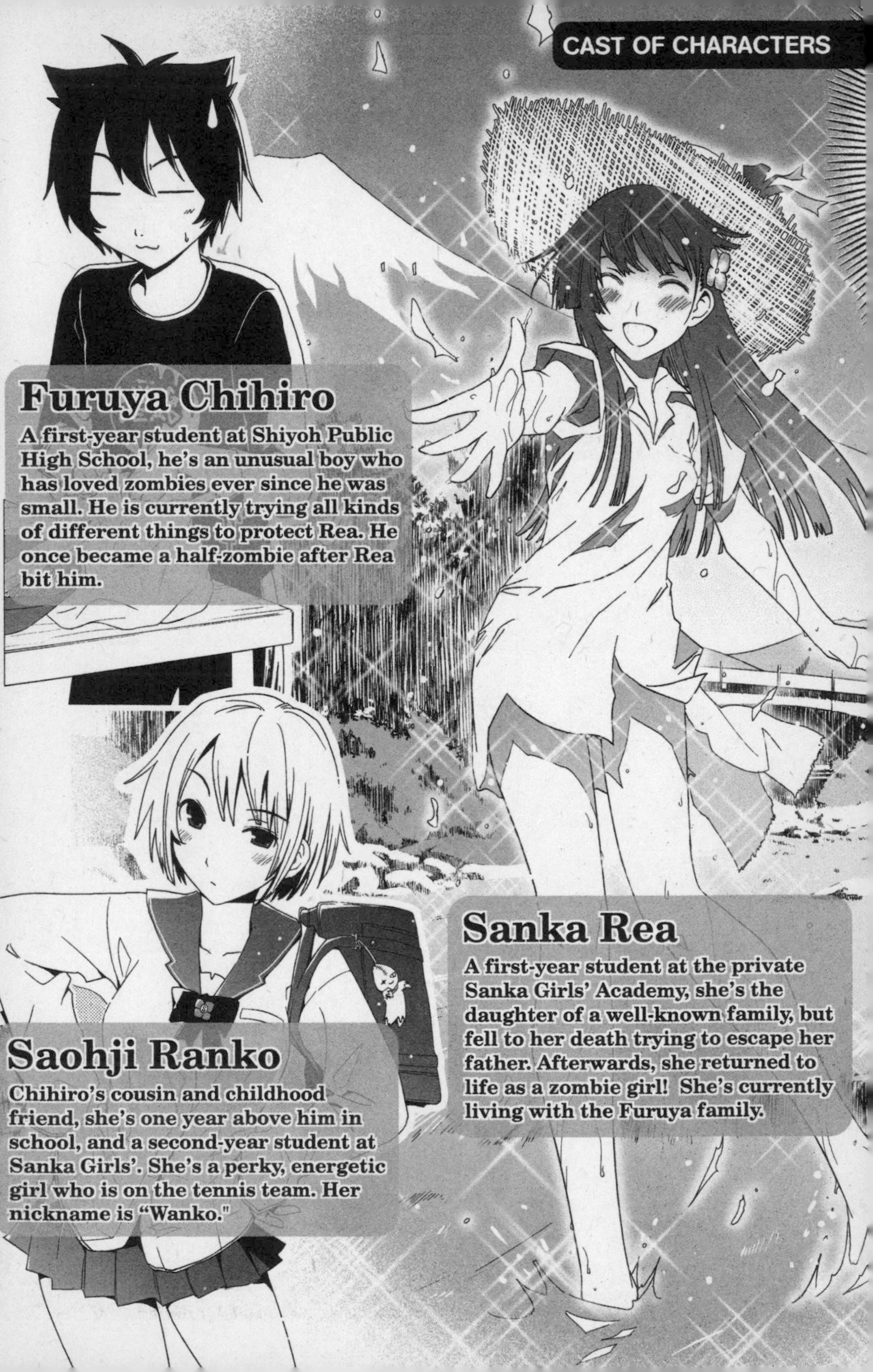

Furuya Chihiro

A first-year student at Shiyoh Public High School, he's an unusual boy who has loved zombies ever since he was small. He is currently trying all kinds of different things to protect Rea. He once became a half-zombie after Rea bit him.

Sanka Rea

A first-year student at the private Sanka Girls' Academy, she's the daughter of a well-known family, but fell to her death trying to escape her father. Afterwards, she returned to life as a zombie girl! She's currently living with the Furuya family.

Saohji Ranko

Chihiro's cousin and childhood friend, she's one year above him in school, and a second-year student at Sanka Girls'. She's a perky, energetic girl who is on the tennis team. Her nickname is "Wanko."

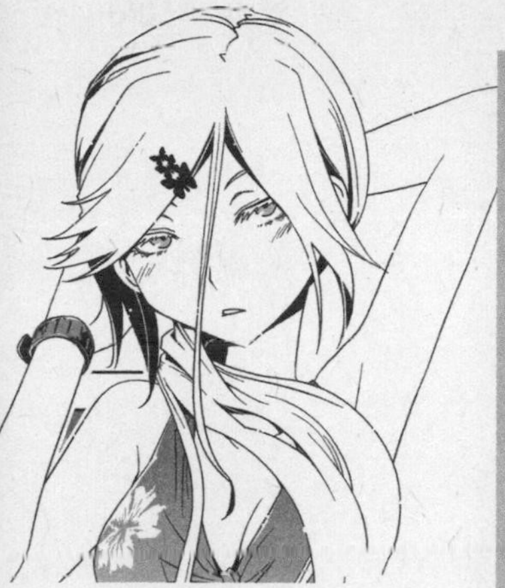

Kurumiya Darin Arciento

An expert in zombie research who came to Japan from the southern islands to visit "Professor Boyle" (Grandpa). She has a strange passion for her research. Despite her looks, she's younger than Rea.

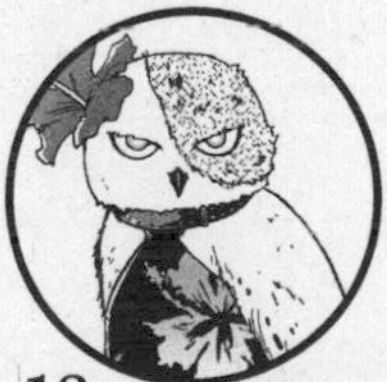

18

Darin's faithful pet. It's been zombified.

THE FURUYA FAMILY

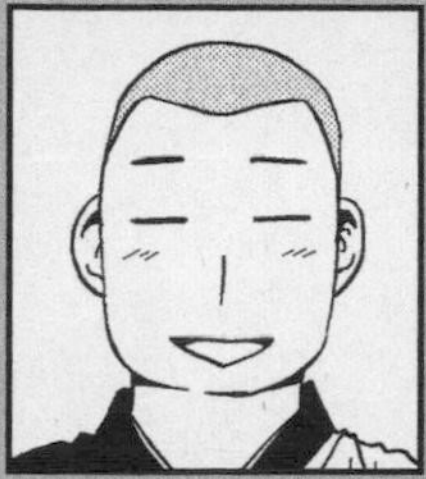

Dad

His real name is Furuya Dohn. He's the head priest at Shiryohji Temple. He agreed to Rea and Darin living in their home, saying only, "Should be fine, right?"

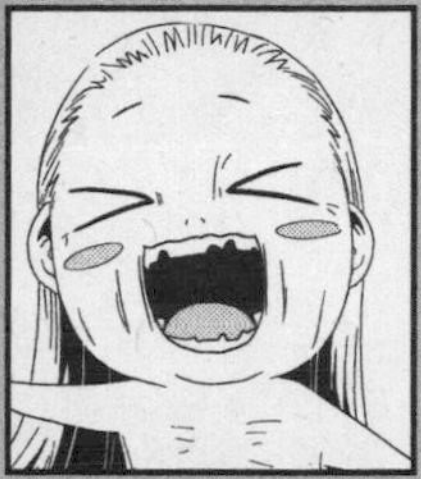

Grandpa

The most mysterious organism (?) of all in "Sankarea". Apparently he has studied zombies at an overseas research facility in the past...

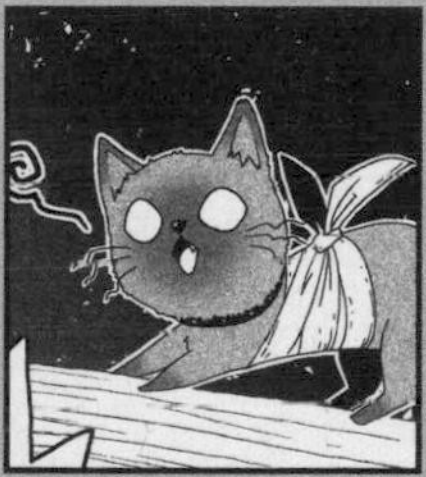

Bub

He was hit by a car and died, but came back to life thanks to the elixir Chihiro and Rea made.

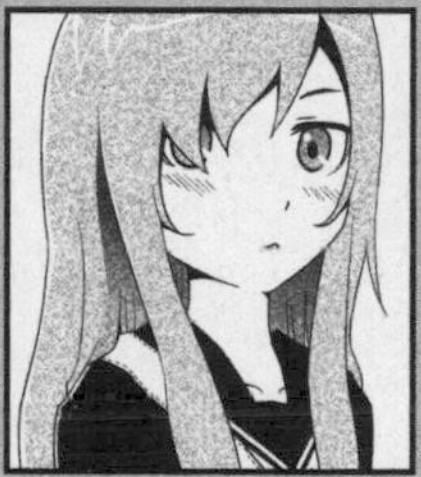

Furuya Mero

A reliable first-year middle school student, she manages all the housework for the Furuya family. She loves to read the Heart Sutra.

STORY

It's the night of the Shiyoh Festival. Following Ranko's advice, Rea faced up to her real feelings and invited Chihiro for a stroll on the riverbank. Enveloped in the mist, the two of them quickly drew close... but at that moment, Rea suddenly and unconsciously bit into Chihiro's neck. Shocked, Rea fled, binding herself in chains and trying to leave behind all her regrets, but Chihiro caught up with her at the ruined hotel where they met. Now a lightning strike causes the building to catch fire, and an irresistible impulse once again assails Rea's body...

MITSURU HATTORI presents

**IF... I WERE TO BECOME...
A ZOMBIE... THEN, I TOO...**

CONTENTS

**SANKAREA
ANECDOTES**

PAGE 106

SERIALIZED IN BESSATSU
SHONEN MAGAZINE,
SEPTEMBER 2011 –
JANUARY 2012.

SANKAREA 5

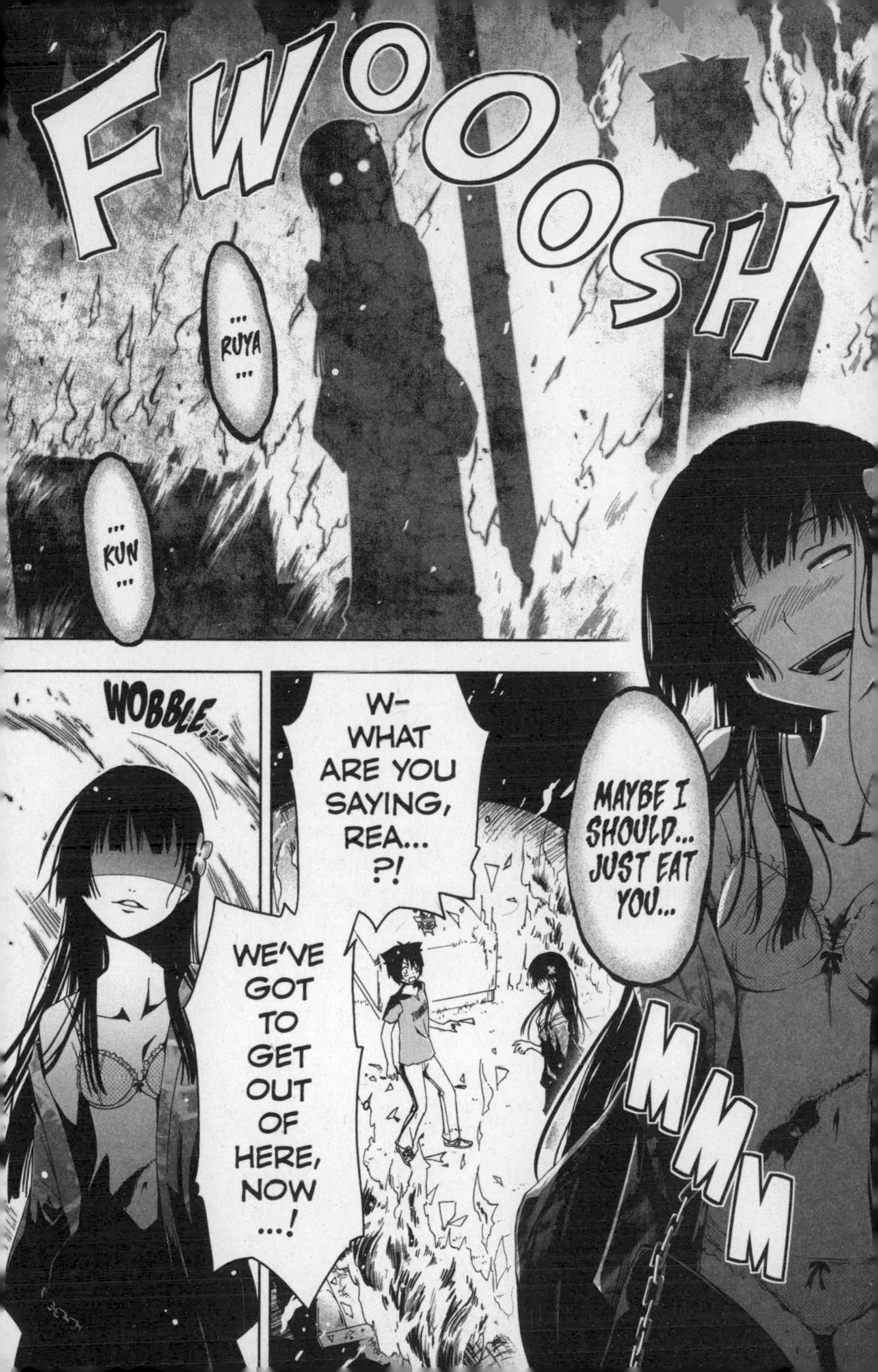
FWOOOSH
...RUYA...
...KUN...
MAYBE I SHOULD... JUST EAT YOU...
MMMM
W- WHAT ARE YOU SAYING, REA...?!
WOBBLE...
WE'VE GOT TO GET OUT OF HERE, NOW...!

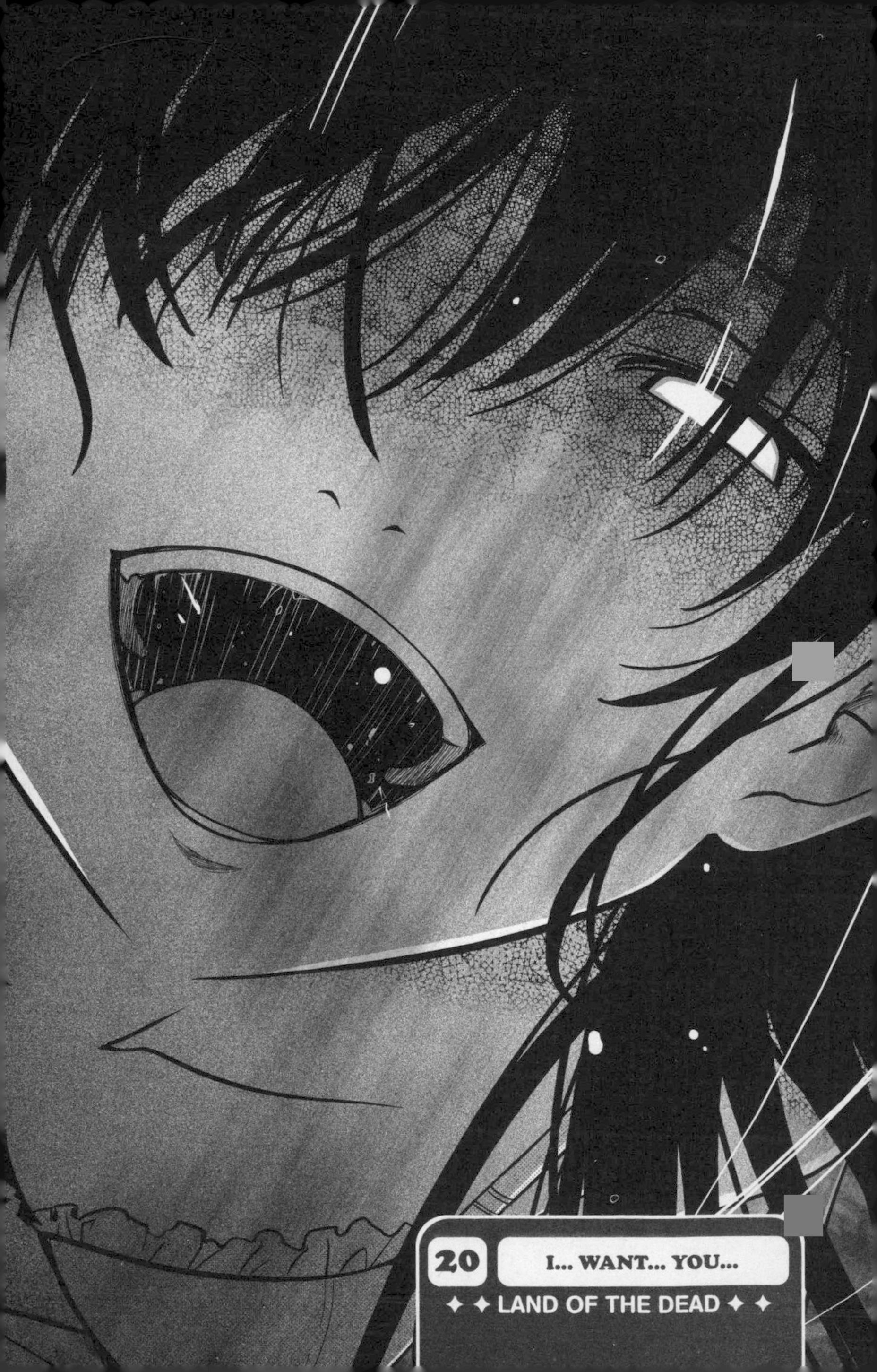
20
I... WANT... YOU...
✦ ✦ LAND OF THE DEAD ✦ ✦

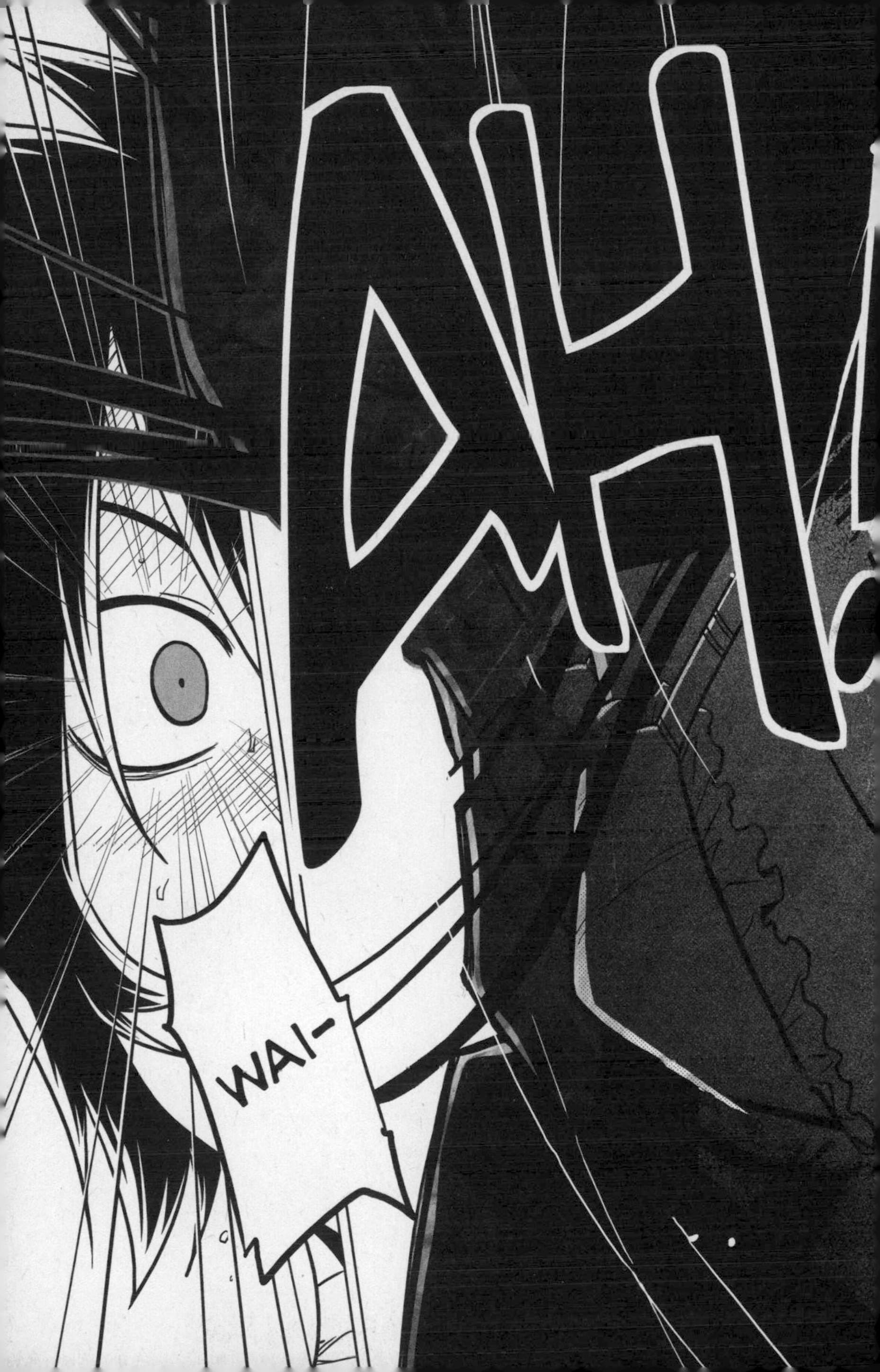
WAI-

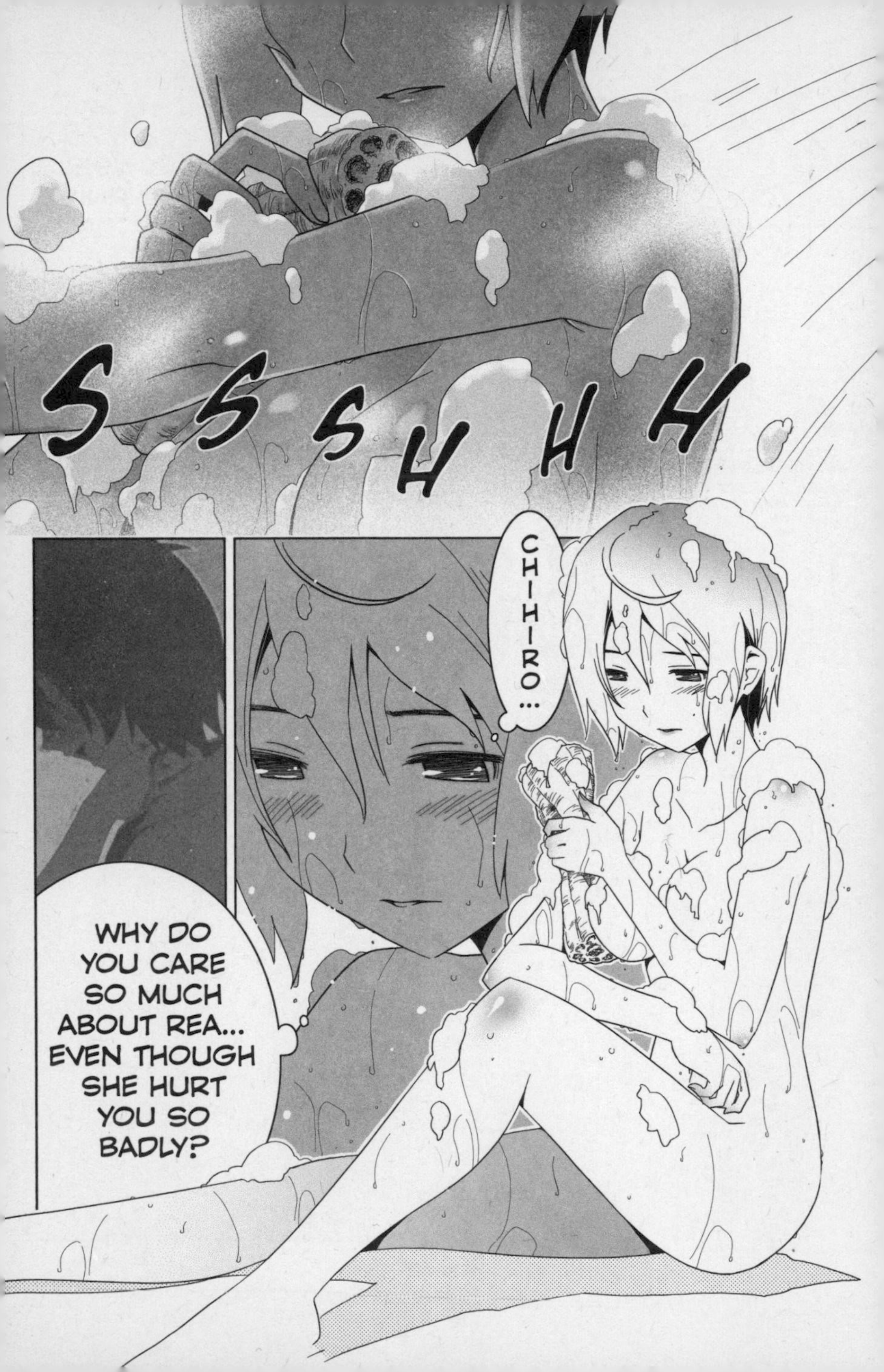
SSSHHH
CHIHIRO...
WHY DO YOU CARE SO MUCH ABOUT REA... EVEN THOUGH SHE HURT YOU SO BADLY?

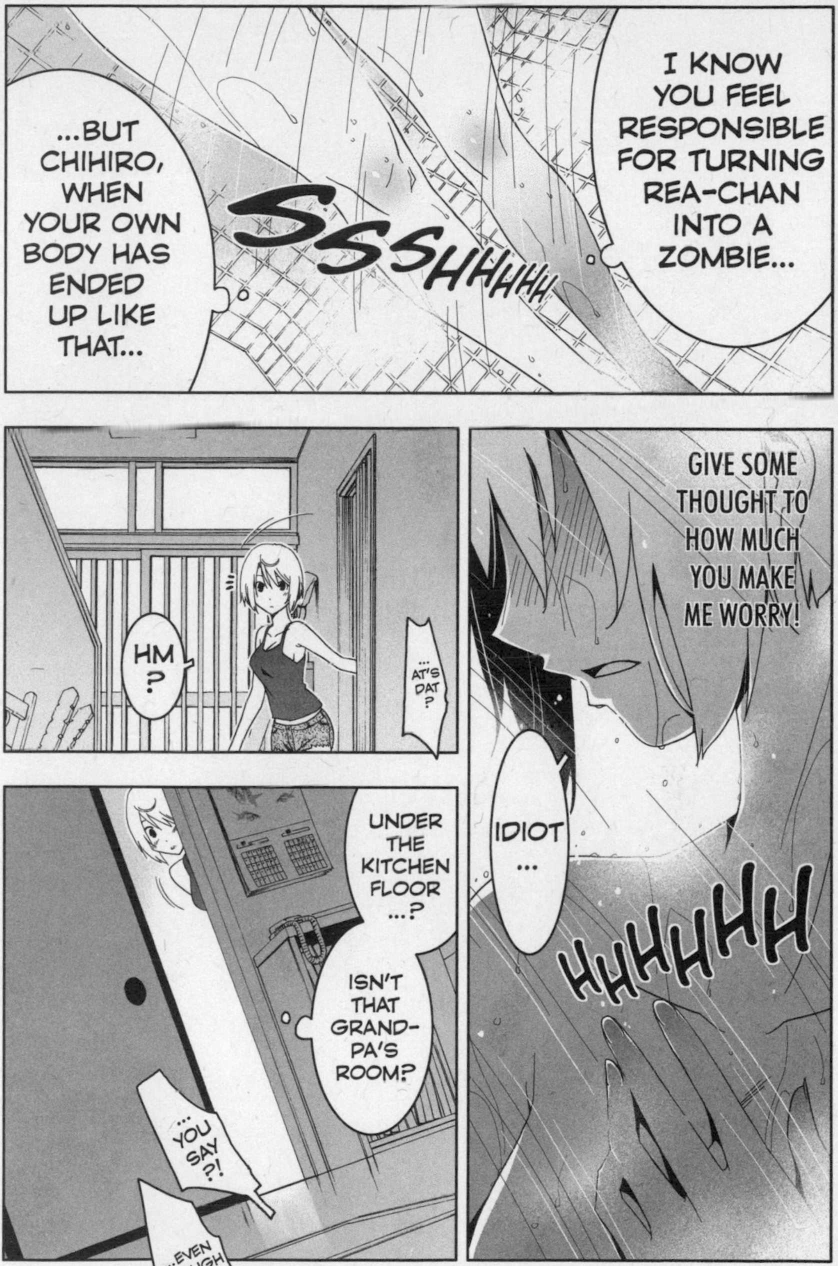
I KNOW YOU FEEL RESPONSIBLE FOR TURNING REA-CHAN INTO A ZOMBIE...
SSSHHHHH
...BUT CHIHIRO, WHEN YOUR OWN BODY HAS ENDED UP LIKE THAT...
GIVE SOME THOUGHT TO HOW MUCH YOU MAKE ME WORRY!
IDIOT ...
HHHHHH
...AT'S DAT?
HM?
UNDER THE KITCHEN FLOOR ...?
ISN'T THAT GRAND-PA'S ROOM?
...YOU SAY?!
...EVEN THOUGH ...!!

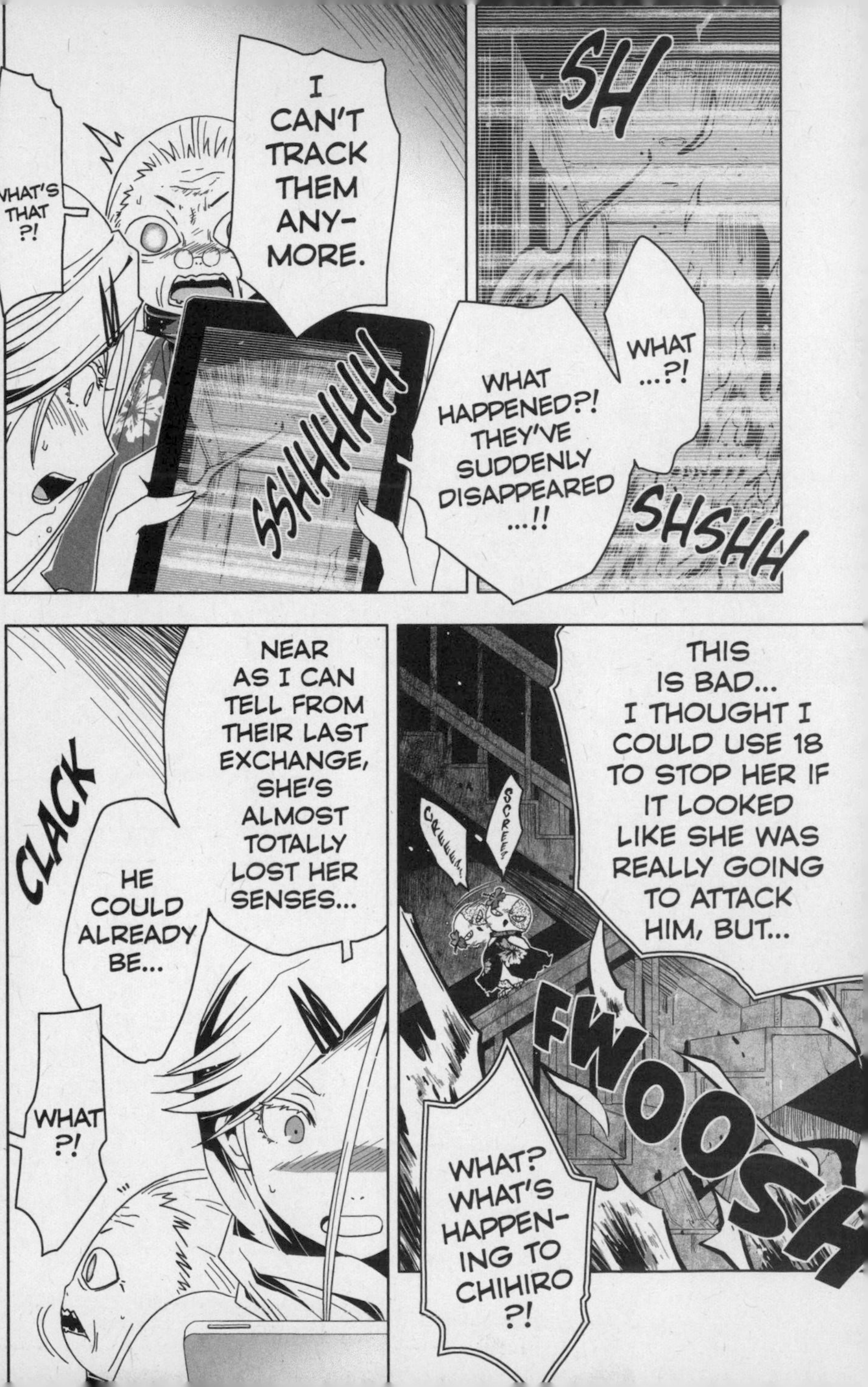
SH
WHAT ...?!
WHAT HAPPENED?! THEY'VE SUDDENLY DISAPPEARED ...!!
SHSHH
I CAN'T TRACK THEM ANY-MORE.
SSHHHH
WHAT'S THAT ?!
THIS IS BAD... I THOUGHT I COULD USE 18 TO STOP HER IF IT LOOKED LIKE SHE WAS REALLY GOING TO ATTACK HIM, BUT...
SCREEE...
CAWWWW...
FWOOSH
WHAT? WHAT'S HAPPEN-ING TO CHIHIRO ?!
NEAR AS I CAN TELL FROM THEIR LAST EXCHANGE, SHE'S ALMOST TOTALLY LOST HER SENSES...
CLACK
HE COULD ALREADY BE...
WHAT ?!

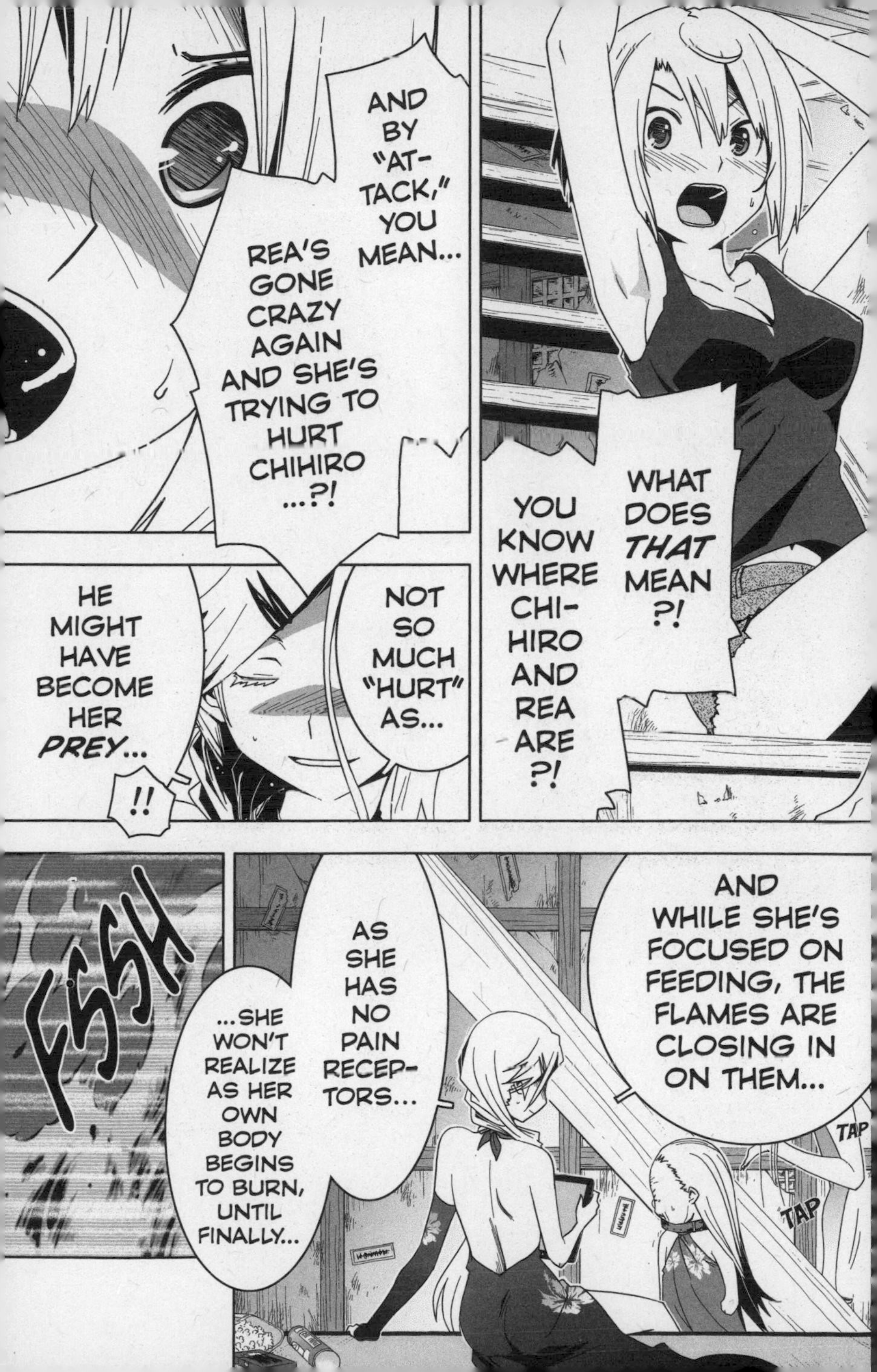
WHAT DOES *THAT* MEAN?!
YOU KNOW WHERE CHIHIRO AND REA ARE?!
AND BY "ATTACK," YOU MEAN...
REA'S GONE CRAZY AGAIN AND SHE'S TRYING TO HURT CHIHIRO...?!
NOT SO MUCH "HURT" AS...
HE MIGHT HAVE BECOME HER *PREY*...
!!
AND WHILE SHE'S FOCUSED ON FEEDING, THE FLAMES ARE CLOSING IN ON THEM...
TAP
TAP
AS SHE HAS NO PAIN RECEPTORS...
...SHE WON'T REALIZE AS HER OWN BODY BEGINS TO BURN, UNTIL FINALLY...
FSSH

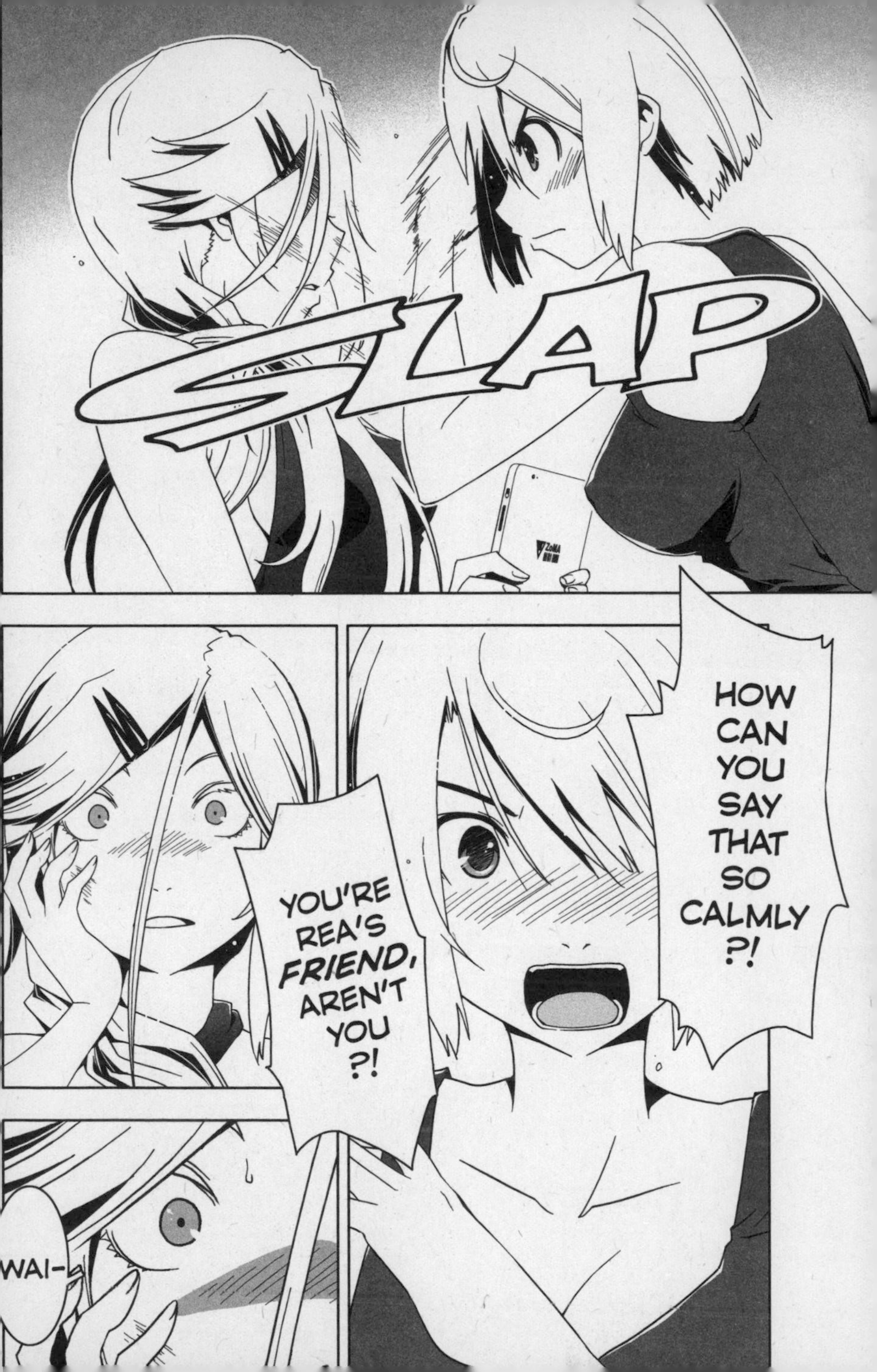
SLAP
HOW CAN YOU SAY THAT SO CALMLY?!
YOU'RE REA'S *FRIEND*, AREN'T YOU?!
WAI-

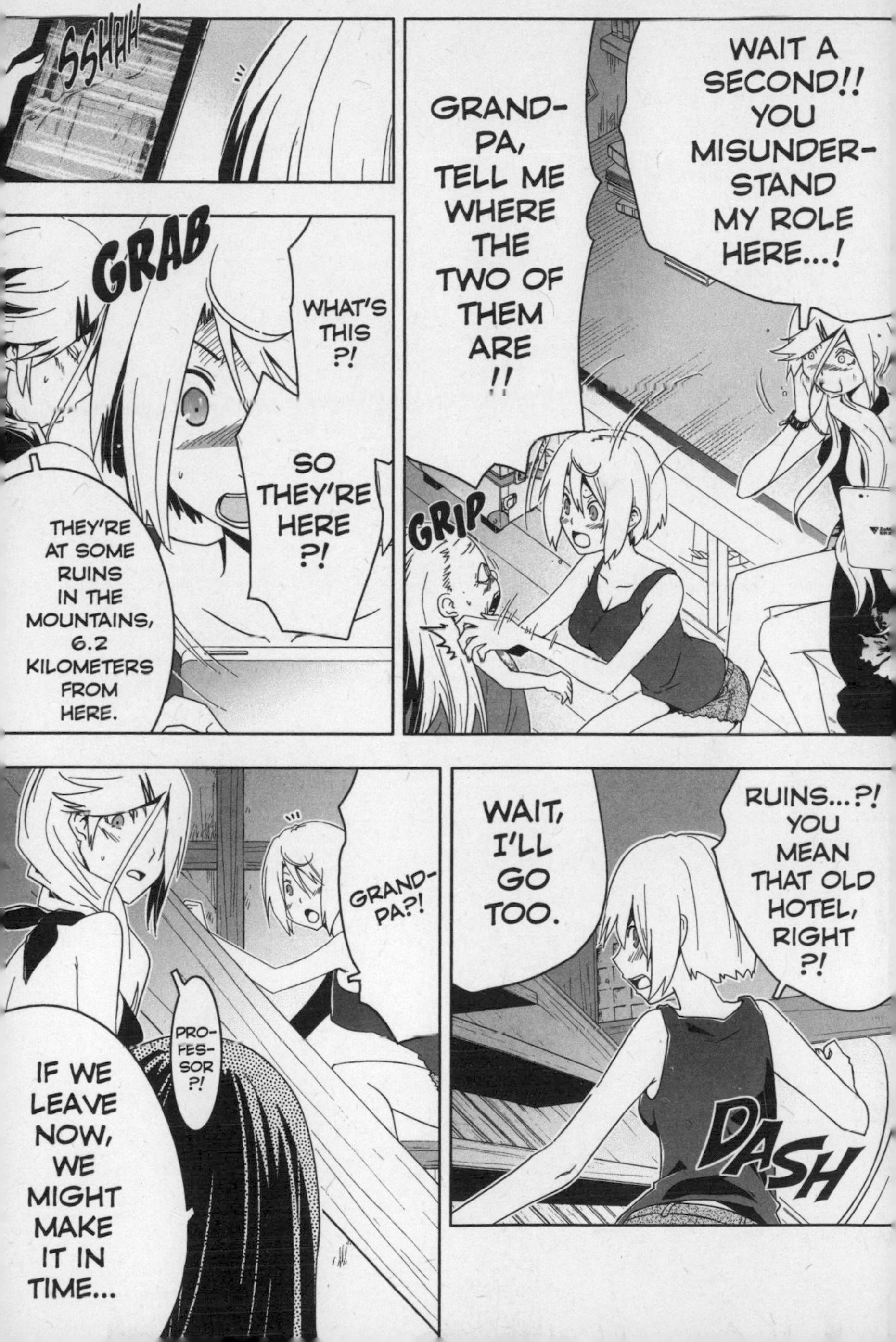
WAIT A SECOND!! YOU MISUNDERSTAND MY ROLE HERE...!
GRANDPA, TELL ME WHERE THE TWO OF THEM ARE!!
GRIP
SSHHH
WHAT'S THIS?!
GRAB
SO THEY'RE HERE?!
THEY'RE AT SOME RUINS IN THE MOUNTAINS, 6.2 KILOMETERS FROM HERE.
RUINS...?! YOU MEAN THAT OLD HOTEL, RIGHT?!
WAIT, I'LL GO TOO.
DASH
GRANDPA?!
PROFESSOR?!
IF WE LEAVE NOW, WE MIGHT MAKE IT IN TIME...

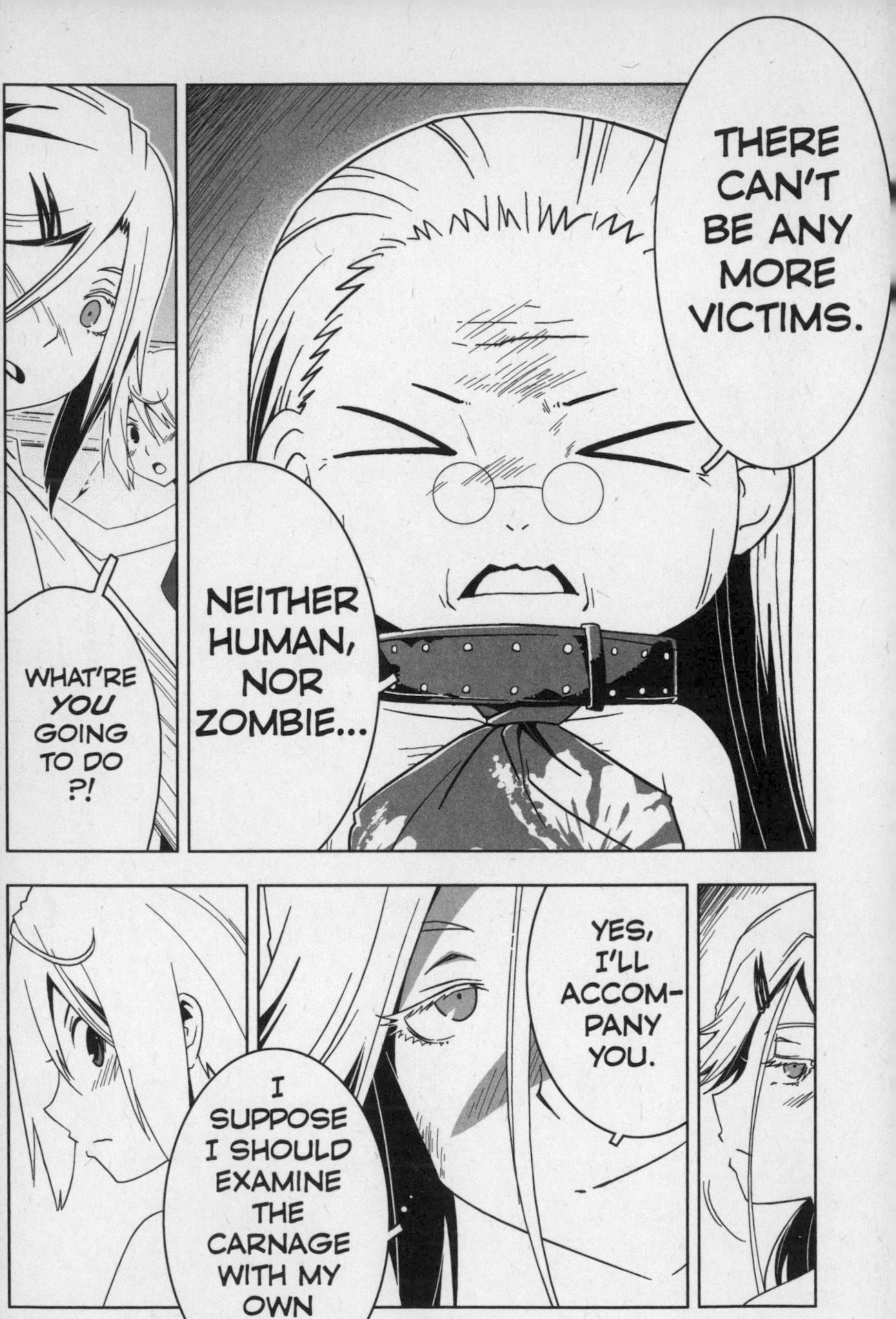
THERE CAN'T BE ANY MORE VICTIMS.
NEITHER HUMAN, NOR ZOMBIE...
WHAT'RE *YOU* GOING TO DO ?!
YES, I'LL ACCOM-PANY YOU.
I SUPPOSE I SHOULD EXAMINE THE CARNAGE WITH MY OWN EYES...

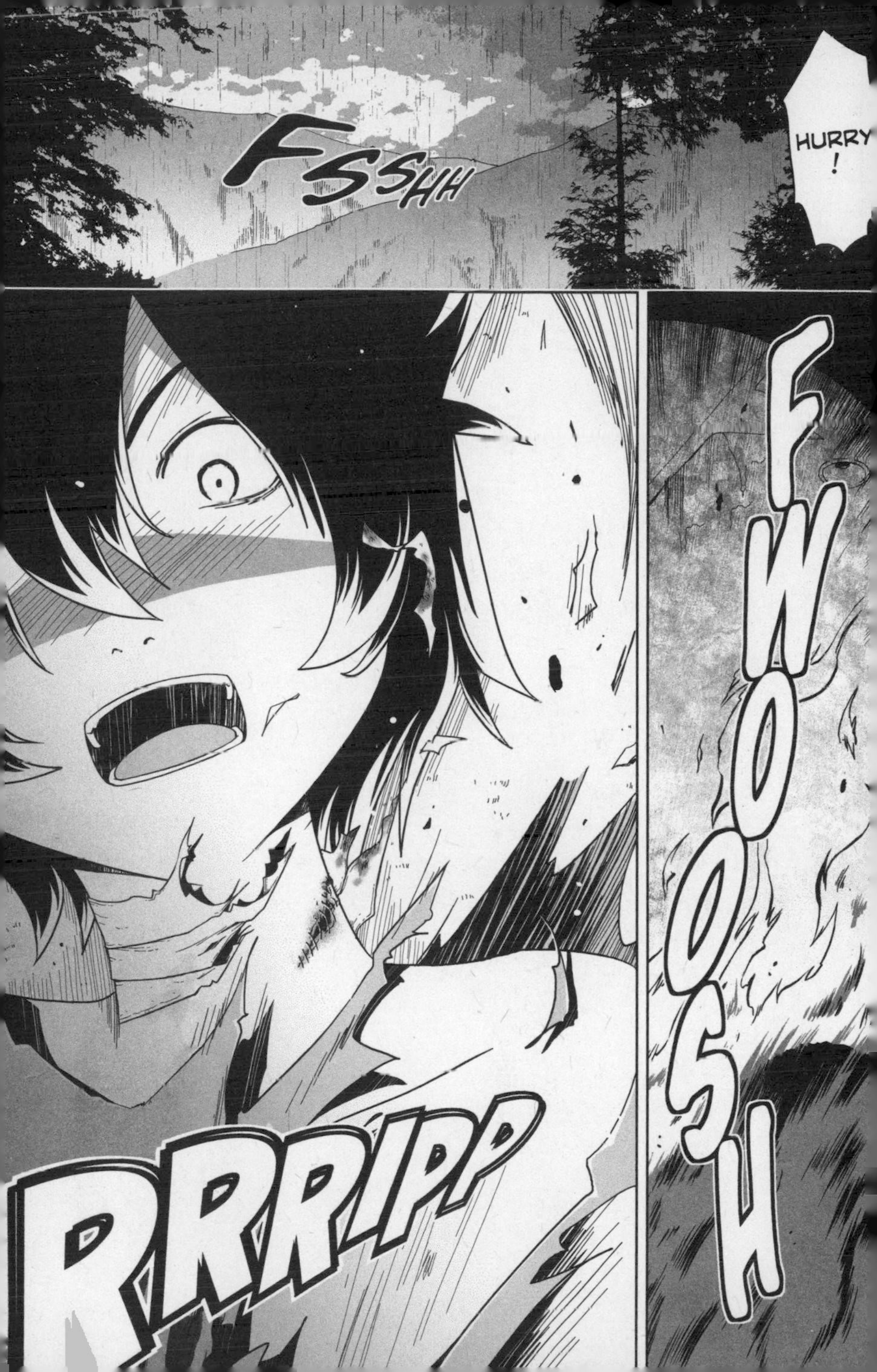
HURRY!
FSSHH
FWOOOSH
RRRIPP

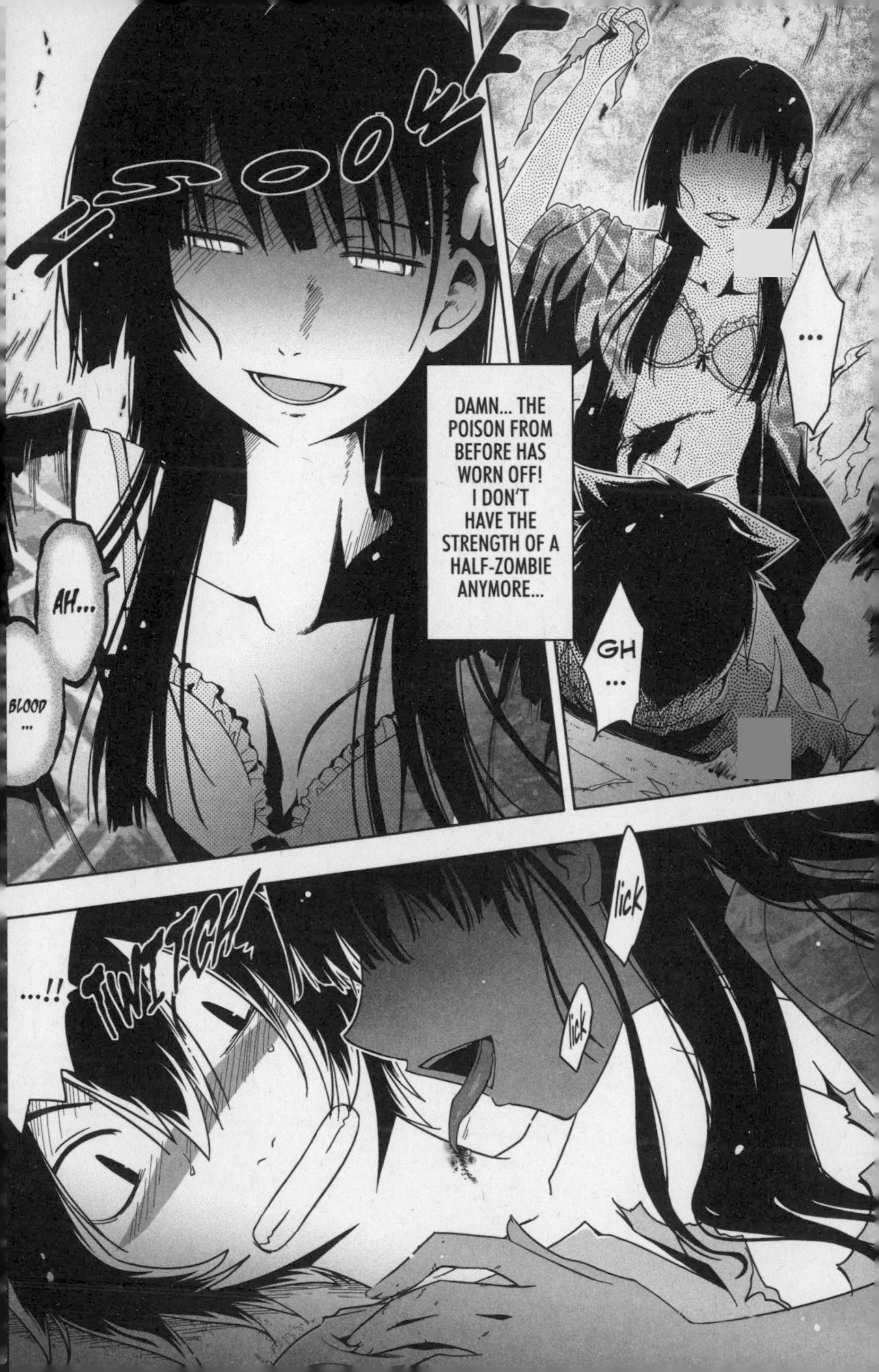
...
DAMN... THE POISON FROM BEFORE HAS WORN OFF! I DON'T HAVE THE STRENGTH OF A HALF-ZOMBIE ANYMORE...
GH ...
HSOOOW!
AH...
BLOOD ...
lick
lick
TWITCH!
...!!

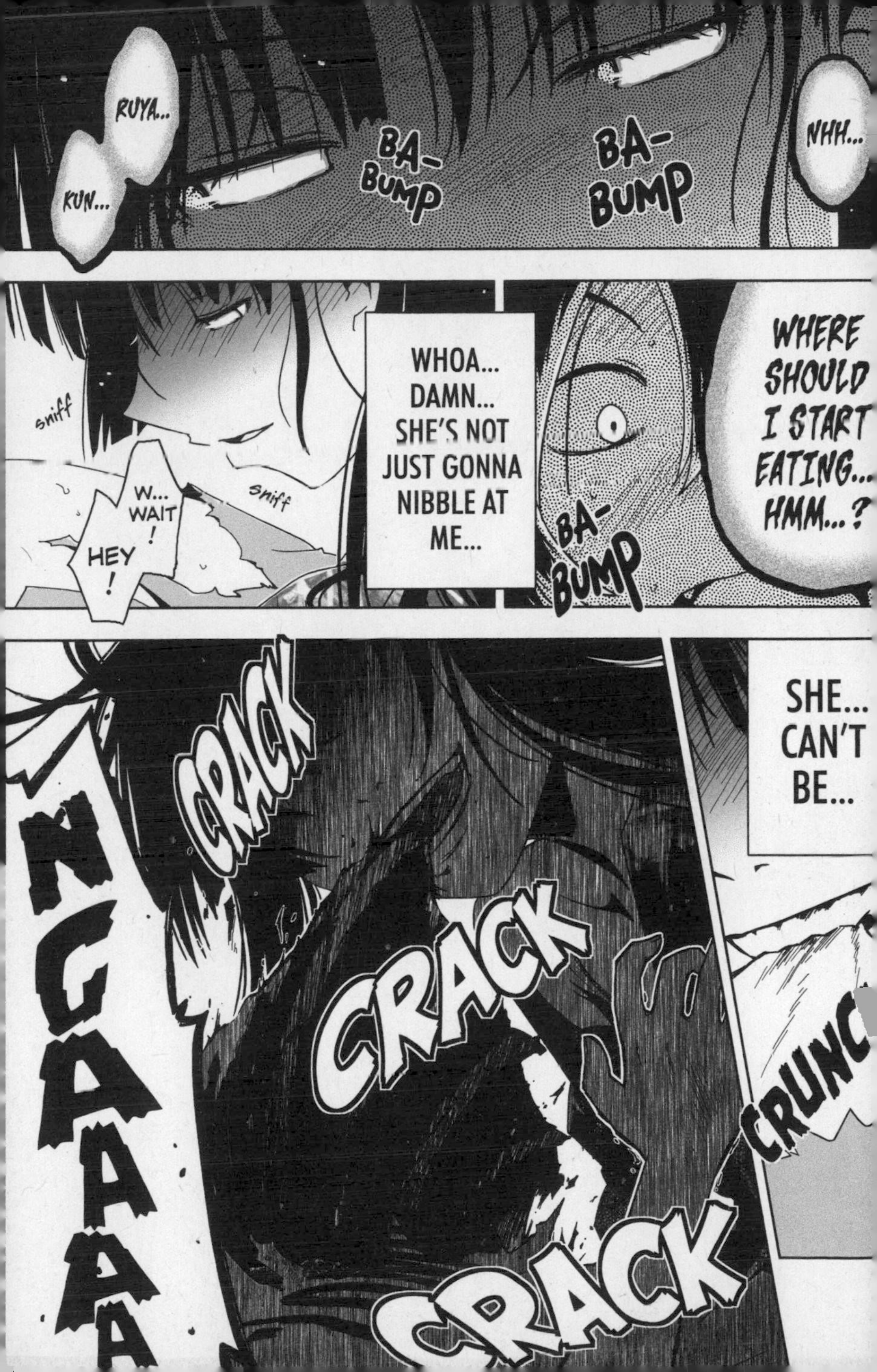
NHH...
BA-BUMP
BA-BUMP
RUYA... KUN...
WHERE SHOULD I START EATING... HMM...?
BA-BUMP
WHOA... DAMN... SHE'S NOT JUST GONNA NIBBLE AT ME...
sniff
sniff
W... WAIT!
HEY!
SHE... CAN'T BE...
CRUNC
CRACK
CRACK
CRACK
NGAAAAA

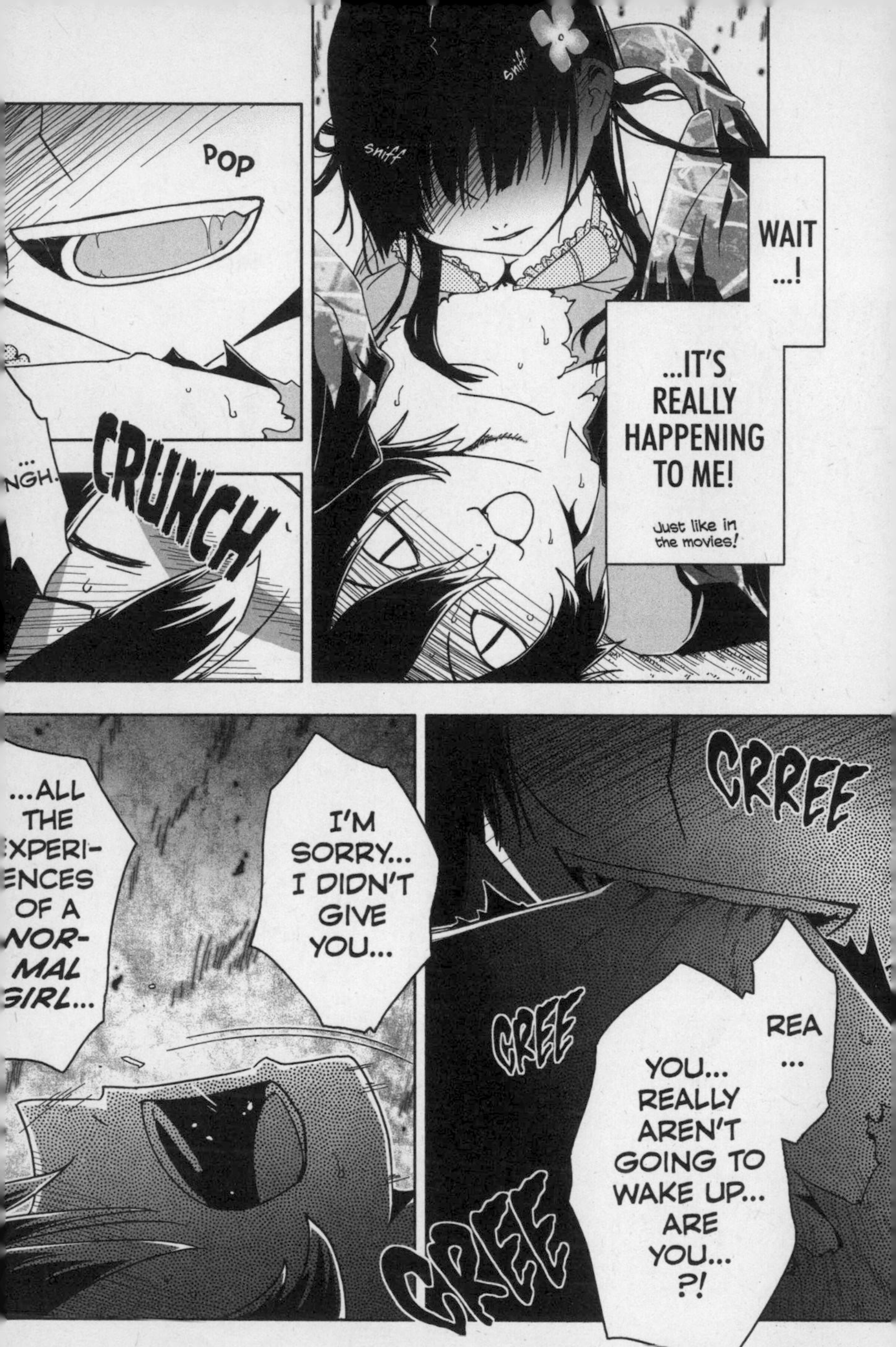
sniff
sniff
WAIT...!
...IT'S REALLY HAPPENING TO ME!
Just like in the movies!
POP
CRUNCH
...NGH!
CRREE
REA...
YOU... REALLY AREN'T GOING TO WAKE UP... ARE YOU...?!
CREE
CREE
I'M SORRY... I DIDN'T GIVE YOU...
...ALL THE XPERI-ENCES OF A NOR-MAL IRL...

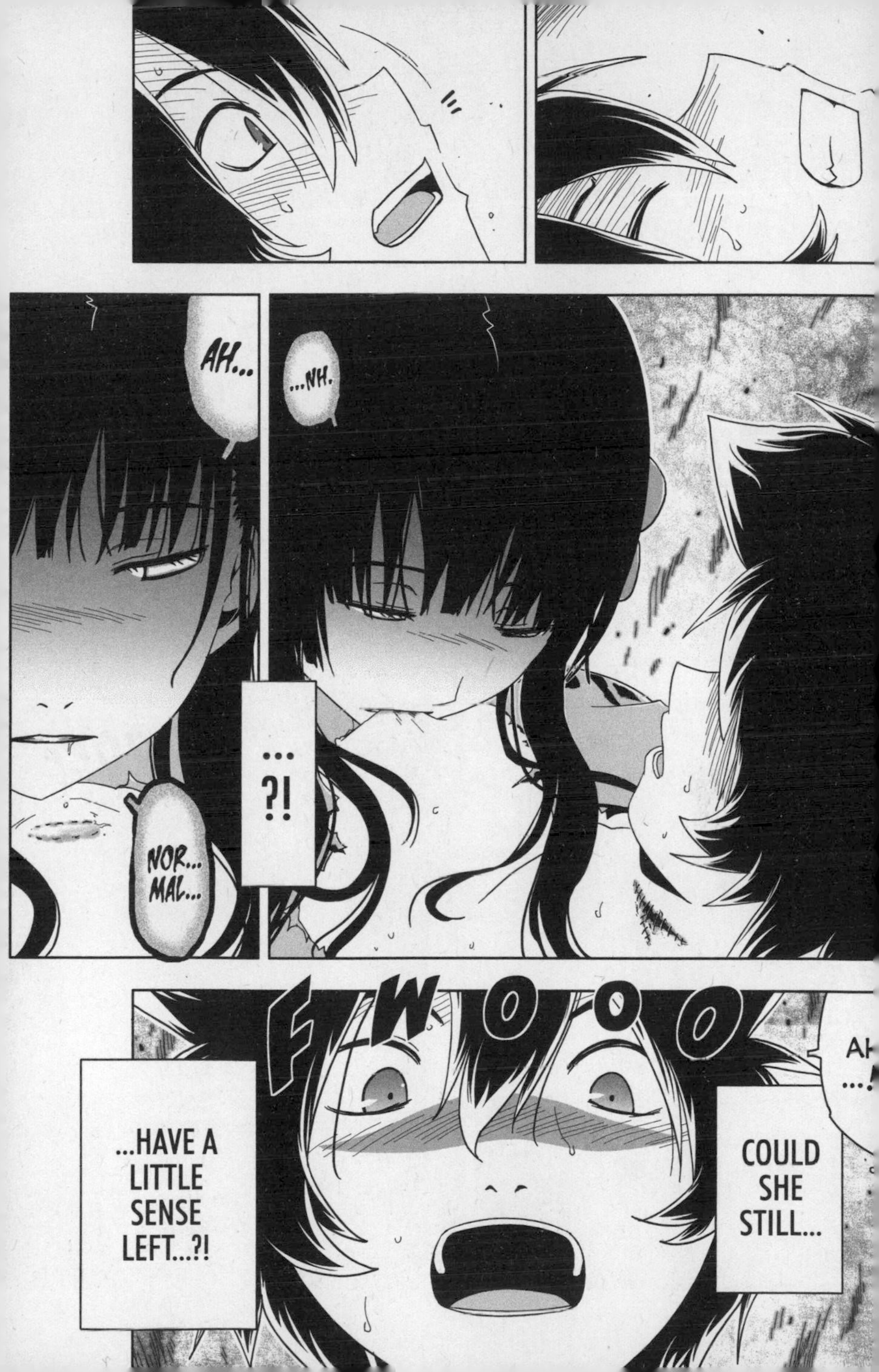
...NH.
...?!
AH...
NOR... MAL...
AH ...!
FWOOO
COULD SHE STILL...
...HAVE A LITTLE SENSE LEFT...?!

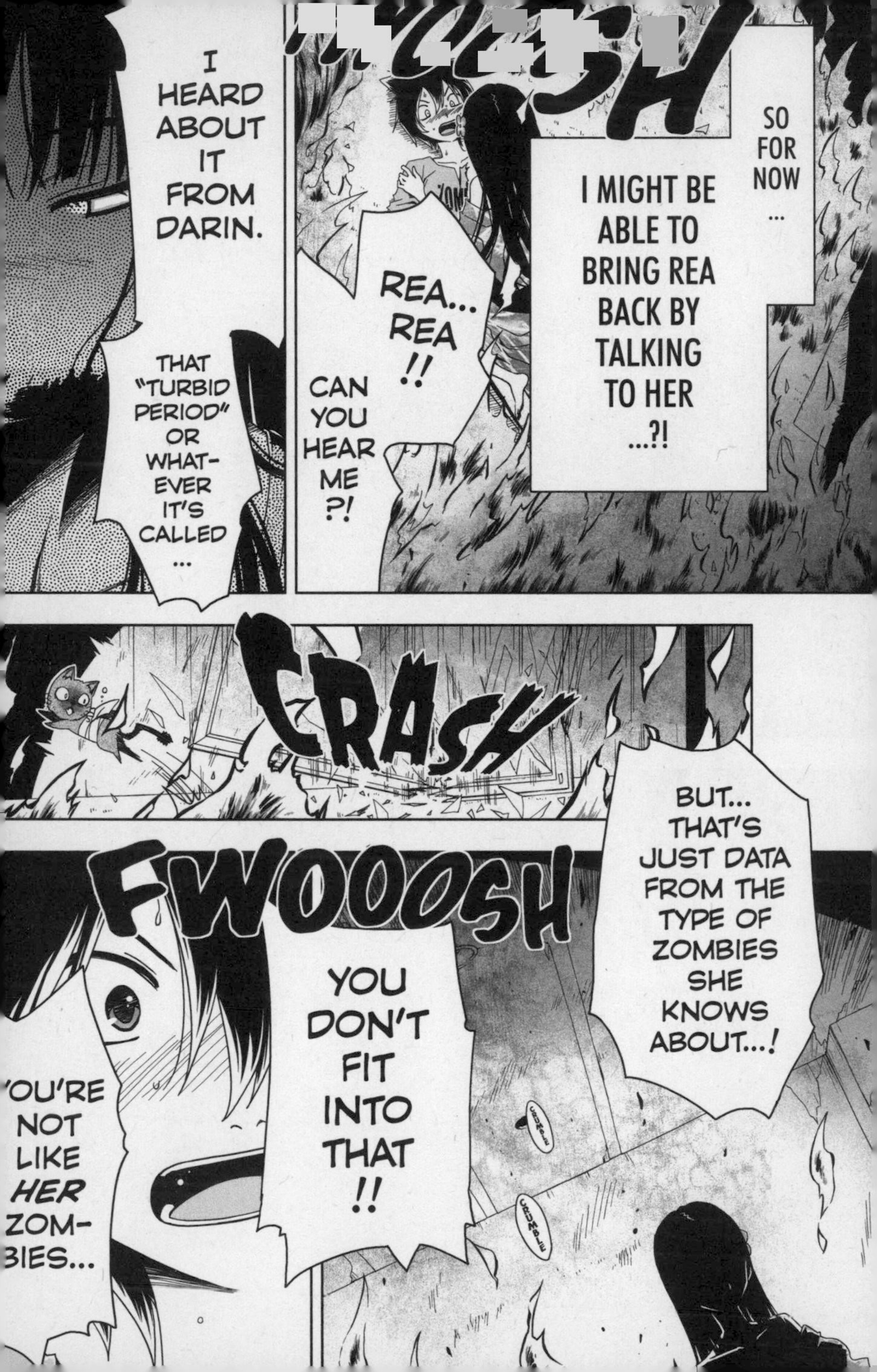
SO FOR NOW ...
I MIGHT BE ABLE TO BRING REA BACK BY TALKING TO HER ...?!
REA... REA !!
CAN YOU HEAR ME ?!
I HEARD ABOUT IT FROM DARIN.
THAT "TURBID PERIOD" OR WHATEVER IT'S CALLED ...
CRASH
BUT... THAT'S JUST DATA FROM THE TYPE OF ZOMBIES SHE KNOWS ABOUT...!
FWOOOSH
YOU DON'T FIT INTO THAT !!
CRUMBLE
CRUMBLE
'OU'RE NOT LIKE *HER* ZOMBIES...

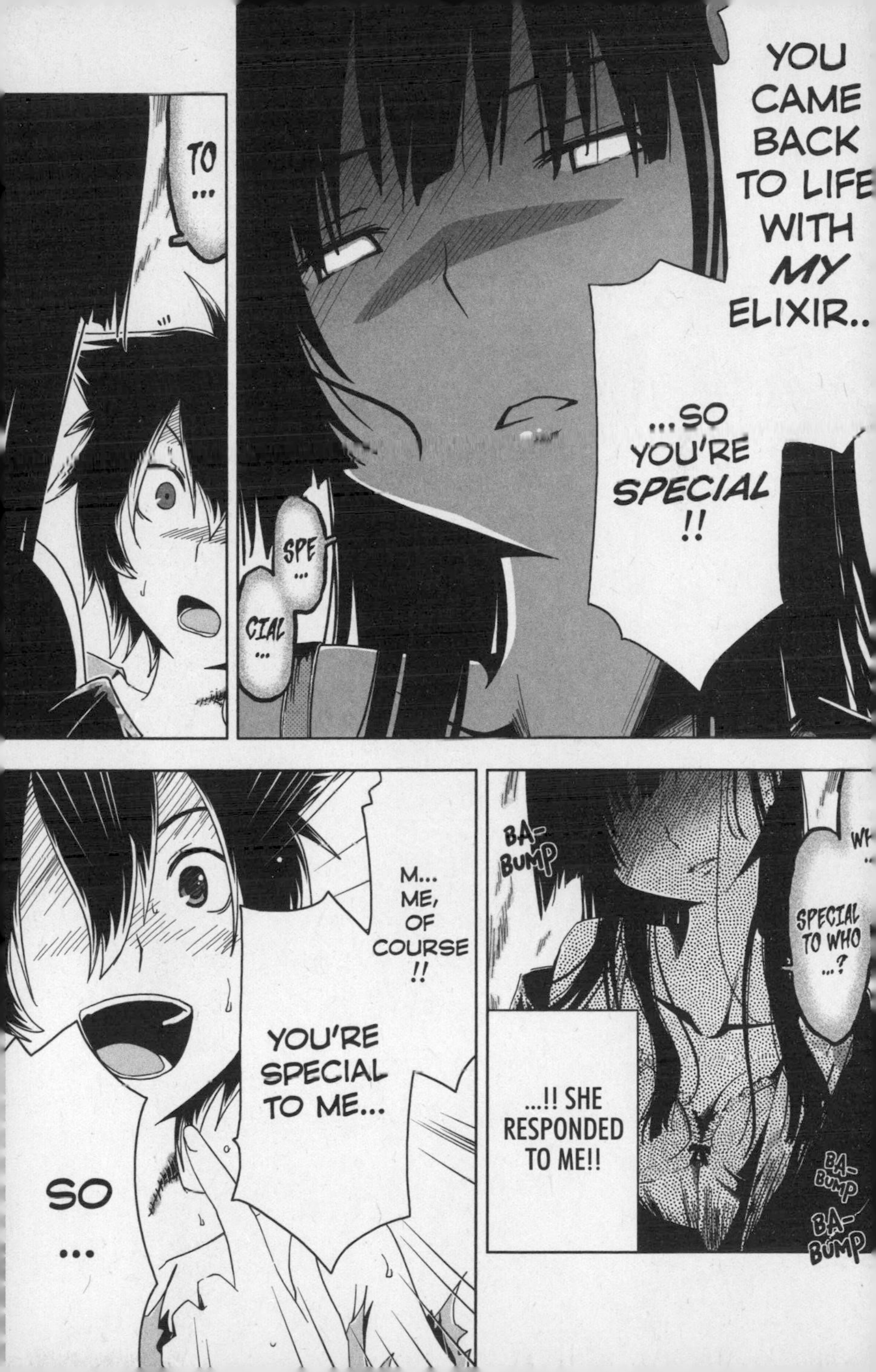
YOU CAME BACK TO LIFE WITH MY ELIXIR..
...SO YOU'RE SPECIAL !!
SPE...
CIAL...
TO...
BA-BUMP
SPECIAL TO WHO ...?
...!! SHE RESPONDED TO ME!!
BA-BUMP
BA-BUMP
M... ME, OF COURSE !!
YOU'RE SPECIAL TO ME...
SO ...

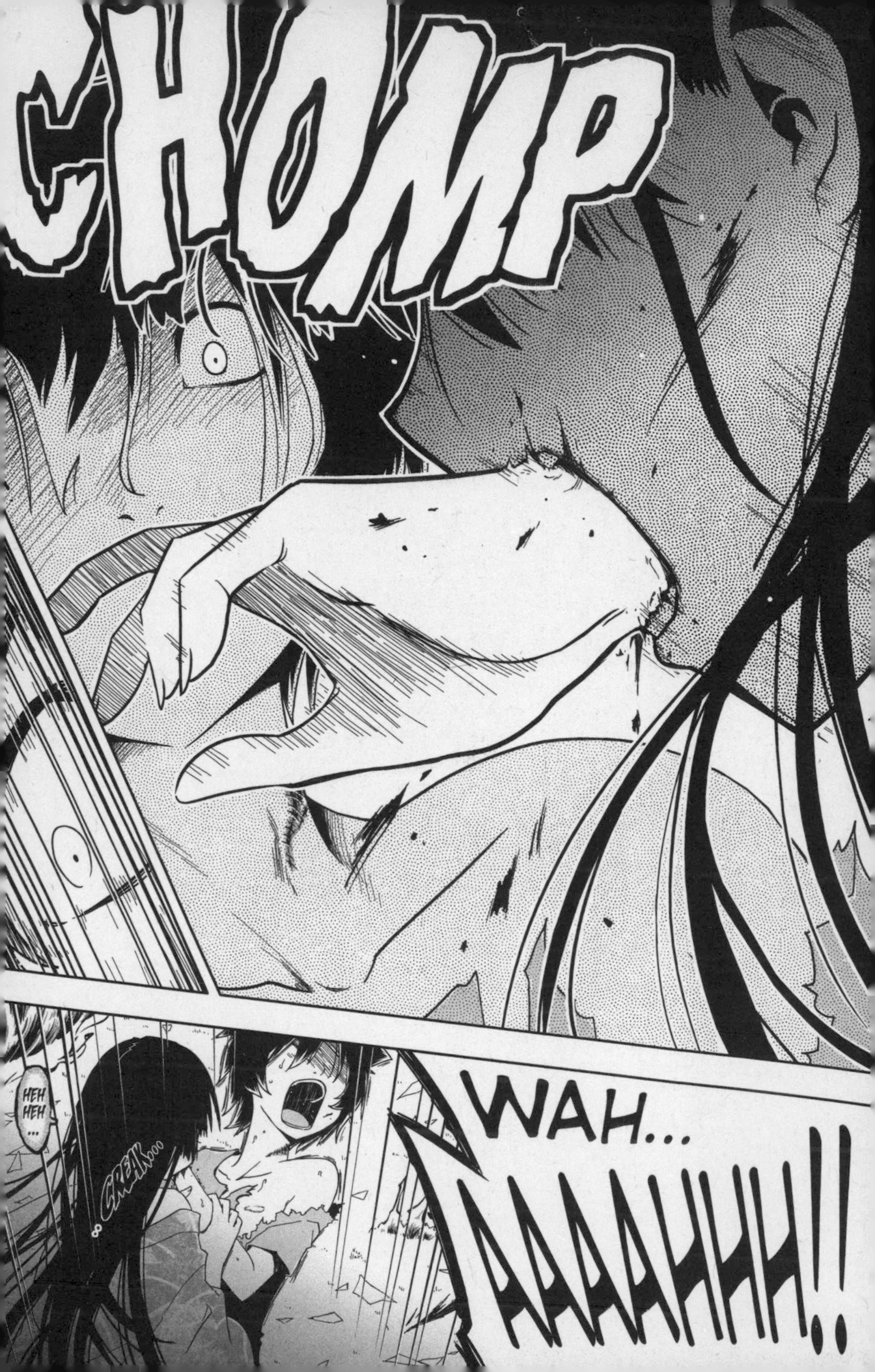
CHOMP
WAH... AAAAHHH!!
CREAK...
HEH HEH ...

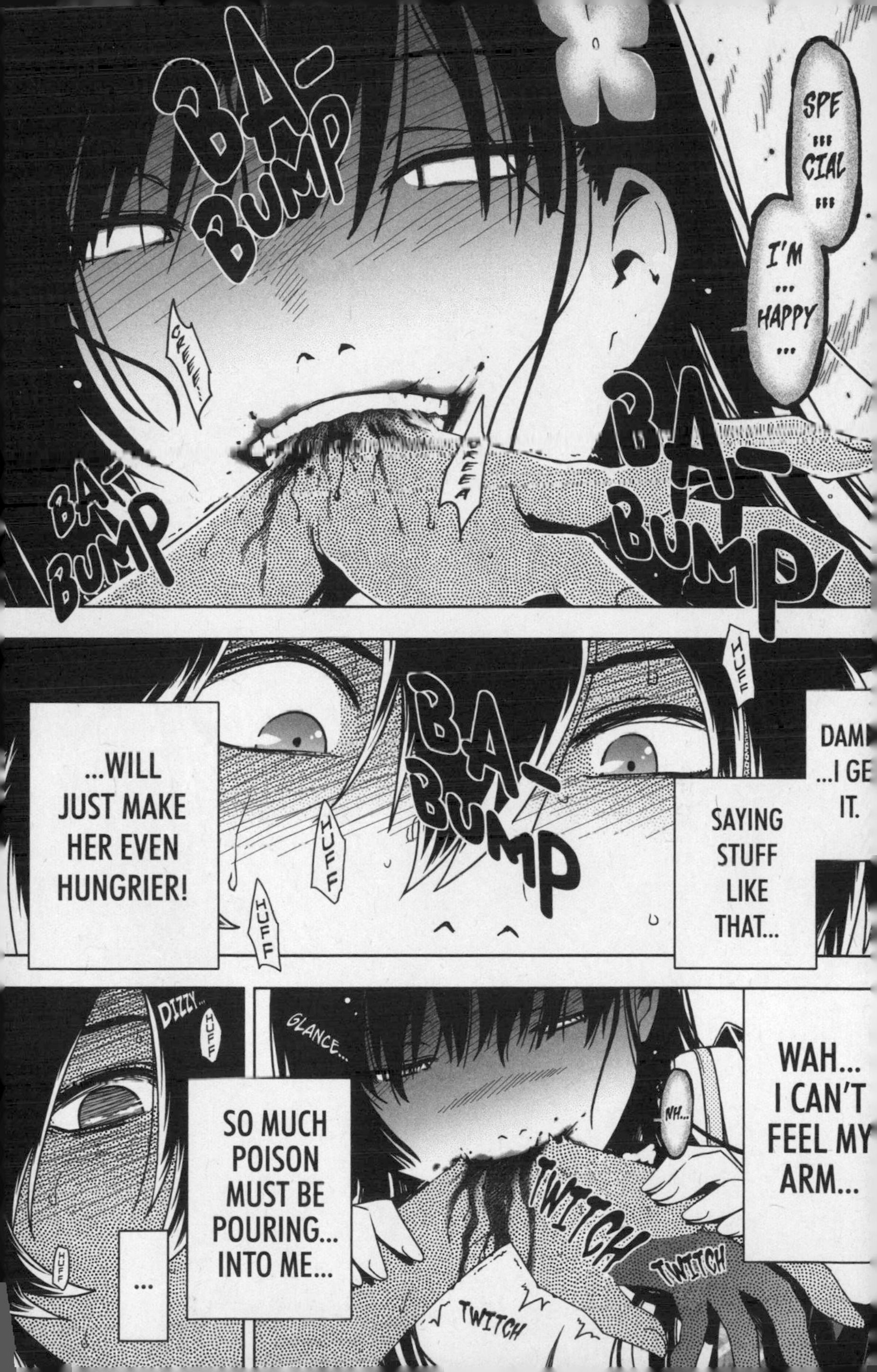
SPE... CIAL... I'M... HAPPY...
BA-BUMP
BA-BUMP
CREEEE...
BA-BUMP
HUFF
DAMN... I GET IT.
SAYING STUFF LIKE THAT...
BA-BUMP
HUFF
HUFF
...WILL JUST MAKE HER EVEN HUNGRIER!
WAH... I CAN'T FEEL MY ARM...
NH...
GLANCE...
TWITCH
TWITCH
TWITCH
SO MUCH POISON MUST BE POURING... INTO ME...
DIZZY...
HUFF
HUFF
...

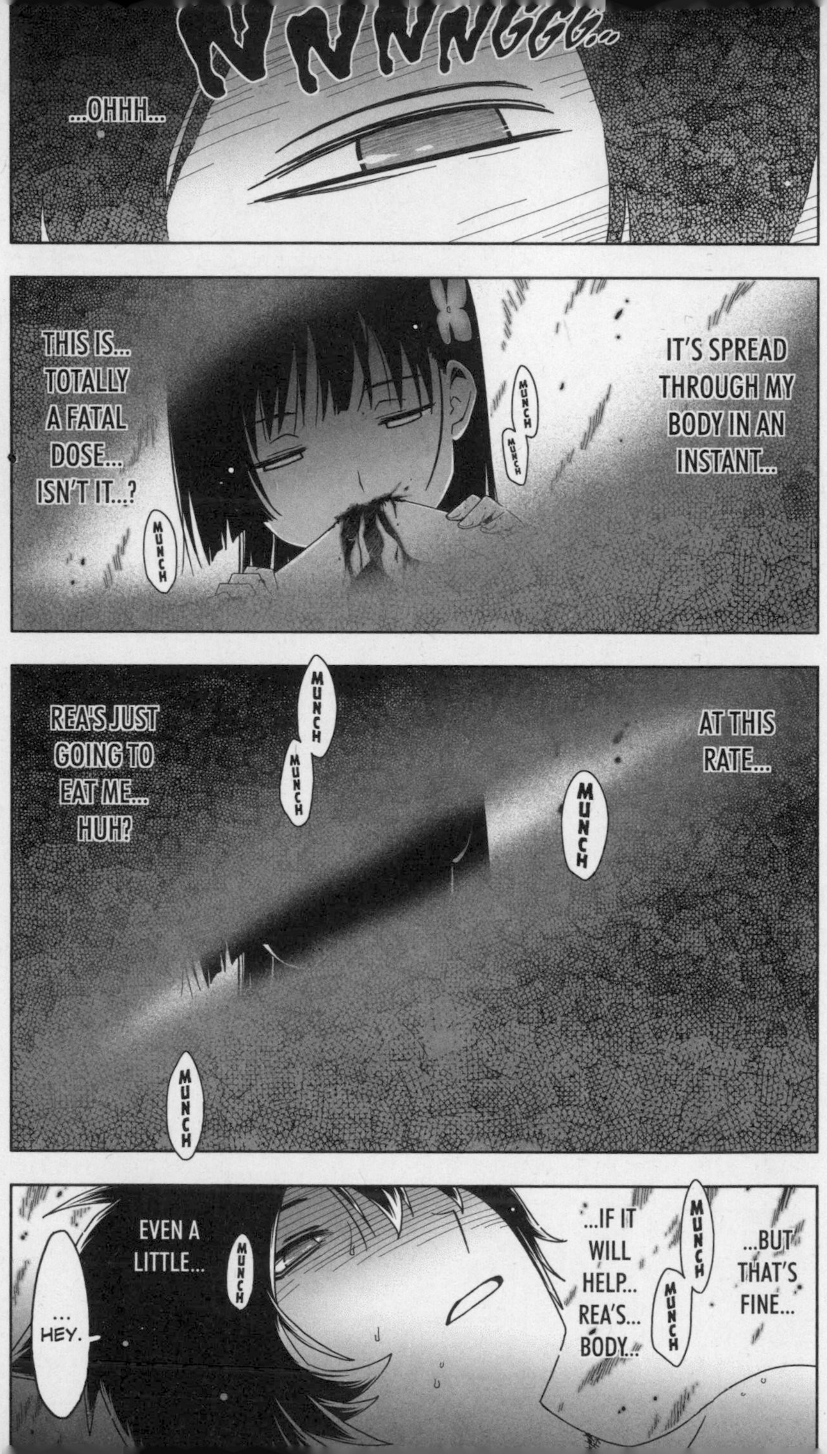
NNNNGGG..
...OHHH...
IT'S SPREAD THROUGH MY BODY IN AN INSTANT...
MUNCH
MUNCH
THIS IS... TOTALLY A FATAL DOSE... ISN'T IT...?
MUNCH
AT THIS RATE...
MUNCH
MUNCH
MUNCH
REA'S JUST GOING TO EAT ME... HUH?
MUNCH
...BUT THAT'S FINE...
MUNCH
MUNCH
...IF IT WILL HELP... REA'S... BODY...
MUNCH
EVEN A LITTLE...
... HEY.

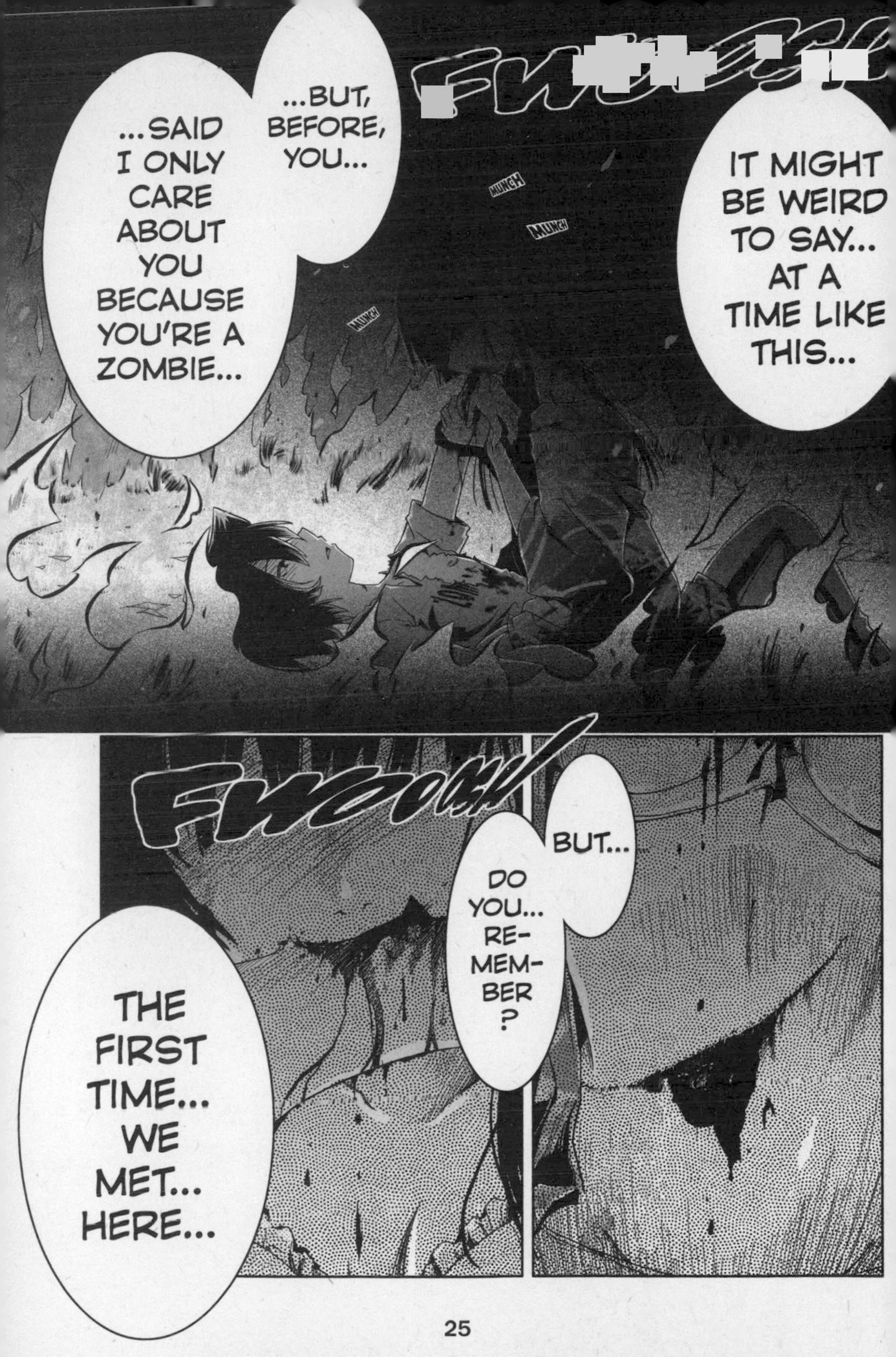
IT MIGHT BE WEIRD TO SAY... AT A TIME LIKE THIS...
MUNCH
MUNCH
MUNCH
...BUT, BEFORE, YOU...
...SAID I ONLY CARE ABOUT YOU BECAUSE YOU'RE A ZOMBIE...
BUT...
DO YOU... RE-MEM-BER?
THE FIRST TIME... WE MET... HERE...

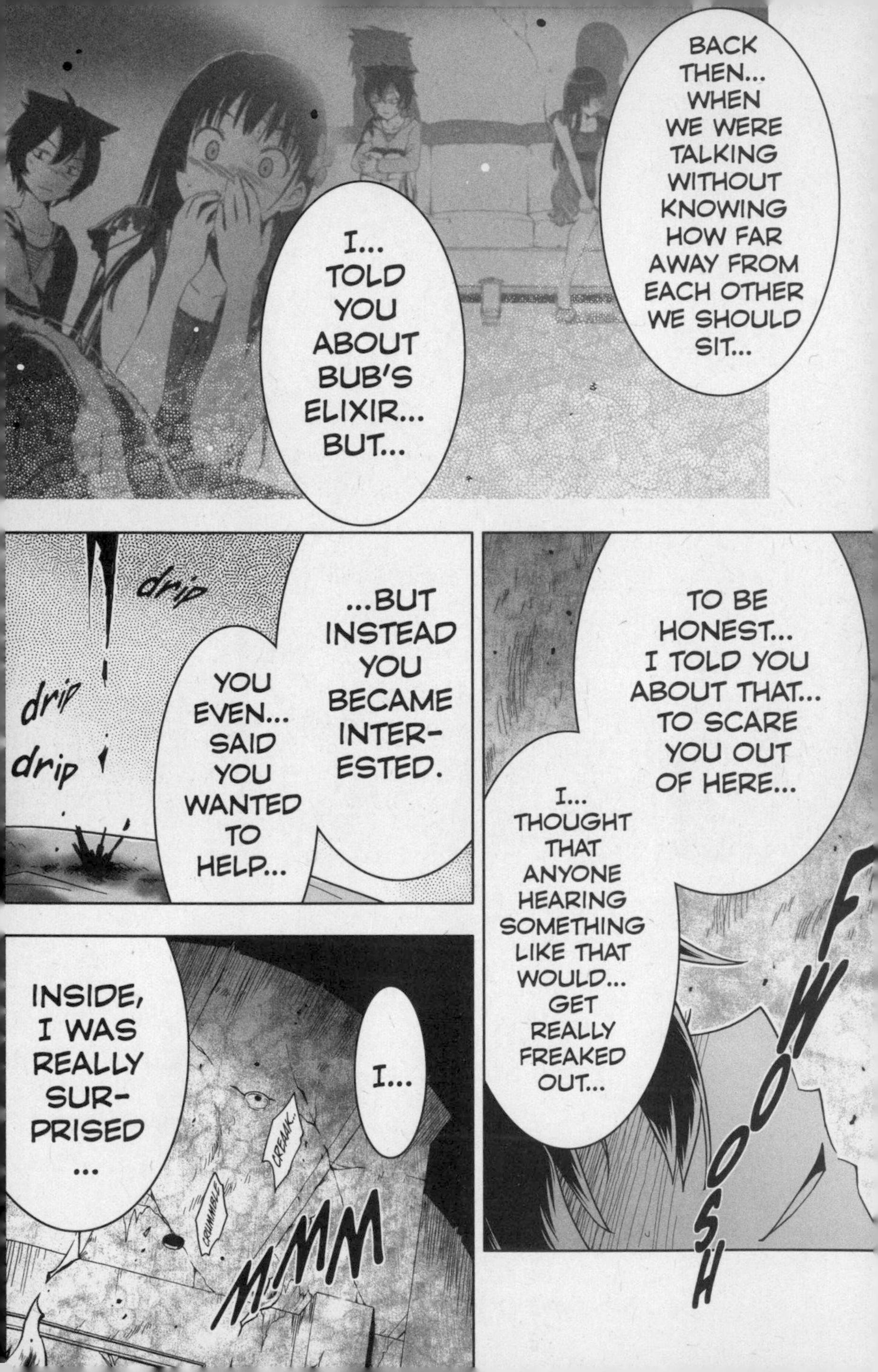
BACK THEN... WHEN WE WERE TALKING WITHOUT KNOWING HOW FAR AWAY FROM EACH OTHER WE SHOULD SIT...
I... TOLD YOU ABOUT BUB'S ELIXIR... BUT...
TO BE HONEST... I TOLD YOU ABOUT THAT... TO SCARE YOU OUT OF HERE...
I... THOUGHT THAT ANYONE HEARING SOMETHING LIKE THAT WOULD... GET REALLY FREAKED OUT...
FWOOOSH
...BUT INSTEAD YOU BECAME INTER-ESTED.
YOU EVEN... SAID YOU WANTED TO HELP...
drip
drip
drip
I...
INSIDE, I WAS REALLY SUR-PRISED...
CREAAK...
CRUMMBLE
MMMM

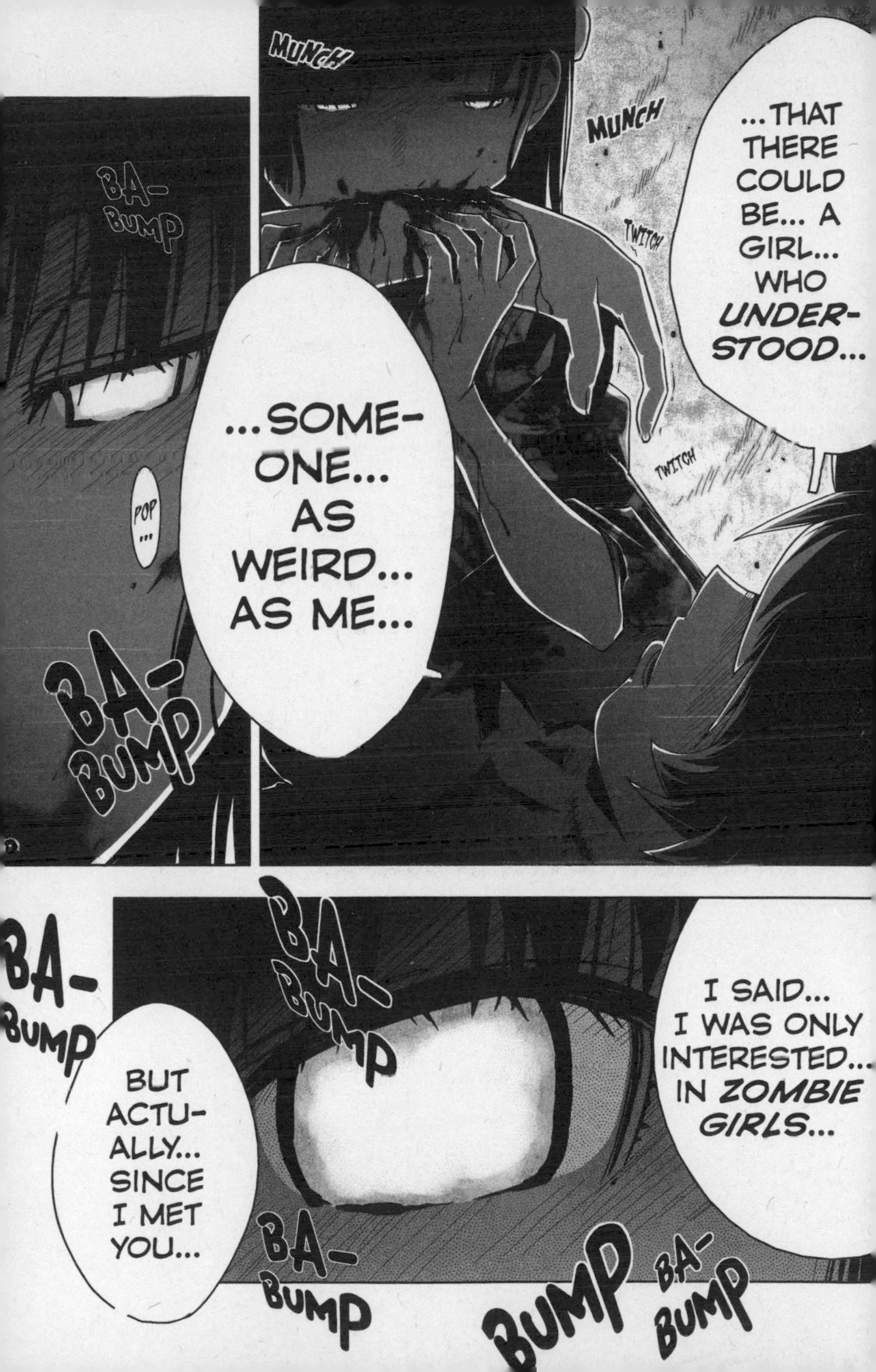
MUNCH
...THAT THERE COULD BE... A GIRL... WHO UNDERSTOOD...
MUNCH
TWITCH
TWITCH
...SOMEONE... AS WEIRD... AS ME...
BA-BUMP
POP...
BA-BUMP
I SAID... I WAS ONLY INTERESTED... IN ZOMBIE GIRLS...
BA-BUMP
BA-BUMP
BUMP
BA-BUMP
BUT ACTUALLY... SINCE I MET YOU...
BA-BUMP
BA-BUMP

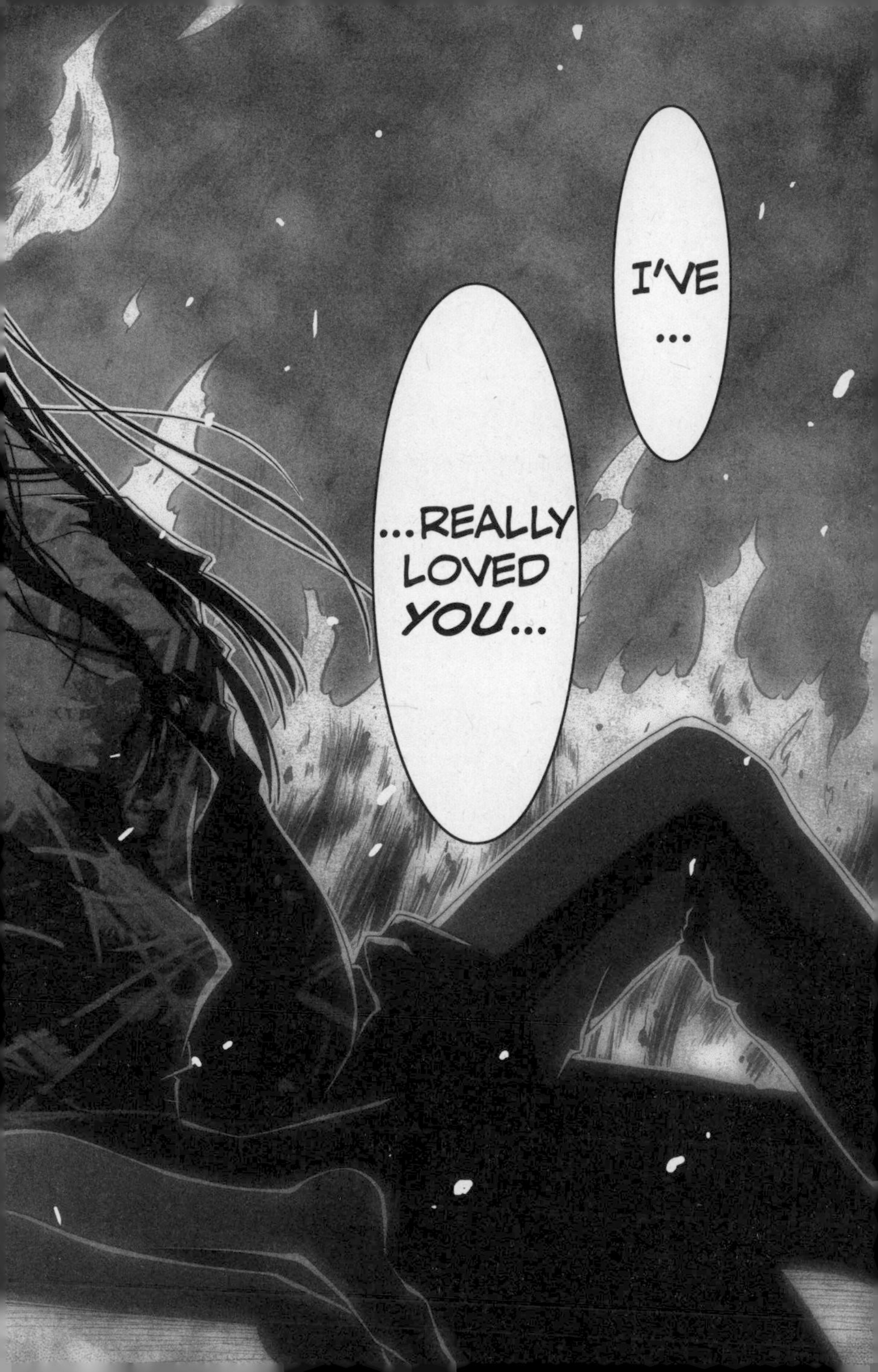
I'VE ...
...REALLY LOVED YOU...

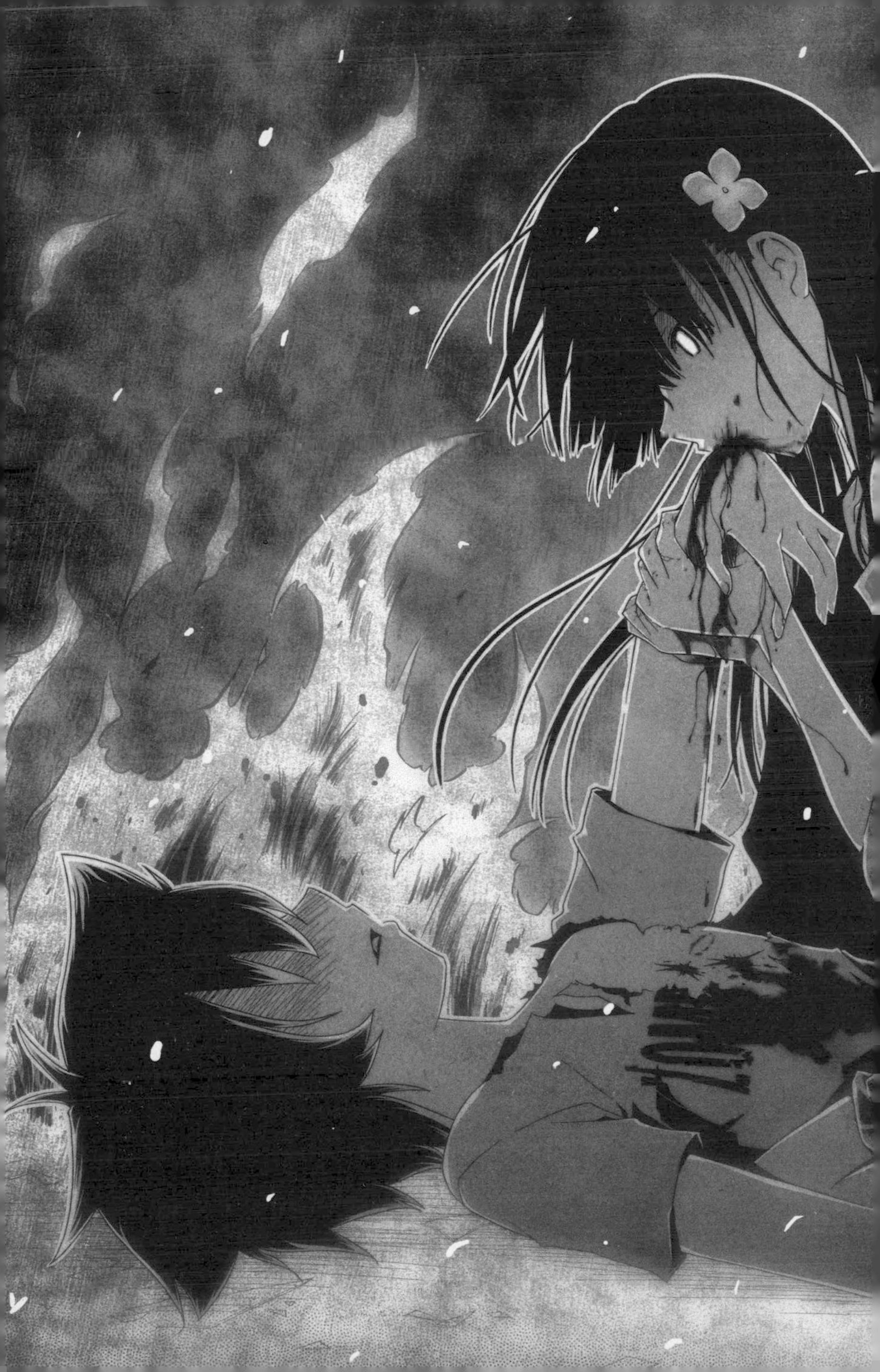

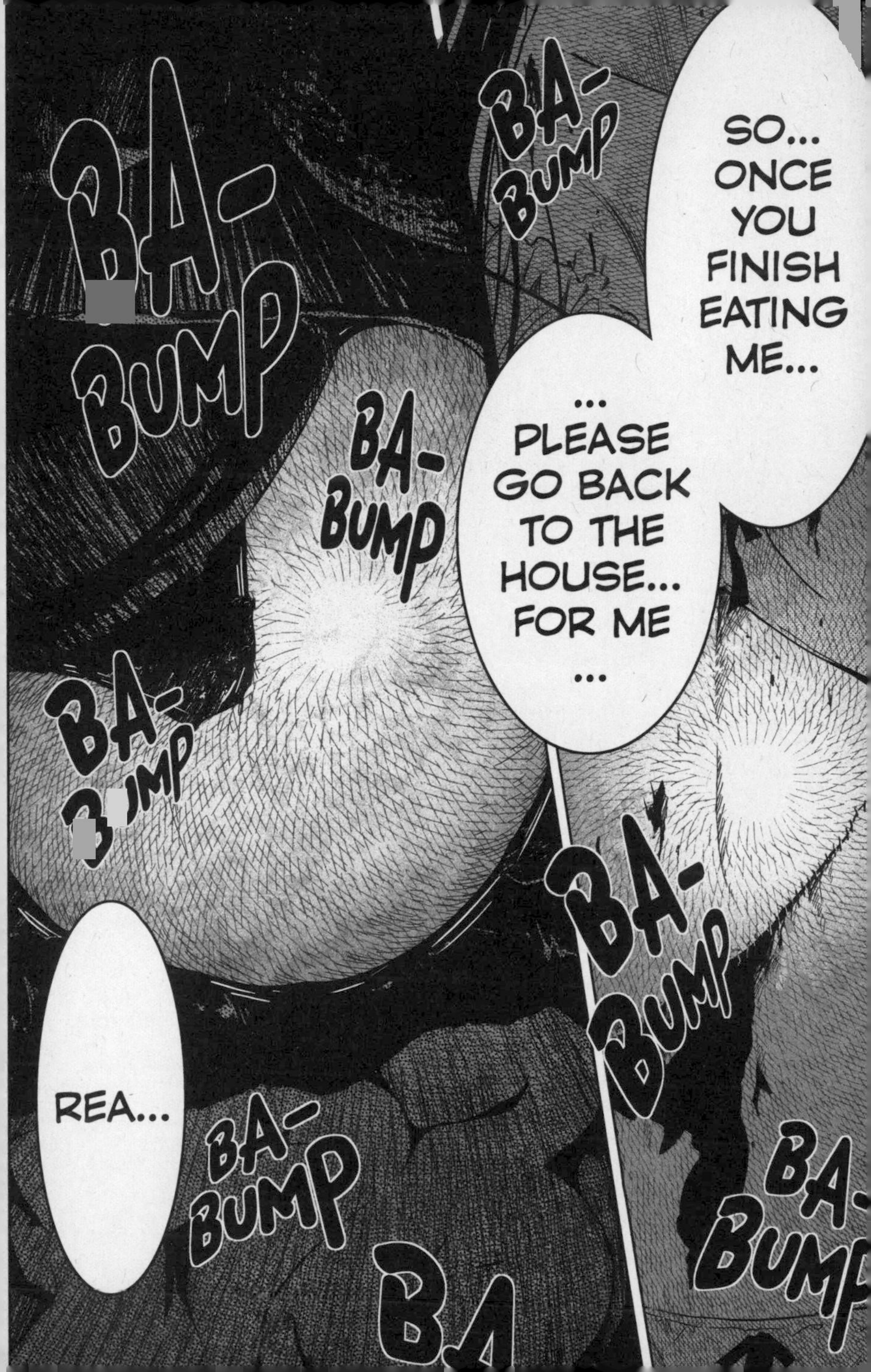
BA-BUMP
SO... ONCE YOU FINISH EATING ME...
... PLEASE GO BACK TO THE HOUSE... FOR ME ...
BA-BUMP
BA-BUMP
BA-BUMP
BA-BUMP
BA-BUMP
BA-BUMP
REA...
BA-BUMP
BA

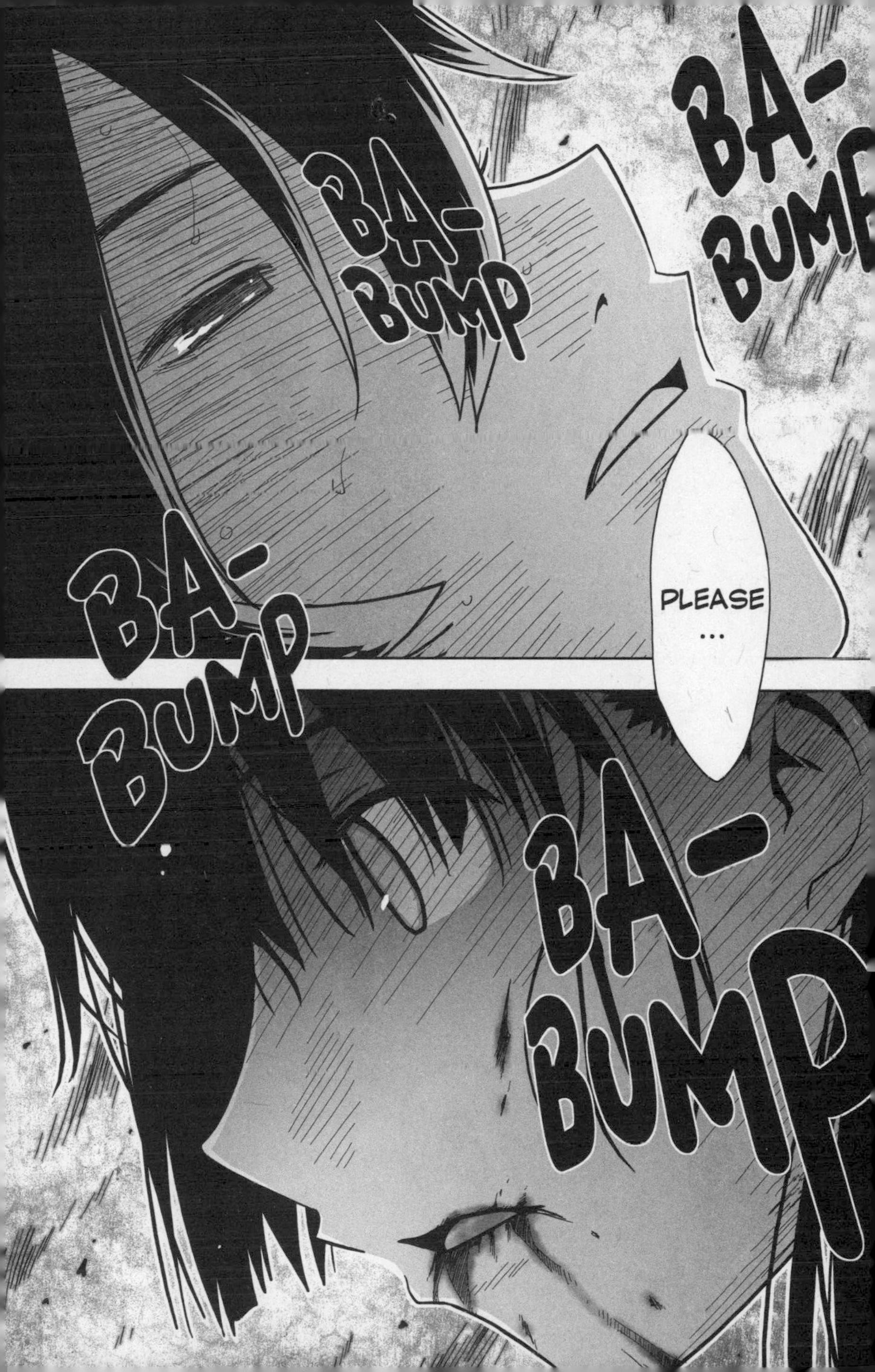
BA-BUMP
BA-BUMP
PLEASE ...
BA-BUMP
BA-BUMP

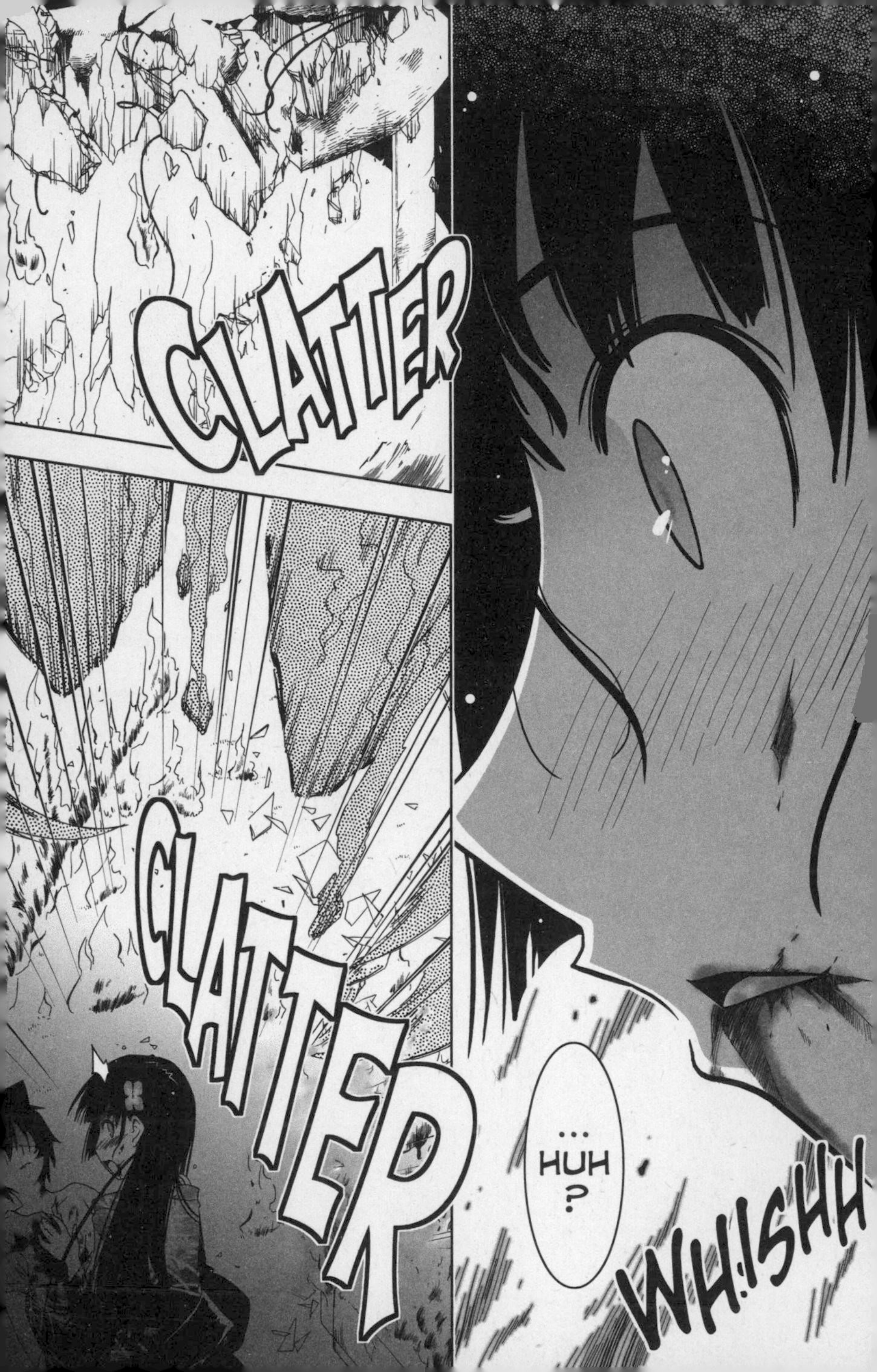
...HUH?
WHISHH
CLATTER
CLATTER

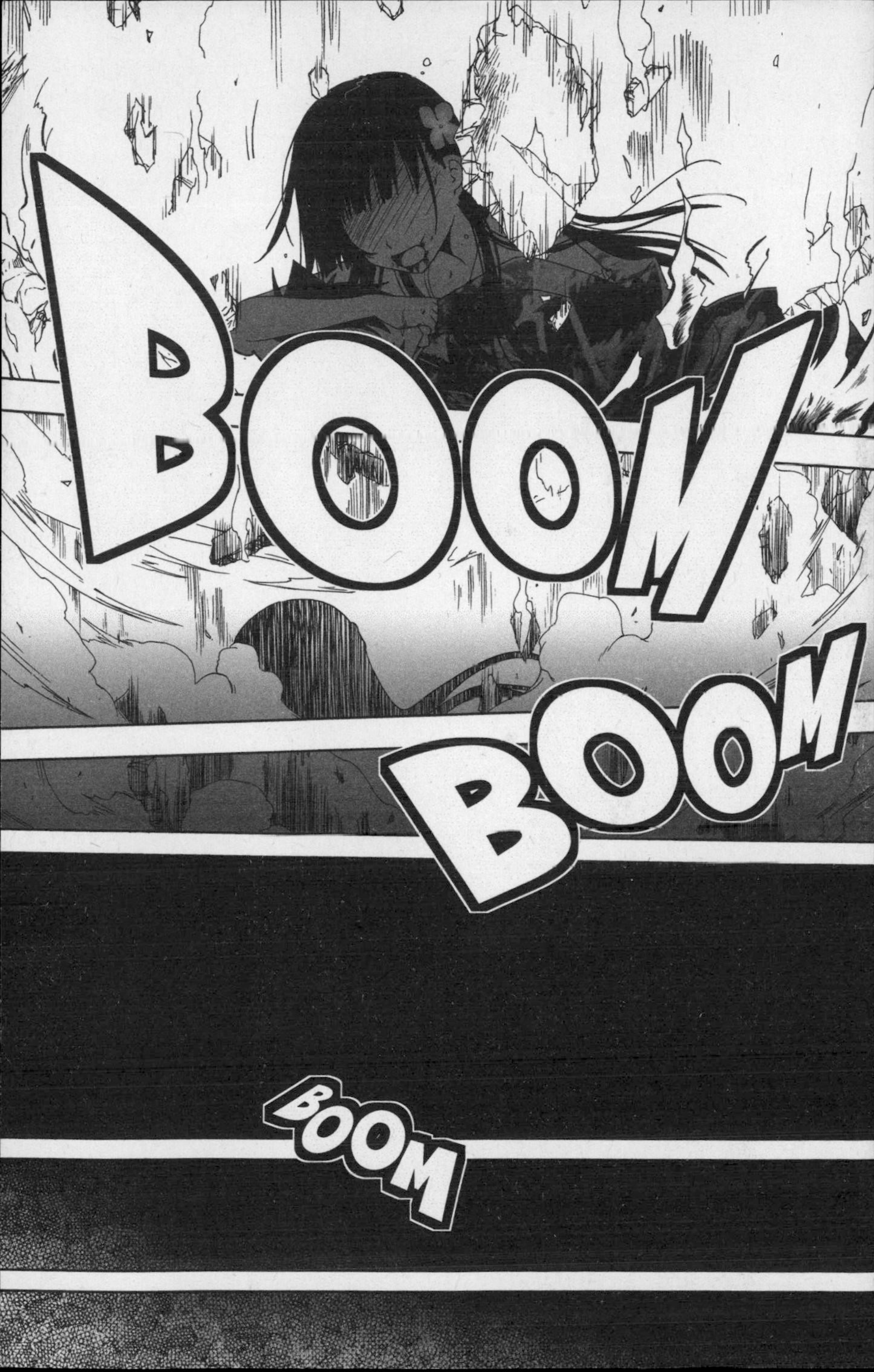
BOOM
BOOM
BOOM

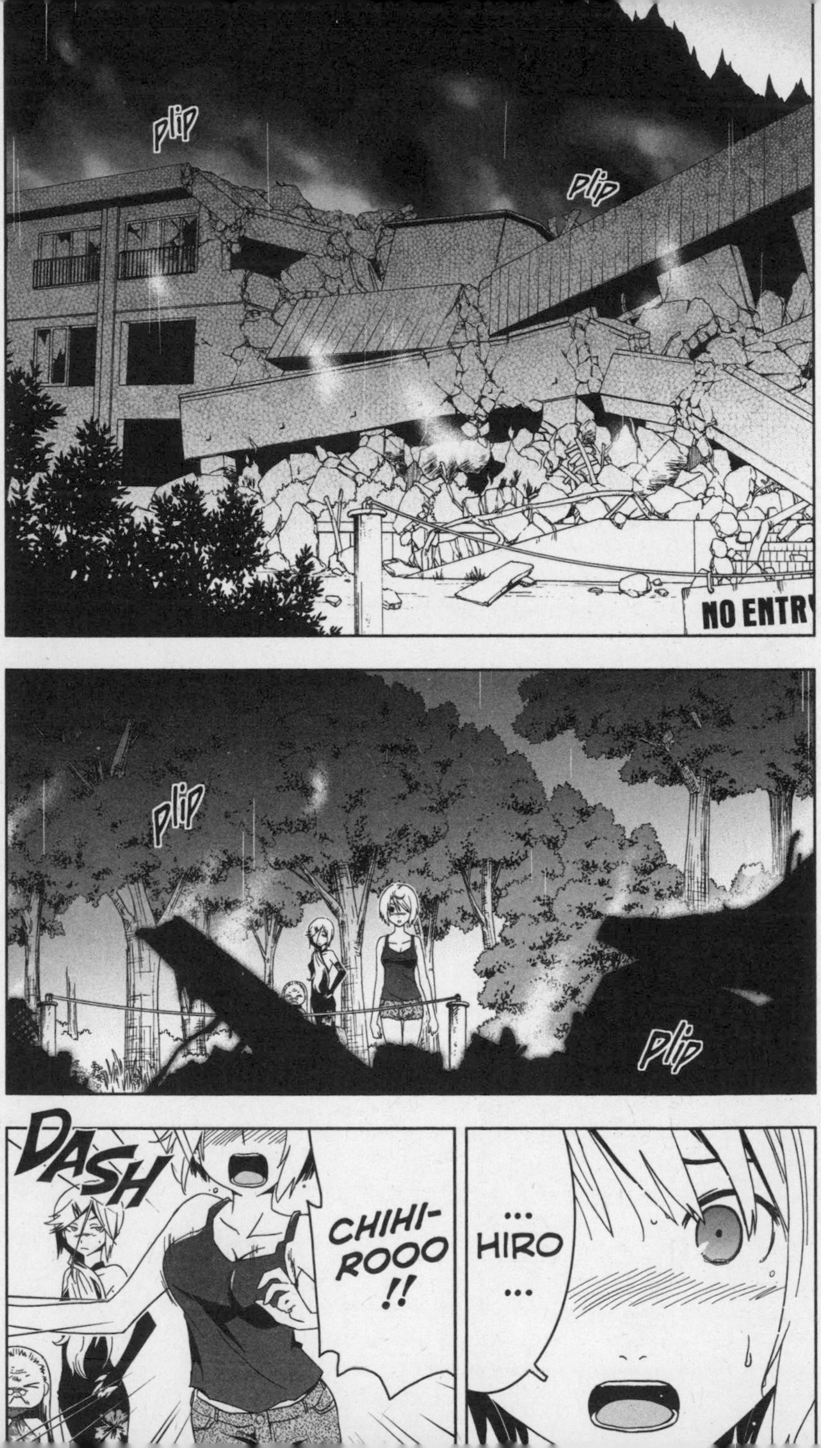
plip
plip
NO ENTRY
plip
plip
... HIRO ...
DASH
CHIHI-ROOO !!

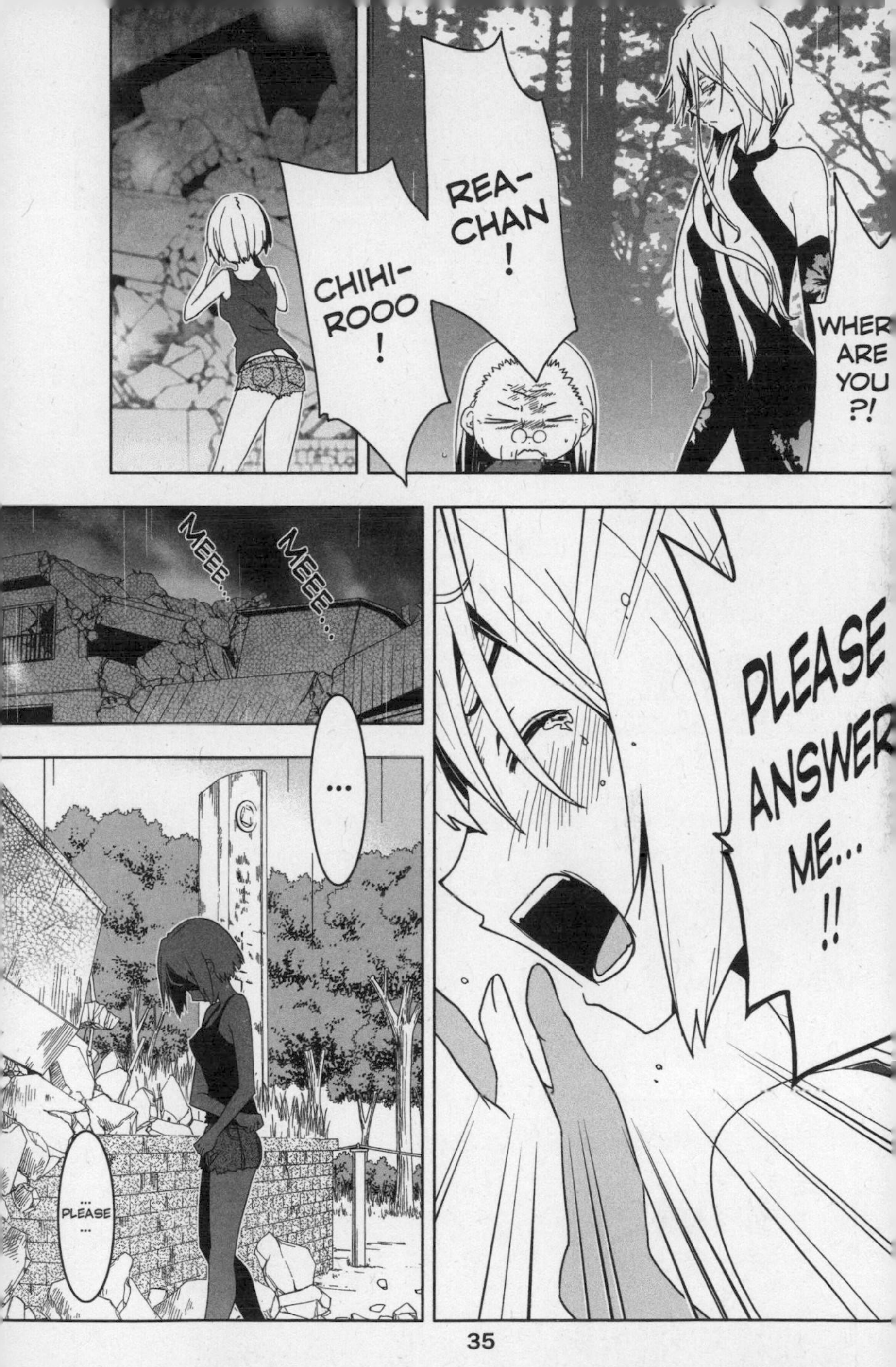
WHER ARE YOU ?!
REA-CHAN !
CHIHI-ROOO !
PLEASE ANSWER ME... !!
MEEE...
MEEE...
...
... PLEASE ...

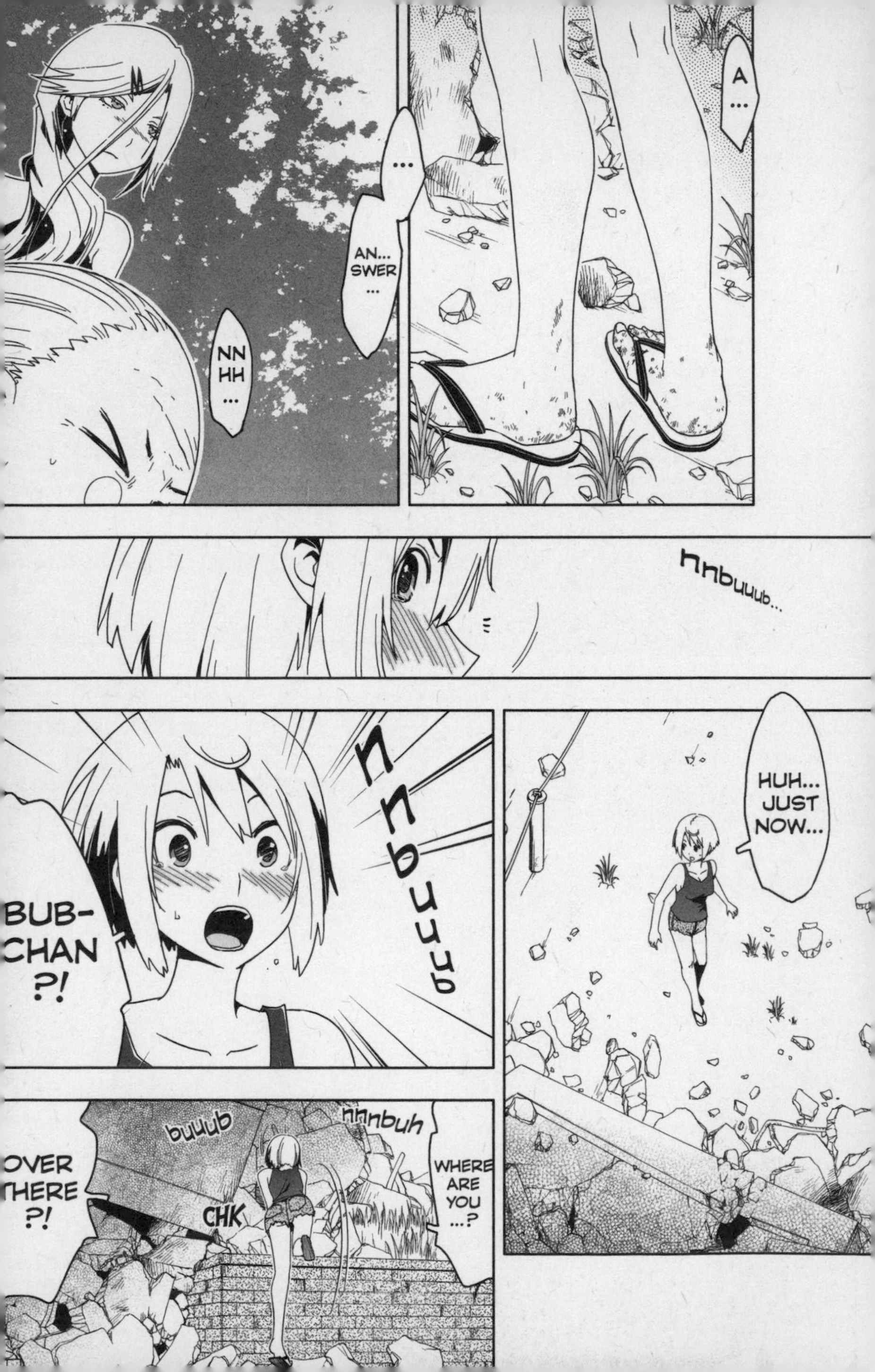
A ...
...
AN... SWER ...
NN HH ...
nnbuuub...
HUH... JUST NOW...
nnbuuub
BUB-CHAN ?!
WHERE ARE YOU ...?
nnnbuh
buuub
CHK
OVER THERE ?!

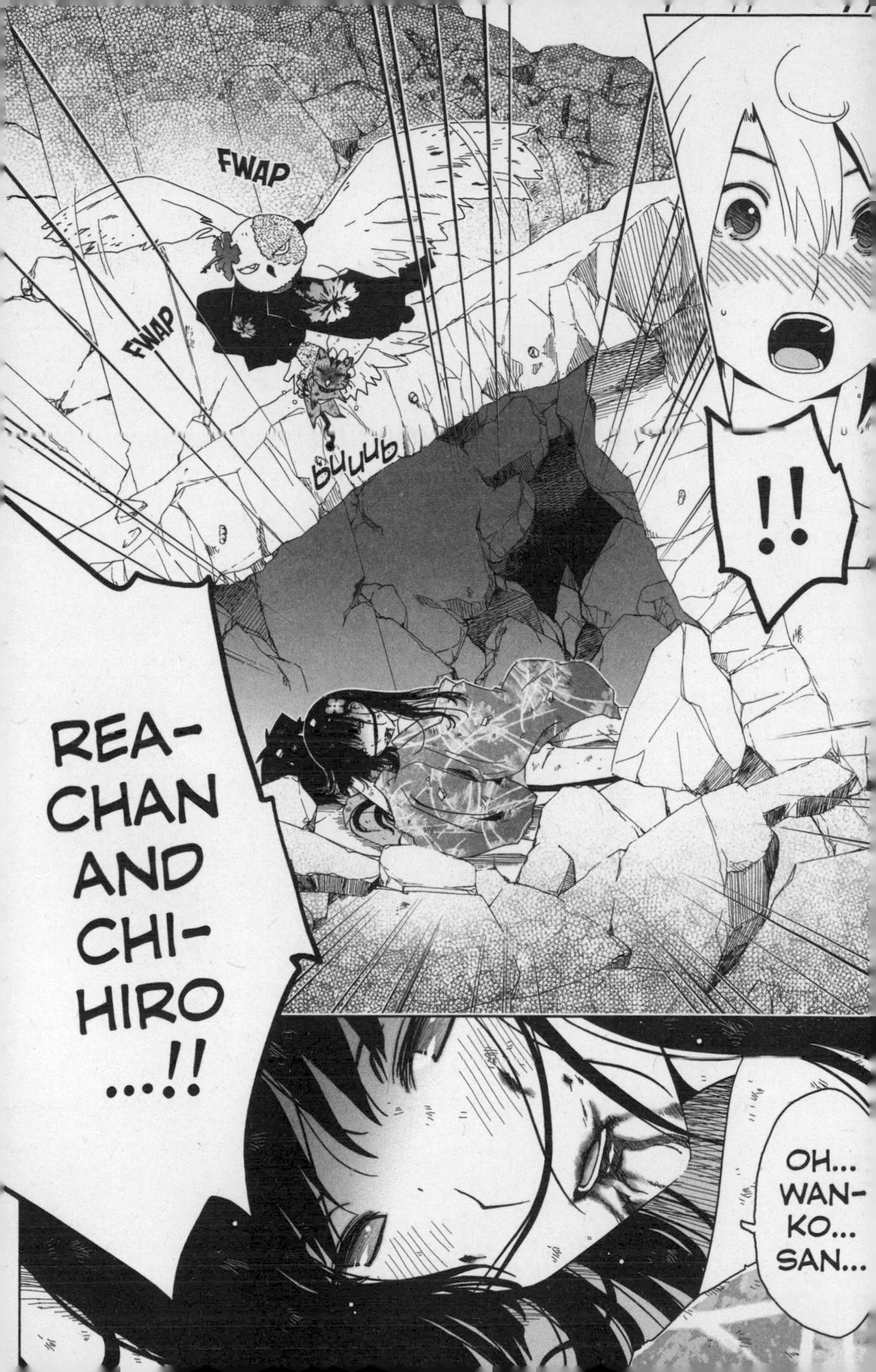
!!
FWAP
FWAP
buuub
REA-CHAN AND CHI-HIRO ...!!
OH... WAN-KO... SAN...

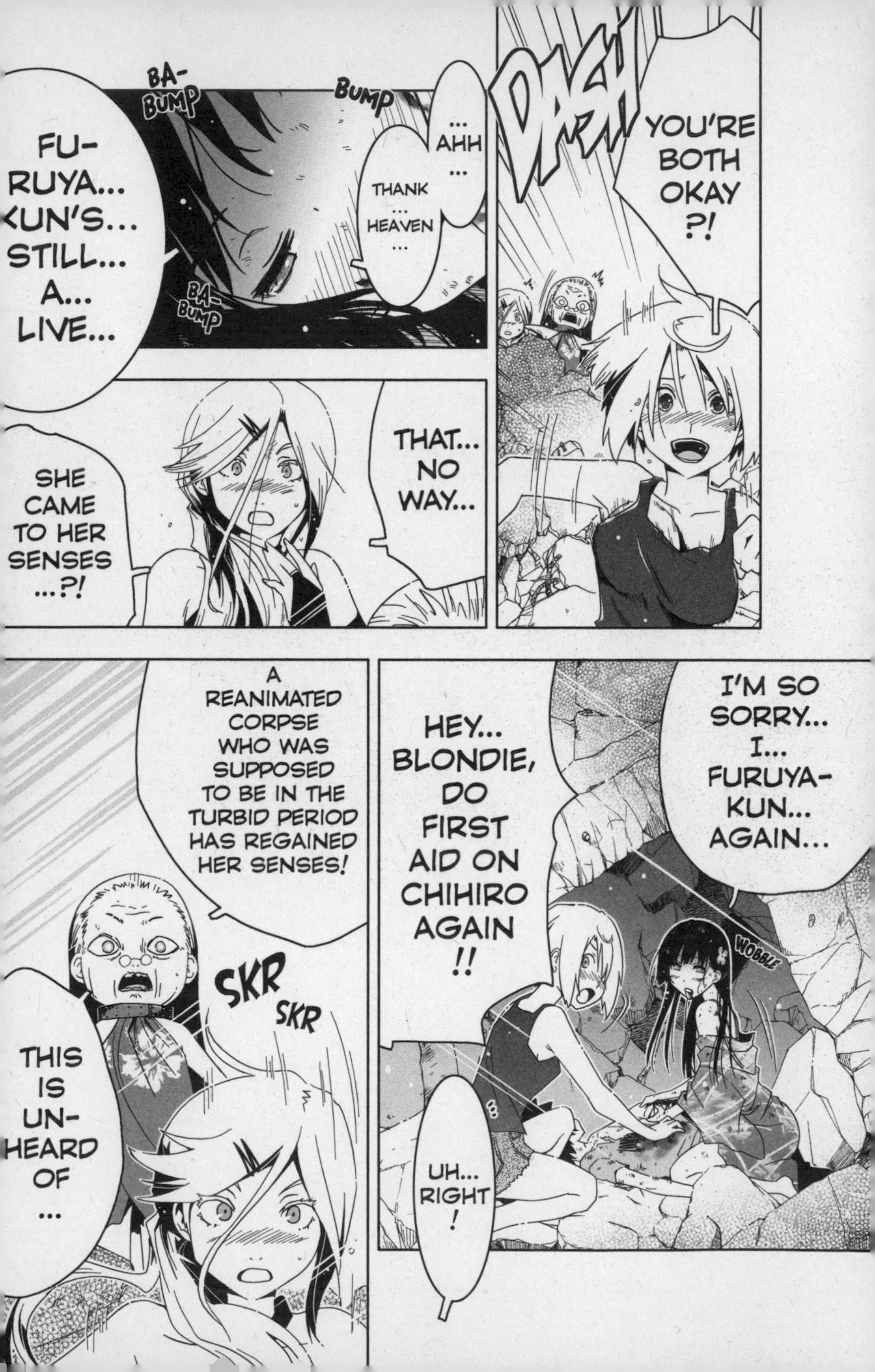
DASH
YOU'RE BOTH OKAY ?!
... AHH ...
THANK ... HEAVEN ...
BUMP
BA-BUMP
FU-RUYA... KUN'S... STILL... A... LIVE...
BA-BUMP
THAT... NO WAY...
SHE CAME TO HER SENSES ...?!
I'M SO SORRY... I... FURUYA-KUN... AGAIN...
HEY... BLONDIE, DO FIRST AID ON CHIHIRO AGAIN !!
WOBBLE
UH... RIGHT !
A REANIMATED CORPSE WHO WAS SUPPOSED TO BE IN THE TURBID PERIOD HAS REGAINED HER SENSES!
SKR
SKR
THIS IS UN-HEARD OF ...

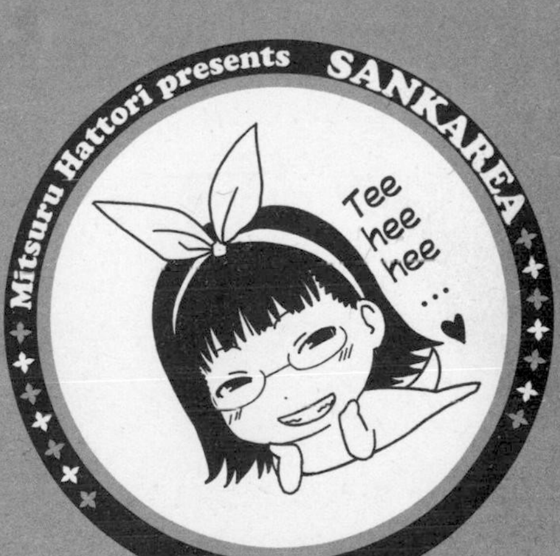
Mitsuru Hattori presents SANKAREA
Tee hee hee ...

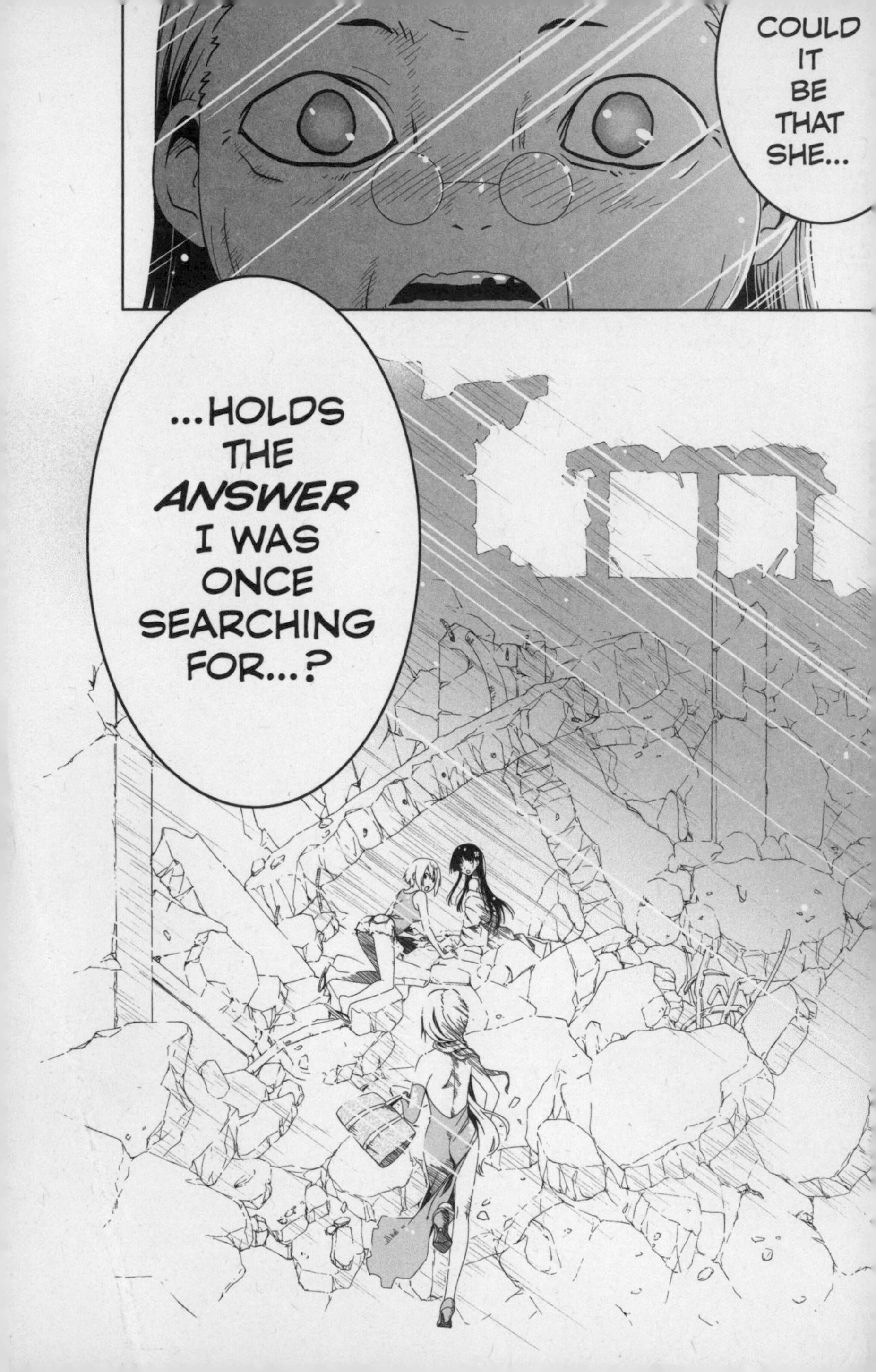
COULD IT BE THAT SHE...
...HOLDS THE *ANSWER* I WAS ONCE SEARCHING FOR...?

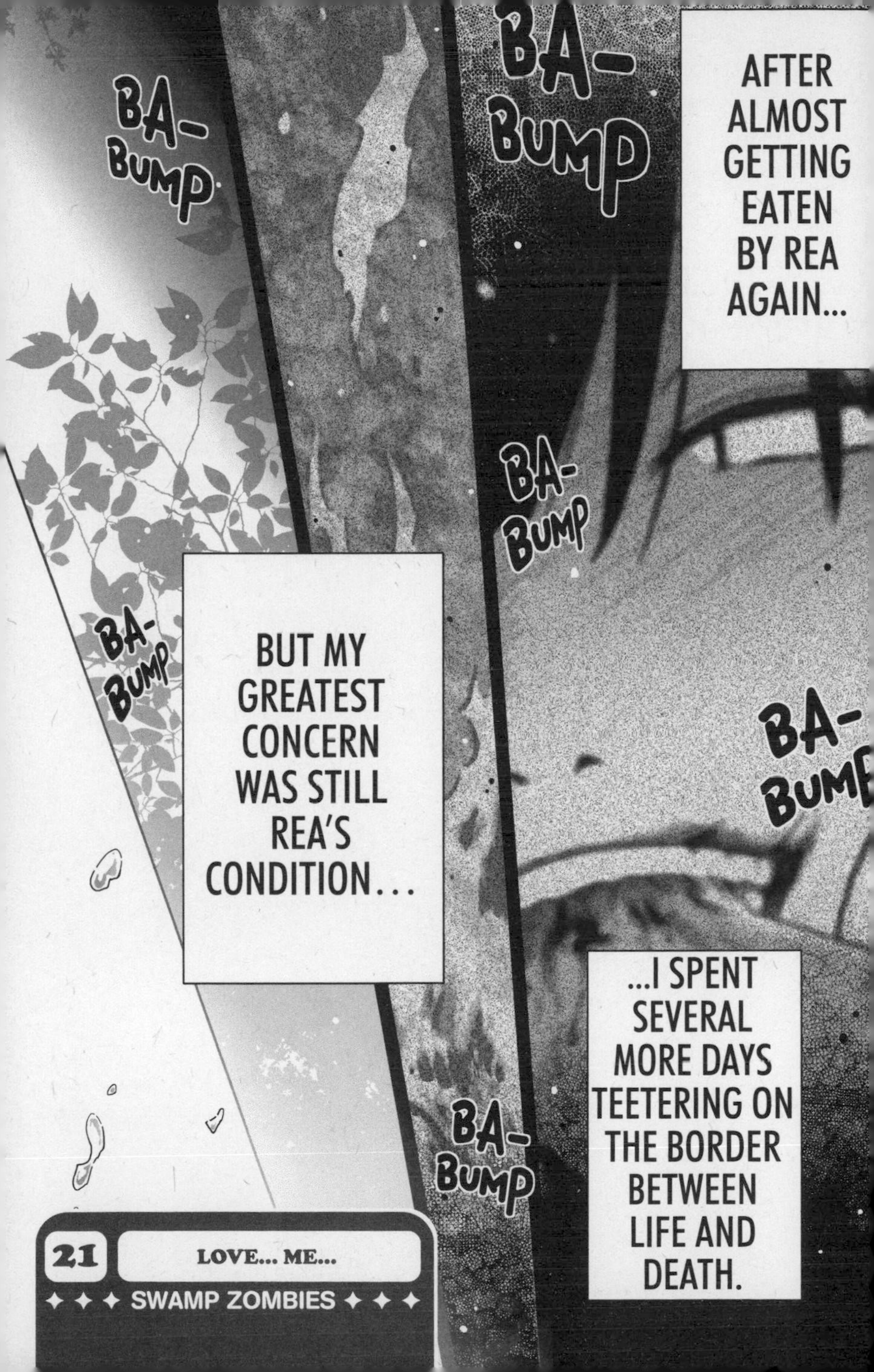
BA-BUMP
AFTER ALMOST GETTING EATEN BY REA AGAIN...
BA-BUMP
BA-BUMP
...I SPENT SEVERAL MORE DAYS TEETERING ON THE BORDER BETWEEN LIFE AND DEATH.
BA-BUMP
BA-BUMP
BA-BUMP
BUT MY GREATEST CONCERN WAS STILL REA'S CONDITION...
21
LOVE... ME...
SWAMP ZOMBIES

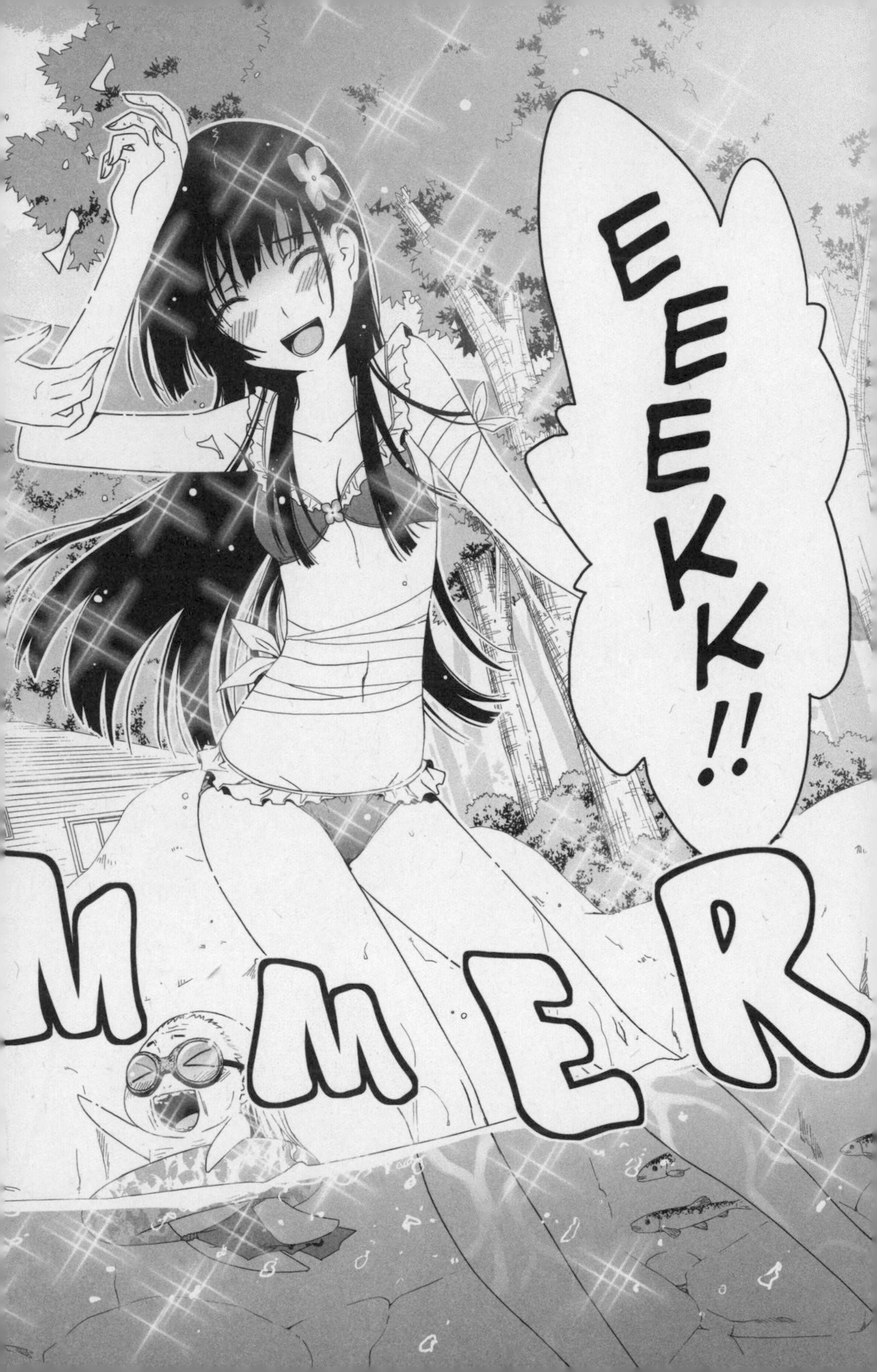
EEEKK!!
MMER

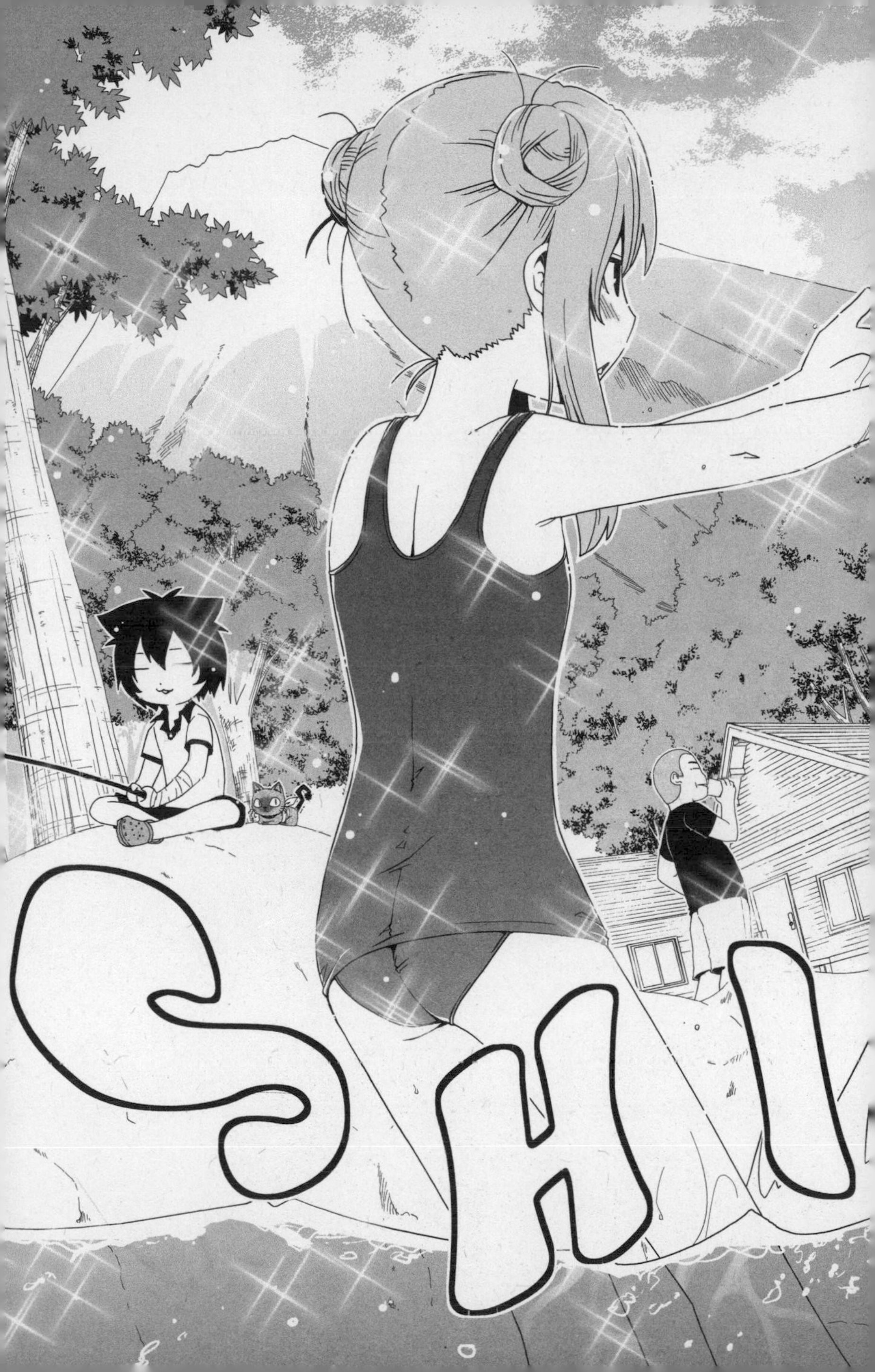
SHU

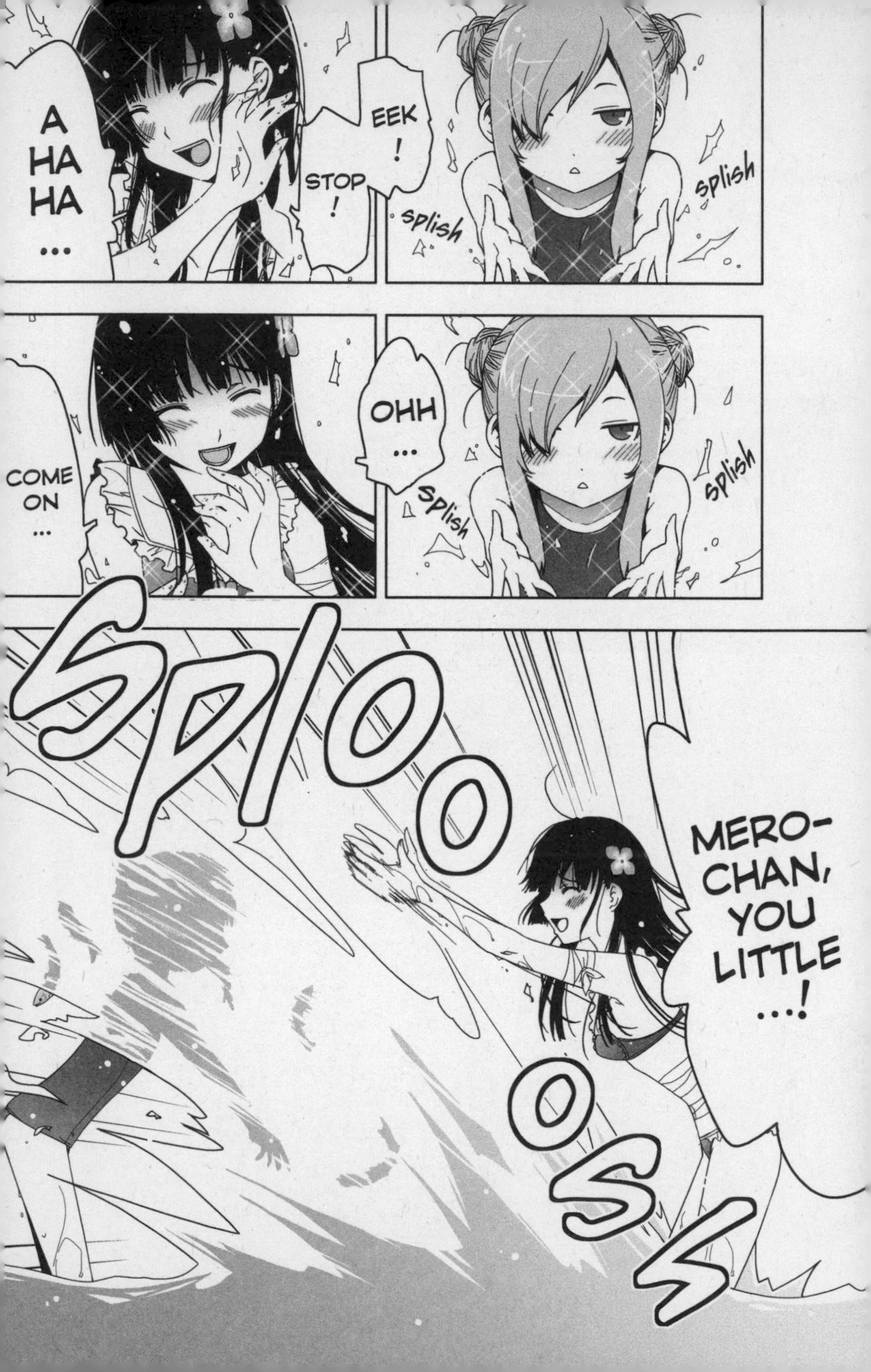
splish
splish
EEK!
STOP!
A HA HA ...
splish
splish
OHH ...
COME ON ...
SPLOOOSH
MERO-CHAN, YOU LITTLE ...!

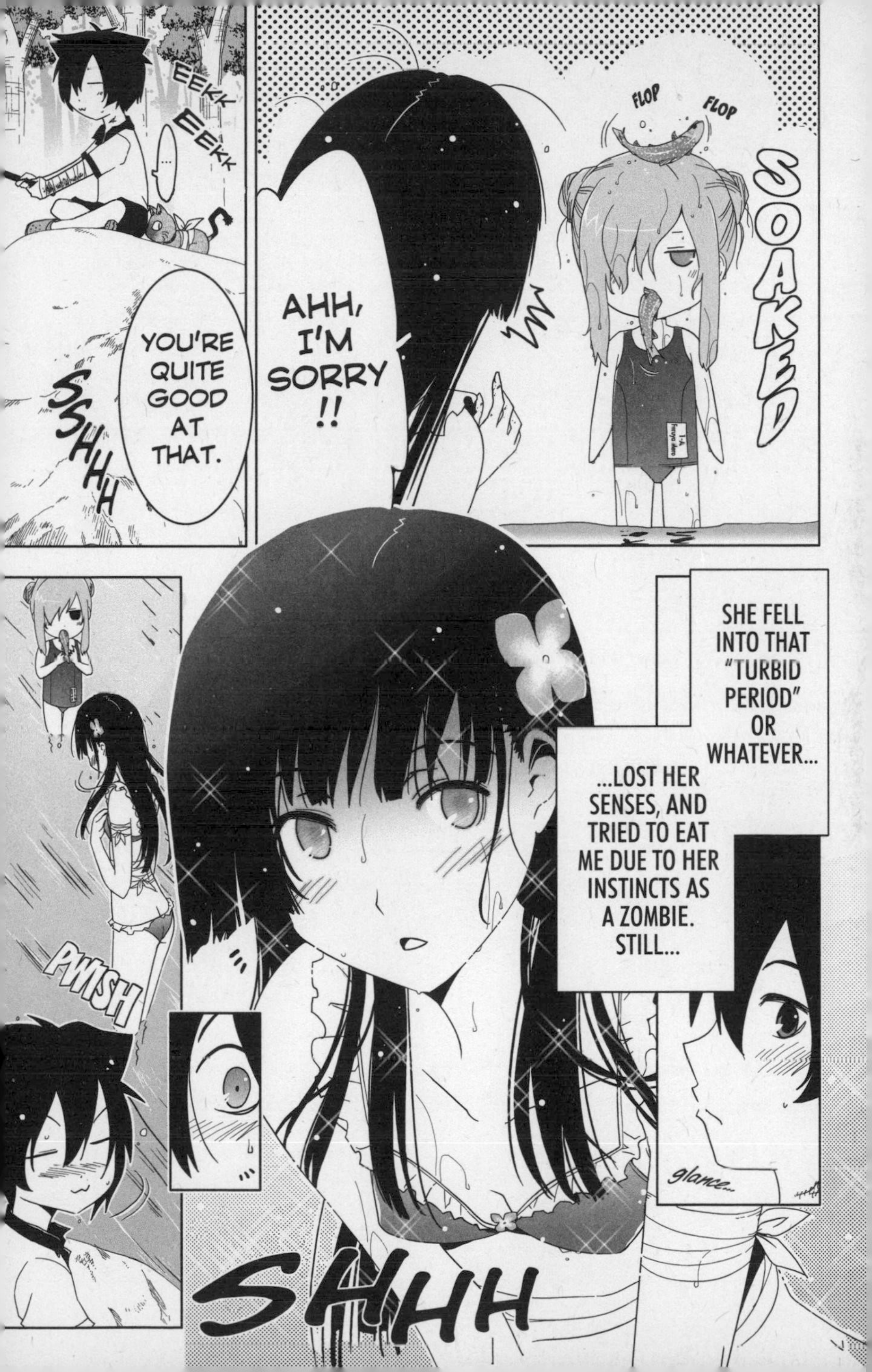
FLOP
FLOP
SOAKED
AHH, I'M SORRY!!
EEKK
EEKK
...
YOU'RE QUITE GOOD AT THAT.
SSHHHH
SHE FELL INTO THAT "TURBID PERIOD" OR WHATEVER...
...LOST HER SENSES, AND TRIED TO EAT ME DUE TO HER INSTINCTS AS A ZOMBIE. STILL...
glance...
SHHH
PWISH

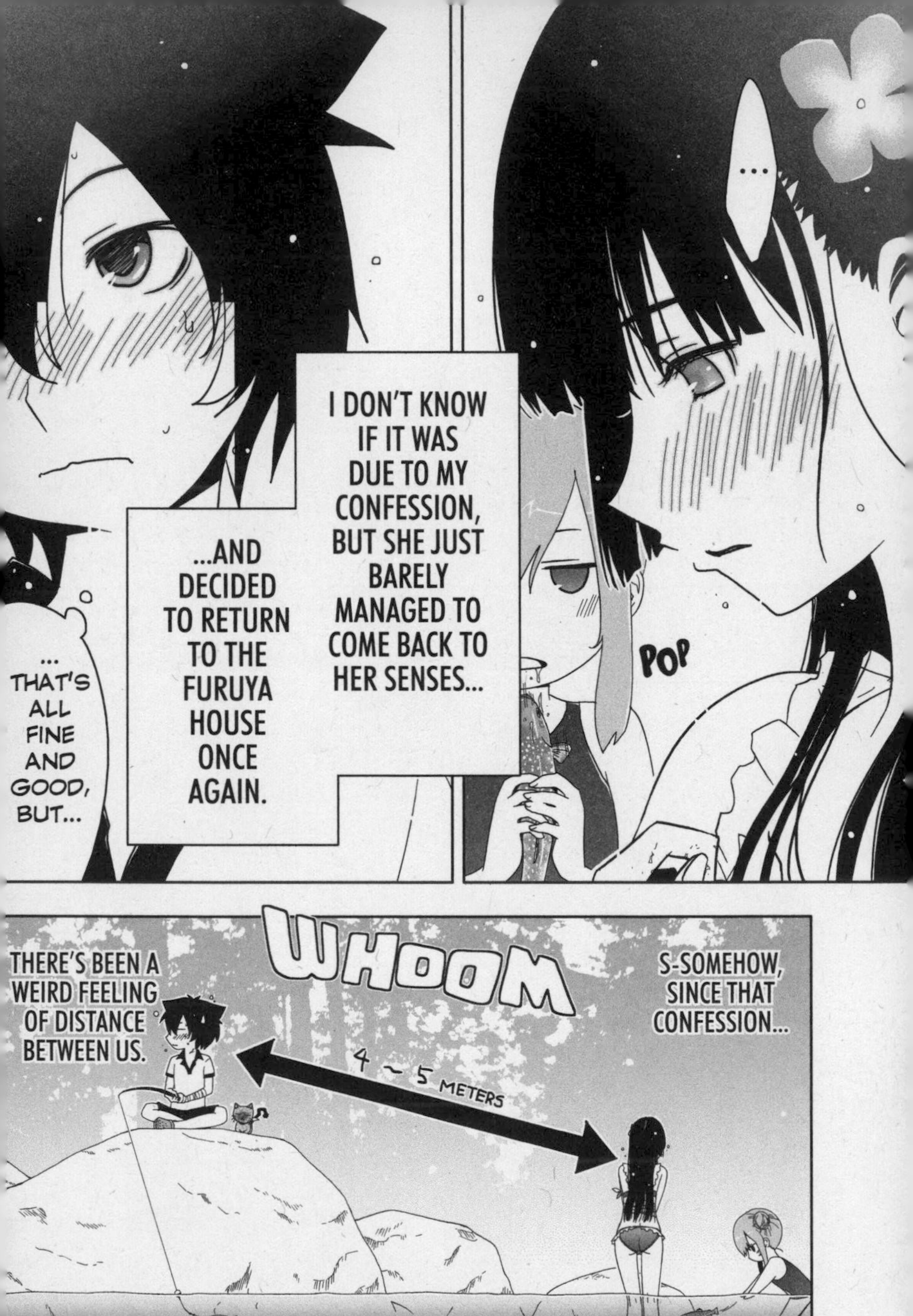
...
I DON'T KNOW IF IT WAS DUE TO MY CONFESSION, BUT SHE JUST BARELY MANAGED TO COME BACK TO HER SENSES...
POP
...AND DECIDED TO RETURN TO THE FURUYA HOUSE ONCE AGAIN.
...THAT'S ALL FINE AND GOOD, BUT...
S-SOMEHOW, SINCE THAT CONFESSION...
WHOOM
4 ~ 5 METERS
THERE'S BEEN A WEIRD FEELING OF DISTANCE BETWEEN US.

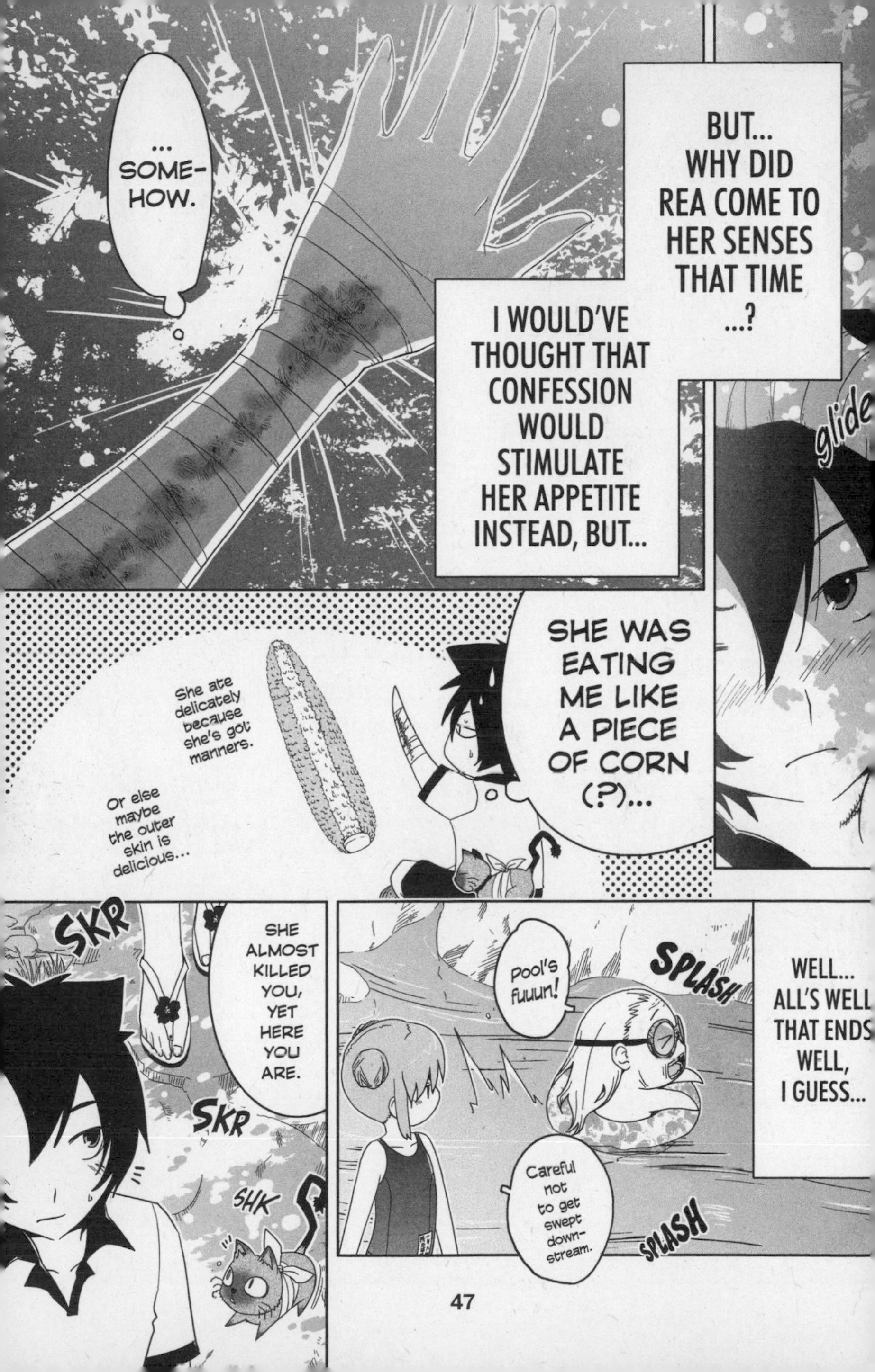
BUT... WHY DID REA COME TO HER SENSES THAT TIME ...?
I WOULD'VE THOUGHT THAT CONFESSION WOULD STIMULATE HER APPETITE INSTEAD, BUT...
glide
... SOME-HOW.
SHE WAS EATING ME LIKE A PIECE OF CORN (?)...
She ate delicately because she's got manners.
Or else maybe the outer skin is delicious...
WELL... ALL'S WELL THAT ENDS WELL, I GUESS...
SPLASH
Pool's fuuun!
Careful not to get swept down-stream.
SPLASH
SKR
SHE ALMOST KILLED YOU, YET HERE YOU ARE.
SKR
SHK

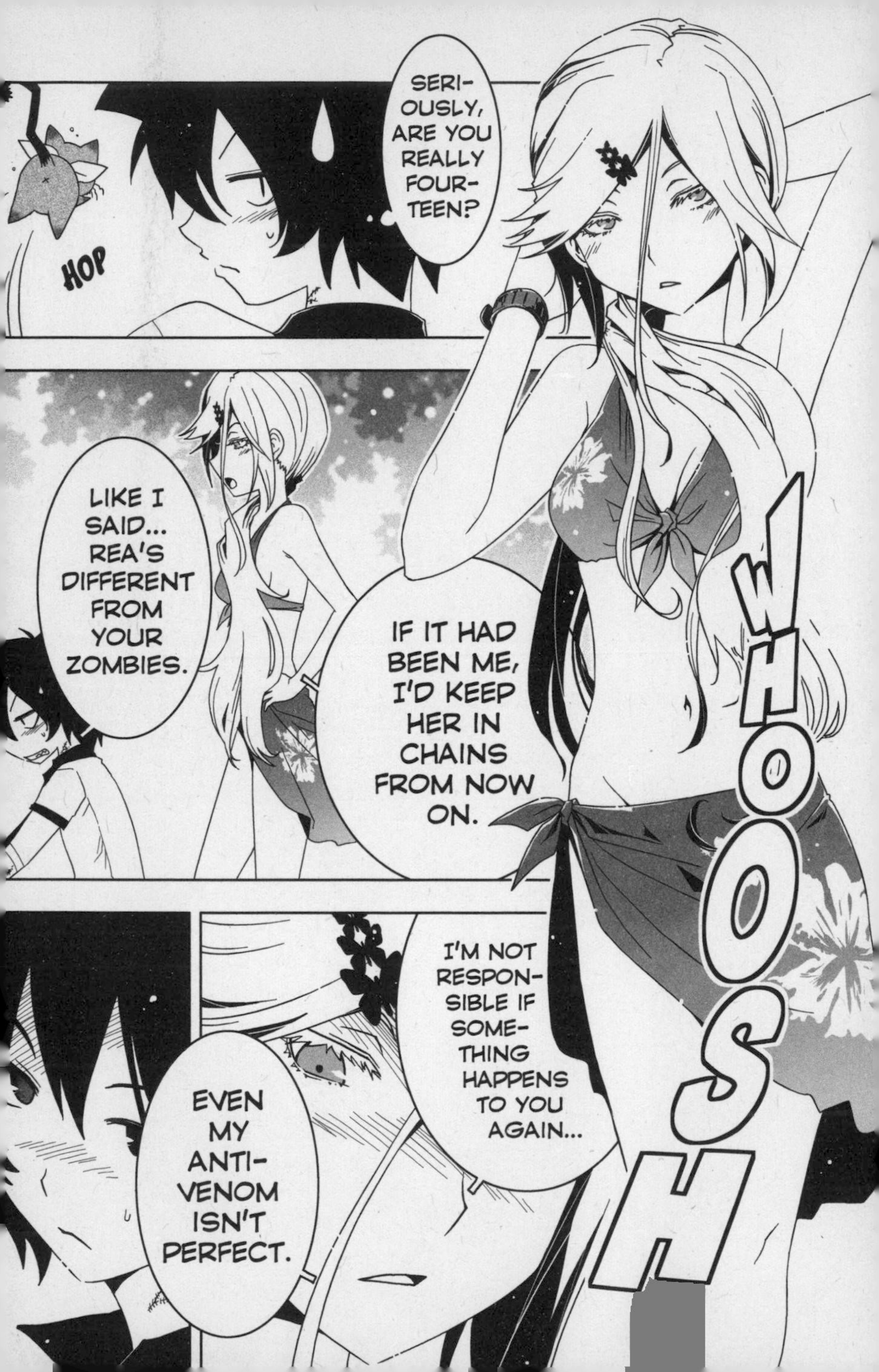
SERIOUSLY, ARE YOU REALLY FOURTEEN?
HOP
LIKE I SAID... REA'S DIFFERENT FROM YOUR ZOMBIES.
IF IT HAD BEEN ME, I'D KEEP HER IN CHAINS FROM NOW ON.
I'M NOT RESPONSIBLE IF SOMETHING HAPPENS TO YOU AGAIN...
EVEN MY ANTI-VENOM ISN'T PERFECT.
WHOOSH

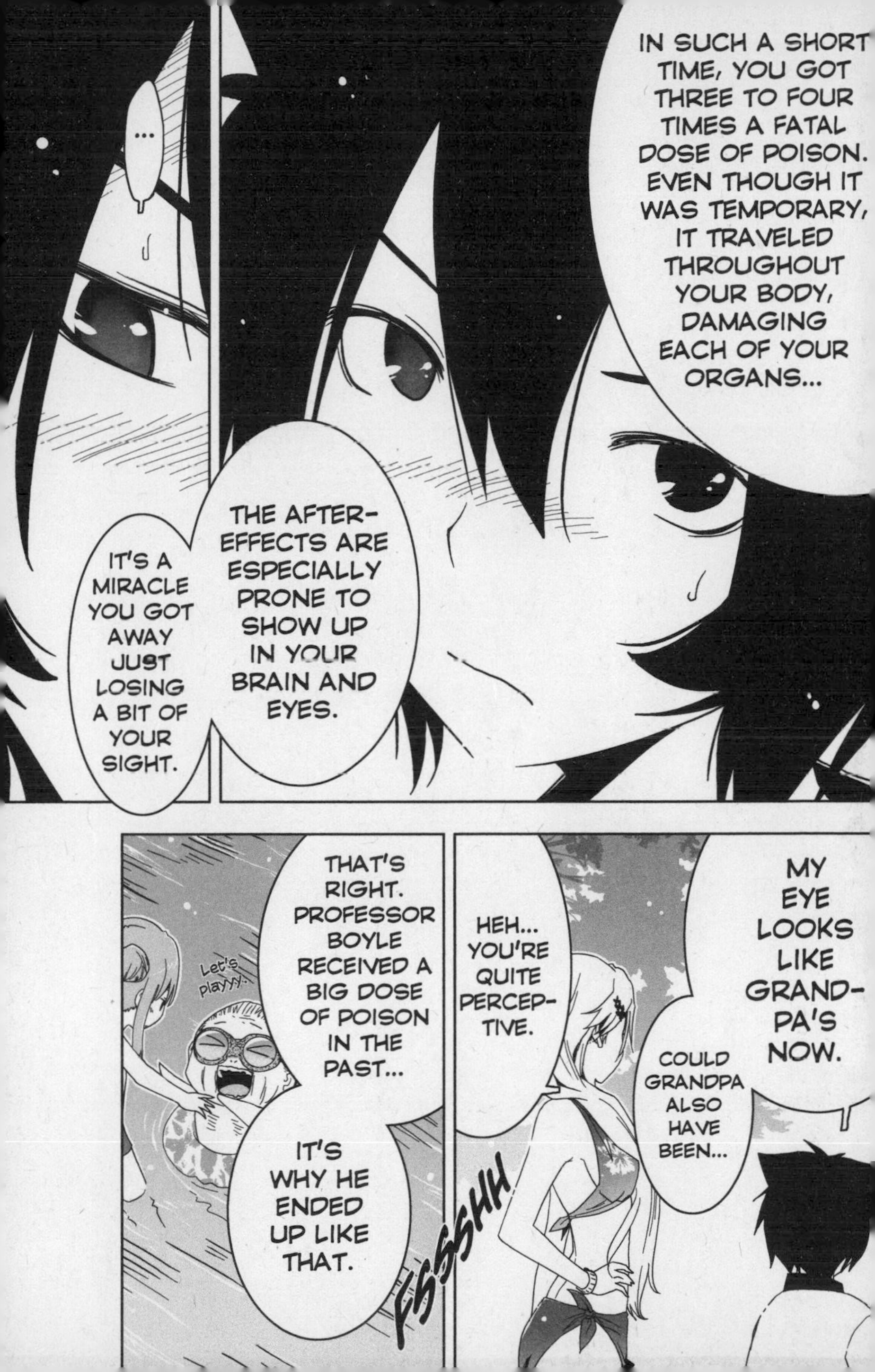
IN SUCH A SHORT TIME, YOU GOT THREE TO FOUR TIMES A FATAL DOSE OF POISON. EVEN THOUGH IT WAS TEMPORARY, IT TRAVELED THROUGHOUT YOUR BODY, DAMAGING EACH OF YOUR ORGANS...
THE AFTER-EFFECTS ARE ESPECIALLY PRONE TO SHOW UP IN YOUR BRAIN AND EYES.
IT'S A MIRACLE YOU GOT AWAY JUST LOSING A BIT OF YOUR SIGHT.
...
MY EYE LOOKS LIKE GRAND-PA'S NOW.
COULD GRANDPA ALSO HAVE BEEN...
HEH... YOU'RE QUITE PERCEP-TIVE.
FSSSHH
THAT'S RIGHT. PROFESSOR BOYLE RECEIVED A BIG DOSE OF POISON IN THE PAST...
Let's playyy.
IT'S WHY HE ENDED UP LIKE THAT.

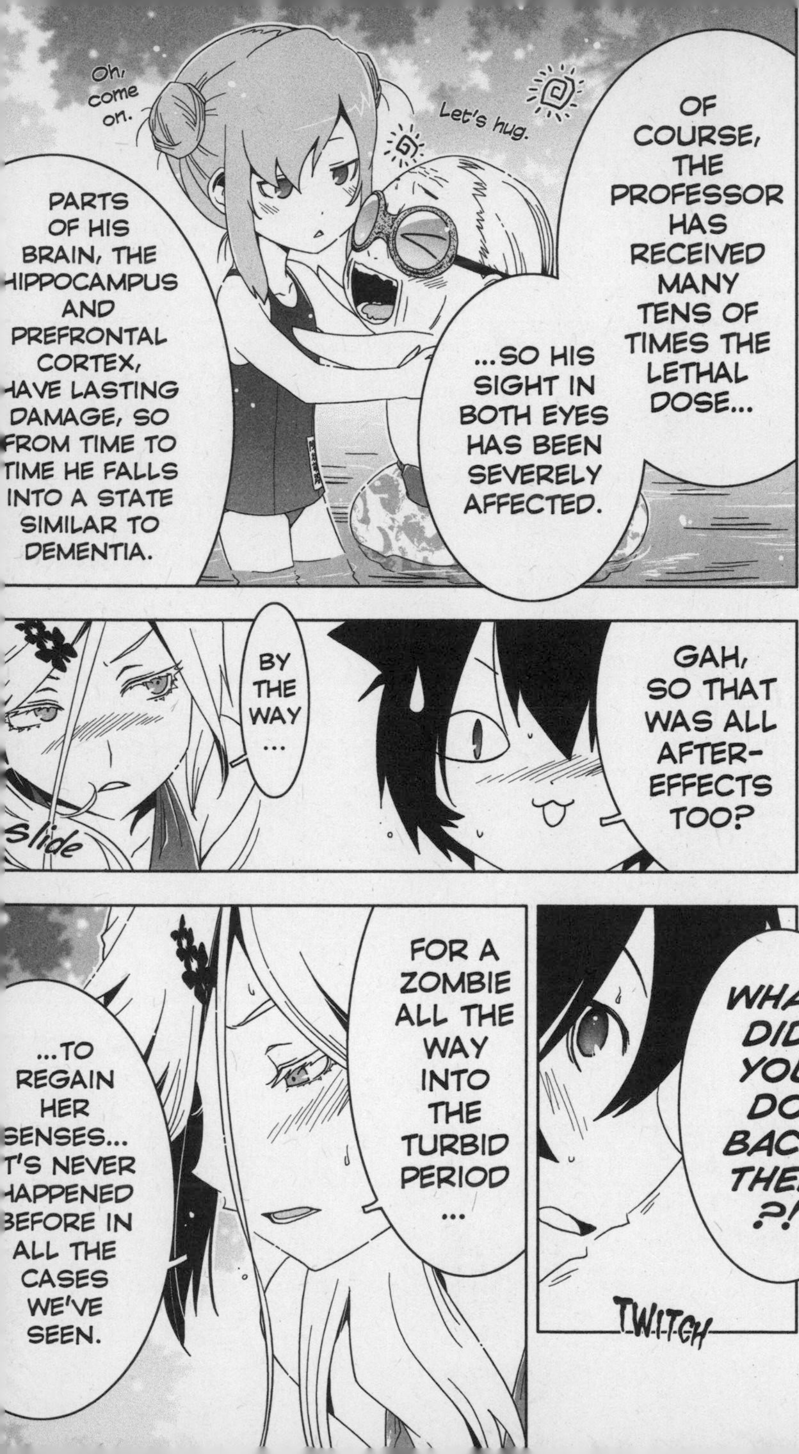
OF COURSE, THE PROFESSOR HAS RECEIVED MANY TENS OF TIMES THE LETHAL DOSE...
Let's hug.
...SO HIS SIGHT IN BOTH EYES HAS BEEN SEVERELY AFFECTED.
Oh, come on.
PARTS OF HIS BRAIN, THE HIPPOCAMPUS AND PREFRONTAL CORTEX, HAVE LASTING DAMAGE, SO FROM TIME TO TIME HE FALLS INTO A STATE SIMILAR TO DEMENTIA.
GAH, SO THAT WAS ALL AFTER-EFFECTS TOO?
BY THE WAY ...
Slide
WHAT DID YOU DO BACK THEN?!
T.W.I.T.C.H
FOR A ZOMBIE ALL THE WAY INTO THE TURBID PERIOD ...
...TO REGAIN HER SENSES... IT'S NEVER HAPPENED BEFORE IN ALL THE CASES WE'VE SEEN.

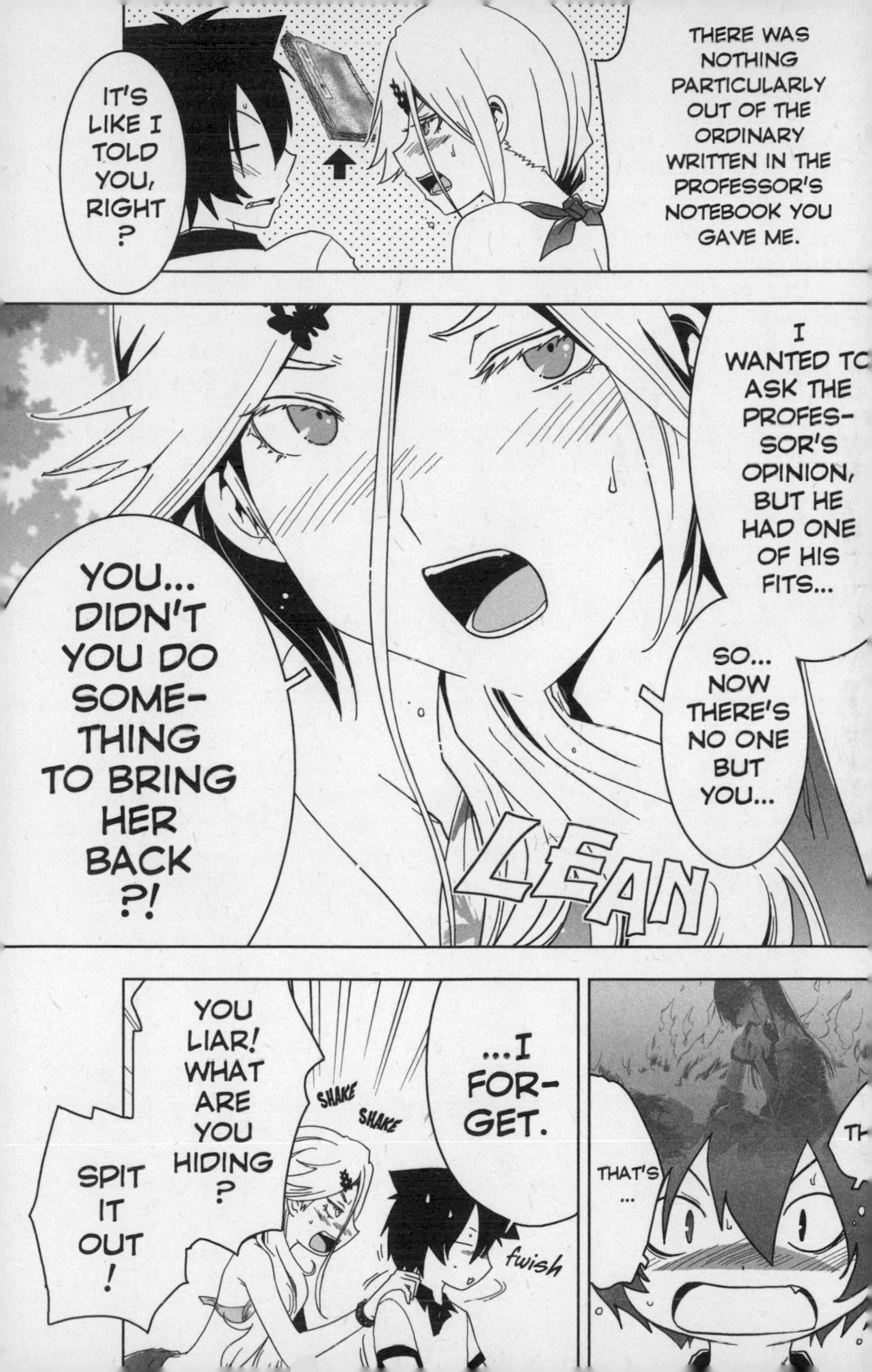
THERE WAS NOTHING PARTICULARLY OUT OF THE ORDINARY WRITTEN IN THE PROFESSOR'S NOTEBOOK YOU GAVE ME.
IT'S LIKE I TOLD YOU, RIGHT?
I WANTED TO ASK THE PROFES-SOR'S OPINION, BUT HE HAD ONE OF HIS FITS...
SO... NOW THERE'S NO ONE BUT YOU...
LEAN
YOU... DIDN'T YOU DO SOME-THING TO BRING HER BACK?!
THAT'S...
...I FOR-GET.
YOU LIAR! WHAT ARE YOU HIDING?
SHAKE
SHAKE
SPIT IT OUT!
fwish

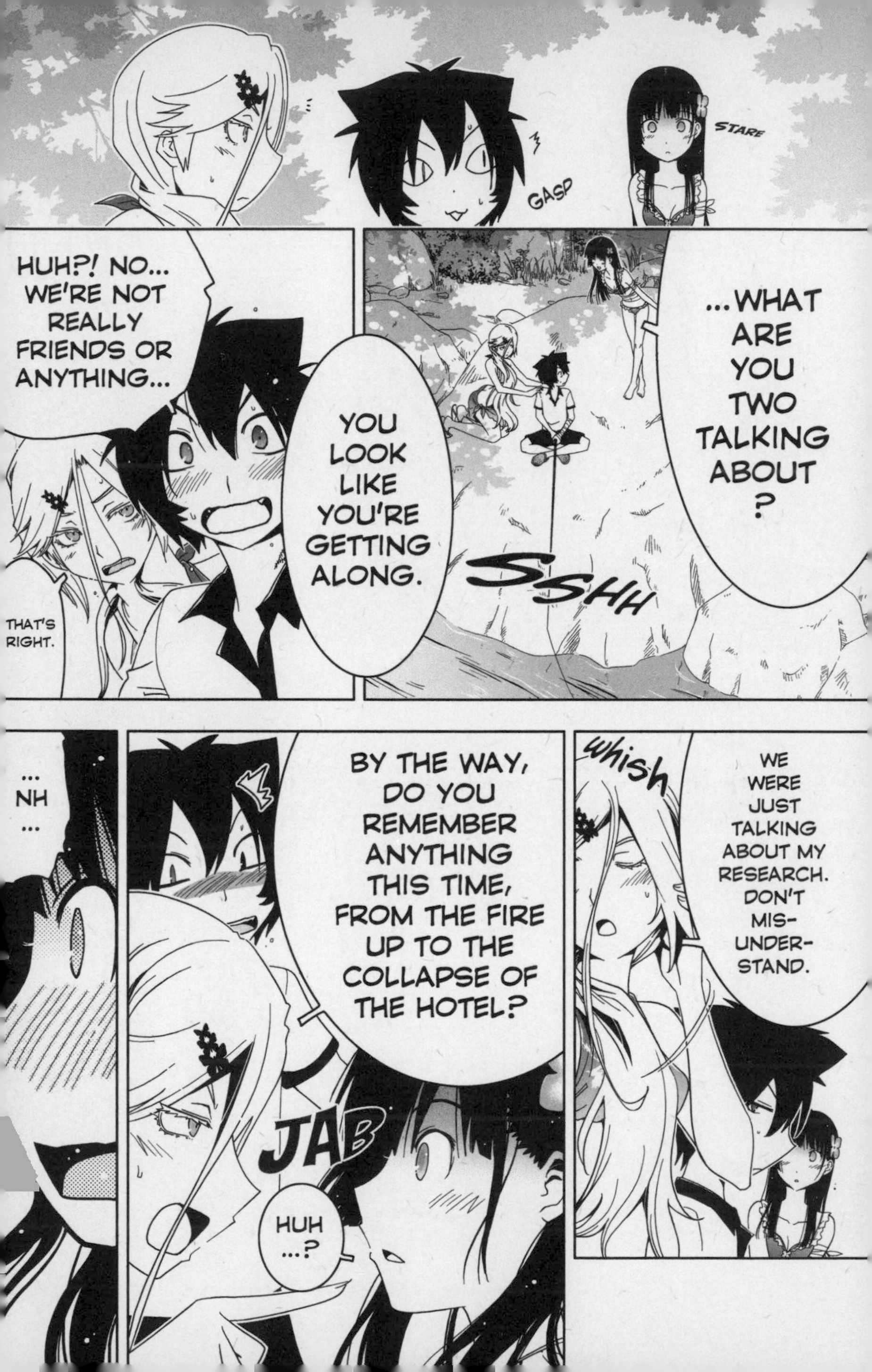
STARE
GASP
...WHAT ARE YOU TWO TALKING ABOUT?
SSHH
YOU LOOK LIKE YOU'RE GETTING ALONG.
HUH?! NO... WE'RE NOT REALLY FRIENDS OR ANYTHING...
THAT'S RIGHT.
whish
WE WERE JUST TALKING ABOUT MY RESEARCH. DON'T MIS-UNDER-STAND.
BY THE WAY, DO YOU REMEMBER ANYTHING THIS TIME, FROM THE FIRE UP TO THE COLLAPSE OF THE HOTEL?
JAB
HUH ...?
... NH ...

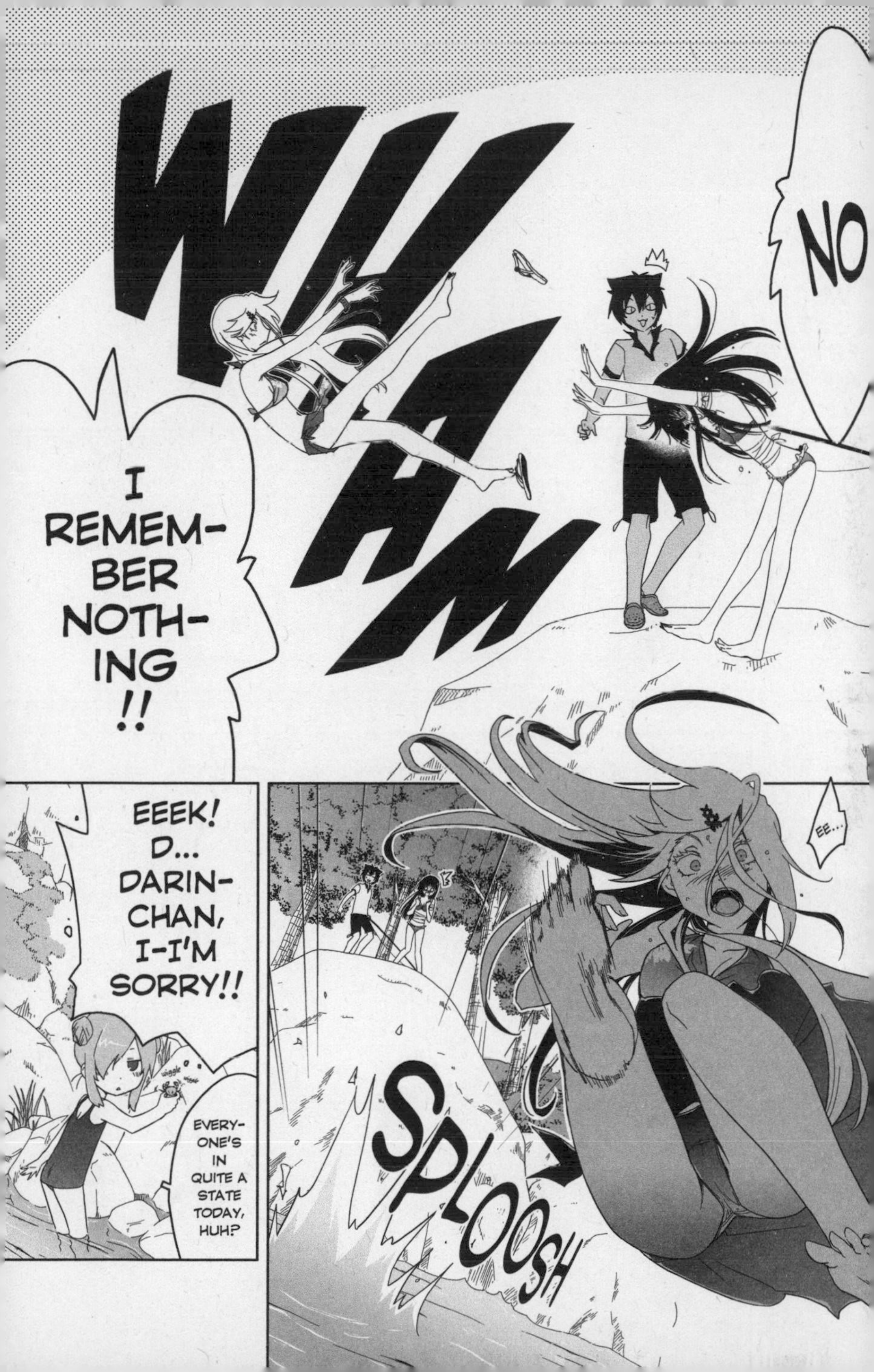
NO
WHAM
I REMEMBER NOTHING!!
EE...
SPLOOSH
EEEK! D... DARIN-CHAN, I-I'M SORRY!!
wiggle wiggle
EVERYONE'S IN QUITE A STATE TODAY, HUH?

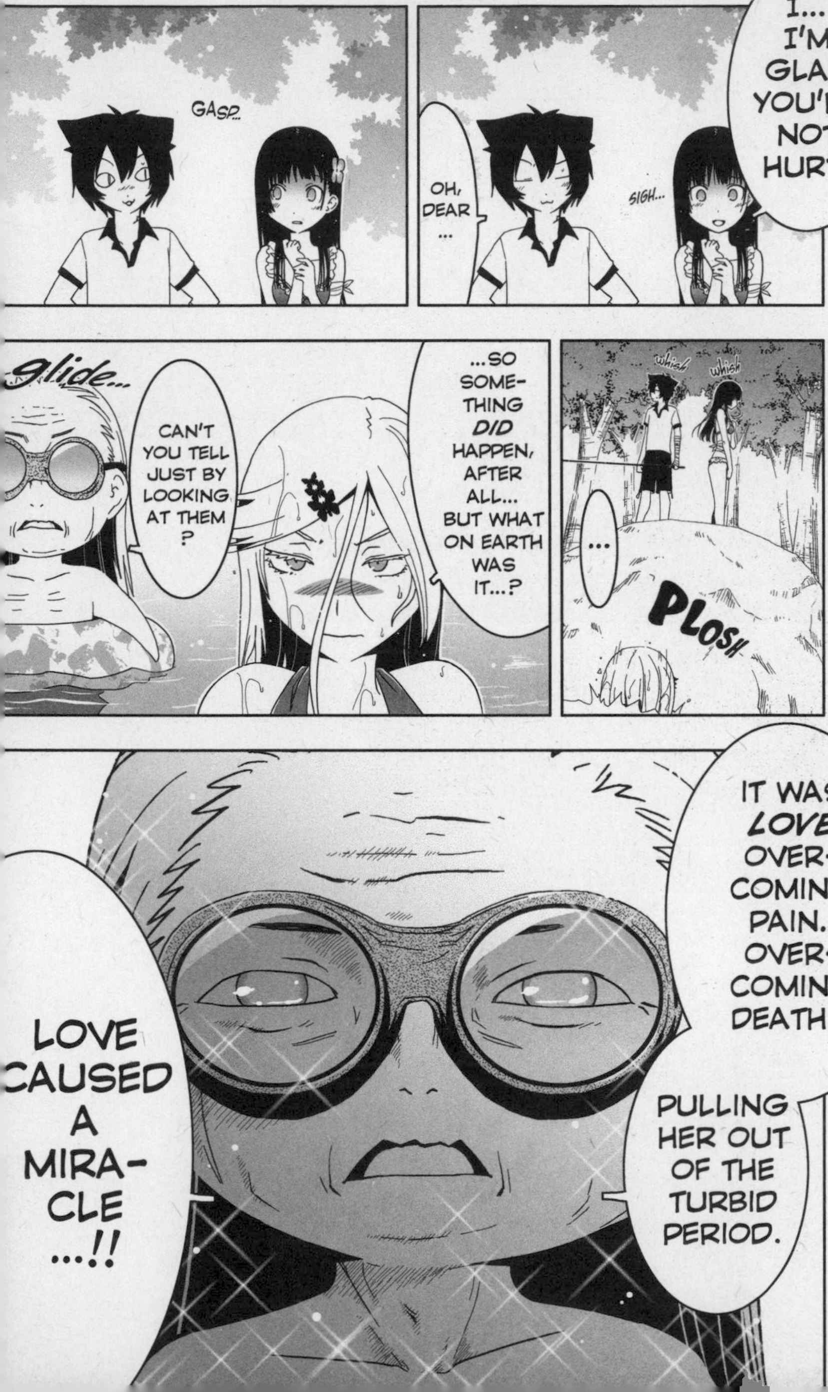
I... I'M GLAD YOU'RE NOT HURT.
SIGH...
OH, DEAR ...
GASP...
whish
whish
...
PLOSH
...SO SOME-THING *DID* HAPPEN, AFTER ALL... BUT WHAT ON EARTH WAS IT...?
CAN'T YOU TELL JUST BY LOOKING AT THEM?
glide...
IT WAS *LOVE* OVER-COMING PAIN... OVER-COMING DEATH...
PULLING HER OUT OF THE TURBID PERIOD.
LOVE CAUSED A MIRA-CLE ...!!

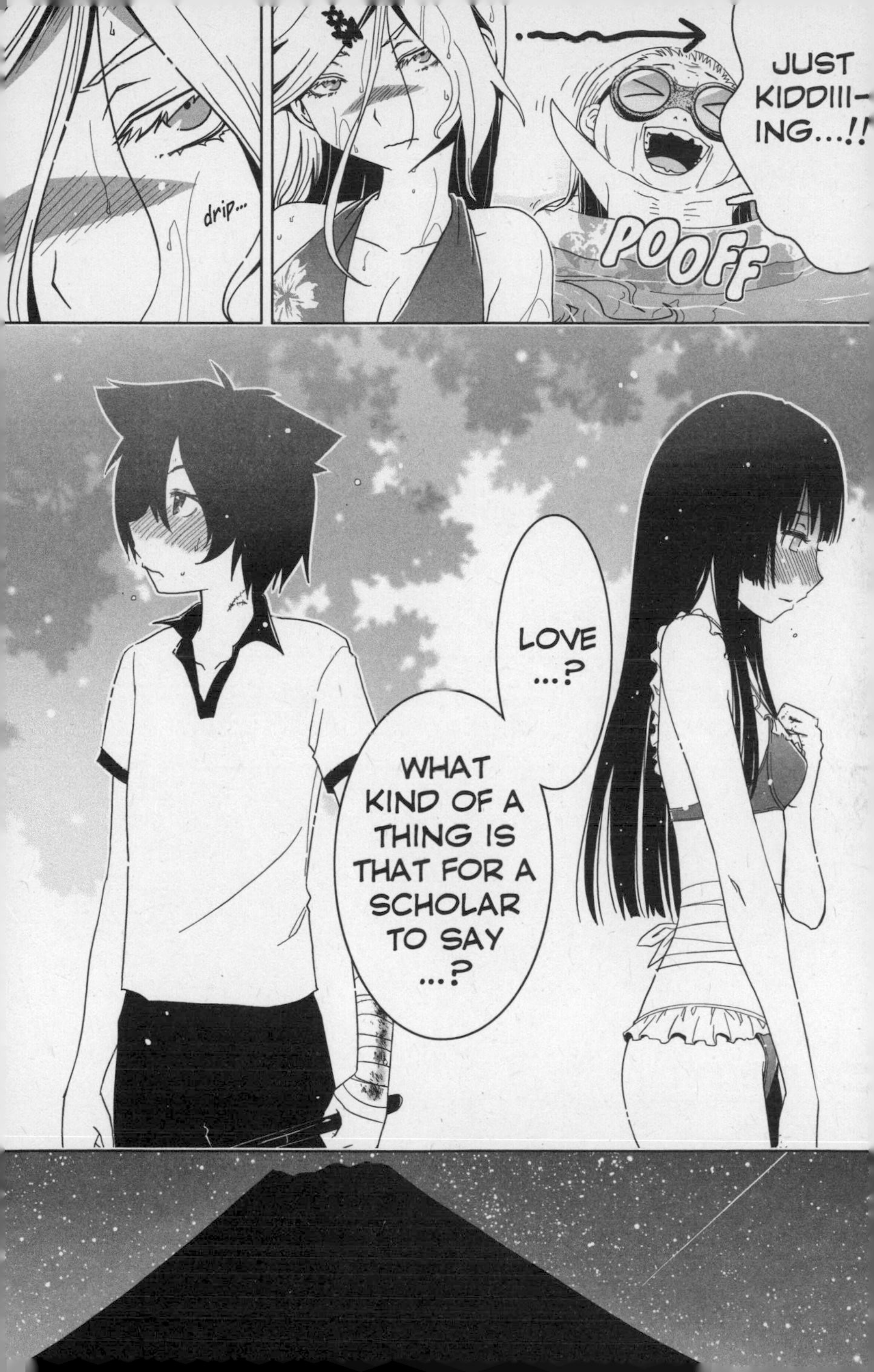
JUST KIDDIIII-ING...!!
POOFF
drip...
LOVE ...?
WHAT KIND OF A THING IS THAT FOR A SCHOLAR TO SAY ...?

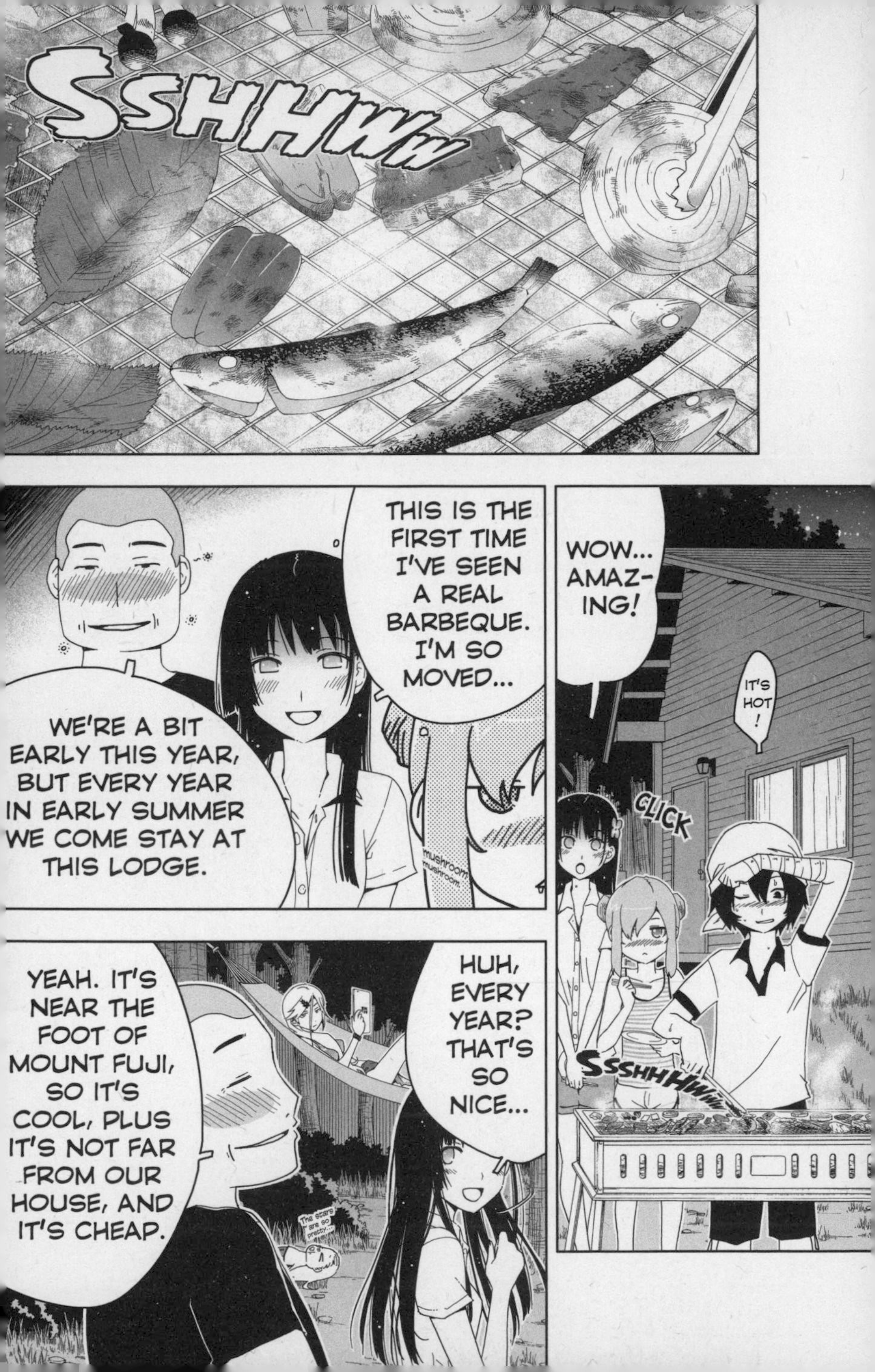
SSHHWW
WOW... AMAZ-ING!
IT'S HOT!
CLICK
SSSHHHWWW
THIS IS THE FIRST TIME I'VE SEEN A REAL BARBEQUE. I'M SO MOVED...
WE'RE A BIT EARLY THIS YEAR, BUT EVERY YEAR IN EARLY SUMMER WE COME STAY AT THIS LODGE.
mushroom mushroom
HUH, EVERY YEAR? THAT'S SO NICE...
YEAH. IT'S NEAR THE FOOT OF MOUNT FUJI, SO IT'S COOL, PLUS IT'S NOT FAR FROM OUR HOUSE, AND IT'S CHEAP.
The stars are so pretty...

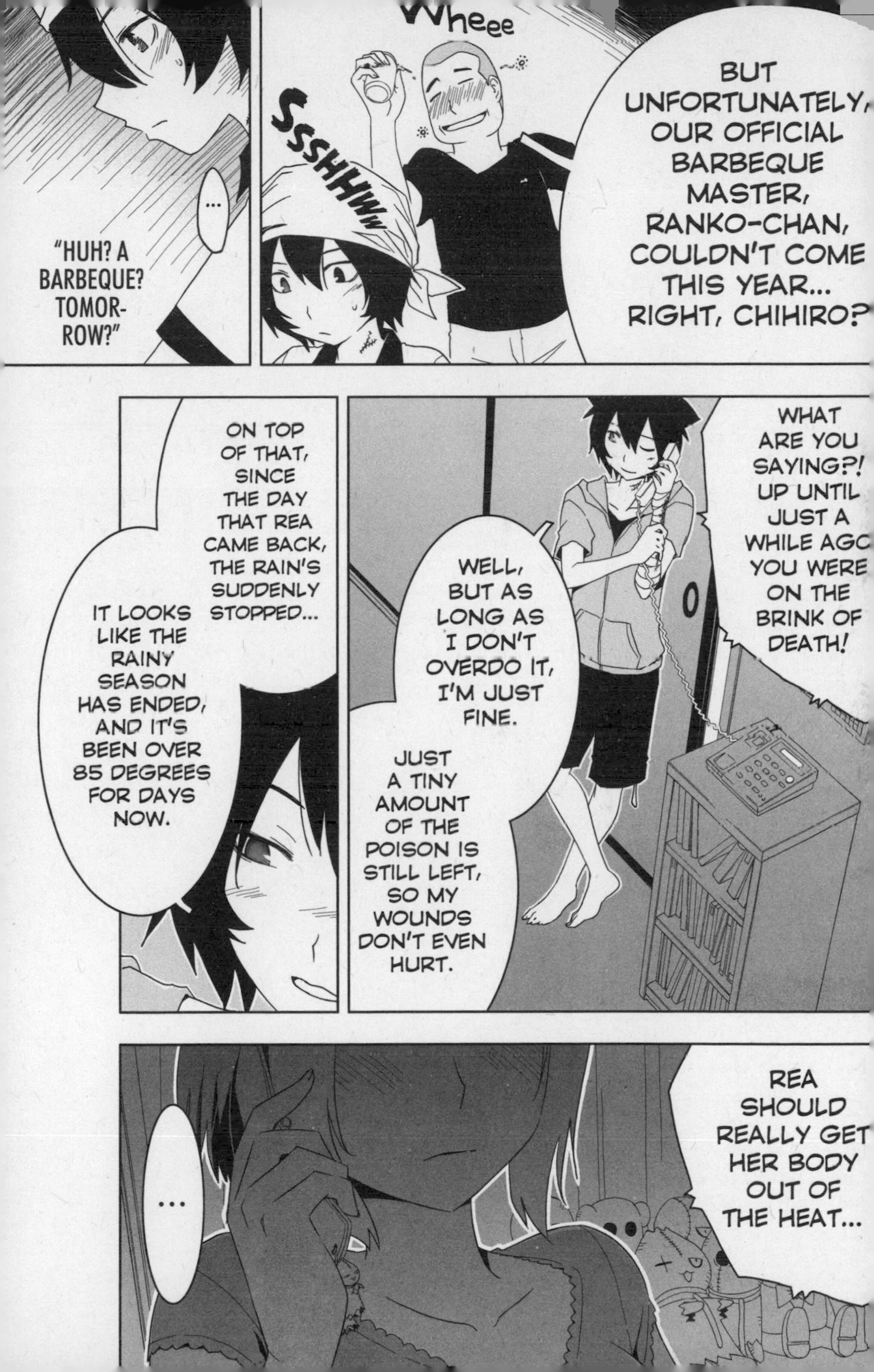

BUT UNFORTUNATELY, OUR OFFICIAL BARBEQUE MASTER, RANKO-CHAN, COULDN'T COME THIS YEAR... RIGHT, CHIHIRO?
Wheee
SSSHHHWW
...
"HUH? A BARBEQUE? TOMOR-ROW?"
WHAT ARE YOU SAYING?! UP UNTIL JUST A WHILE AGO YOU WERE ON THE BRINK OF DEATH!
WELL, BUT AS LONG AS I DON'T OVERDO IT, I'M JUST FINE.
JUST A TINY AMOUNT OF THE POISON IS STILL LEFT, SO MY WOUNDS DON'T EVEN HURT.
ON TOP OF THAT, SINCE THE DAY THAT REA CAME BACK, THE RAIN'S SUDDENLY STOPPED...
IT LOOKS LIKE THE RAINY SEASON HAS ENDED, AND IT'S BEEN OVER 85 DEGREES FOR DAYS NOW.
REA SHOULD REALLY GET HER BODY OUT OF THE HEAT...
...

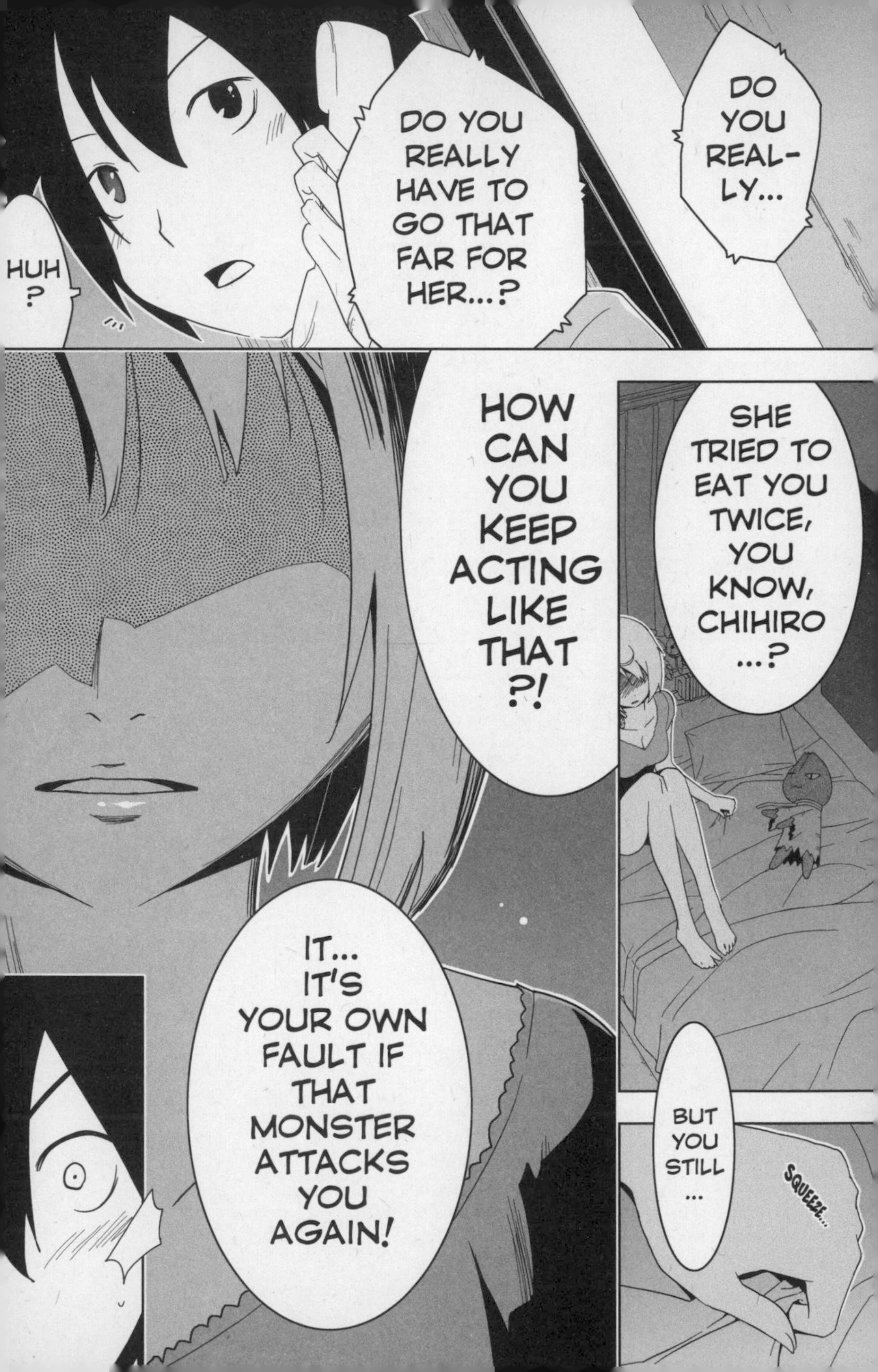
DO YOU REAL-LY...
DO YOU REALLY HAVE TO GO THAT FAR FOR HER...?
HUH?
SHE TRIED TO EAT YOU TWICE, YOU KNOW, CHIHIRO...?
BUT YOU STILL...
SQUEEZE...
HOW CAN YOU KEEP ACTING LIKE THAT?!
IT... IT'S YOUR OWN FAULT IF THAT MONSTER ATTACKS YOU AGAIN!

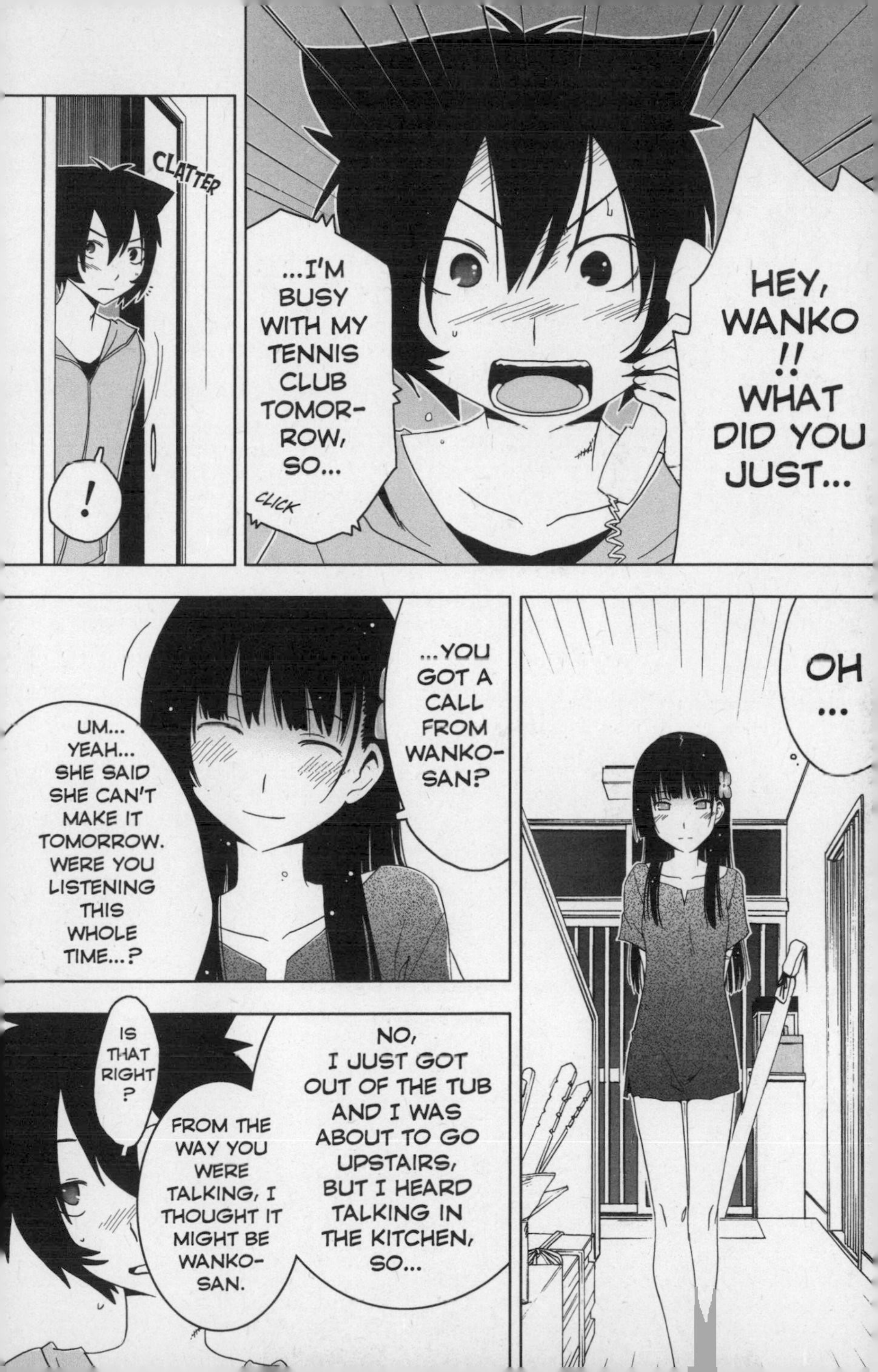
HEY, WANKO!! WHAT DID YOU JUST...
...I'M BUSY WITH MY TENNIS CLUB TOMORROW, SO...
CLICK
CLATTER
!
OH...
...YOU GOT A CALL FROM WANKO-SAN?
UM... YEAH... SHE SAID SHE CAN'T MAKE IT TOMORROW. WERE YOU LISTENING THIS WHOLE TIME...?
NO, I JUST GOT OUT OF THE TUB AND I WAS ABOUT TO GO UPSTAIRS, BUT I HEARD TALKING IN THE KITCHEN, SO...
IS THAT RIGHT?
FROM THE WAY YOU WERE TALKING, I THOUGHT IT MIGHT BE WANKO-SAN.

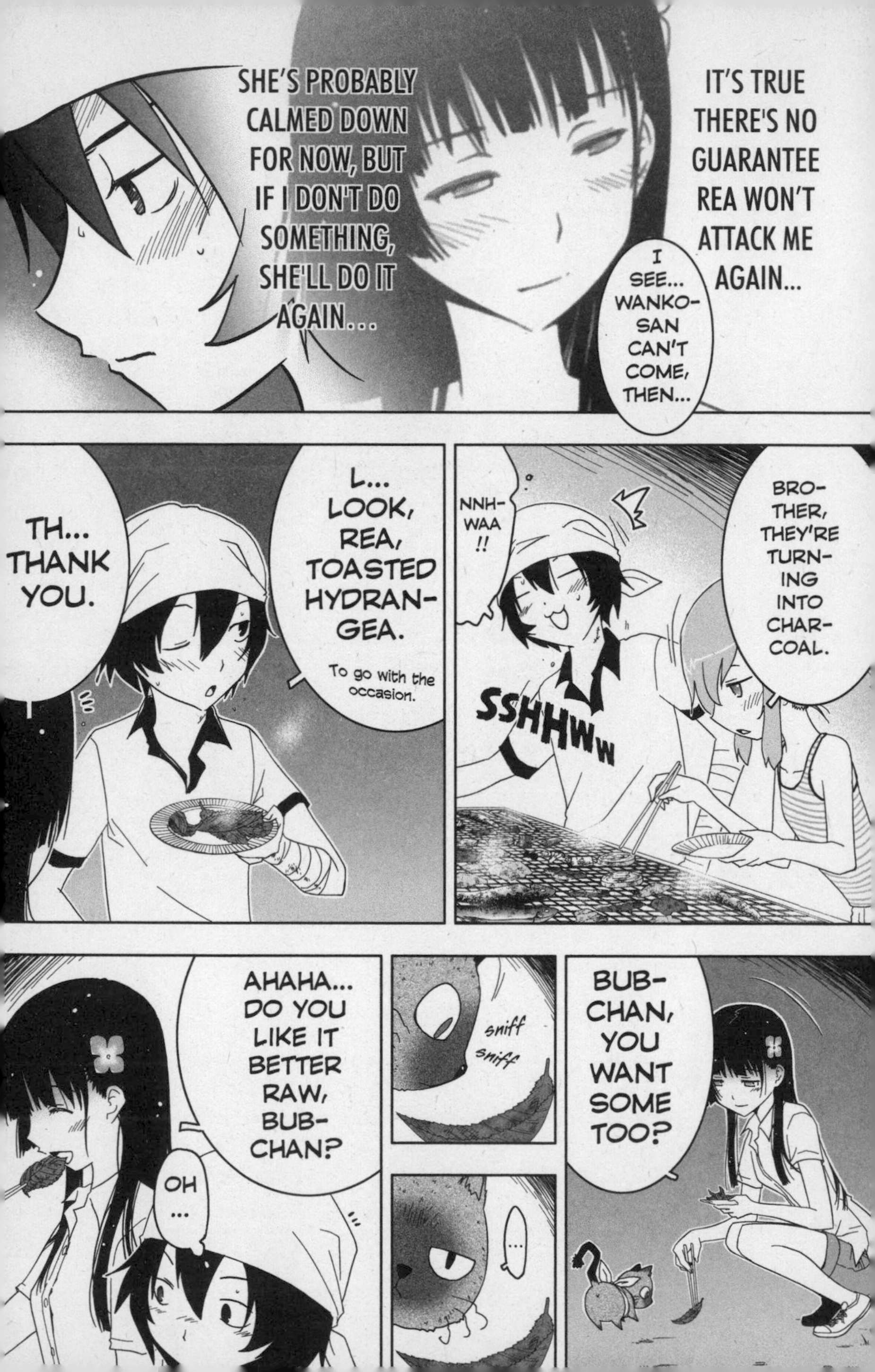
IT'S TRUE THERE'S NO GUARANTEE REA WON'T ATTACK ME AGAIN...
I SEE... WANKO-SAN CAN'T COME, THEN...
SHE'S PROBABLY CALMED DOWN FOR NOW, BUT IF I DON'T DO SOMETHING, SHE'LL DO IT AGAIN...
BROTHER, THEY'RE TURNING INTO CHARCOAL.
NNH-WAA!!
SSHHWWW
L... LOOK, REA, TOASTED HYDRANGEA.
To go with the occasion.
TH... THANK YOU.
BUB-CHAN, YOU WANT SOME TOO?
sniff sniff
...
AHAHA... DO YOU LIKE IT BETTER RAW, BUB-CHAN?
OH ...

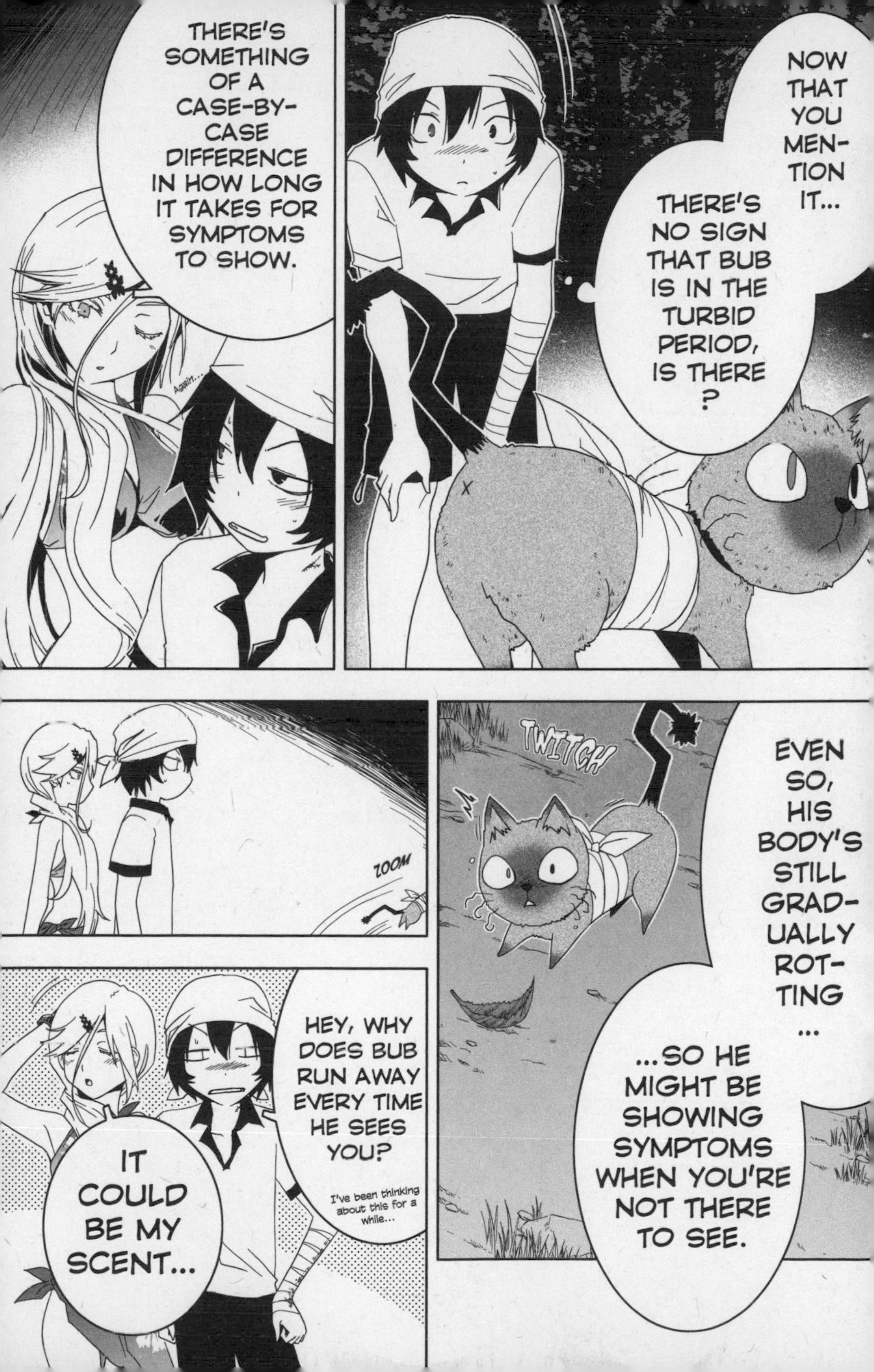
NOW THAT YOU MENTION IT...
THERE'S NO SIGN THAT BUB IS IN THE TURBID PERIOD, IS THERE?
THERE'S SOMETHING OF A CASE-BY-CASE DIFFERENCE IN HOW LONG IT TAKES FOR SYMPTOMS TO SHOW.
Again...
TWITCH
EVEN SO, HIS BODY'S STILL GRADUALLY ROTTING...
...SO HE MIGHT BE SHOWING SYMPTOMS WHEN YOU'RE NOT THERE TO SEE.
ZOOM
HEY, WHY DOES BUB RUN AWAY EVERY TIME HE SEES YOU?
I've been thinking about this for a while...
IT COULD BE MY SCENT...

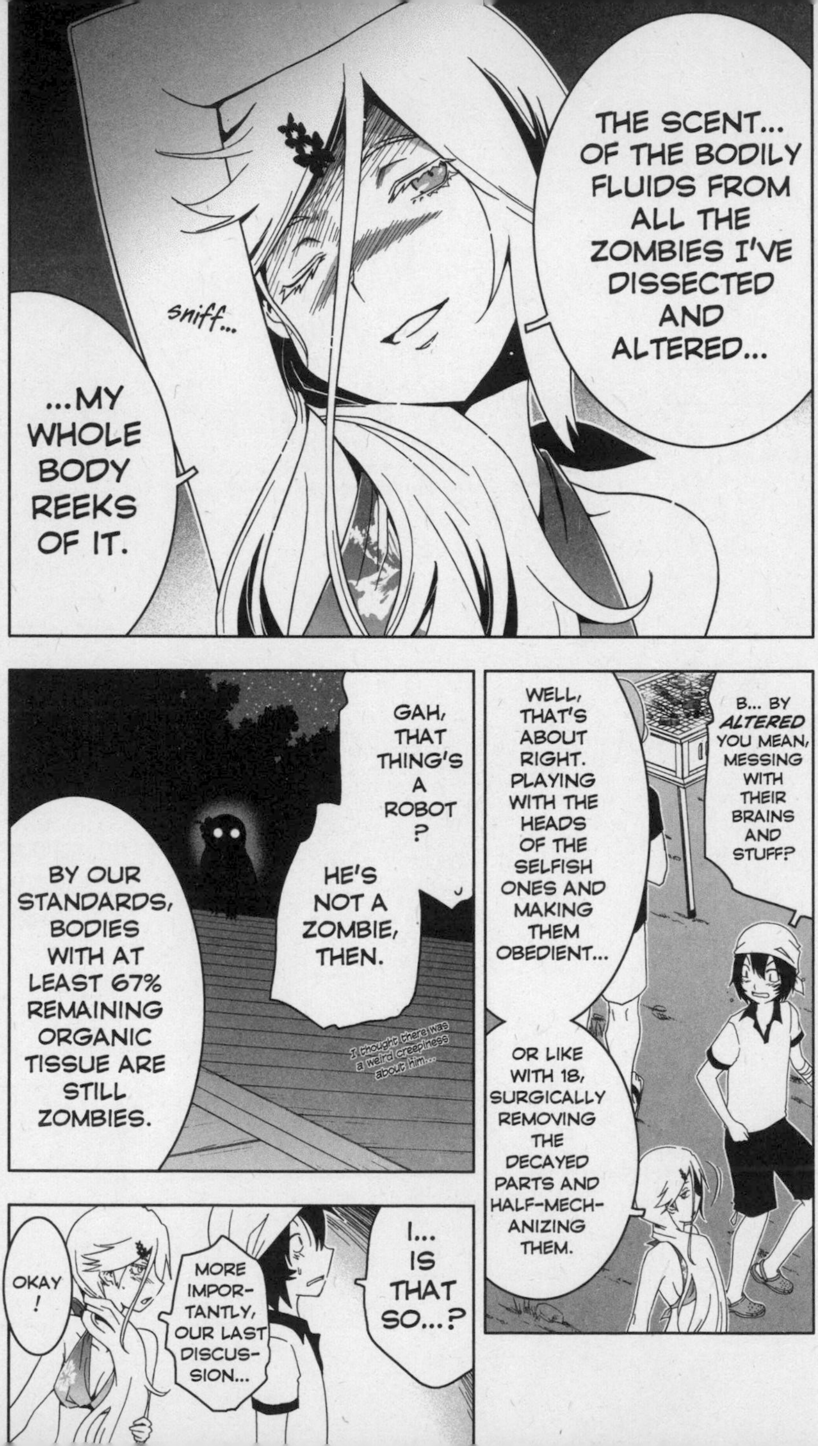
THE SCENT... OF THE BODILY FLUIDS FROM ALL THE ZOMBIES I'VE DISSECTED AND ALTERED...
sniff...
...MY WHOLE BODY REEKS OF IT.
B... BY *ALTERED* YOU MEAN, MESSING WITH THEIR BRAINS AND STUFF?
WELL, THAT'S ABOUT RIGHT. PLAYING WITH THE HEADS OF THE SELFISH ONES AND MAKING THEM OBEDIENT...
OR LIKE WITH 18, SURGICALLY REMOVING THE DECAYED PARTS AND HALF-MECHANIZING THEM.
GAH, THAT THING'S A ROBOT?
HE'S NOT A ZOMBIE, THEN.
BY OUR STANDARDS, BODIES WITH AT LEAST 67% REMAINING ORGANIC TISSUE ARE STILL ZOMBIES.
I thought there was a weird creepiness about him...
I... IS THAT SO...?
MORE IMPORTANTLY, OUR LAST DISCUSSION...
OKAY!

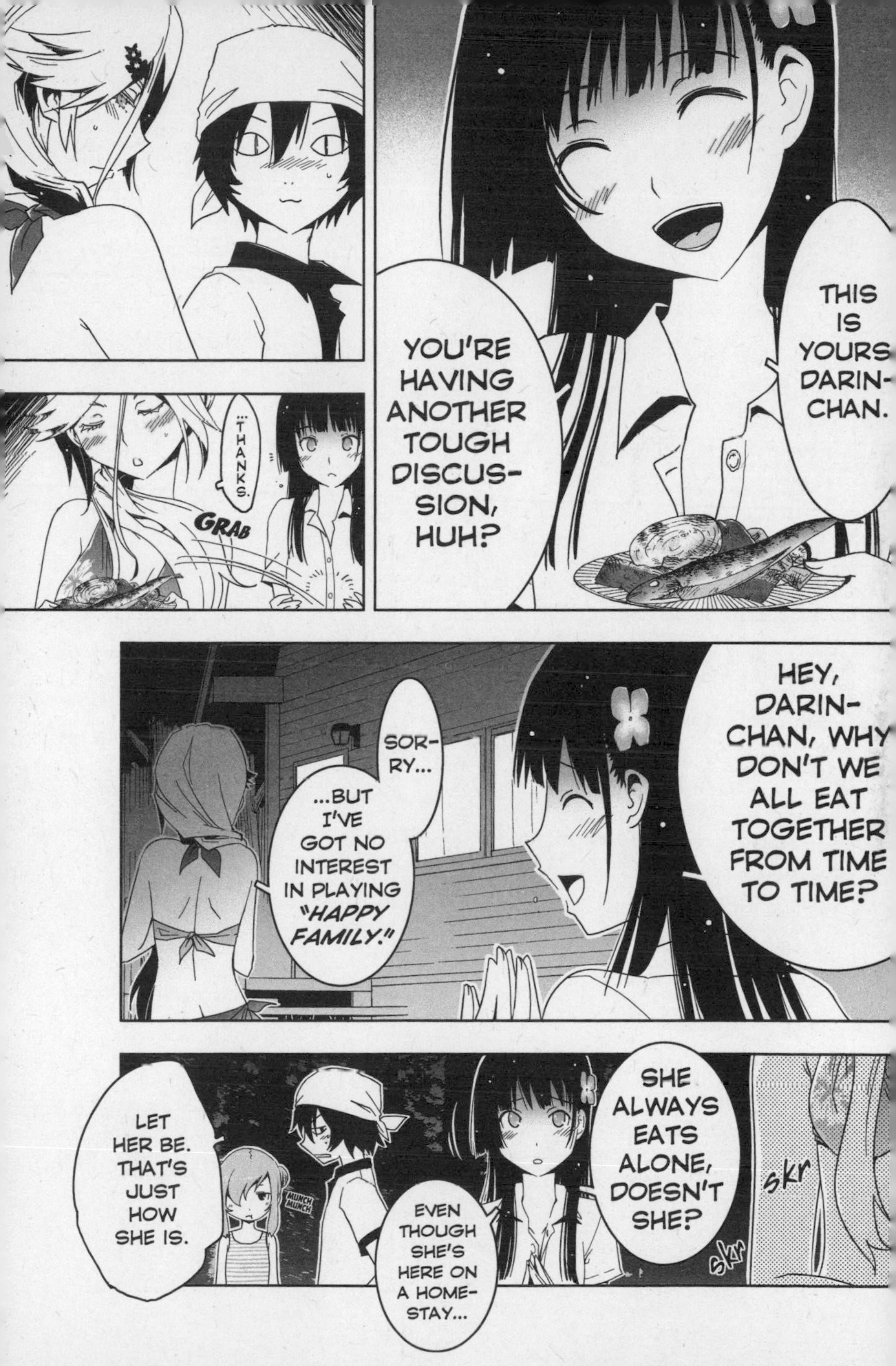
THIS IS YOURS DARIN-CHAN.
YOU'RE HAVING ANOTHER TOUGH DISCUSSION, HUH?
...THANKS.
GRAB
HEY, DARIN-CHAN, WHY DON'T WE ALL EAT TOGETHER FROM TIME TO TIME?
SORRY...
...BUT I'VE GOT NO INTEREST IN PLAYING "HAPPY FAMILY."
skr
skr
SHE ALWAYS EATS ALONE, DOESN'T SHE?
EVEN THOUGH SHE'S HERE ON A HOME-STAY...
MUNCH MUNCH
LET HER BE. THAT'S JUST HOW SHE IS.

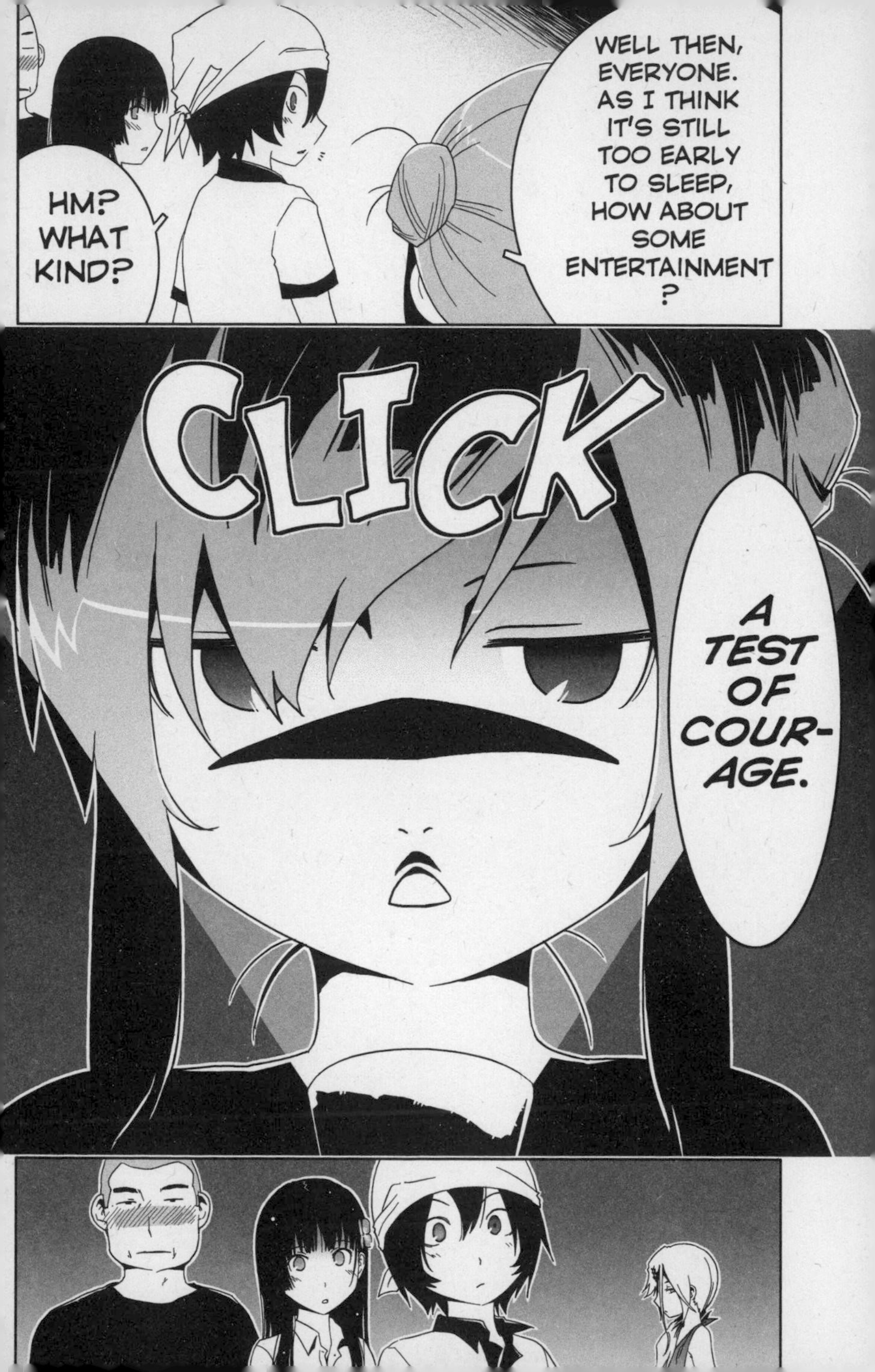
WELL THEN, EVERYONE. AS I THINK IT'S STILL TOO EARLY TO SLEEP, HOW ABOUT SOME ENTERTAINMENT?
HM? WHAT KIND?
CLICK
A TEST OF COUR-AGE.

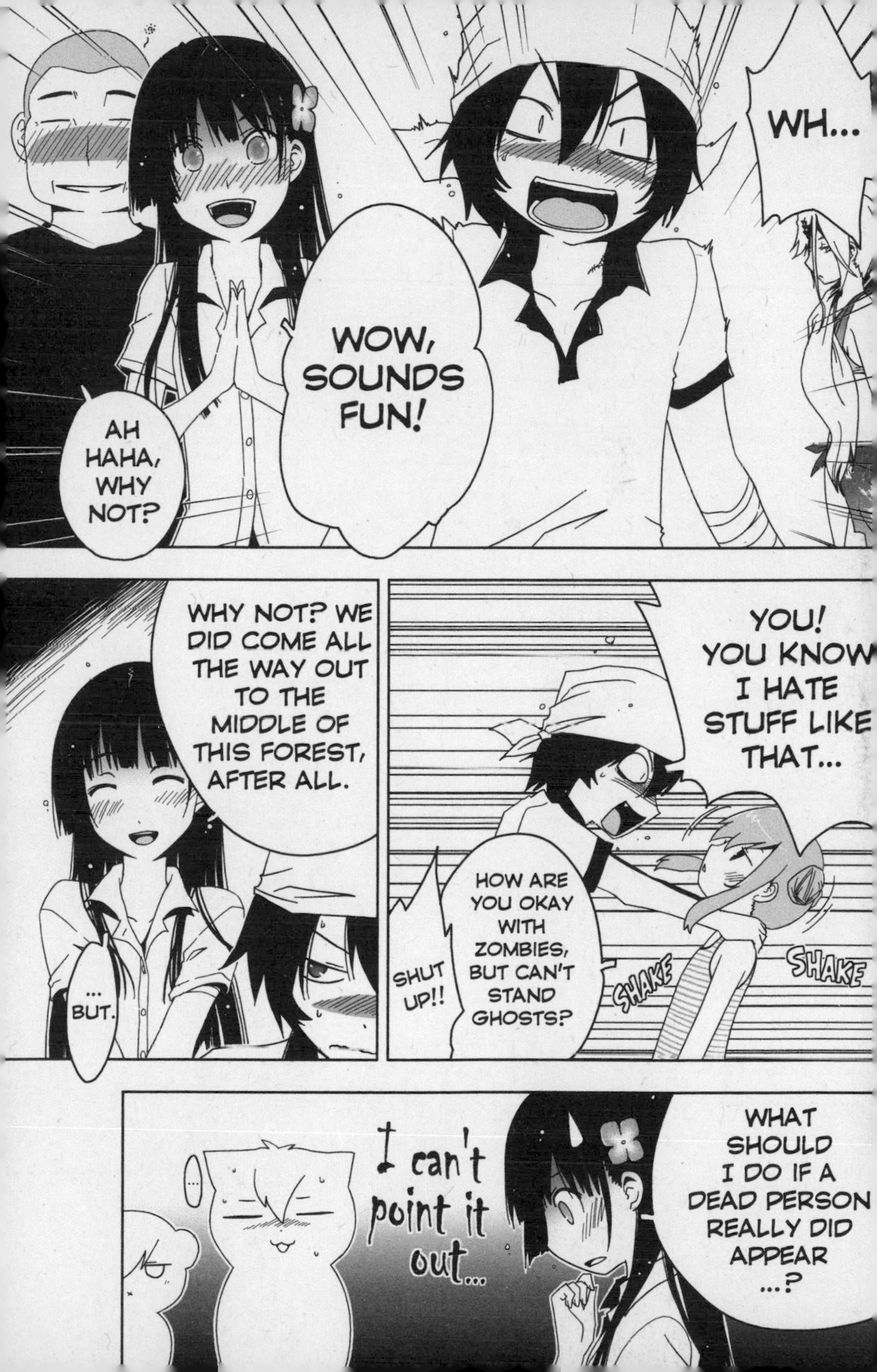
WH...
WOW, SOUNDS FUN!
AH HAHA, WHY NOT?
YOU! YOU KNOW I HATE STUFF LIKE THAT...
SHAKE
HOW ARE YOU OKAY WITH ZOMBIES, BUT CAN'T STAND GHOSTS?
SHAKE
SHUT UP!!
WHY NOT? WE DID COME ALL THE WAY OUT TO THE MIDDLE OF THIS FOREST, AFTER ALL.
... BUT.
WHAT SHOULD I DO IF A DEAD PERSON REALLY DID APPEAR ...?
I can't point it out...
...

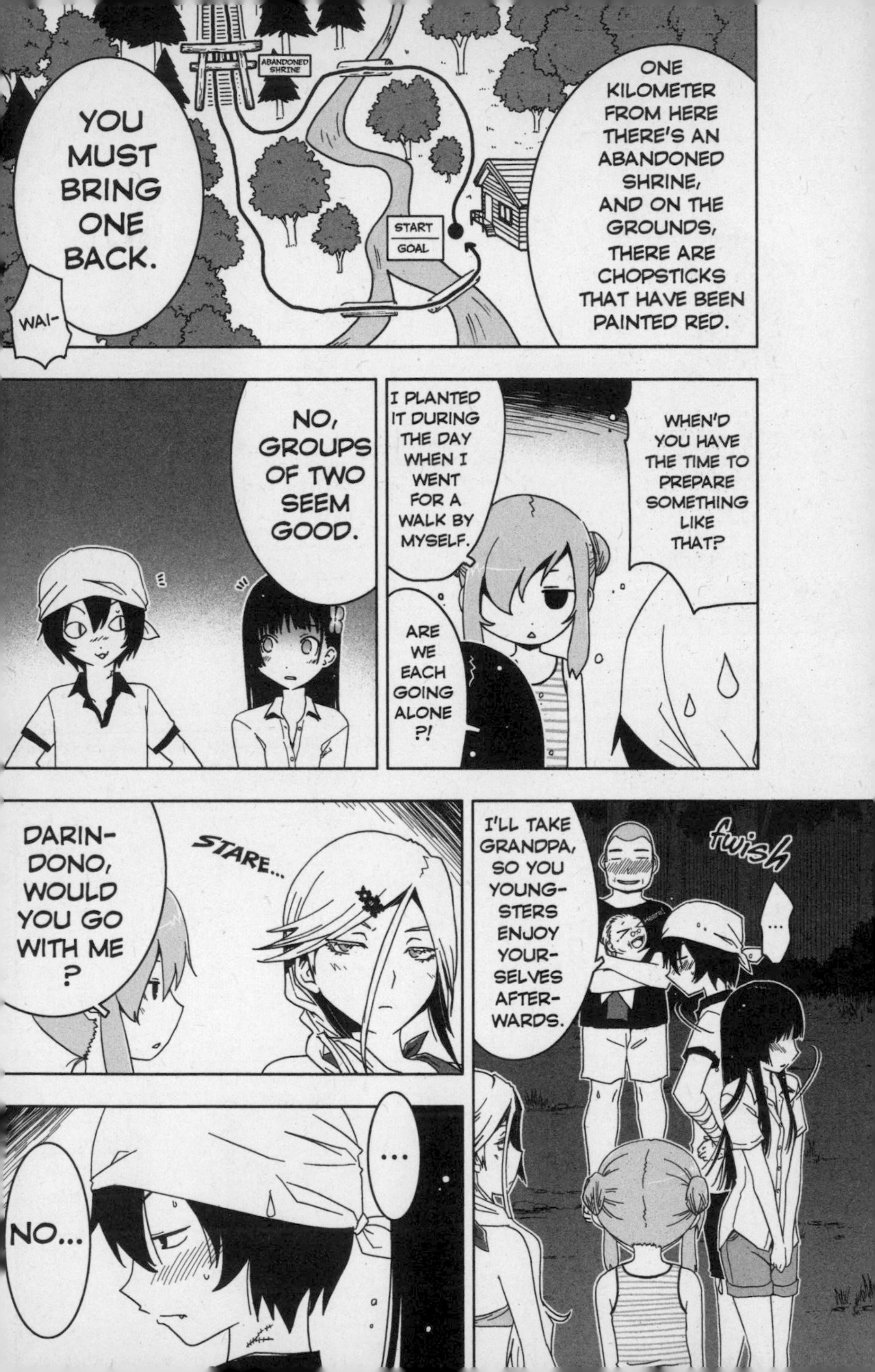
ONE KILOMETER FROM HERE THERE'S AN ABANDONED SHRINE, AND ON THE GROUNDS, THERE ARE CHOPSTICKS THAT HAVE BEEN PAINTED RED.
ABANDONED SHRINE
START
GOAL
YOU MUST BRING ONE BACK.
WAI-
WHEN'D YOU HAVE THE TIME TO PREPARE SOMETHING LIKE THAT?
I PLANTED IT DURING THE DAY WHEN I WENT FOR A WALK BY MYSELF.
ARE WE EACH GOING ALONE ?!
NO, GROUPS OF TWO SEEM GOOD.
I'LL TAKE GRANDPA, SO YOU YOUNG-STERS ENJOY YOUR-SELVES AFTER-WARDS.
fwish
...
DARIN-DONO, WOULD YOU GO WITH ME ?
STARE...
...
NO...

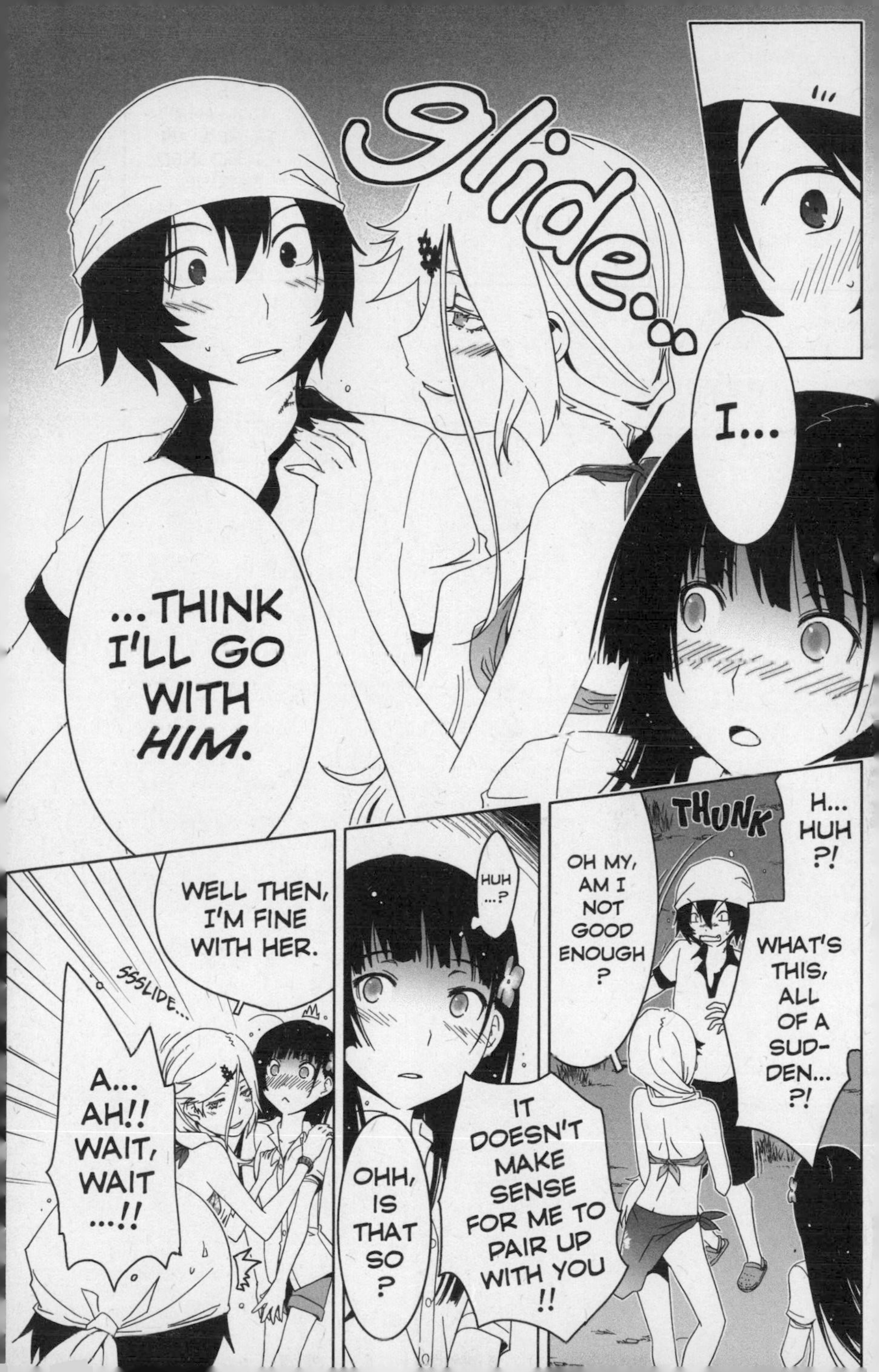
glide...
I...
...THINK I'LL GO WITH *HIM*.
H... HUH ?!
THUNK
OH MY, AM I NOT GOOD ENOUGH ?
WHAT'S THIS, ALL OF A SUD-DEN... ?!
HUH ...?
IT DOESN'T MAKE SENSE FOR ME TO PAIR UP WITH YOU !!
OHH, IS THAT SO ?
WELL THEN, I'M FINE WITH HER.
SSSLIDE...
A... AH!! WAIT, WAIT ...!!

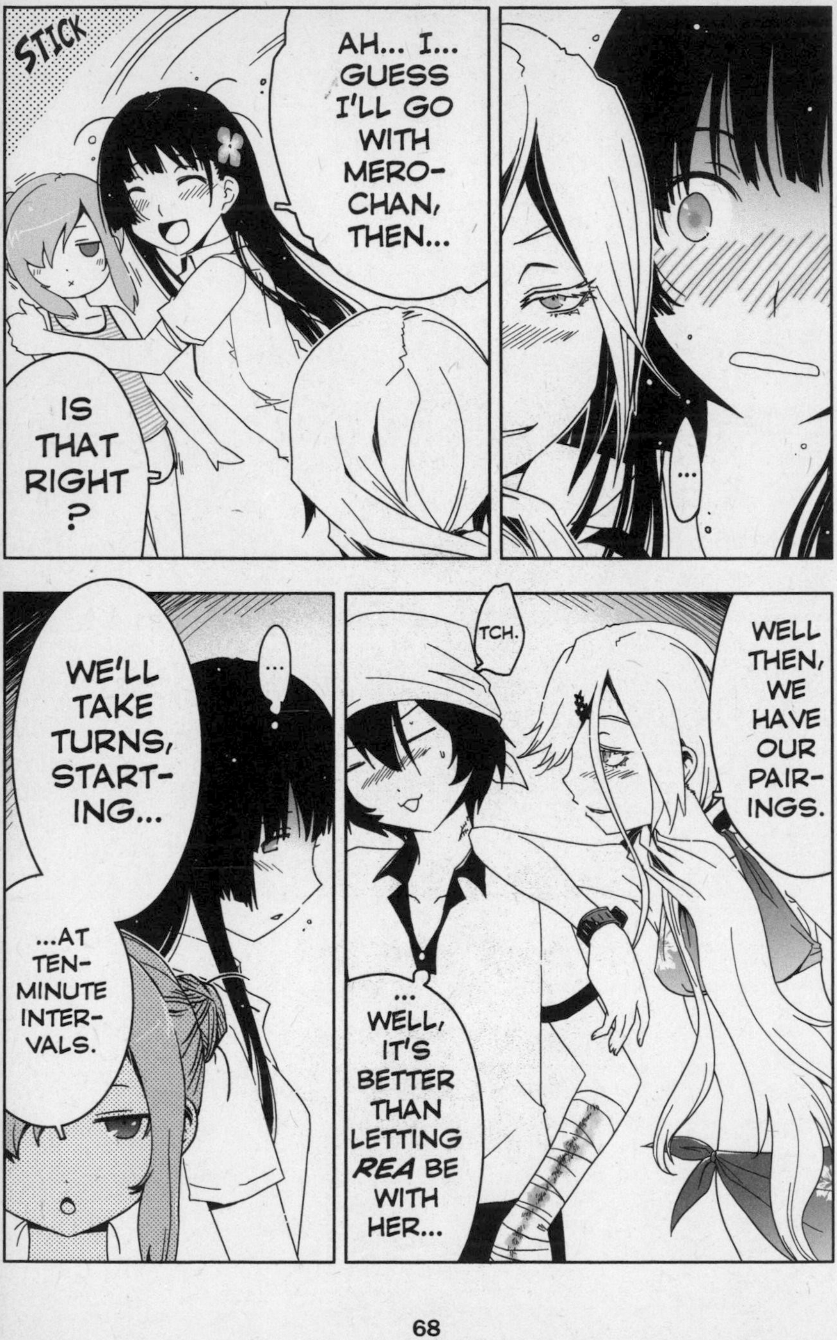
...
AH... I... GUESS I'LL GO WITH MERO-CHAN, THEN...
STICK
IS THAT RIGHT?
WELL THEN, WE HAVE OUR PAIRINGS.
TCH.
...WELL, IT'S BETTER THAN LETTING *REA* BE WITH HER...
...
WE'LL TAKE TURNS, STARTING...
...AT TEN-MINUTE INTERVALS.

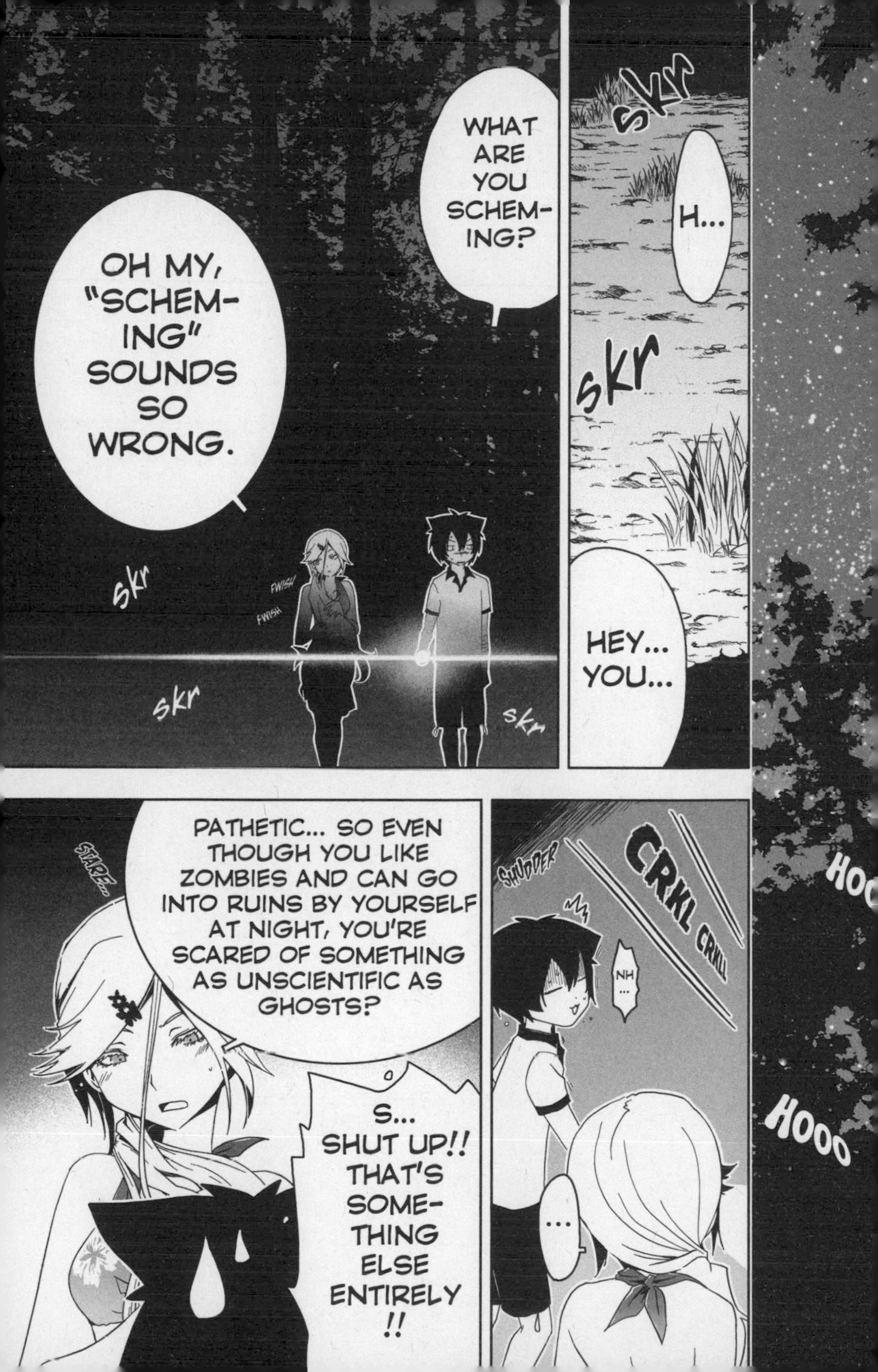
HOO
HOOO
skr
H...
skr
HEY... YOU...
WHAT ARE YOU SCHEMING?
OH MY, "SCHEMING" SOUNDS SO WRONG.
skr
FWISH FWISH
skr
skr
CRKL CRKL
SHUDDER
NH...
...
PATHETIC... SO EVEN THOUGH YOU LIKE ZOMBIES AND CAN GO INTO RUINS BY YOURSELF AT NIGHT, YOU'RE SCARED OF SOMETHING AS UNSCIENTIFIC AS GHOSTS?
STARE...
S... SHUT UP!! THAT'S SOMETHING ELSE ENTIRELY!!

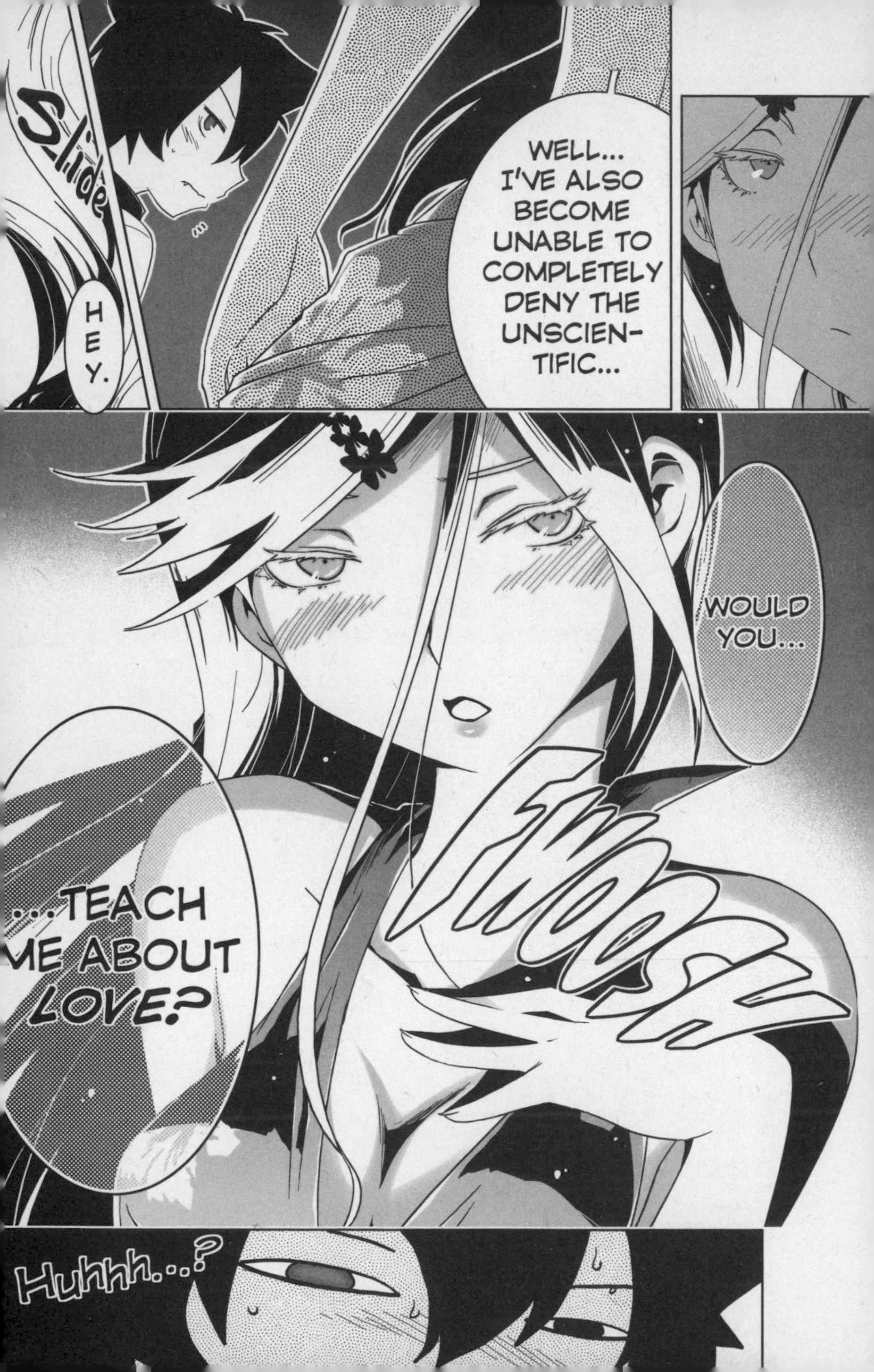
WELL... I'VE ALSO BECOME UNABLE TO COMPLETELY DENY THE UNSCIEN-TIFIC...
Slide
HEY.
WOULD YOU...
Whoosh
...TEACH ME ABOUT LOVE?
Huhhh...?

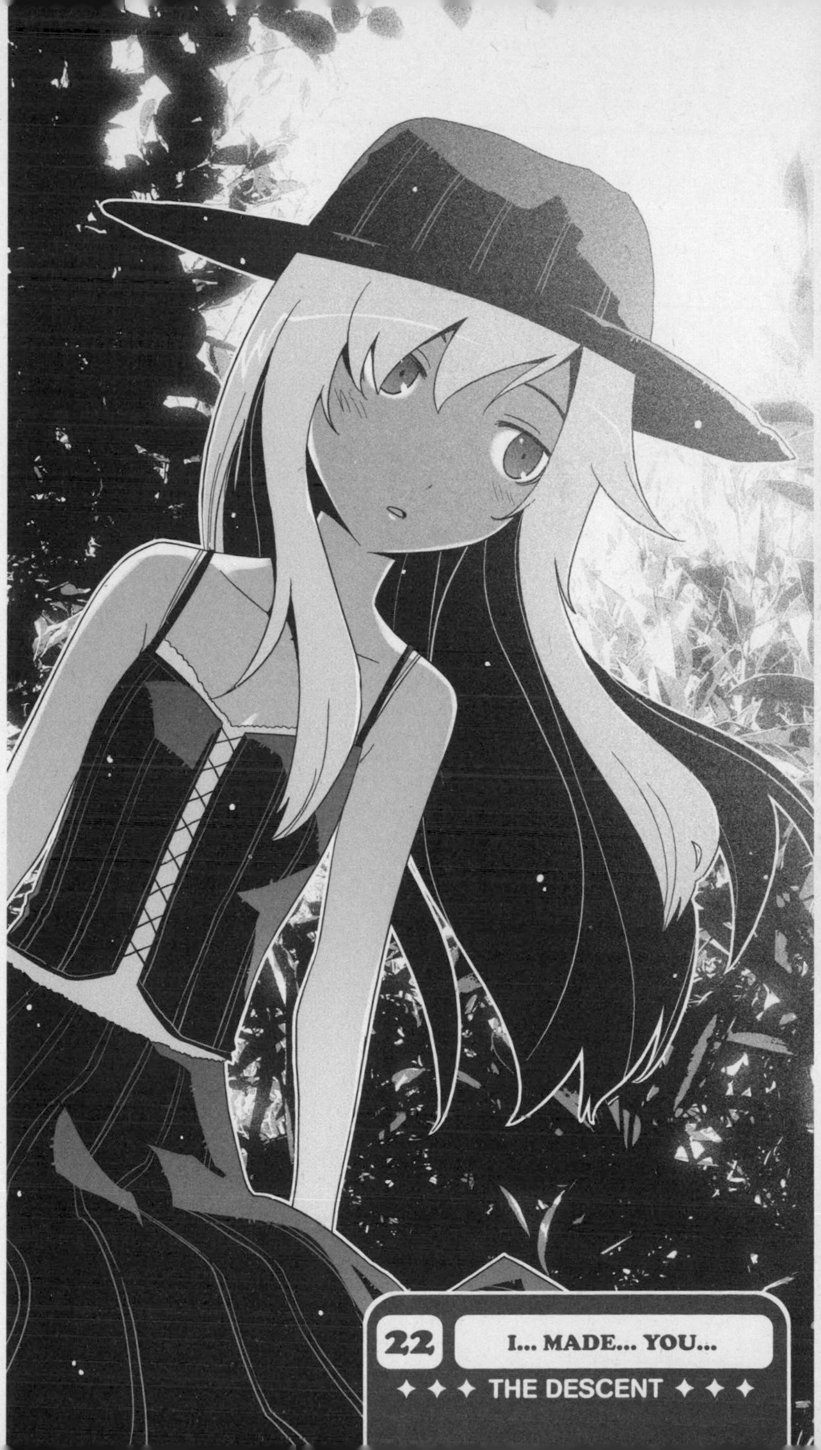
22
I... MADE... YOU...
✦ ✦ ✦ THE DESCENT ✦ ✦ ✦

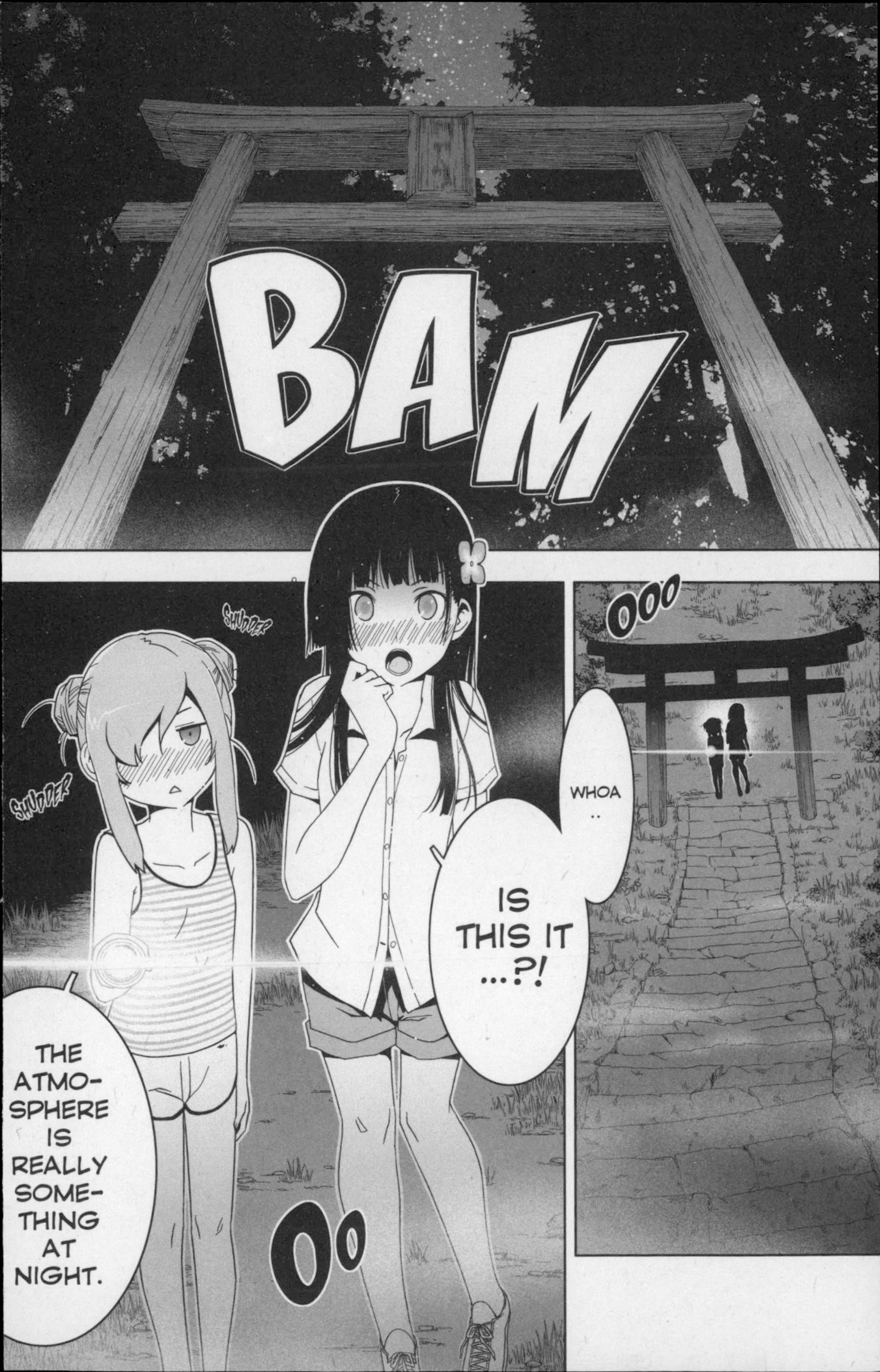
BAM
OOO
WHOA..
IS THIS IT ...?!
SHUDDER
SHUDDER
THE ATMOSPHERE IS REALLY SOMETHING AT NIGHT.
Oo

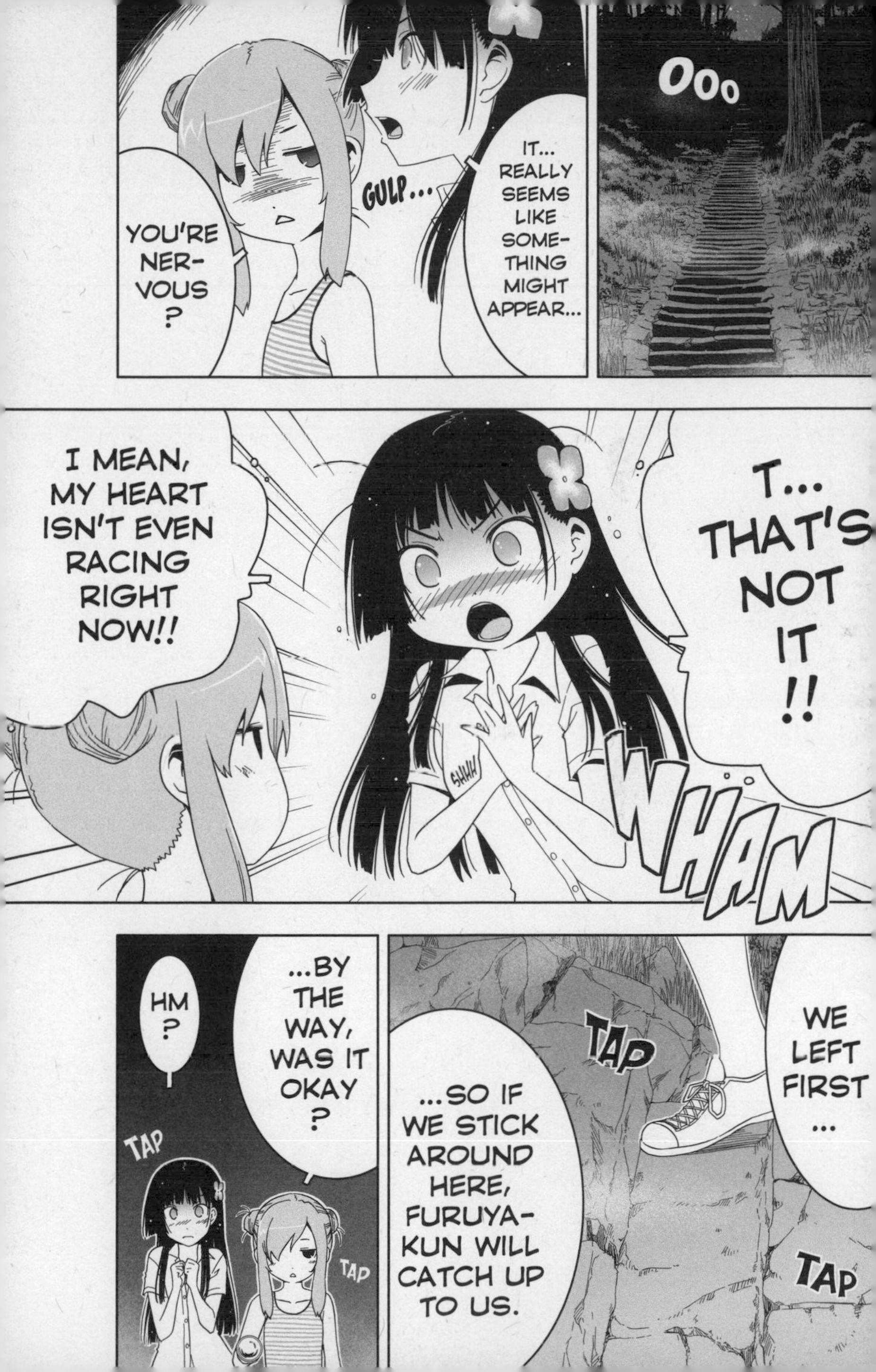
Ooo
IT... REALLY SEEMS LIKE SOME-THING MIGHT APPEAR...
GULP...
YOU'RE NER-VOUS?
T... THAT'S NOT IT!!
WHAM
SHHH
I MEAN, MY HEART ISN'T EVEN RACING RIGHT NOW!!
WE LEFT FIRST...
TAP
...SO IF WE STICK AROUND HERE, FURUYA-KUN WILL CATCH UP TO US.
TAP
...BY THE WAY, WAS IT OKAY?
HM?
TAP
TAP

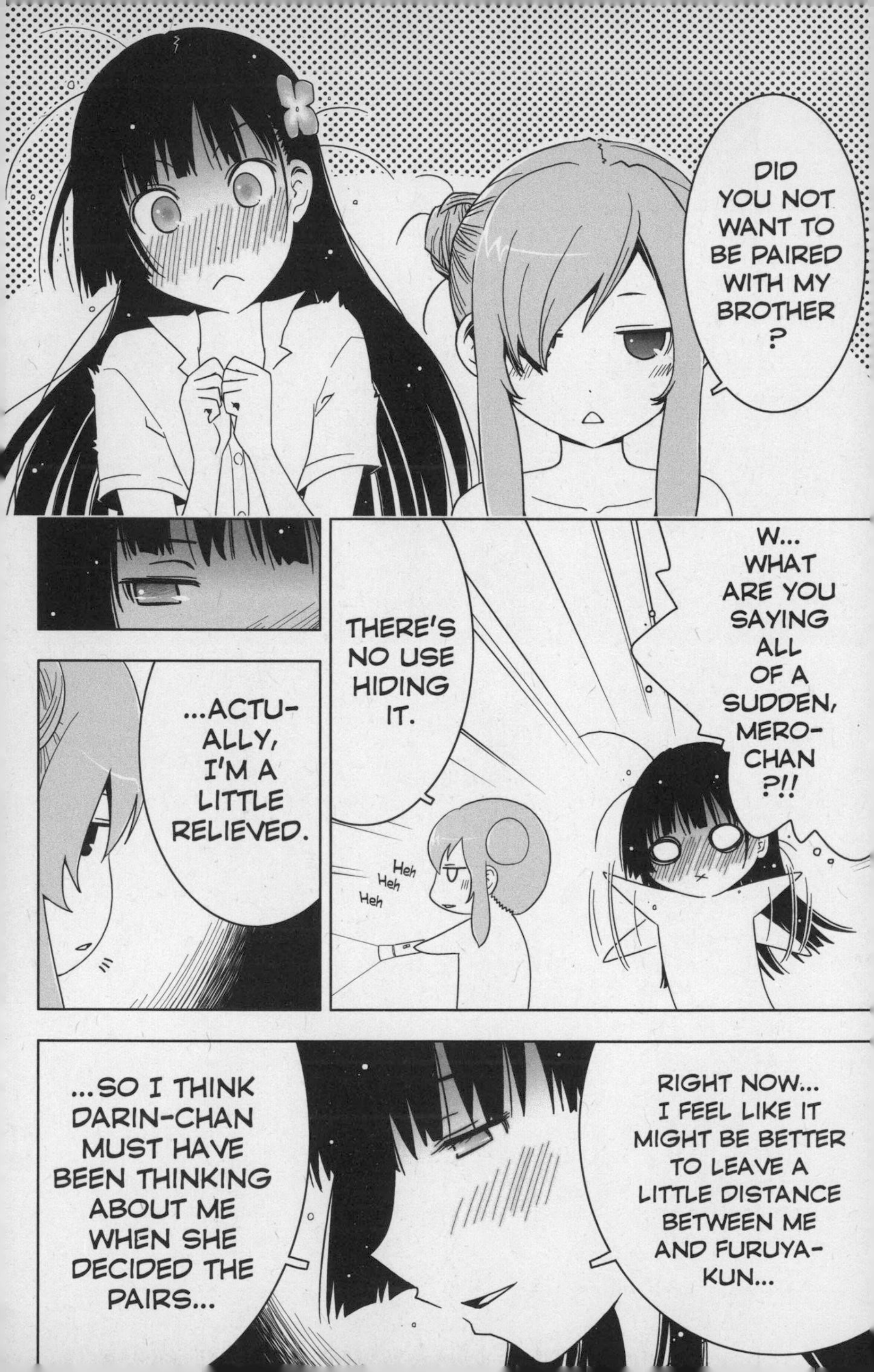
DID YOU NOT WANT TO BE PAIRED WITH MY BROTHER?
W... WHAT ARE YOU SAYING ALL OF A SUDDEN, MERO-CHAN?!!
THERE'S NO USE HIDING IT.
Heh Heh Heh
...ACTU-ALLY, I'M A LITTLE RELIEVED.
RIGHT NOW... I FEEL LIKE IT MIGHT BE BETTER TO LEAVE A LITTLE DISTANCE BETWEEN ME AND FURUYA-KUN...
...SO I THINK DARIN-CHAN MUST HAVE BEEN THINKING ABOUT ME WHEN SHE DECIDED THE PAIRS...

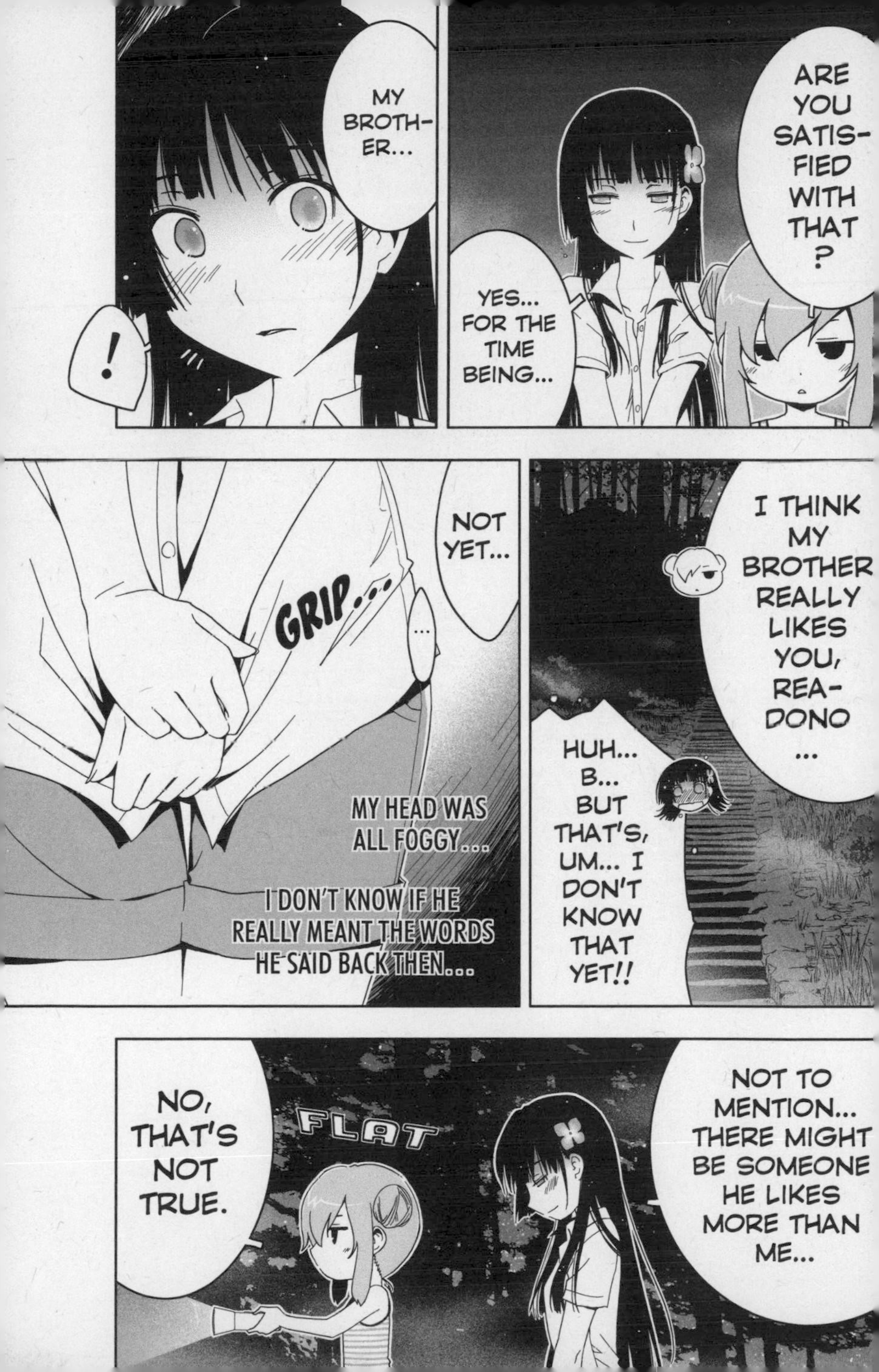
ARE YOU SATISFIED WITH THAT?
YES... FOR THE TIME BEING...
MY BROTHER...
!
I THINK MY BROTHER REALLY LIKES YOU, REA-DONO...
HUH... B... BUT THAT'S, UM... I DON'T KNOW THAT YET!!
NOT YET...
...
GRIP...
MY HEAD WAS ALL FOGGY...
I DON'T KNOW IF HE REALLY MEANT THE WORDS HE SAID BACK THEN...
NOT TO MENTION... THERE MIGHT BE SOMEONE HE LIKES MORE THAN ME...
FLAT
NO, THAT'S NOT TRUE.

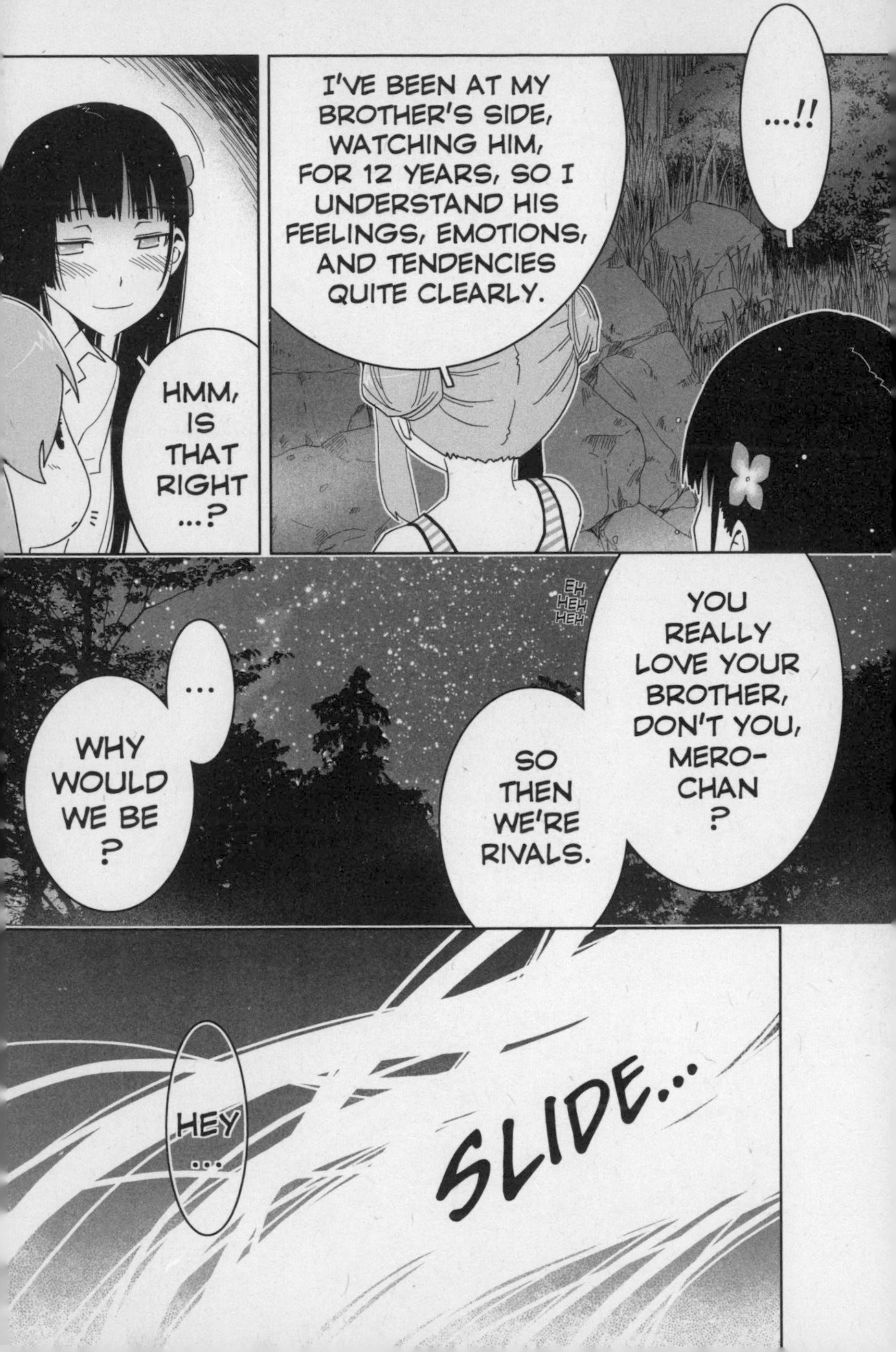
...!!
I'VE BEEN AT MY BROTHER'S SIDE, WATCHING HIM, FOR 12 YEARS, SO I UNDERSTAND HIS FEELINGS, EMOTIONS, AND TENDENCIES QUITE CLEARLY.
HMM, IS THAT RIGHT...?
YOU REALLY LOVE YOUR BROTHER, DON'T YOU, MERO-CHAN?
EH HEH HEH
SO THEN WE'RE RIVALS.
...
WHY WOULD WE BE?
SLIDE...
HEY...

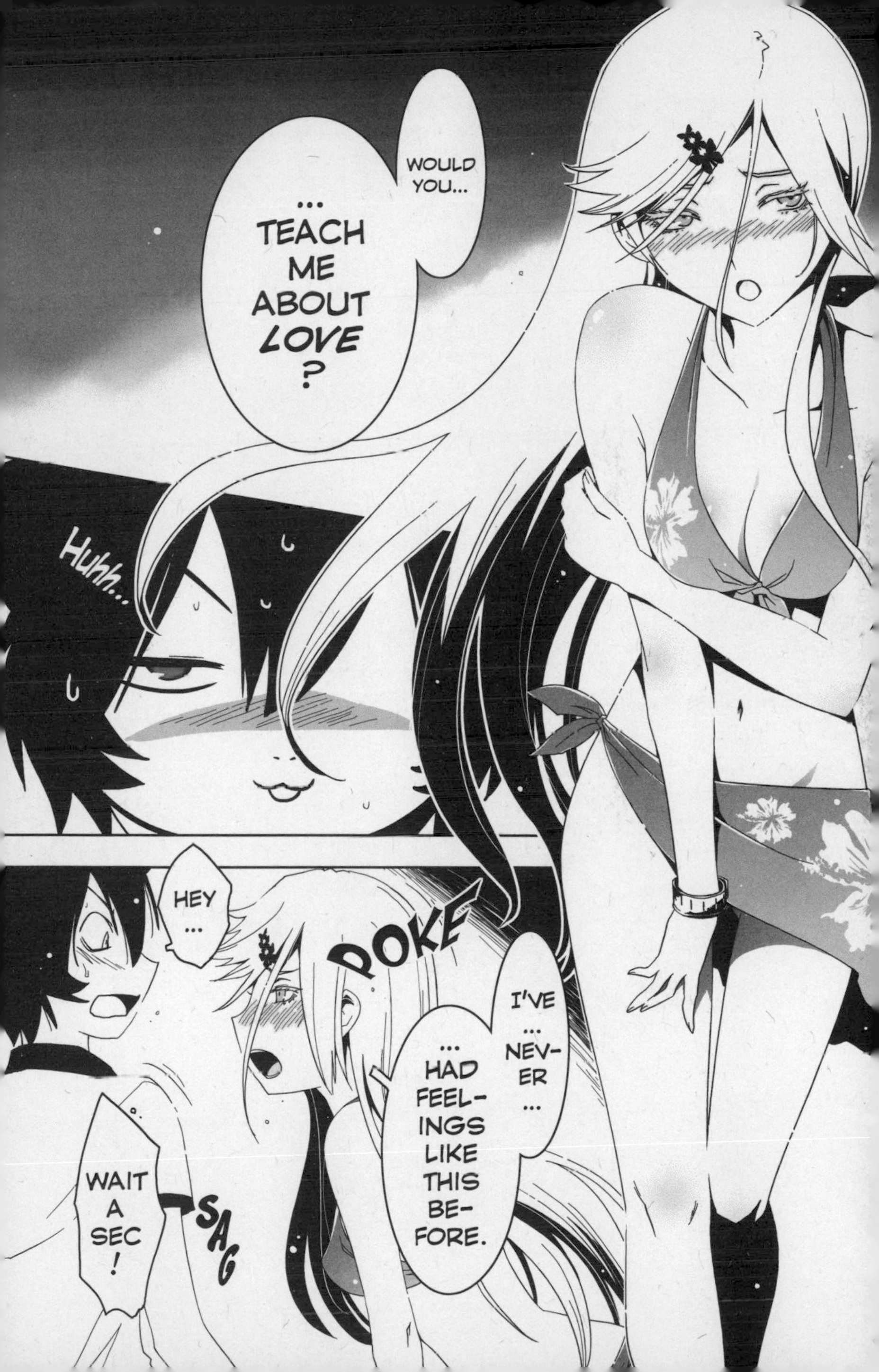
WOULD YOU...
...TEACH ME ABOUT LOVE?
Huhh...
I'VE... NEVER... ...HAD FEELINGS LIKE THIS BEFORE.
POKE
HEY...
SAG
WAIT A SEC!

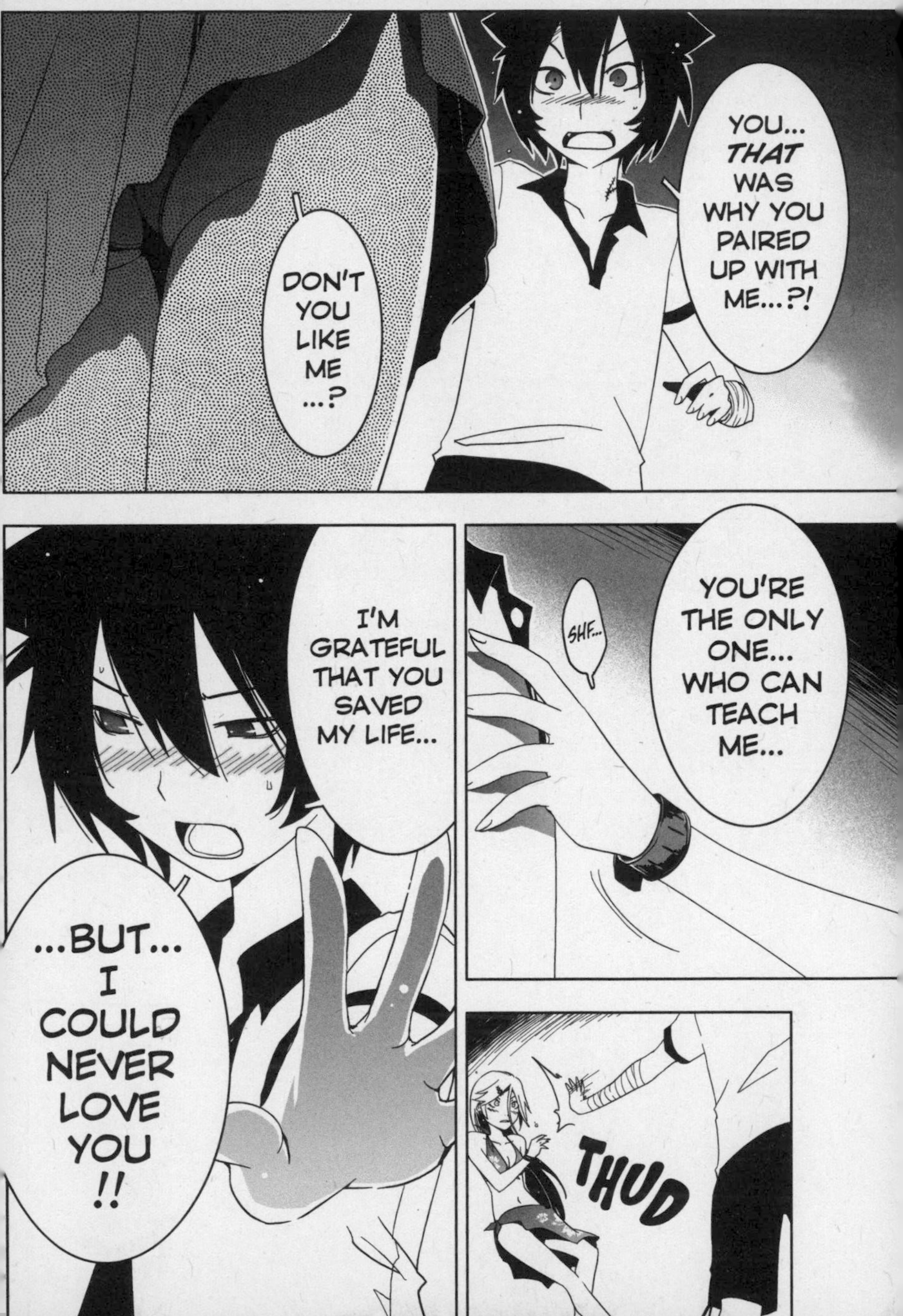
YOU... *THAT* WAS WHY YOU PAIRED UP WITH ME...?!
DON'T YOU LIKE ME ...?
YOU'RE THE ONLY ONE... WHO CAN TEACH ME...
SHF...
THUD
I'M GRATEFUL THAT YOU SAVED MY LIFE...
...BUT... I COULD NEVER LOVE YOU !!

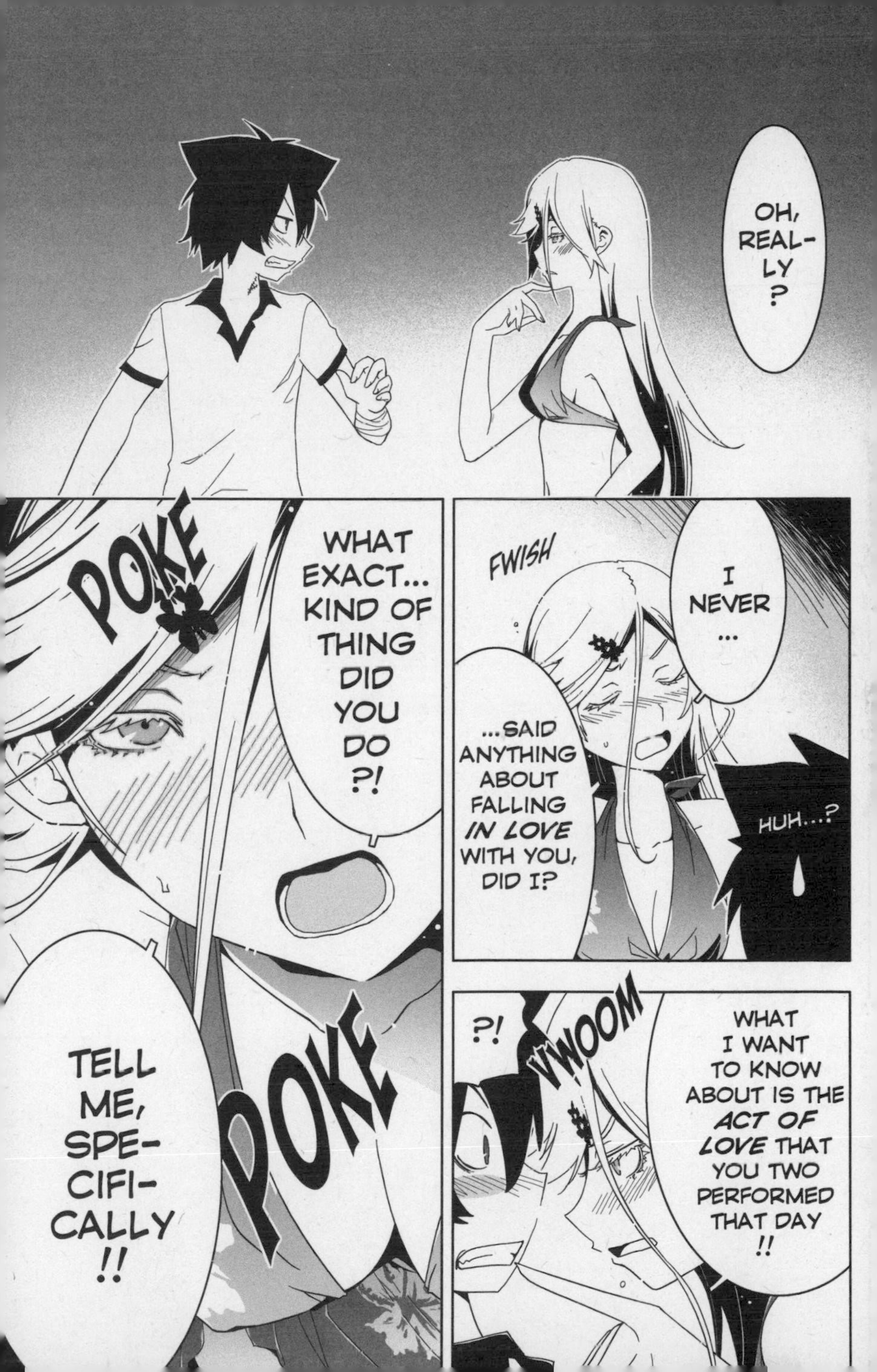
OH, REAL-LY?
FWISH
I NEVER ...
...SAID ANYTHING ABOUT FALLING *IN LOVE* WITH YOU, DID I?
HUH...?
WHAT I WANT TO KNOW ABOUT IS THE *ACT OF LOVE* THAT YOU TWO PERFORMED THAT DAY!!
VWOOM
?!
POKE
WHAT EXACT... KIND OF THING DID YOU DO?!
TELL ME, SPE-CIFI-CALLY!!
POKE

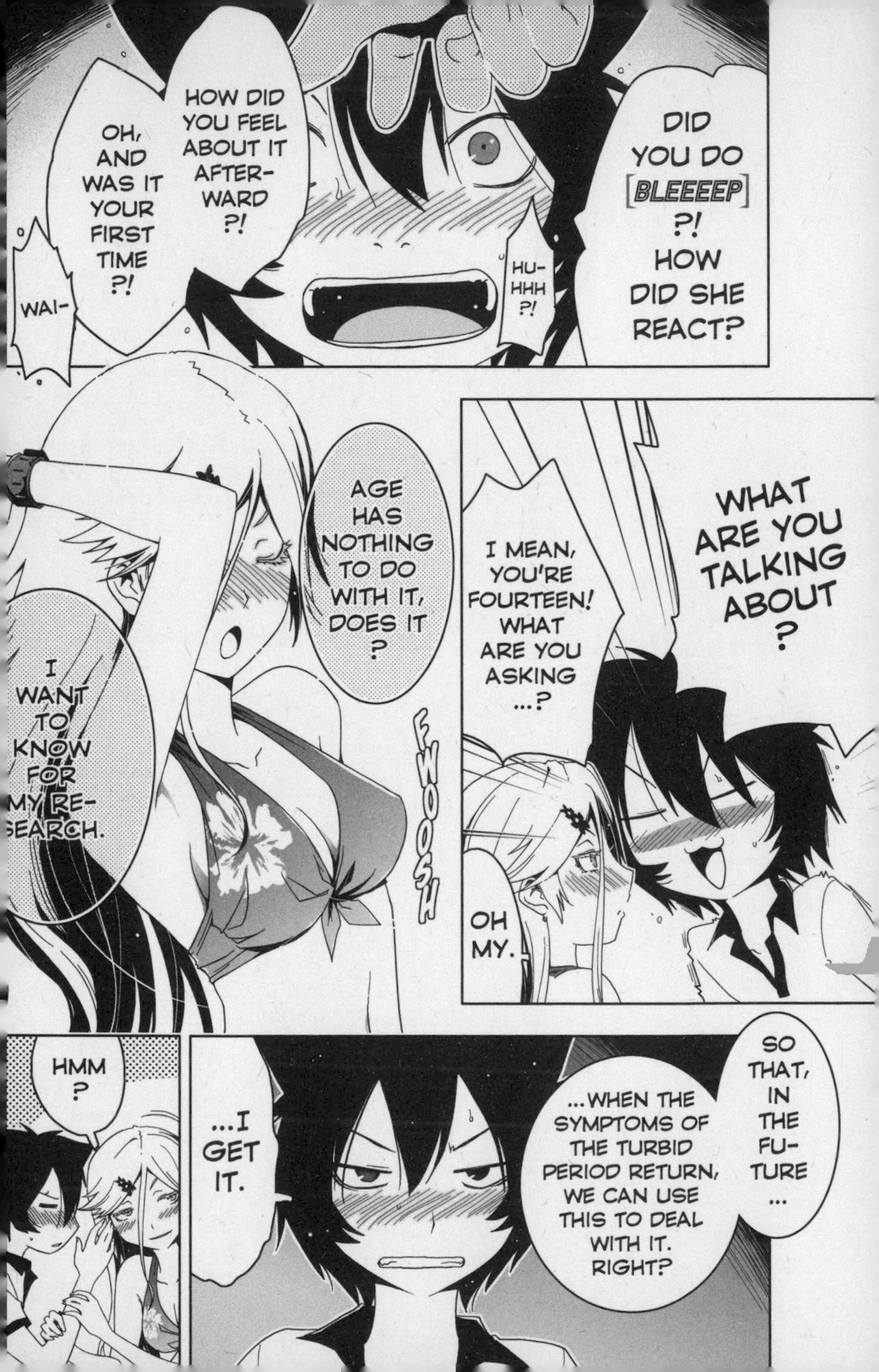

DID YOU DO [BLEEEEP]?! HOW DID SHE REACT?
HU-HHH?!
HOW DID YOU FEEL ABOUT IT AFTER-WARD?!
OH, AND WAS IT YOUR FIRST TIME?!
WAI-
WHAT ARE YOU TALKING ABOUT?
I MEAN, YOU'RE FOURTEEN! WHAT ARE YOU ASKING...?
OH MY.
AGE HAS NOTHING TO DO WITH IT, DOES IT?
FWOOSH
I WANT TO KNOW FOR MY RE-SEARCH.
SO THAT, IN THE FUTURE...
...WHEN THE SYMPTOMS OF THE TURBID PERIOD RETURN, WE CAN USE THIS TO DEAL WITH IT. RIGHT?
...I GET IT.
HMM?

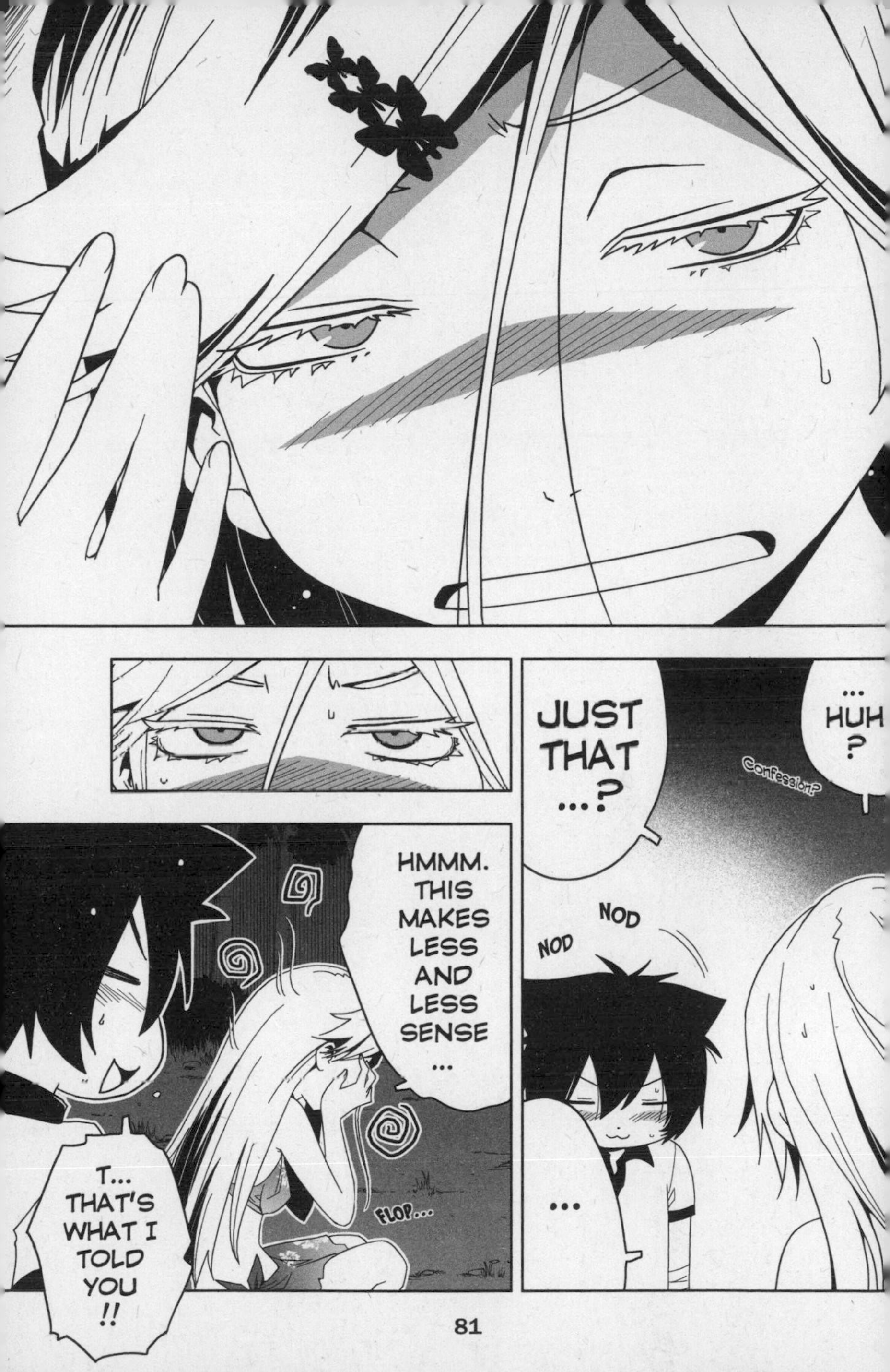
... HUH ?
Confession?
JUST THAT ...?
NOD
NOD
...
HMMM. THIS MAKES LESS AND LESS SENSE ...
T... THAT'S WHAT I TOLD YOU !!
FLOP...

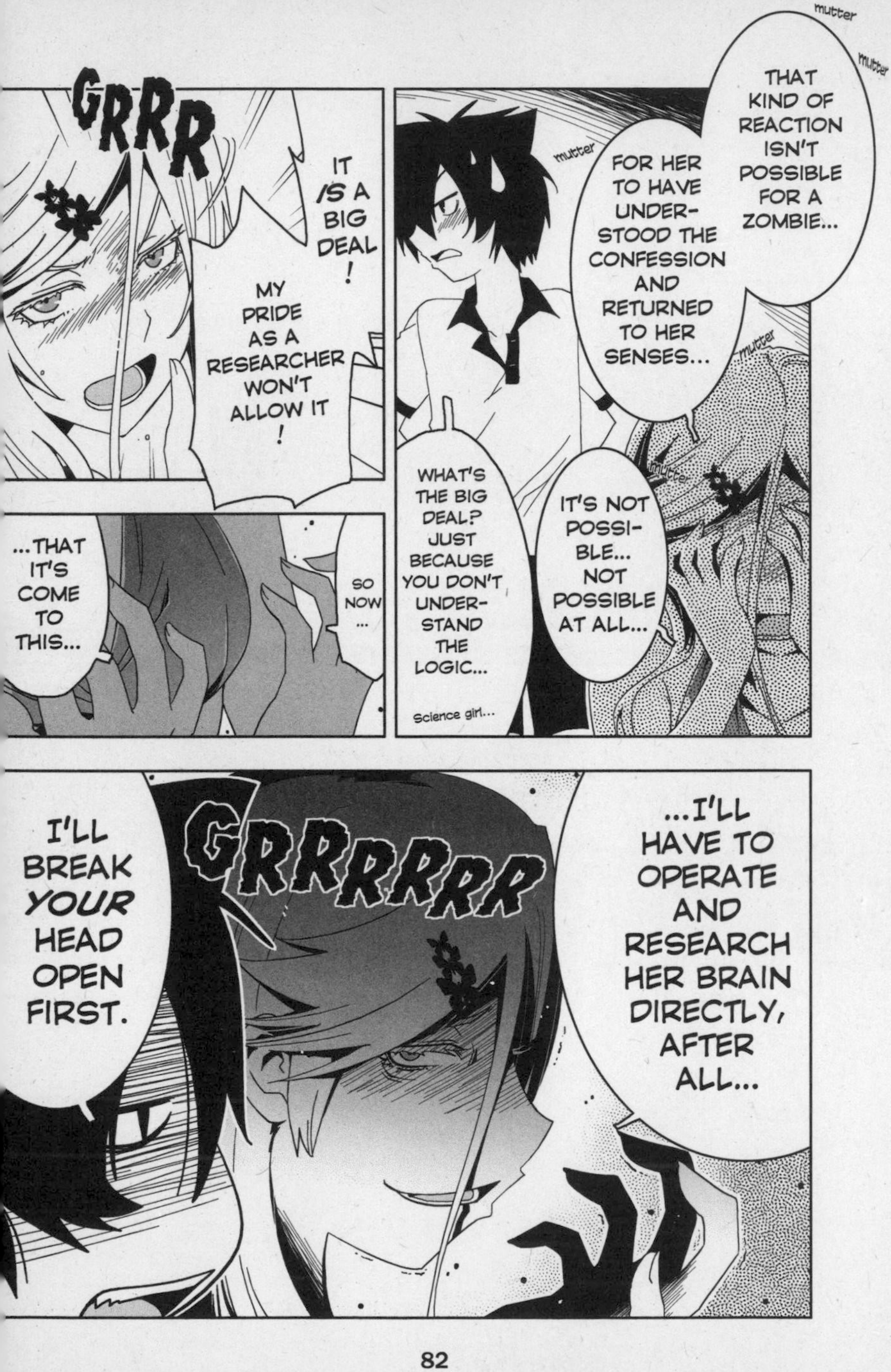
mutter
mutter
THAT KIND OF REACTION ISN'T POSSIBLE FOR A ZOMBIE...
mutter
FOR HER TO HAVE UNDER-STOOD THE CONFESSION AND RETURNED TO HER SENSES...
mutter
mutter
IT'S NOT POSSI-BLE... NOT POSSIBLE AT ALL...
WHAT'S THE BIG DEAL? JUST BECAUSE YOU DON'T UNDER-STAND THE LOGIC...
Science girl...
GRRR
IT *IS* A BIG DEAL!
MY PRIDE AS A RESEARCHER WON'T ALLOW IT!
SO NOW...
...THAT IT'S COME TO THIS...
...I'LL HAVE TO OPERATE AND RESEARCH HER BRAIN DIRECTLY, AFTER ALL...
GRRRRRR
I'LL BREAK *YOUR* HEAD OPEN FIRST.

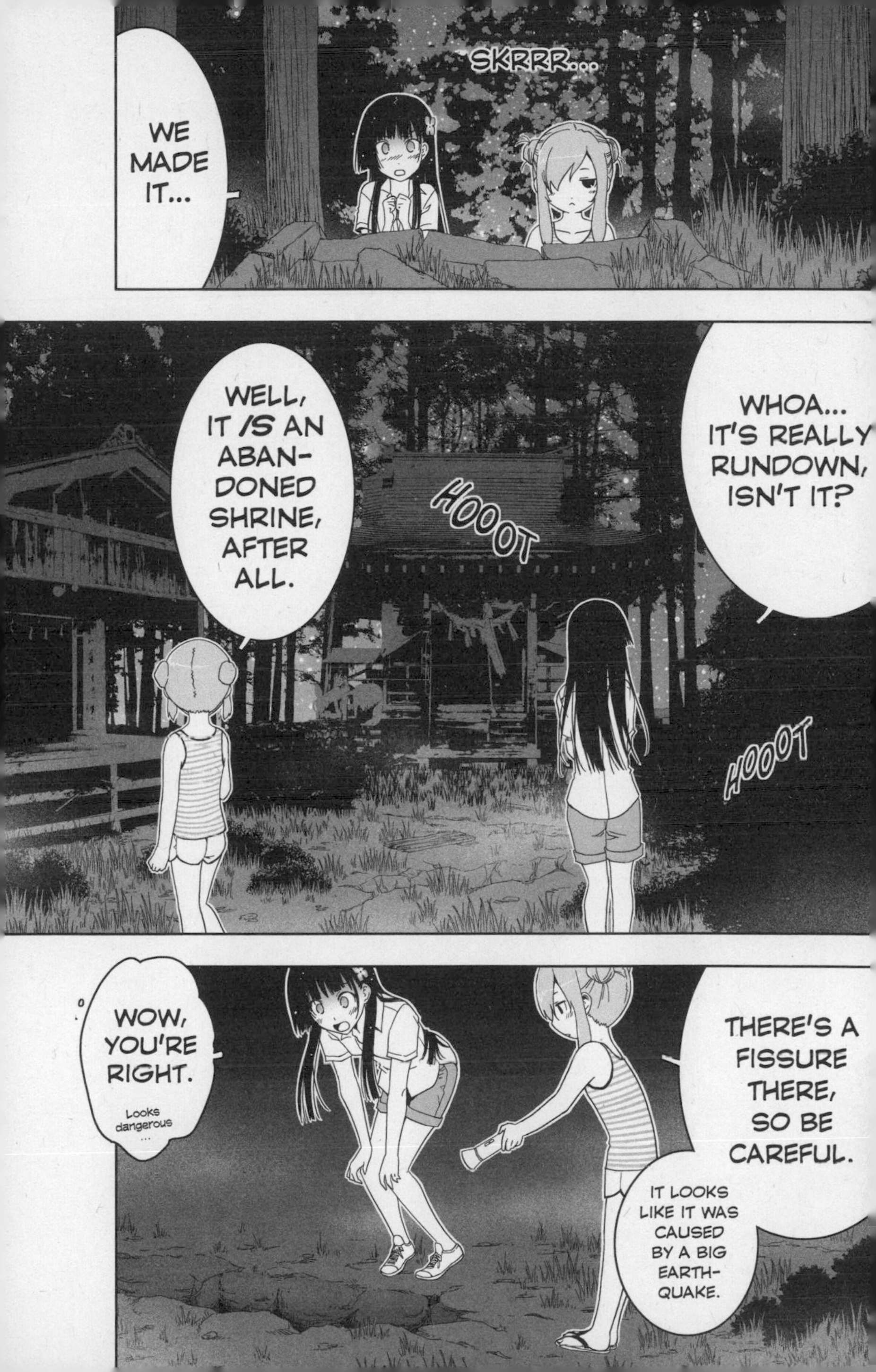
SKRRR...
WE MADE IT...
WHOA... IT'S REALLY RUNDOWN, ISN'T IT?
HOOOT
HOOOT
WELL, IT IS AN ABAN-DONED SHRINE, AFTER ALL.
THERE'S A FISSURE THERE, SO BE CAREFUL.
IT LOOKS LIKE IT WAS CAUSED BY A BIG EARTH-QUAKE.
WOW, YOU'RE RIGHT.
Looks dangerous ...

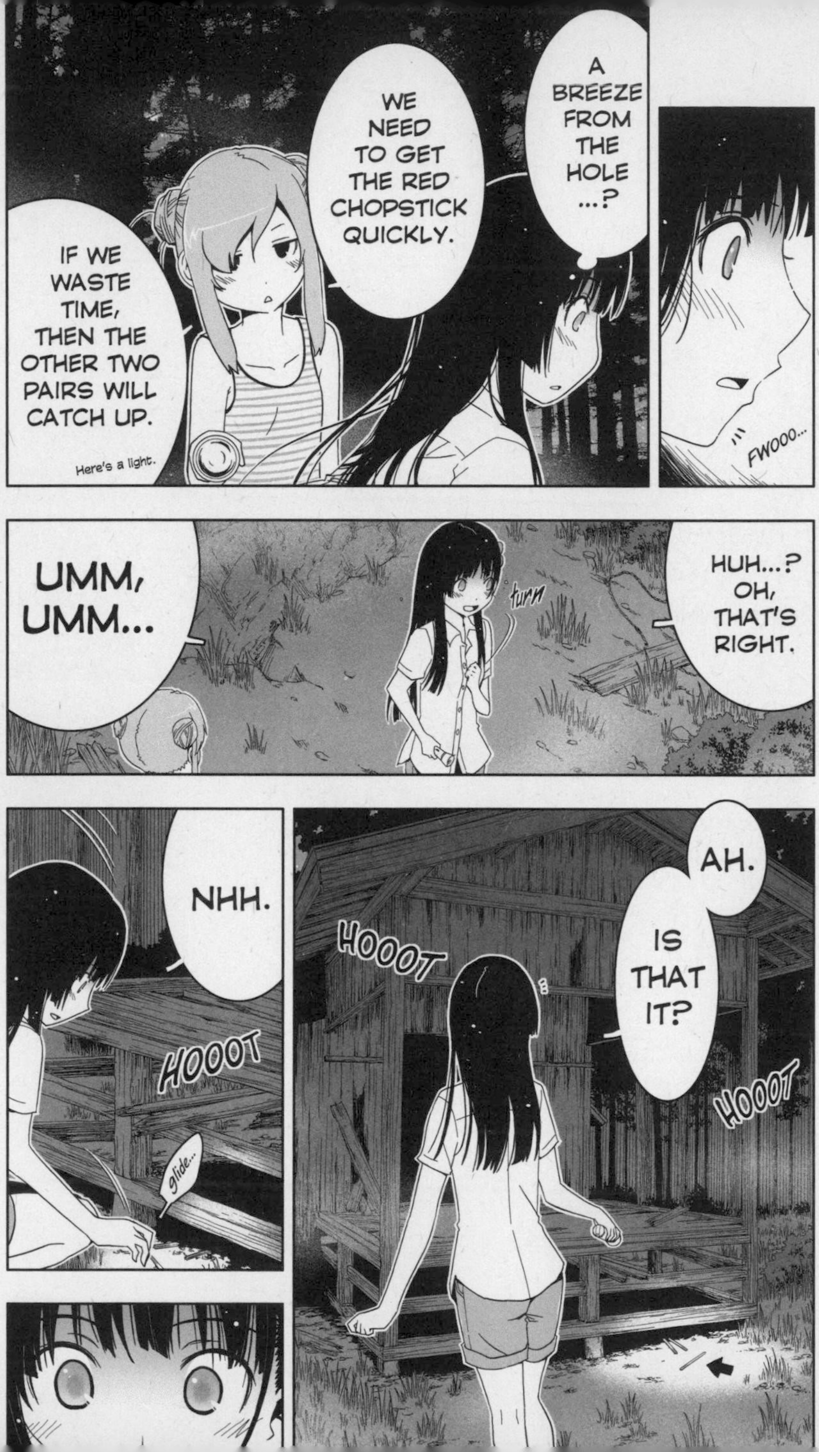
FWOOO...
A BREEZE FROM THE HOLE ...?
WE NEED TO GET THE RED CHOPSTICK QUICKLY.
IF WE WASTE TIME, THEN THE OTHER TWO PAIRS WILL CATCH UP.
Here's a light.
HUH...? OH, THAT'S RIGHT.
turn
UMM, UMM...
AH.
IS THAT IT?
HOOOT
HOOOT
NHH.
HOOOT
glide...

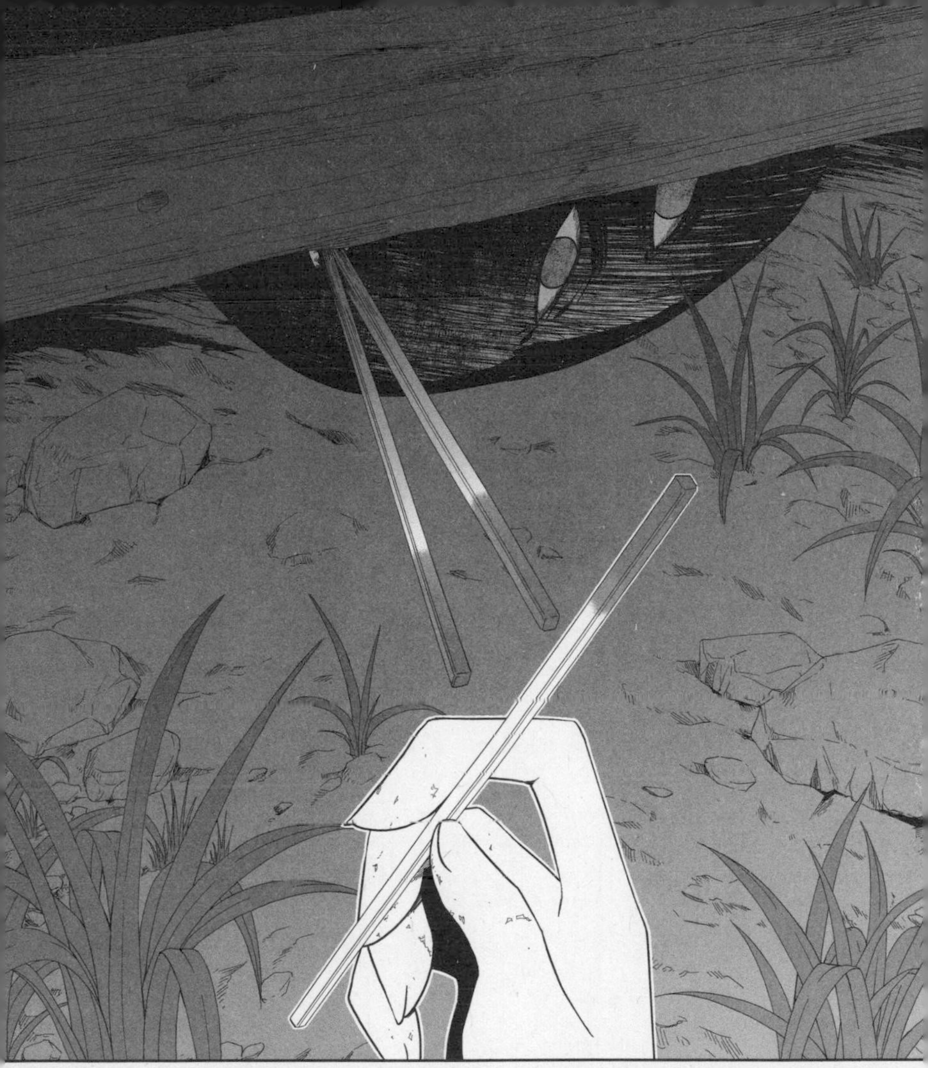
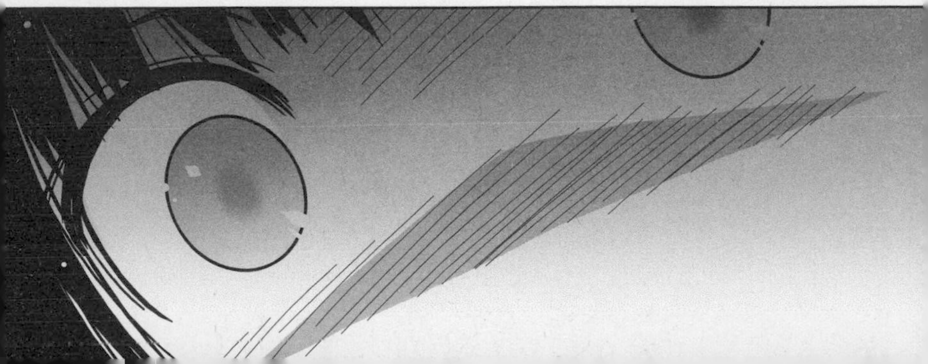

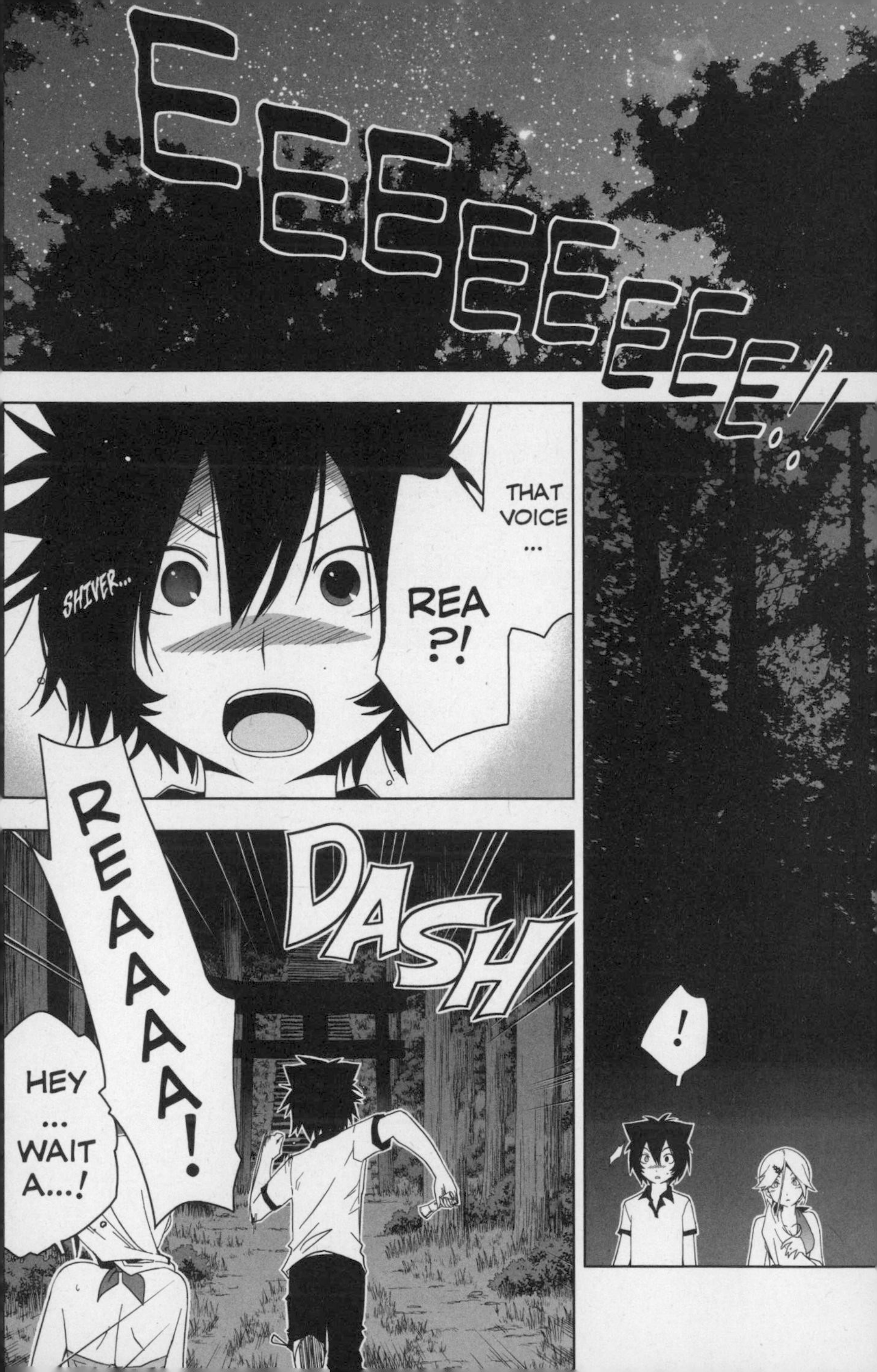
EEEEEEEEEE!!
!
THAT VOICE ...
REA ?!
SHIVER...
REAAAAA!
DASH
HEY ... WAIT A...!

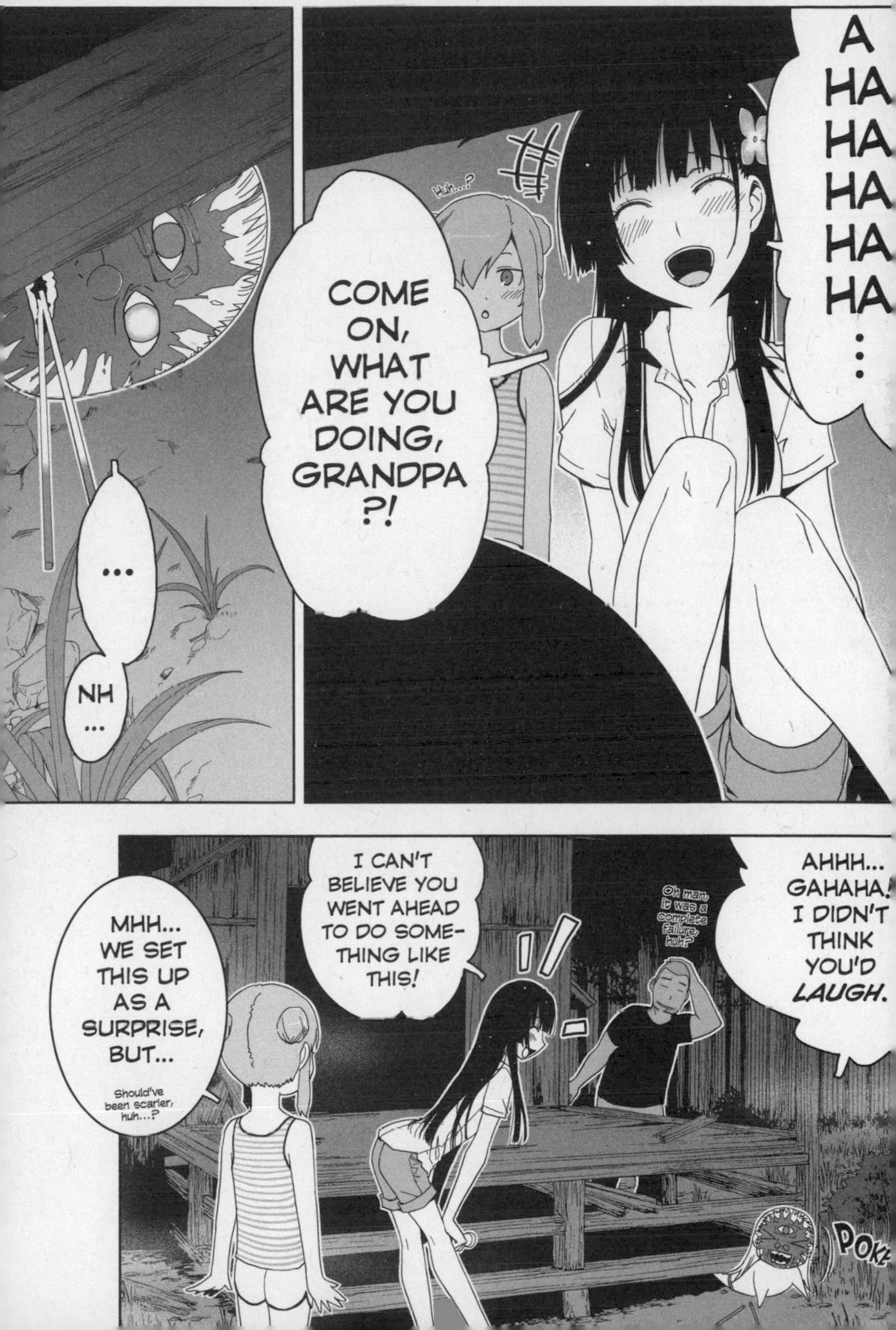
AHAHAHAHAHA...
Huh...?
COME ON, WHAT ARE YOU DOING, GRANDPA?!
...
NH...
AHHH... GAHAHA! I DIDN'T THINK YOU'D LAUGH.
Oh man, it was a complete failure, huh?
I CAN'T BELIEVE YOU WENT AHEAD TO DO SOMETHING LIKE THIS!
MHH... WE SET THIS UP AS A SURPRISE, BUT...
Should've been scarier, huh...?
POKE

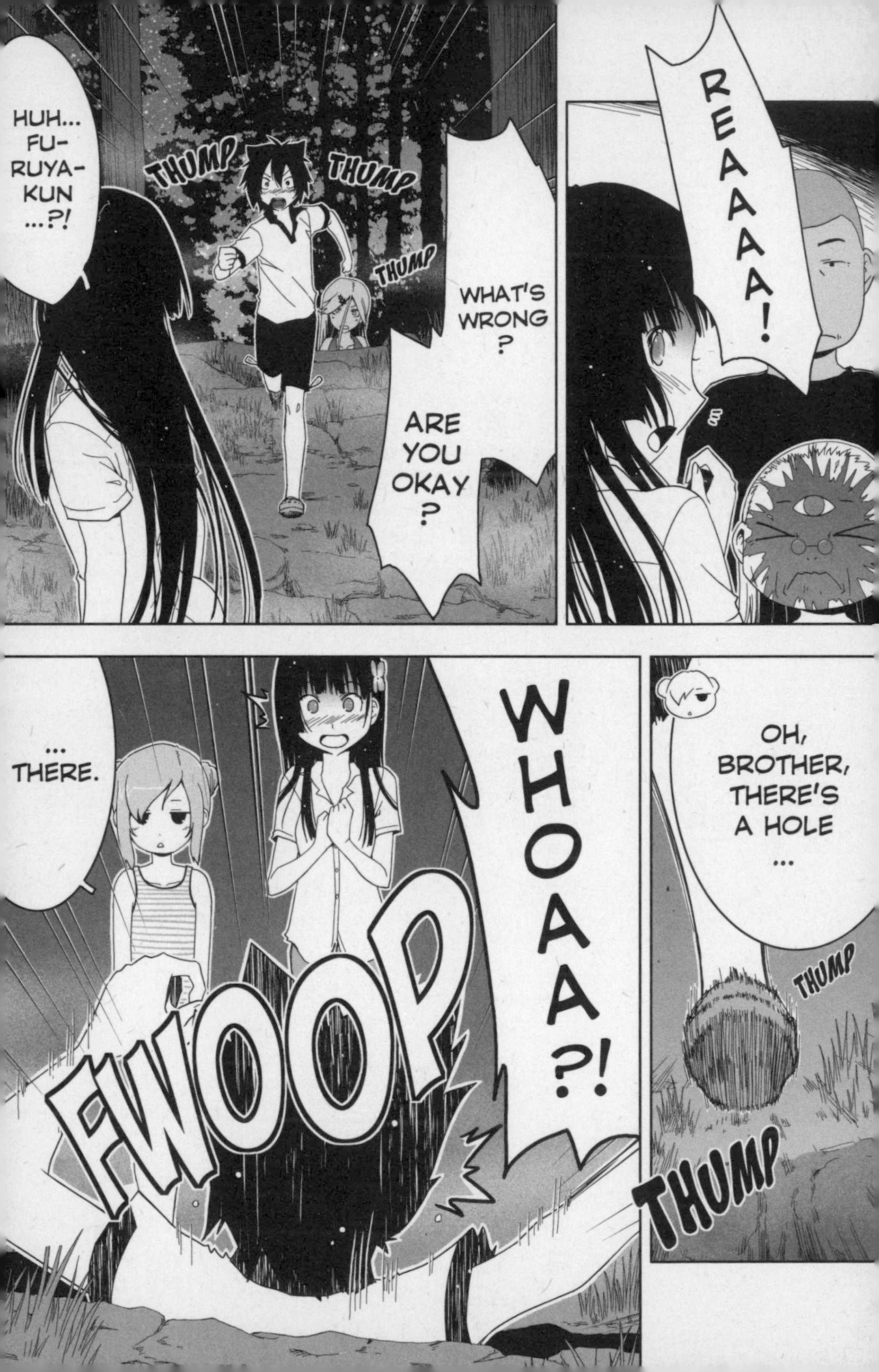
REAAAA!
WHAT'S WRONG?
ARE YOU OKAY?
THUMP
THUMP
THUMP
HUH... FU-RUYA-KUN...?!
OH, BROTHER, THERE'S A HOLE...
THUMP
THUMP
WHOAA?!
FWOOP
... THERE.

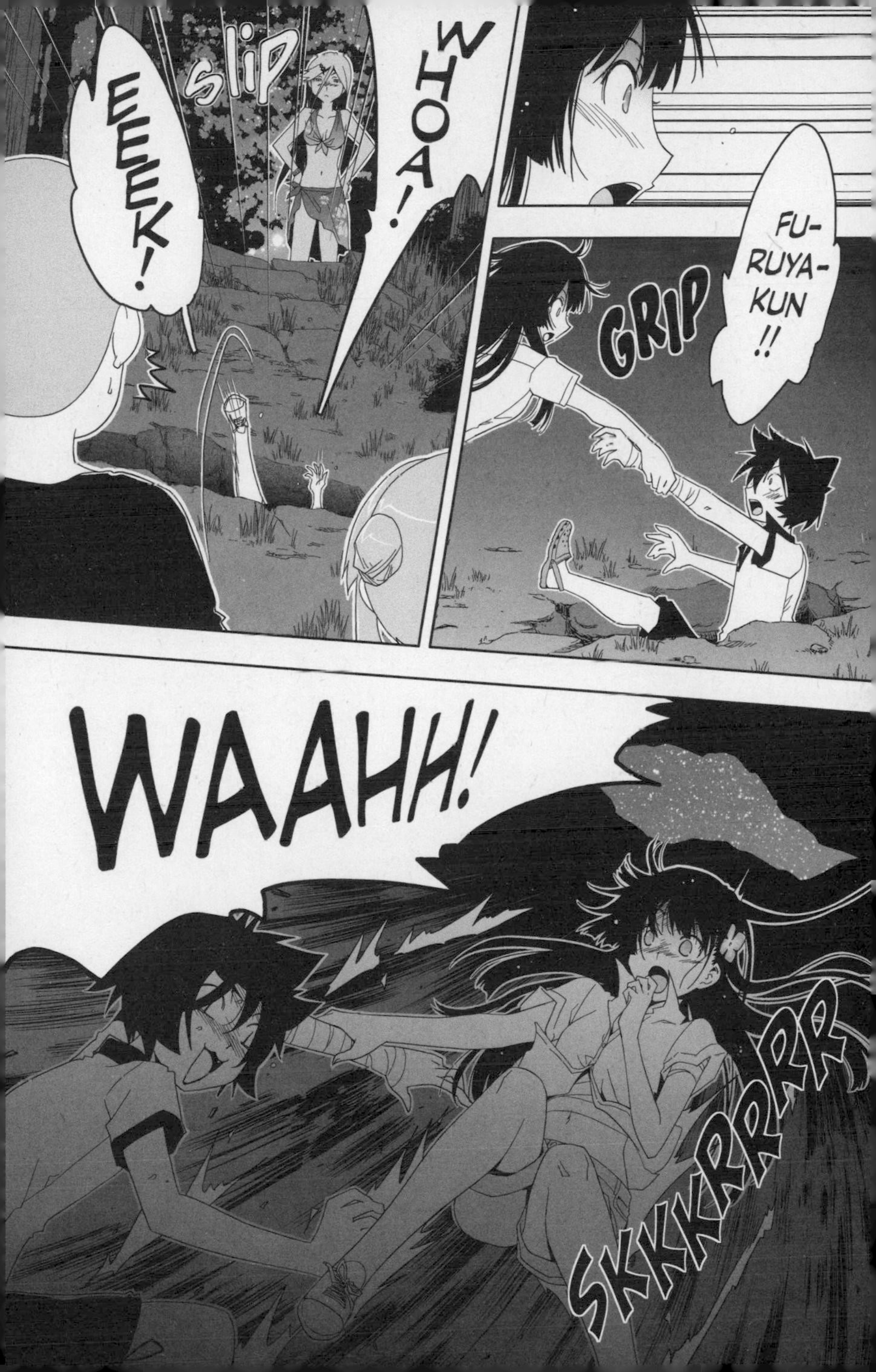
FU-
RUYA-
KUN
!!
GRIP
WHOA!
slip
EEEEK!
WAAHH!
SKKKRRRR

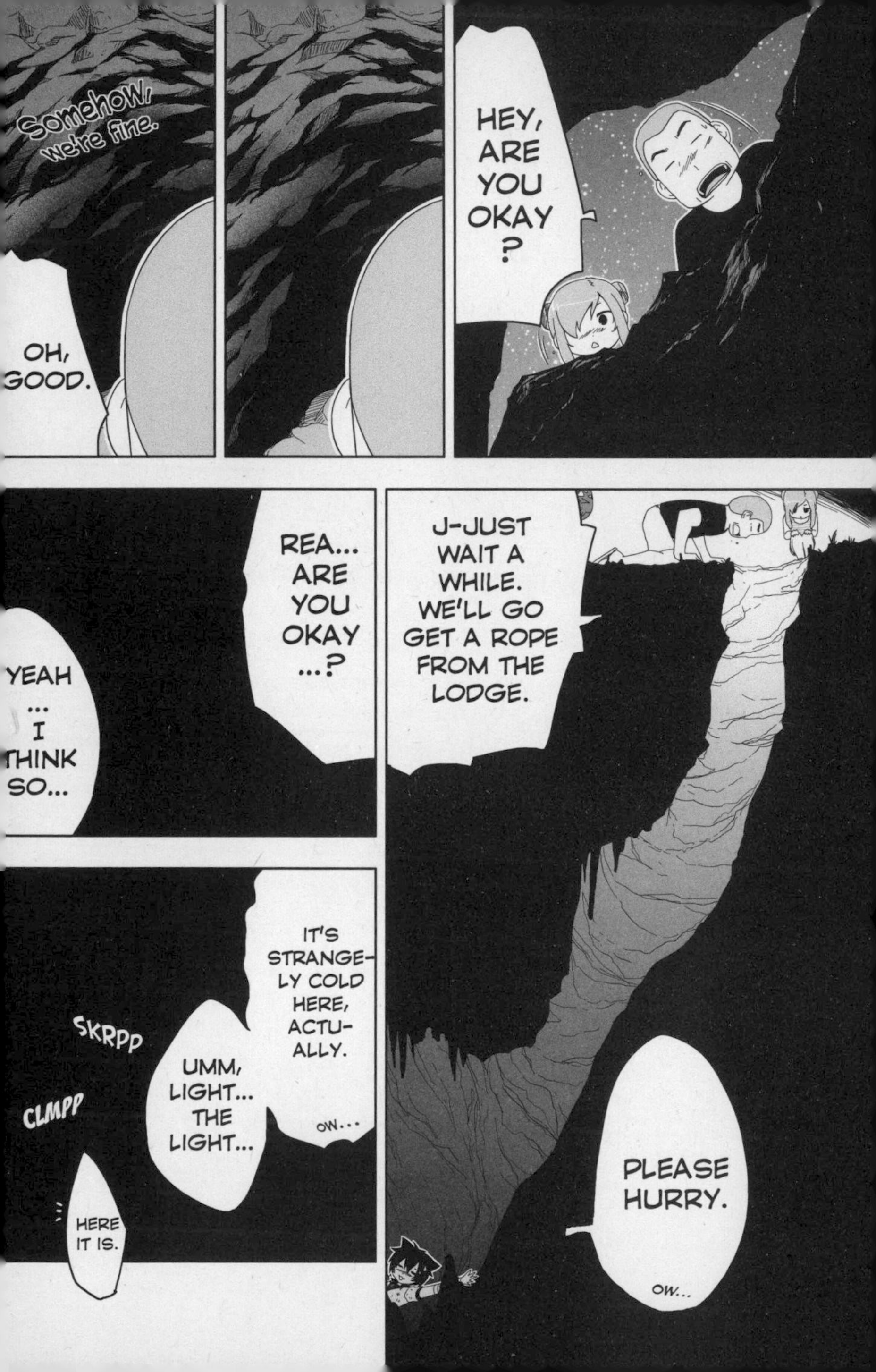
HEY, ARE YOU OKAY?
Somehow, we're fine.
OH, GOOD.
J-JUST WAIT A WHILE. WE'LL GO GET A ROPE FROM THE LODGE.
PLEASE HURRY.
OW...
REA... ARE YOU OKAY...?
YEAH... I THINK SO...
IT'S STRANGELY COLD HERE, ACTUALLY.
OW...
UMM, LIGHT... THE LIGHT...
SKRPP
CLMPP
HERE IT IS.

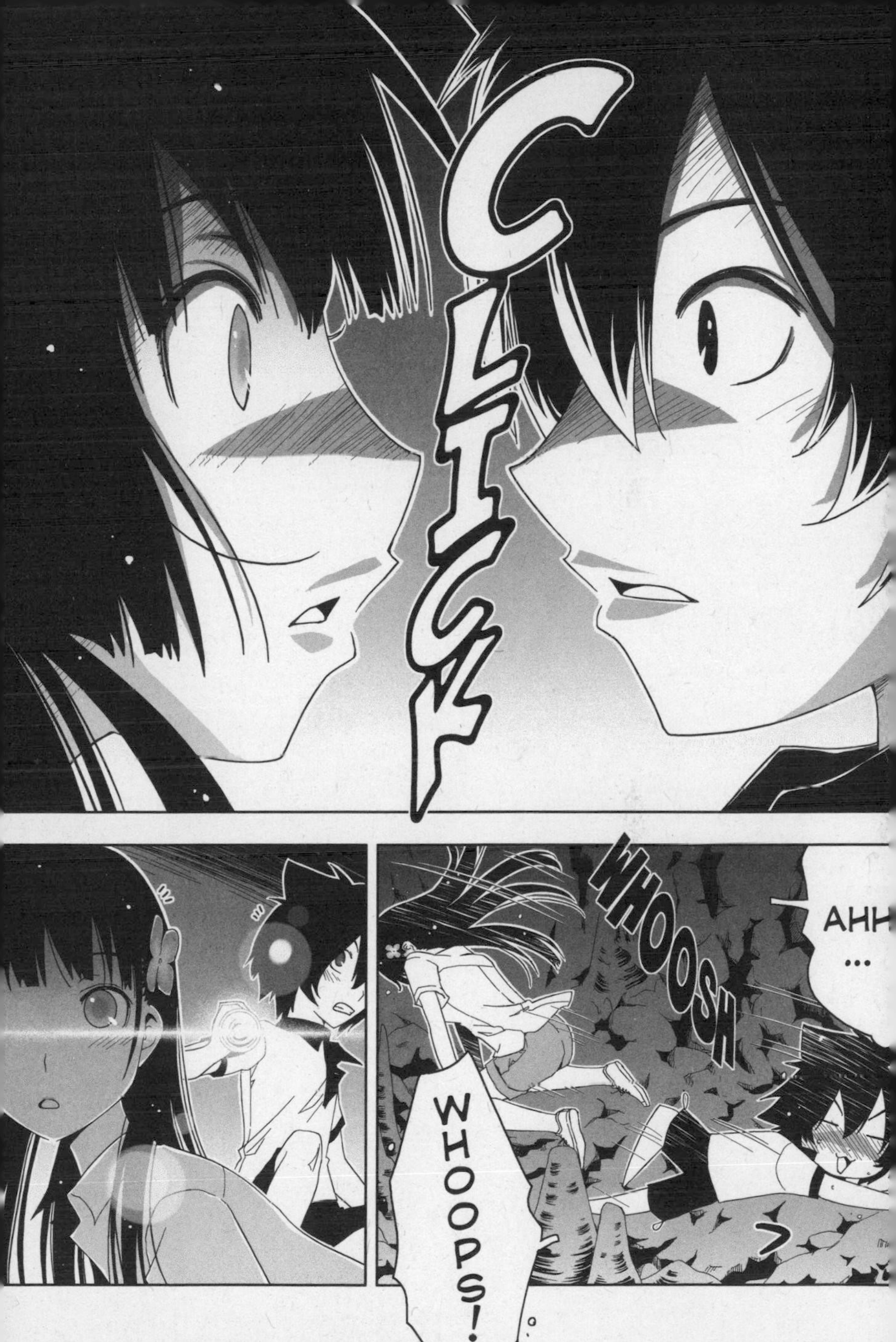
CLICK
WHOOSH
AHH ...
WHOOPS!

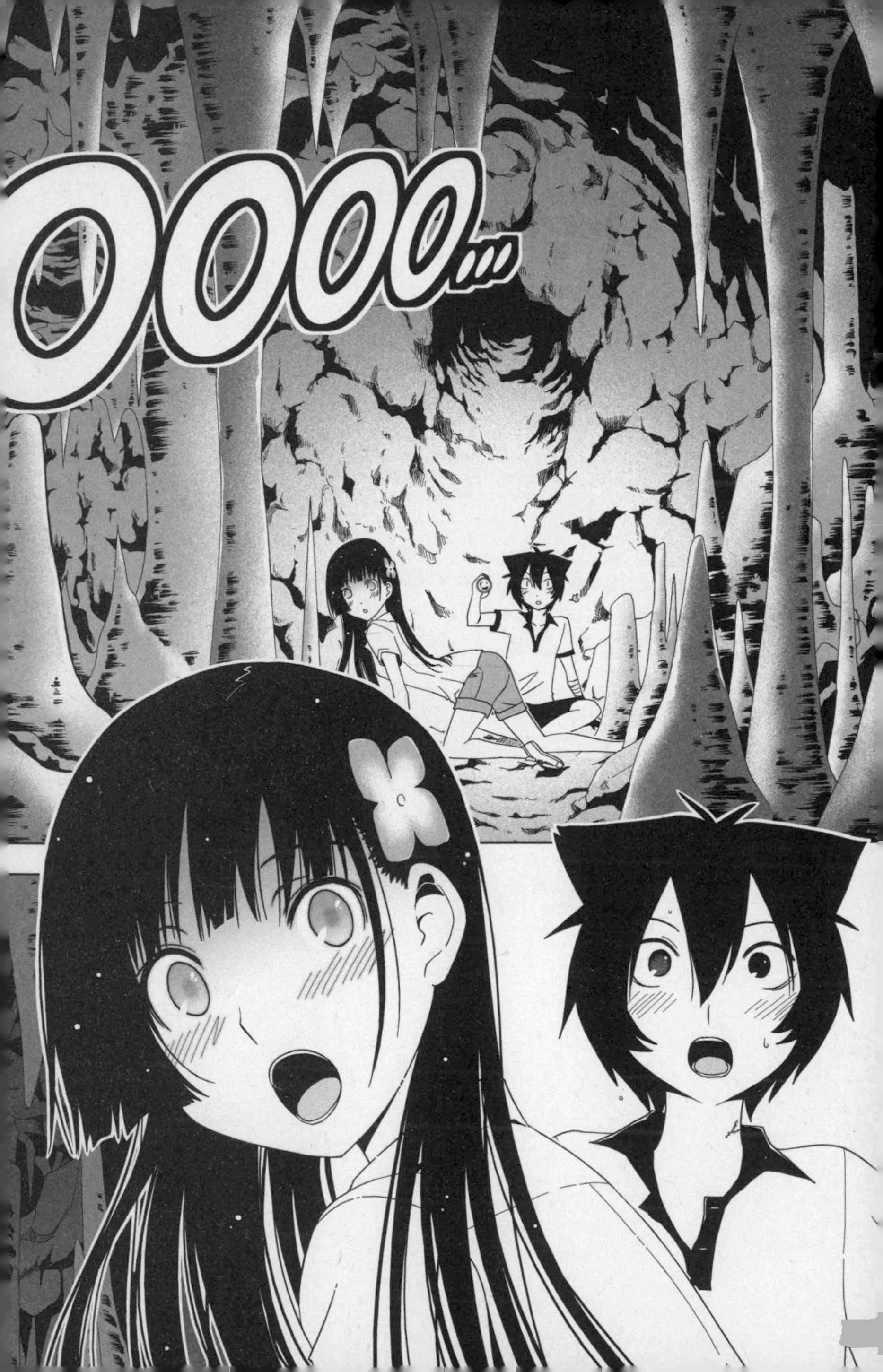
OOOO...

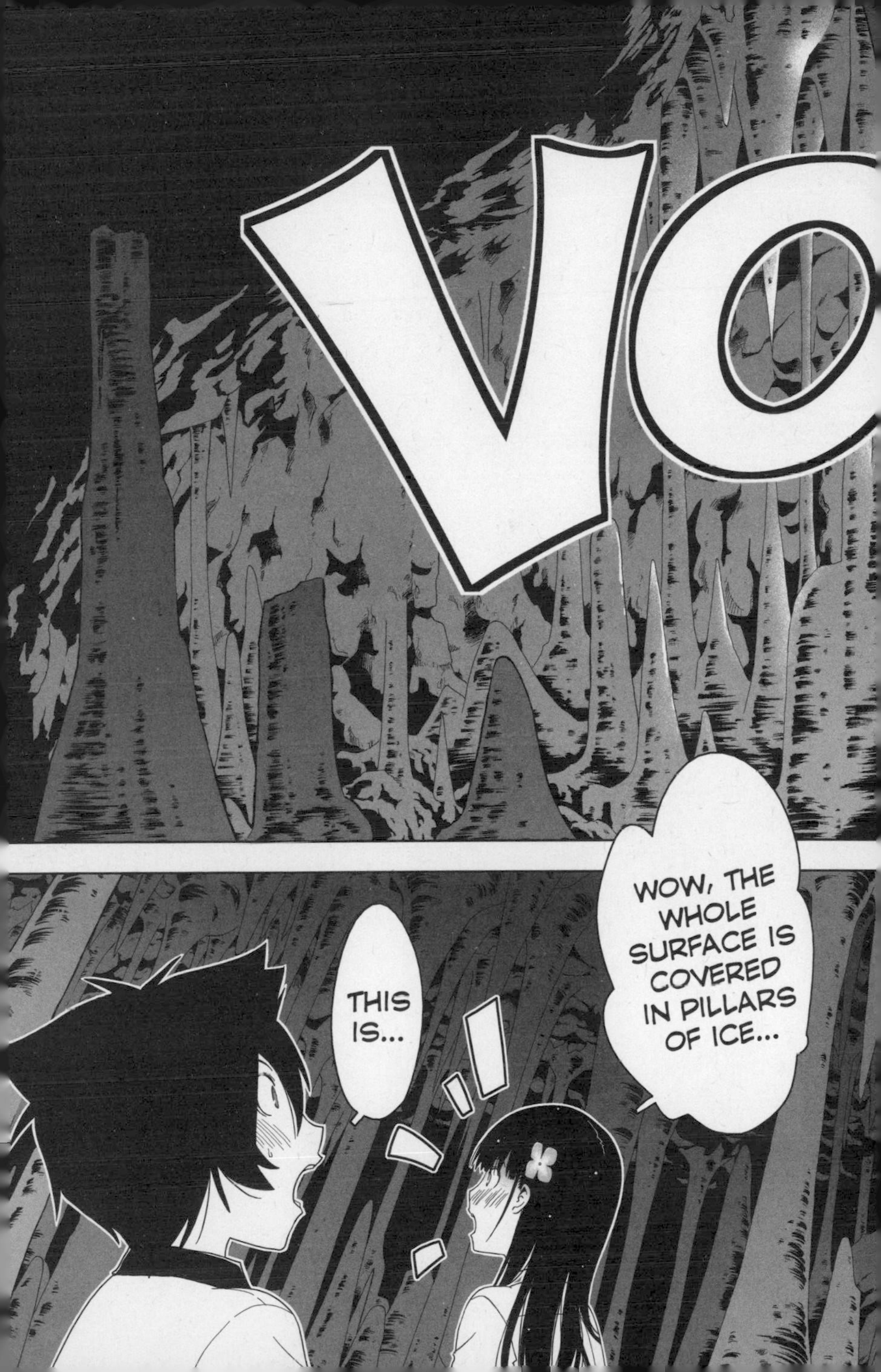
VO
WOW, THE WHOLE SURFACE IS COVERED IN PILLARS OF ICE...
THIS IS...

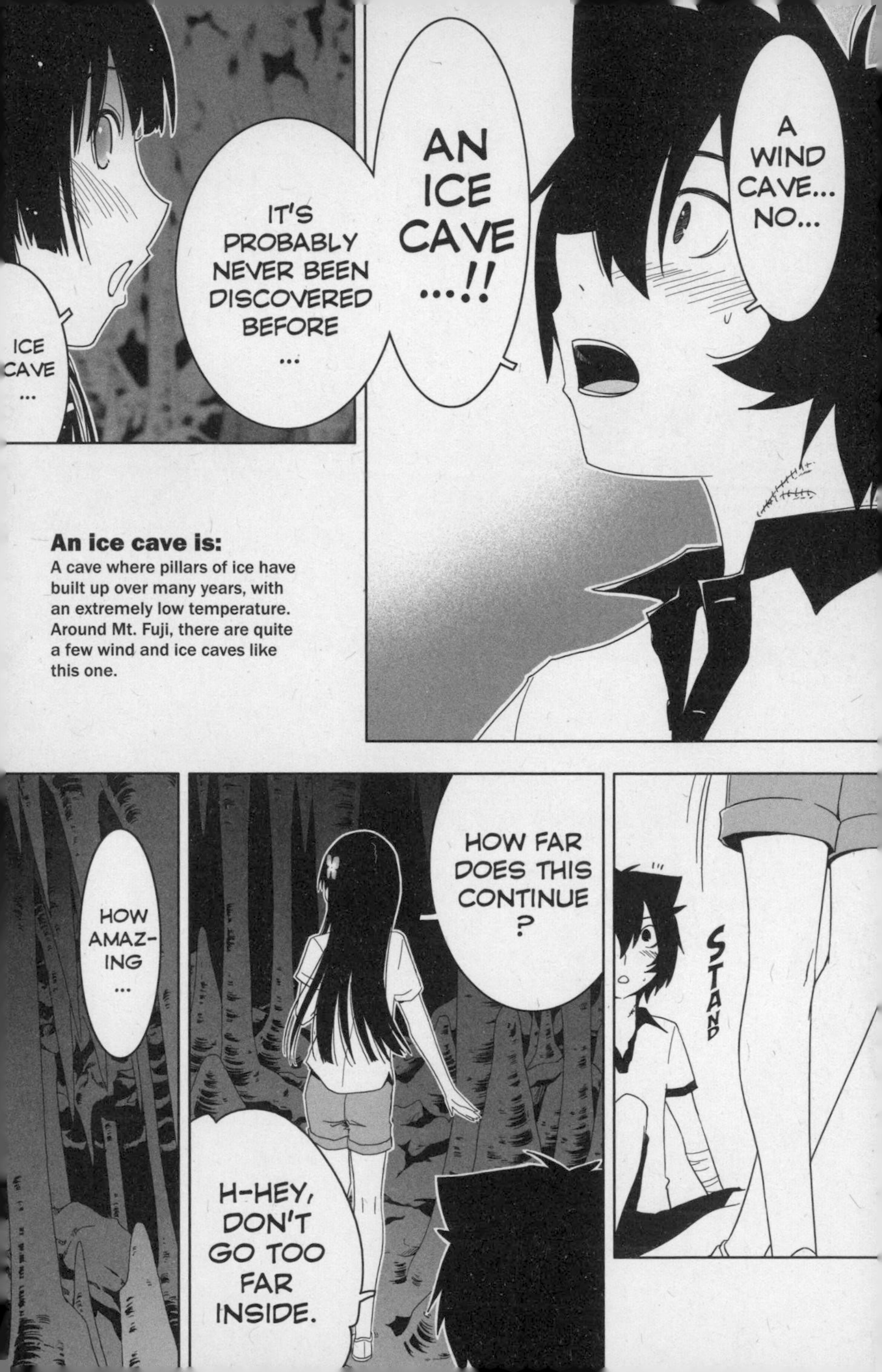
A WIND CAVE... NO...
AN ICE CAVE...!!
IT'S PROBABLY NEVER BEEN DISCOVERED BEFORE...
ICE CAVE...
STAND
HOW FAR DOES THIS CONTINUE?
H-HEY, DON'T GO TOO FAR INSIDE.
HOW AMAZ-ING...

An ice cave is:
A cave where pillars of ice have built up over many years, with an extremely low temperature. Around Mt. Fuji, there are quite a few wind and ice caves like this one.

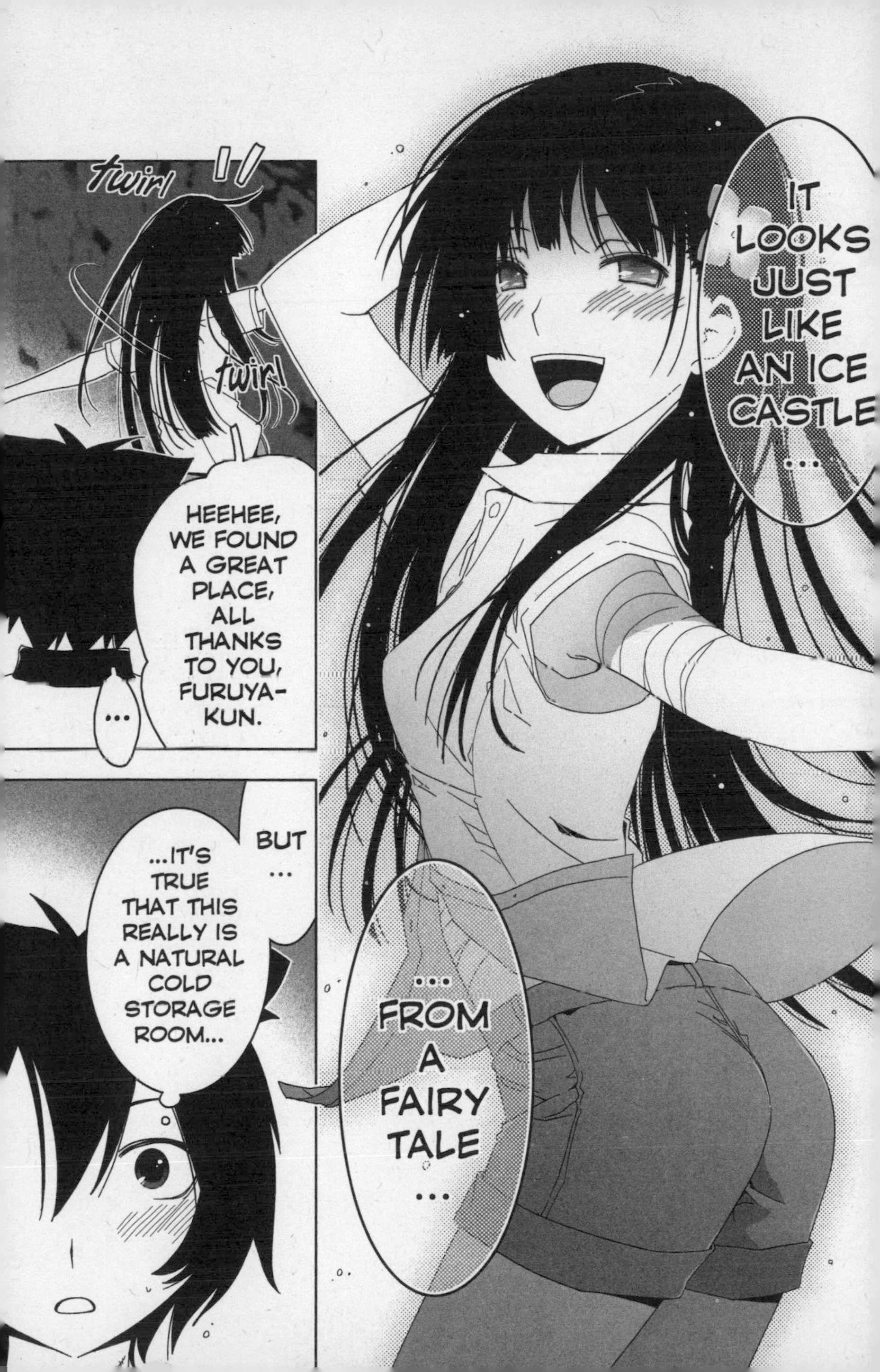
IT LOOKS JUST LIKE AN ICE CASTLE ...
... FROM A FAIRY TALE ...
twirl
!!
twirl
HEEHEE, WE FOUND A GREAT PLACE, ALL THANKS TO YOU, FURUYA-KUN.
...
BUT ...
...IT'S TRUE THAT THIS REALLY IS A NATURAL COLD STORAGE ROOM...

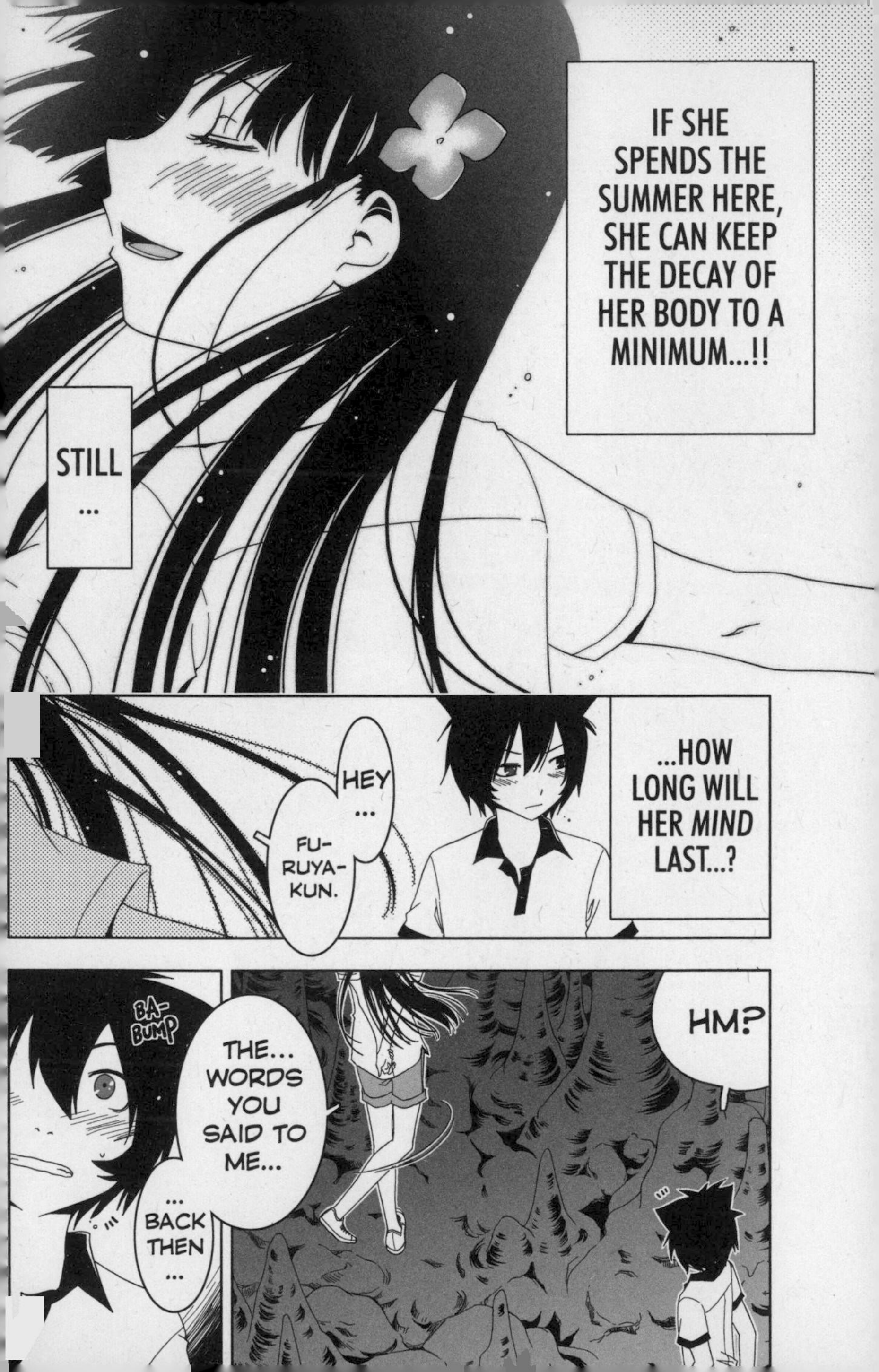
IF SHE SPENDS THE SUMMER HERE, SHE CAN KEEP THE DECAY OF HER BODY TO A MINIMUM...!!
STILL ...
...HOW LONG WILL HER *MIND* LAST...?
HEY ... FU-RUYA-KUN.
HM?
THE... WORDS YOU SAID TO ME...
BA-BUMP
... BACK THEN ...

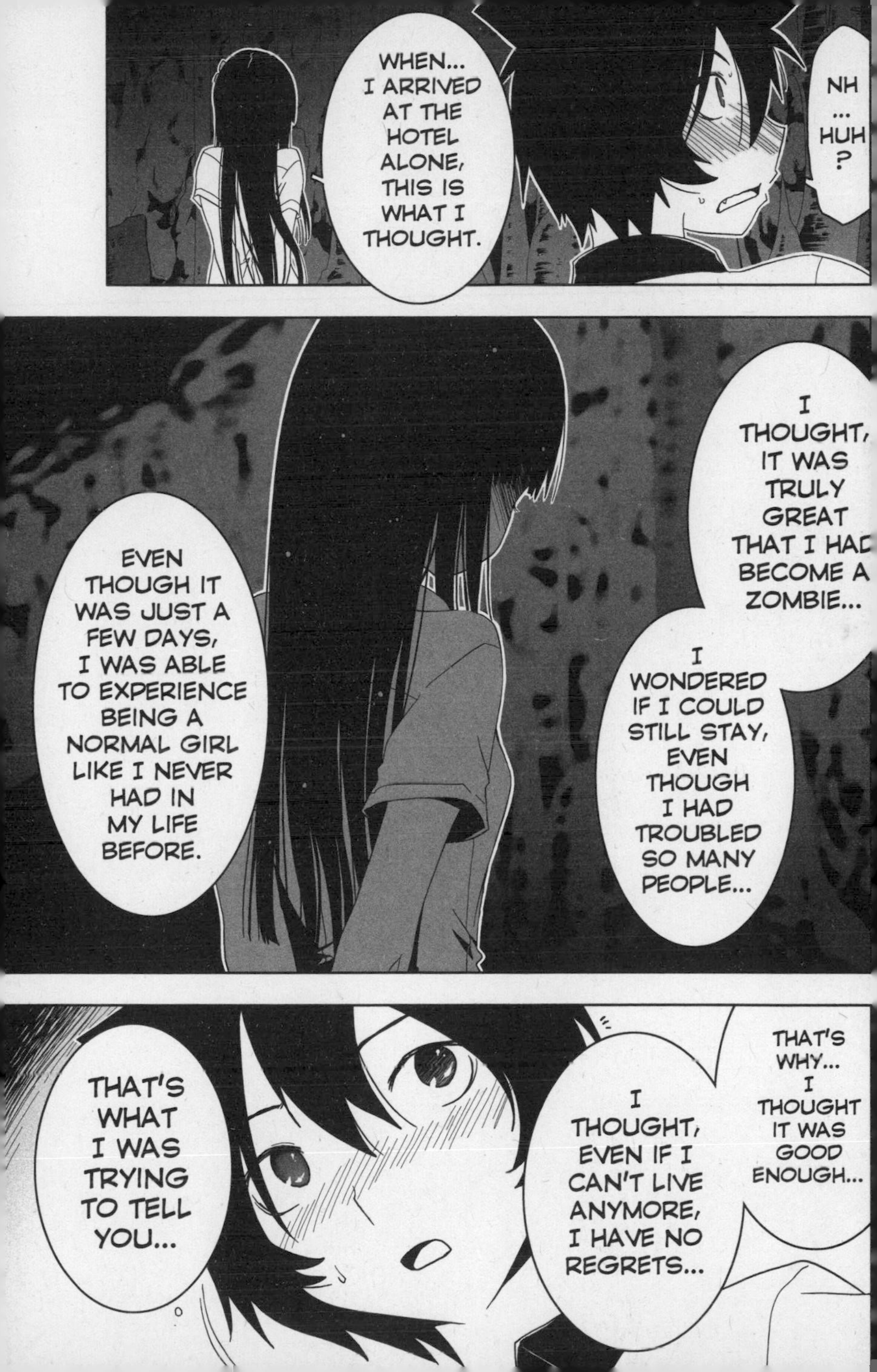
NH ... HUH ?
WHEN... I ARRIVED AT THE HOTEL ALONE, THIS IS WHAT I THOUGHT.
I THOUGHT, IT WAS TRULY GREAT THAT I HAD BECOME A ZOMBIE...
I WONDERED IF I COULD STILL STAY, EVEN THOUGH I HAD TROUBLED SO MANY PEOPLE...
EVEN THOUGH IT WAS JUST A FEW DAYS, I WAS ABLE TO EXPERIENCE BEING A NORMAL GIRL LIKE I NEVER HAD IN MY LIFE BEFORE.
THAT'S WHY... I THOUGHT IT WAS GOOD ENOUGH...
I THOUGHT, EVEN IF I CAN'T LIVE ANYMORE, I HAVE NO REGRETS...
THAT'S WHAT I WAS TRYING TO TELL YOU...

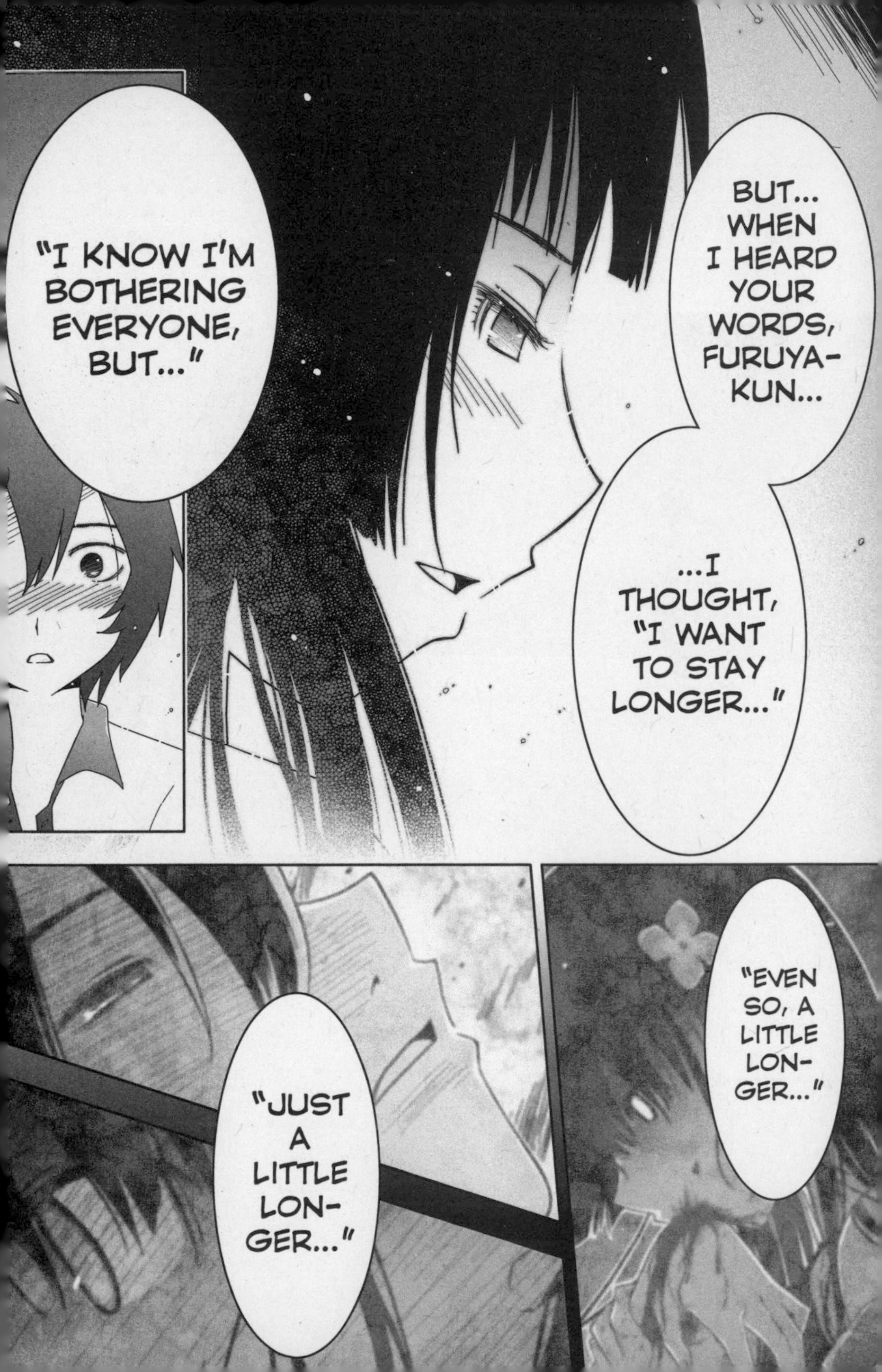
BUT... WHEN I HEARD YOUR WORDS, FURUYA-KUN...
...I THOUGHT, "I WANT TO STAY LONGER..."
"I KNOW I'M BOTHERING EVERYONE, BUT..."
"EVEN SO, A LITTLE LON-GER..."
"JUST A LITTLE LON-GER..."

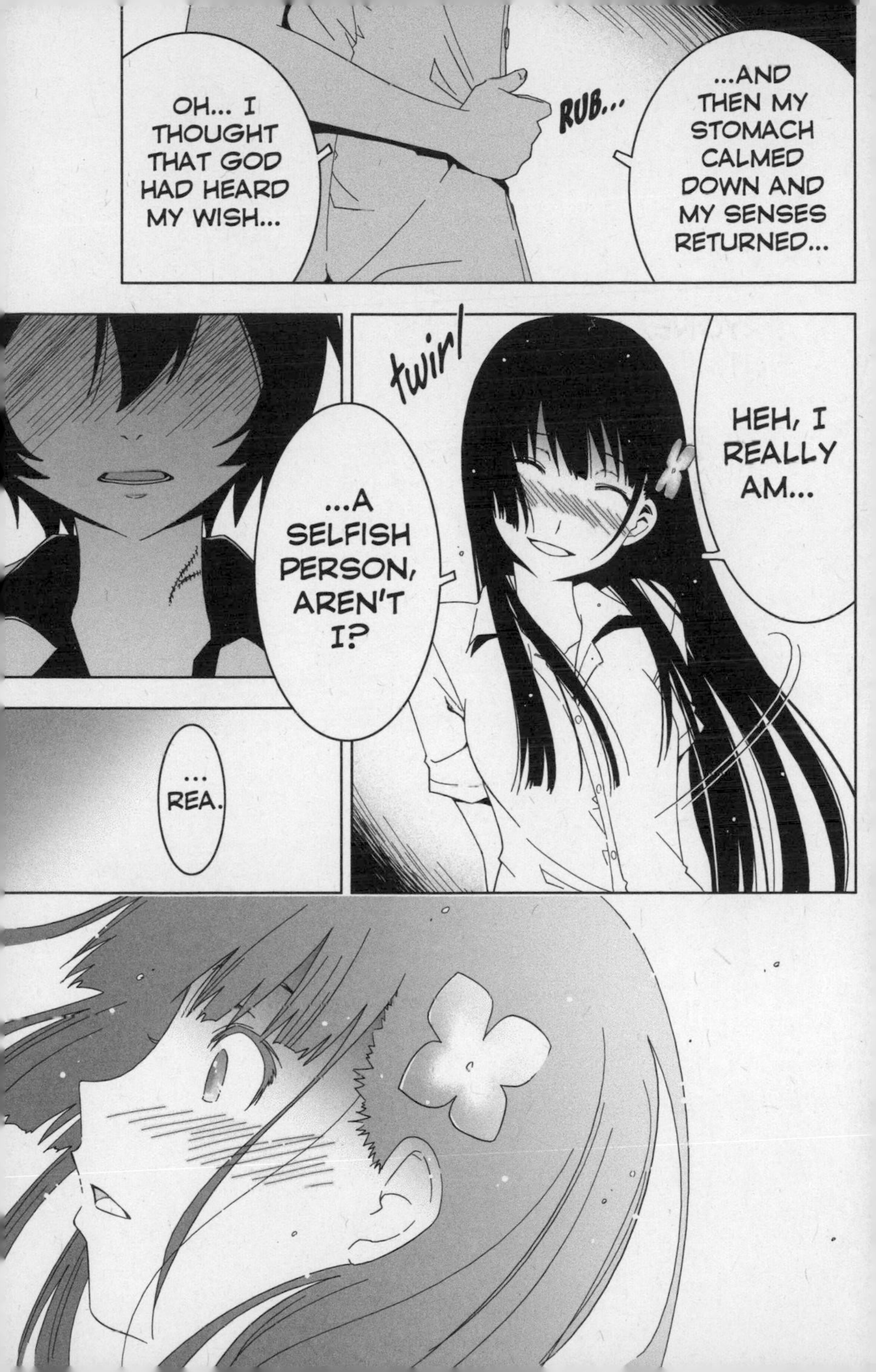
...AND THEN MY STOMACH CALMED DOWN AND MY SENSES RETURNED...
RUB...
OH... I THOUGHT THAT GOD HAD HEARD MY WISH...
HEH, I REALLY AM...
twirl
...A SELFISH PERSON, AREN'T I?
... REA.

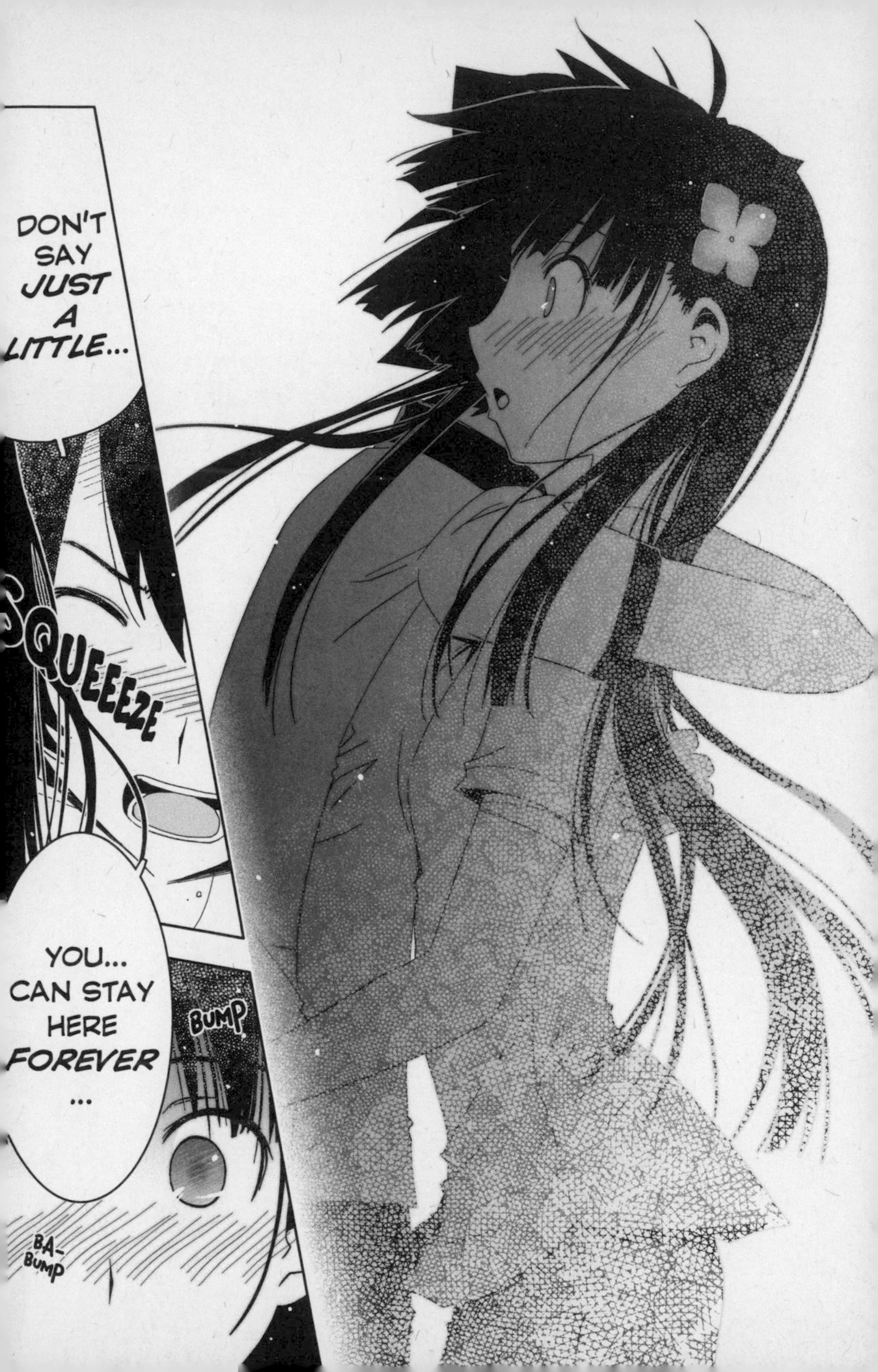
DON'T SAY JUST A LITTLE...
SQUEEEEZE
YOU... CAN STAY HERE FOREVER ...
BUMP
BA-BUMP

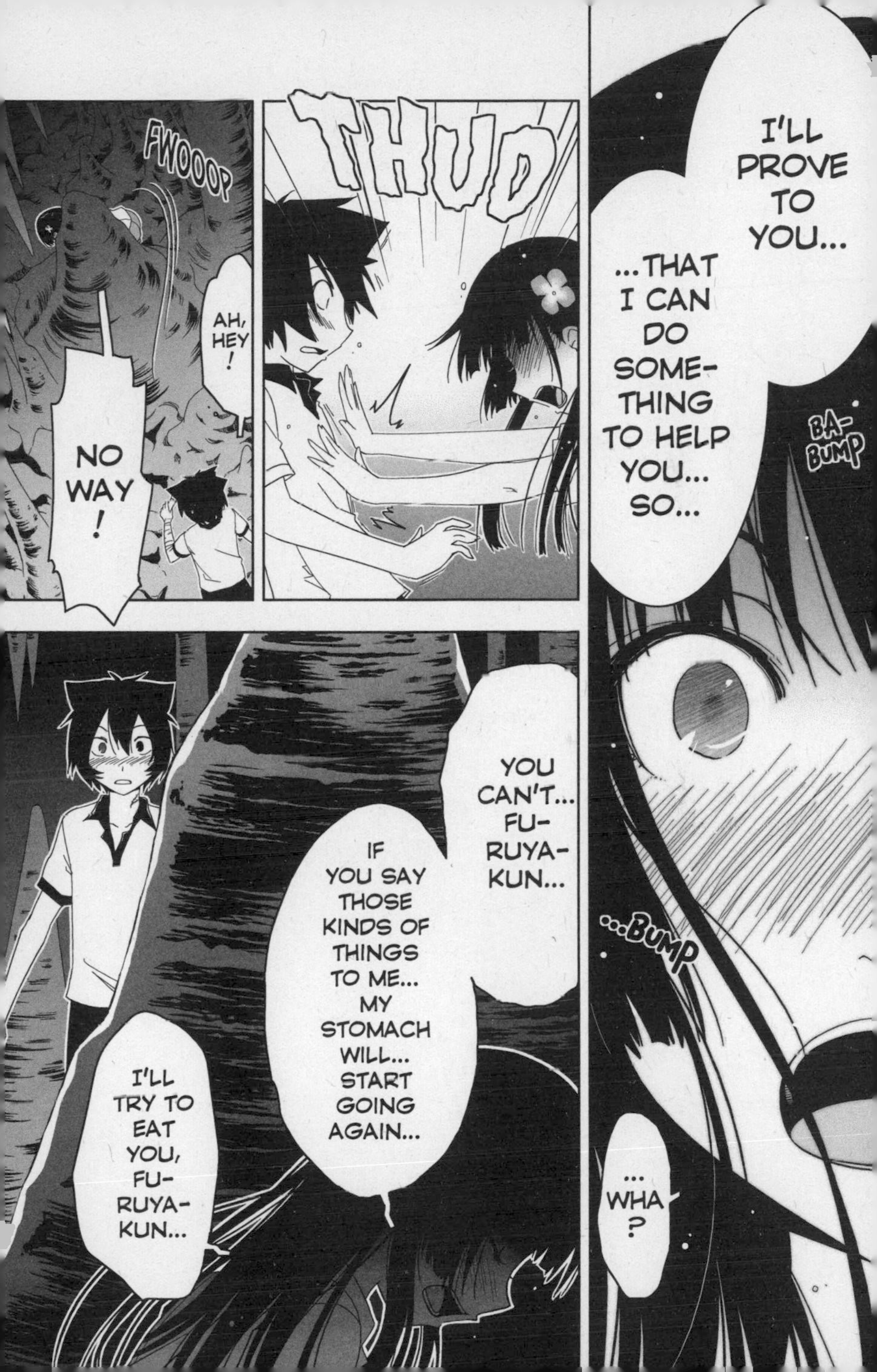
I'LL PROVE TO YOU...
...THAT I CAN DO SOMETHING TO HELP YOU... SO...
BA-BUMP
...BUMP
...WHA?
THUD
FWOOOP
AH, HEY!
NO WAY!
YOU CAN'T... FURUYA-KUN...
IF YOU SAY THOSE KINDS OF THINGS TO ME... MY STOMACH WILL... START GOING AGAIN...
I'LL TRY TO EAT YOU, FURUYA-KUN...

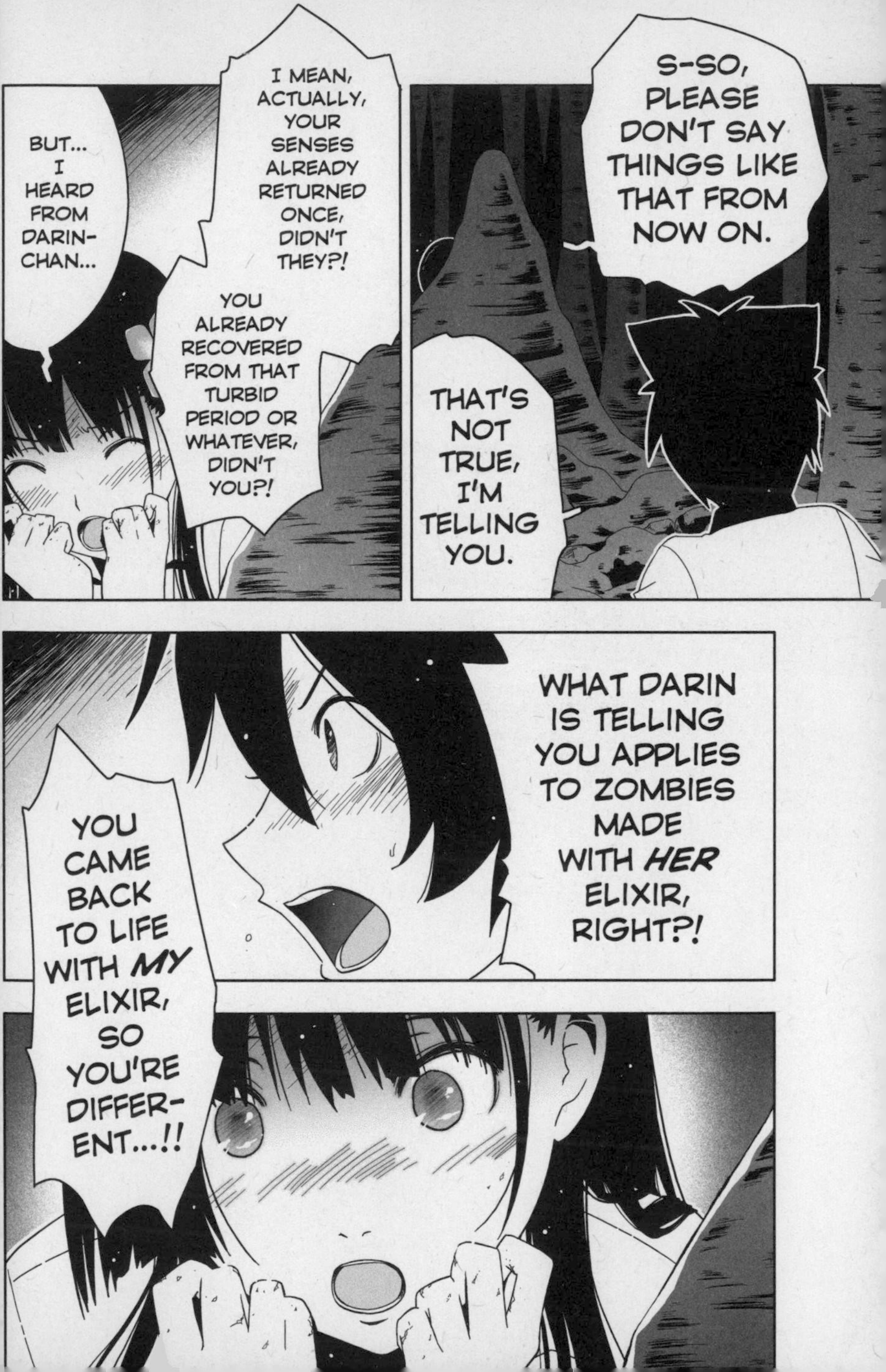
S-SO, PLEASE DON'T SAY THINGS LIKE THAT FROM NOW ON.
THAT'S NOT TRUE, I'M TELLING YOU.
I MEAN, ACTUALLY, YOUR SENSES ALREADY RETURNED ONCE, DIDN'T THEY?!
BUT... I HEARD FROM DARIN-CHAN...
YOU ALREADY RECOVERED FROM THAT TURBID PERIOD OR WHATEVER, DIDN'T YOU?!
WHAT DARIN IS TELLING YOU APPLIES TO ZOMBIES MADE WITH *HER* ELIXIR, RIGHT?!
YOU CAME BACK TO LIFE WITH *MY* ELIXIR, SO YOU'RE DIFFER-ENT...!!

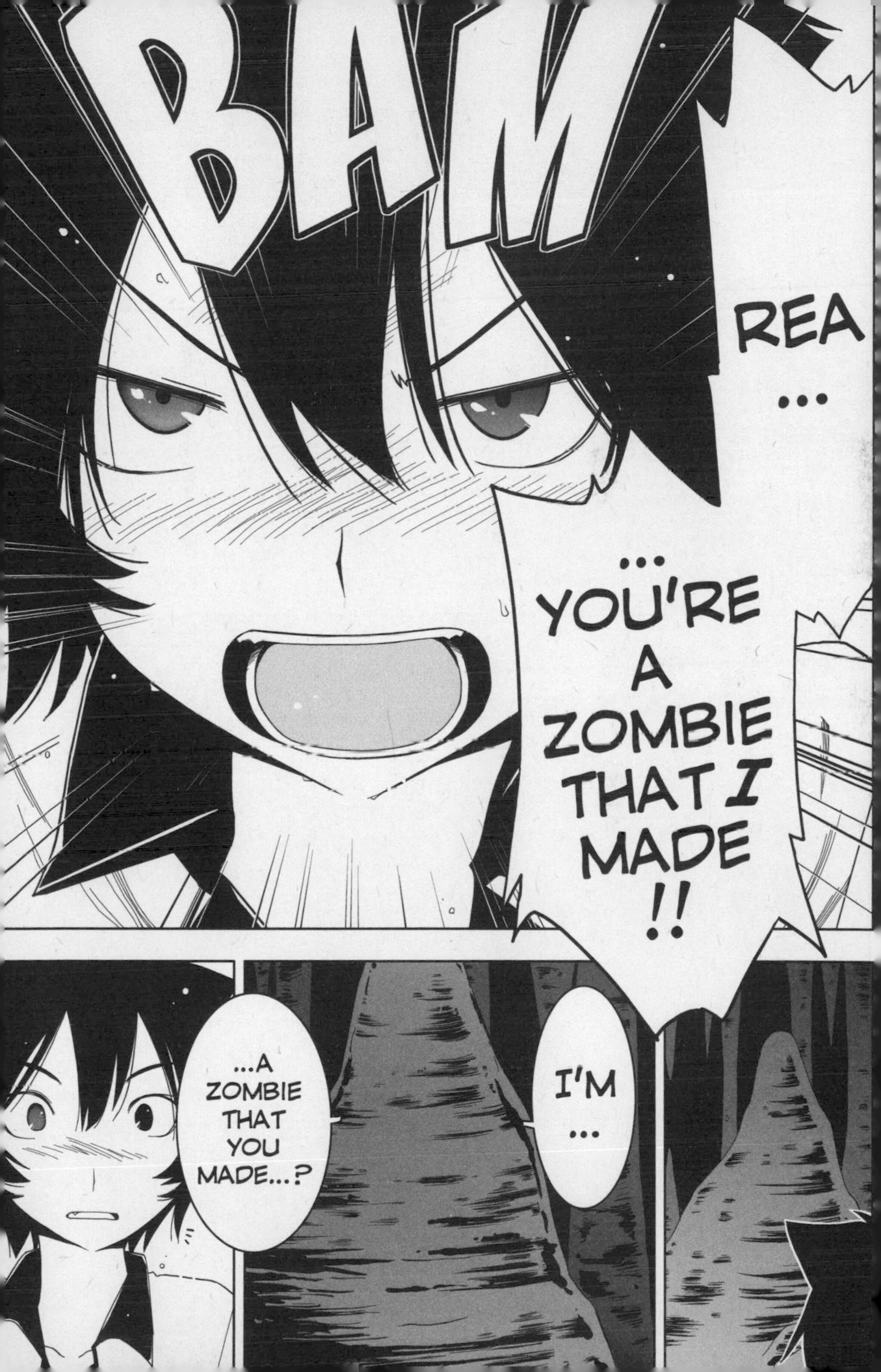
BAM
REA... ...YOU'RE A ZOMBIE THAT *I* MADE!!
I'M...
...A ZOMBIE THAT YOU MADE...?

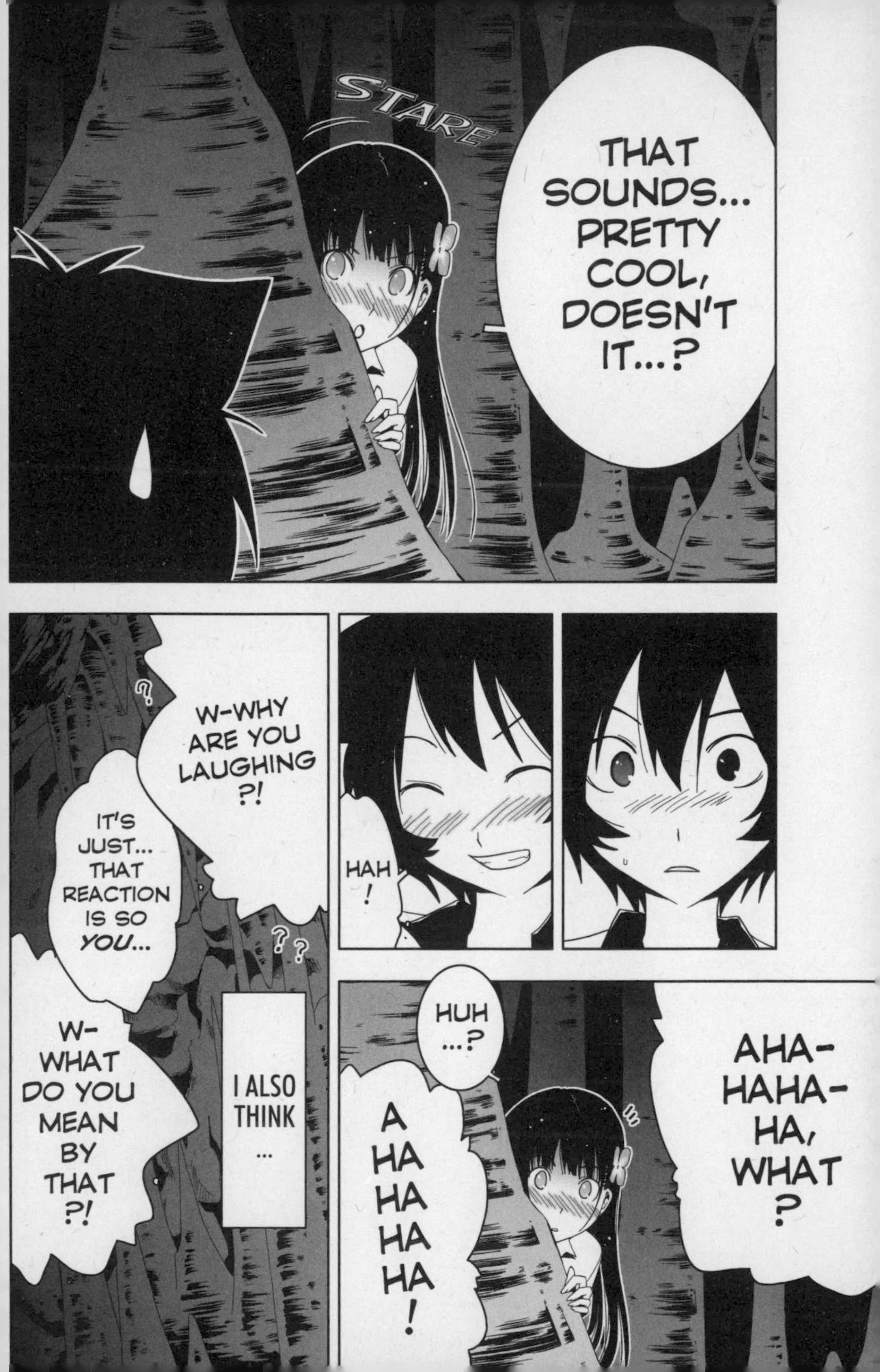
STARE
THAT SOUNDS... PRETTY COOL, DOESN'T IT...?
HAH!
AHA-HAHA-HA, WHAT?
HUH...?
A HA HA HA HA!
W-WHY ARE YOU LAUGHING?!
IT'S JUST... THAT REACTION IS SO *YOU*...
I ALSO THINK...
W-WHAT DO YOU MEAN BY THAT?!

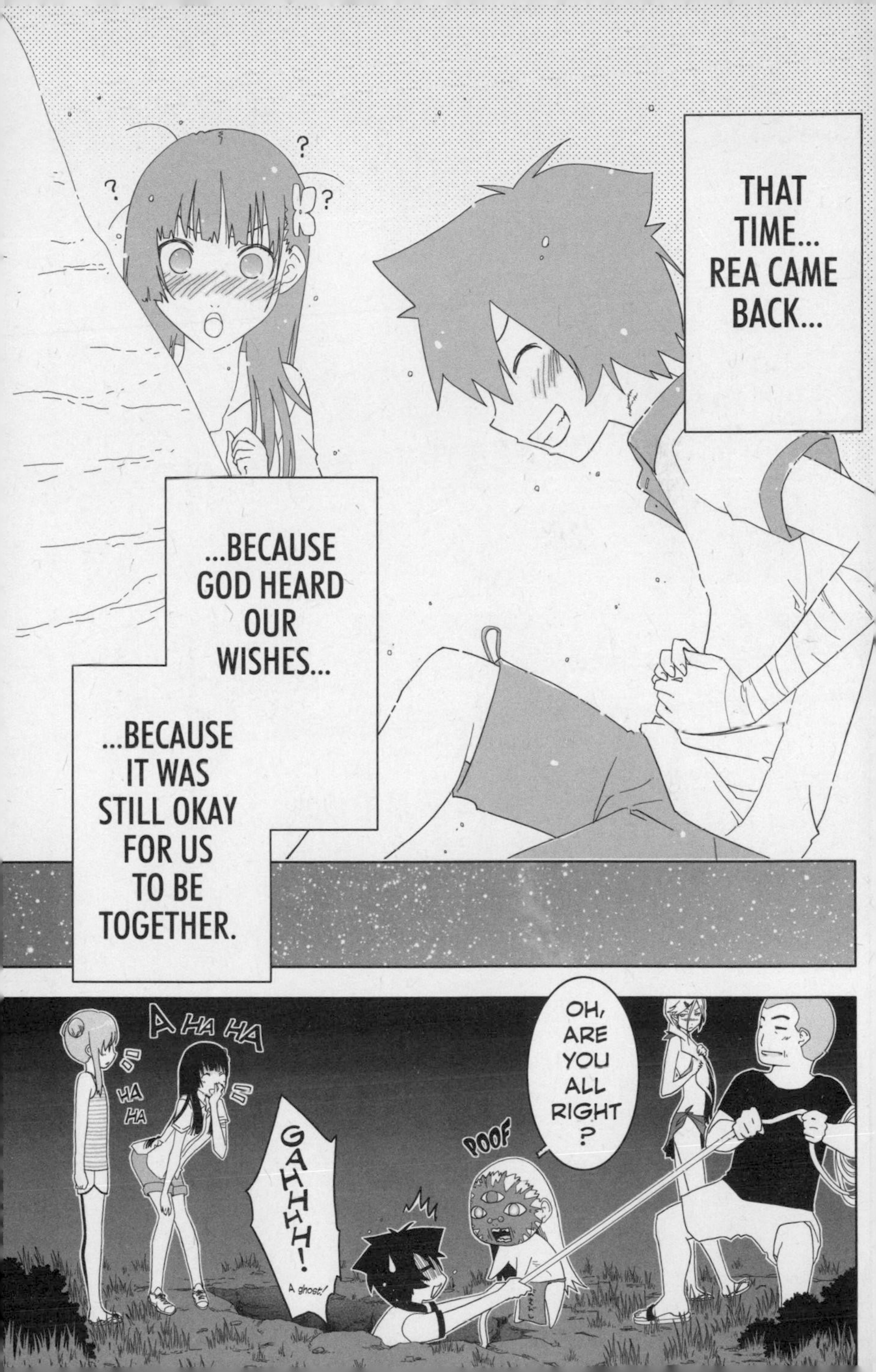
THAT TIME... REA CAME BACK...
...BECAUSE GOD HEARD OUR WISHES...
...BECAUSE IT WAS STILL OKAY FOR US TO BE TOGETHER.
OH, ARE YOU ALL RIGHT?
POOF
GAHHH!
A ghost!
A HA HA
HA HA

SANKAREA ANECDOTES 5

About Mero

This time around is about the changes in Mero's character. In reality… before publication, in the rather early steps, the setting actually had Mero as Chihiro's *older sister!* Or rather, not only her age but also her personality and her appearance were different, so she was a completely different character…

Afterwards, when I decided to make Ranko the cousin character, in order to balance it out, Mero was changed into a younger sister character. If publication had started with this version, I wonder what kind of answers big sister Mero would have given in "Mero's Zen Riddles"…?

By the way, I've drawn a convenience store or whatever below, but in the very beginning, the Furuya family was supposed to run a convenience store, not a temple. (I just remembered this.)

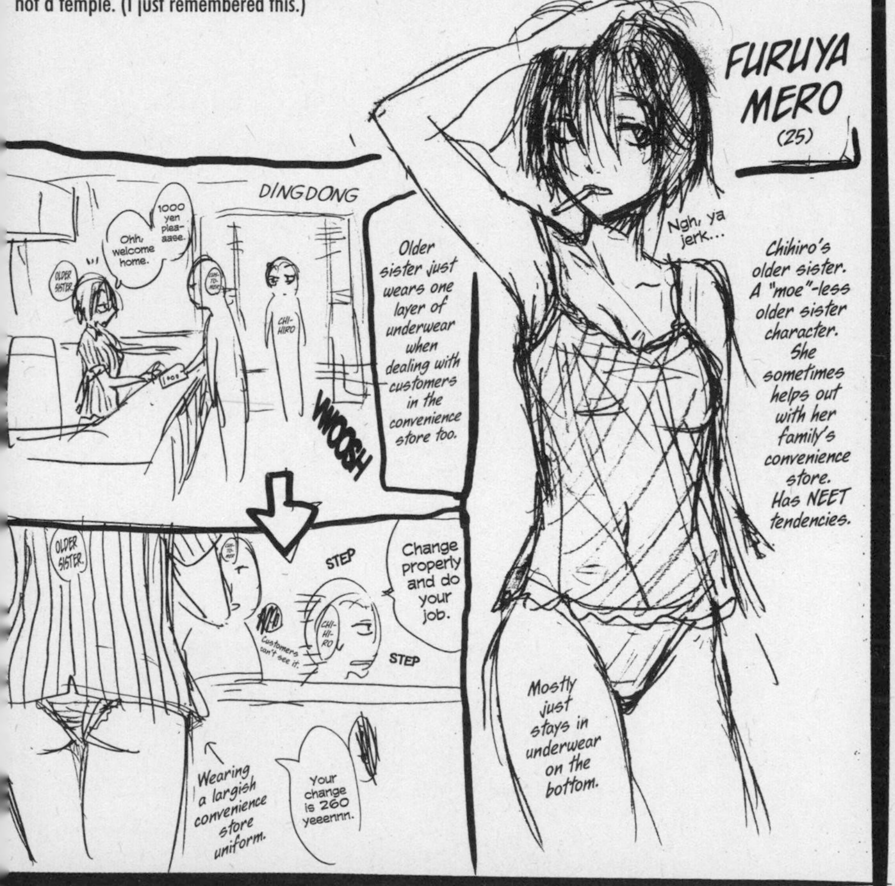
FURUYA MERO
(25)
Chihiro's older sister. A "moe"-less older sister character. She sometimes helps out with her family's convenience store. Has NEET tendencies.
Ngh, ya jerk…
Mostly just stays in underwear on the bottom.
Older sister just wears one layer of underwear when dealing with customers in the convenience store too.
DINGDONG
1000 yen pleaaase.
Ohh, welcome home.
OLDER SISTER
CHIHIRO
VWOOSH
Change properly and do your job.
STEP
STEP
CHI-HIRO
Customers can't see it.
OLDER SISTER
Your change is 260 yeeennn.
Wearing a largish convenience store uniform.

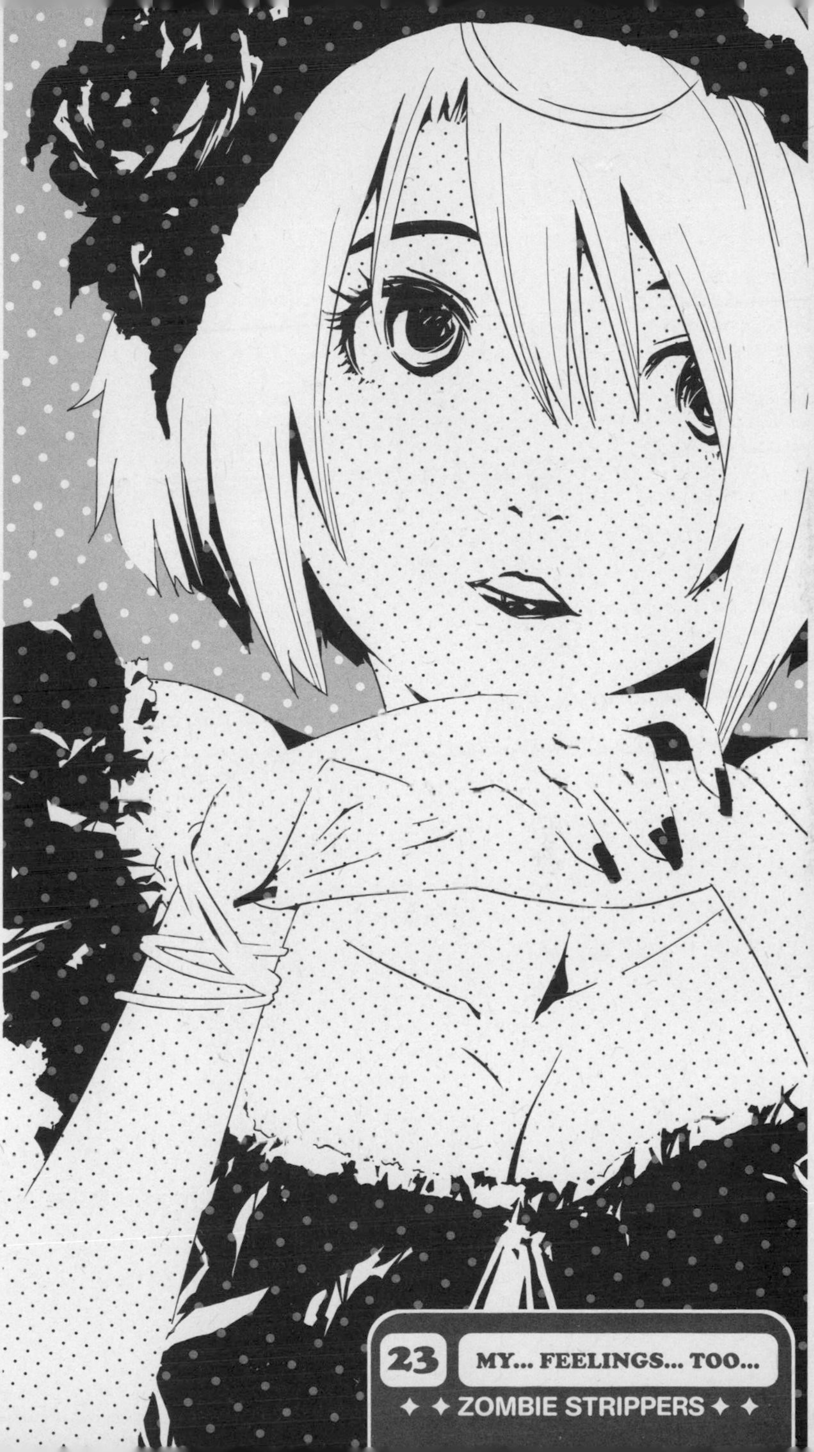
23
MY... FEELINGS... TOO...
✦ ✦ ZOMBIE STRIPPERS ✦ ✦

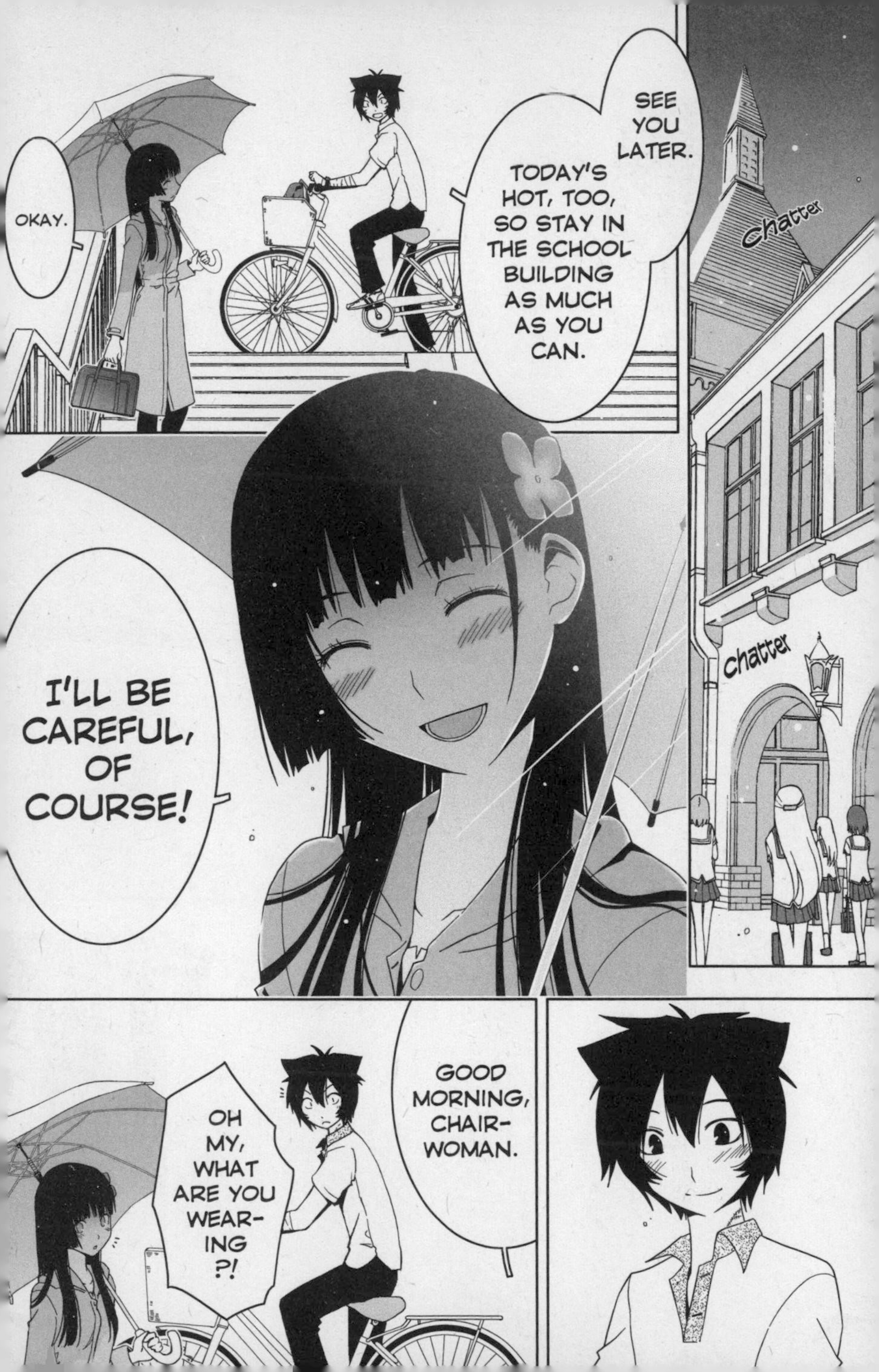
Chatter
Chatter
SEE YOU LATER.
TODAY'S HOT, TOO, SO STAY IN THE SCHOOL BUILDING AS MUCH AS YOU CAN.
OKAY.
I'LL BE CAREFUL, OF COURSE!
GOOD MORNING, CHAIR-WOMAN.
OH MY, WHAT ARE YOU WEAR-ING ?!

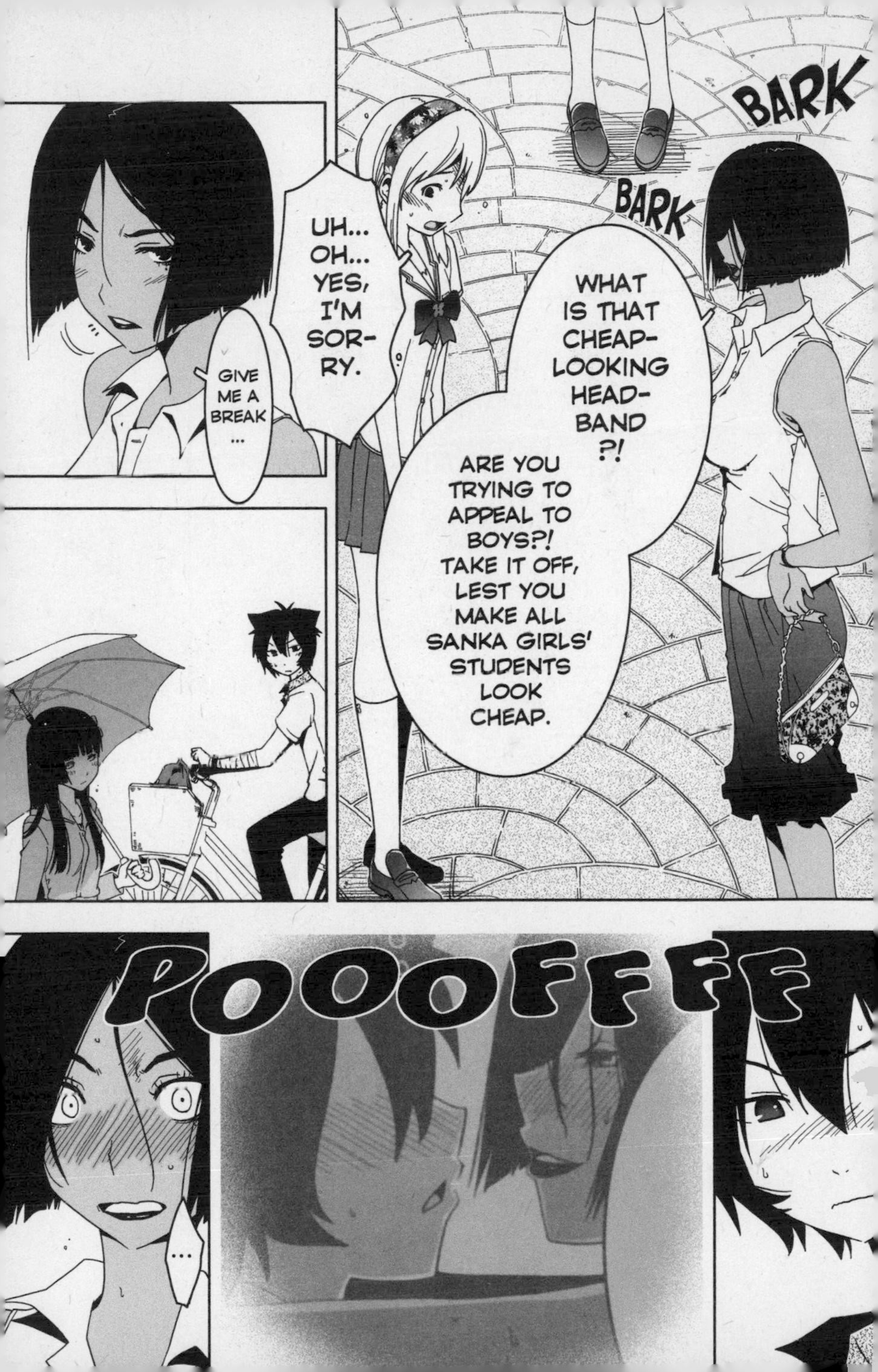
BARK
BARK
WHAT IS THAT CHEAP-LOOKING HEAD-BAND?!
ARE YOU TRYING TO APPEAL TO BOYS?! TAKE IT OFF, LEST YOU MAKE ALL SANKA GIRLS' STUDENTS LOOK CHEAP.
UH... OH... YES, I'M SOR-RY.
GIVE ME A BREAK...
POOOFFFF
...

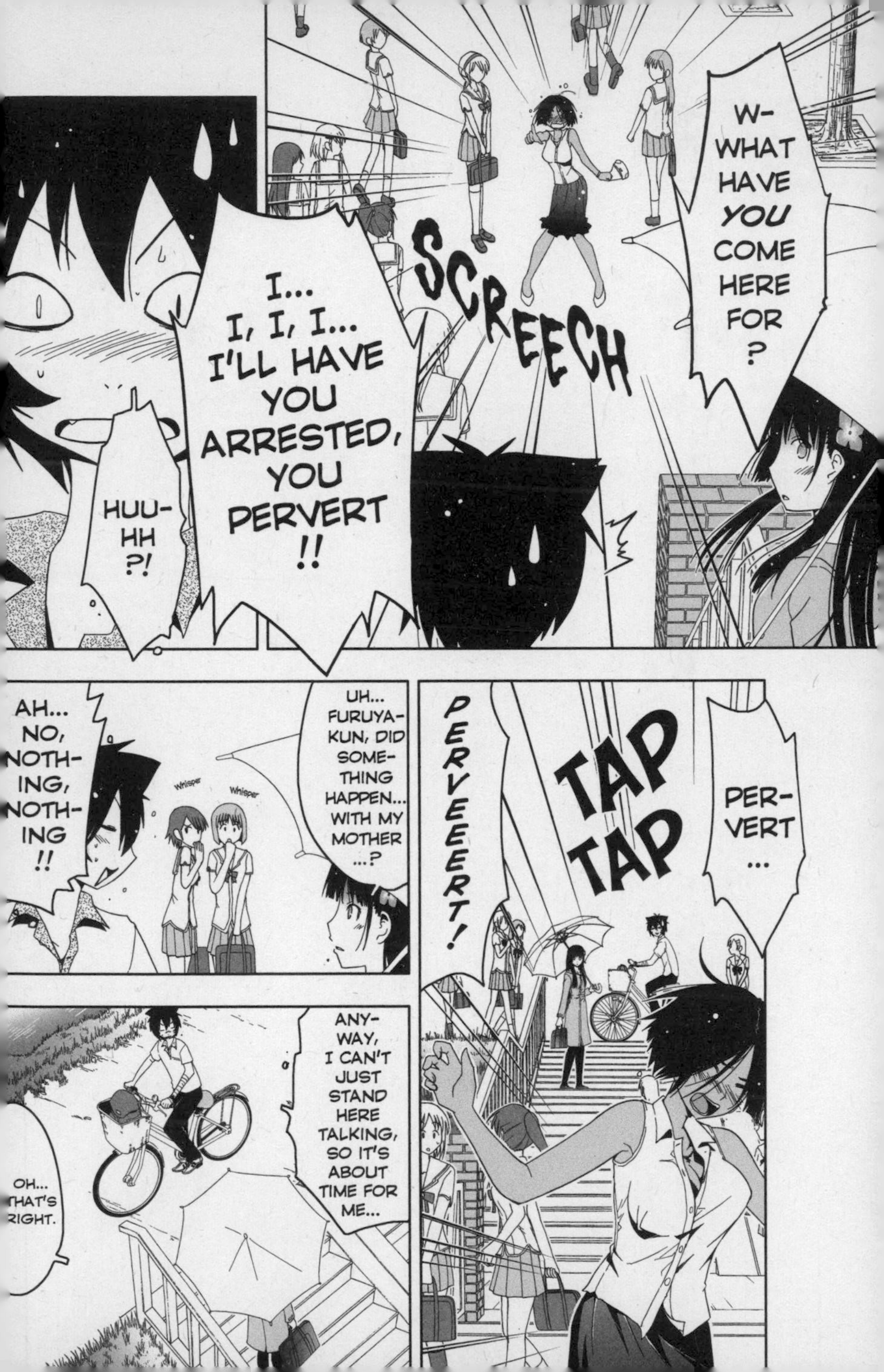
W-WHAT HAVE YOU COME HERE FOR?
SCREECH
I... I, I, I... I'LL HAVE YOU ARRESTED, YOU PERVERT!!
HUU-HH?!
PER-VERT...
TAP TAP
PERVEEERT!
UH... FURUYA-KUN, DID SOME-THING HAPPEN... WITH MY MOTHER...?
Whisper
Whisper
AH... NO, NOTH-ING, NOTH-ING!!
ANY-WAY, I CAN'T JUST STAND HERE TALKING, SO IT'S ABOUT TIME FOR ME...
OH... THAT'S RIGHT.

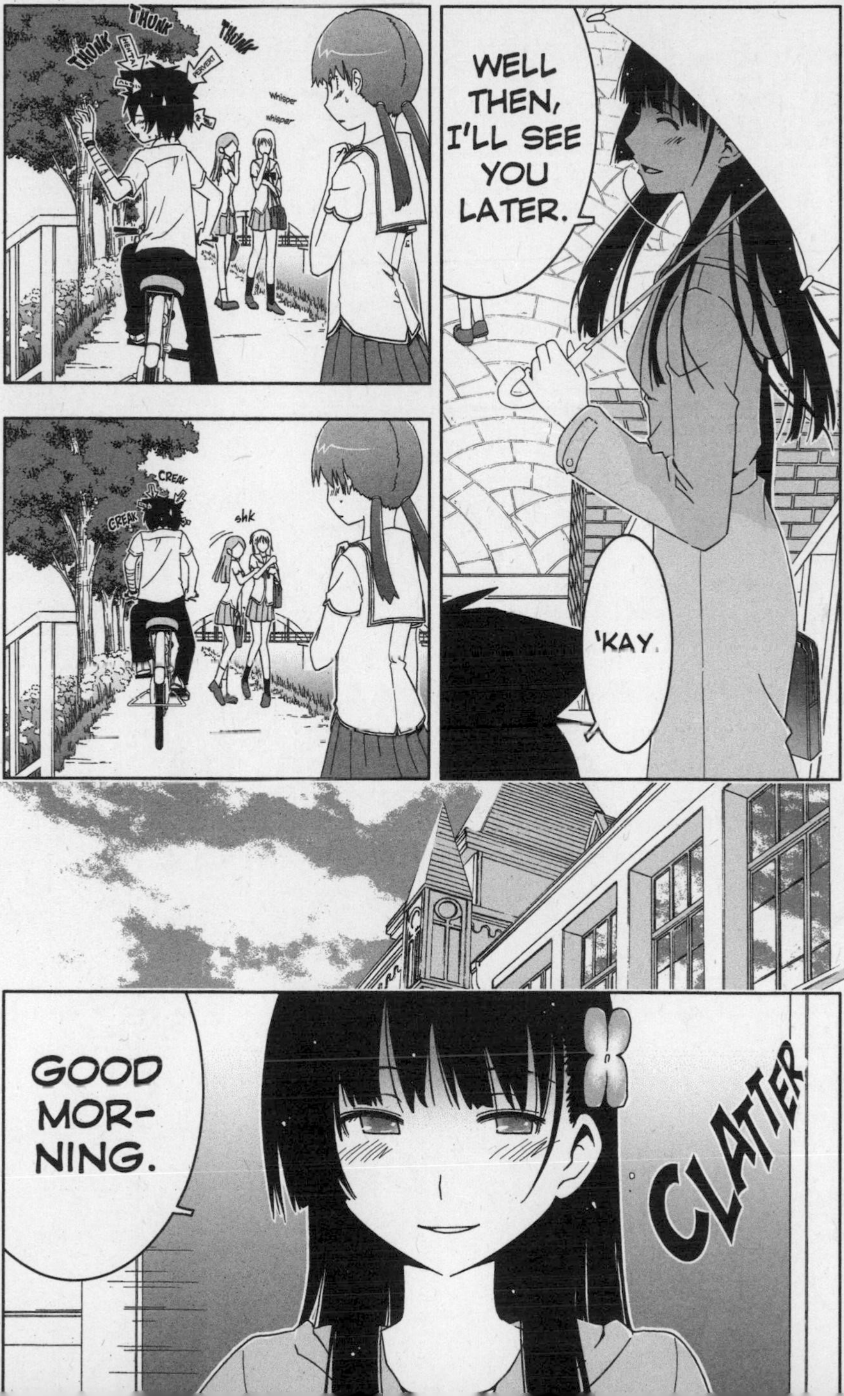
WELL THEN, I'LL SEE YOU LATER.
'KAY.
THUNK
THUNK
THUNK
HENTAI!
PERVERT!
whisper
whisper
CREAK
CREAK
shk
GOOD MORNING.
CLATTER

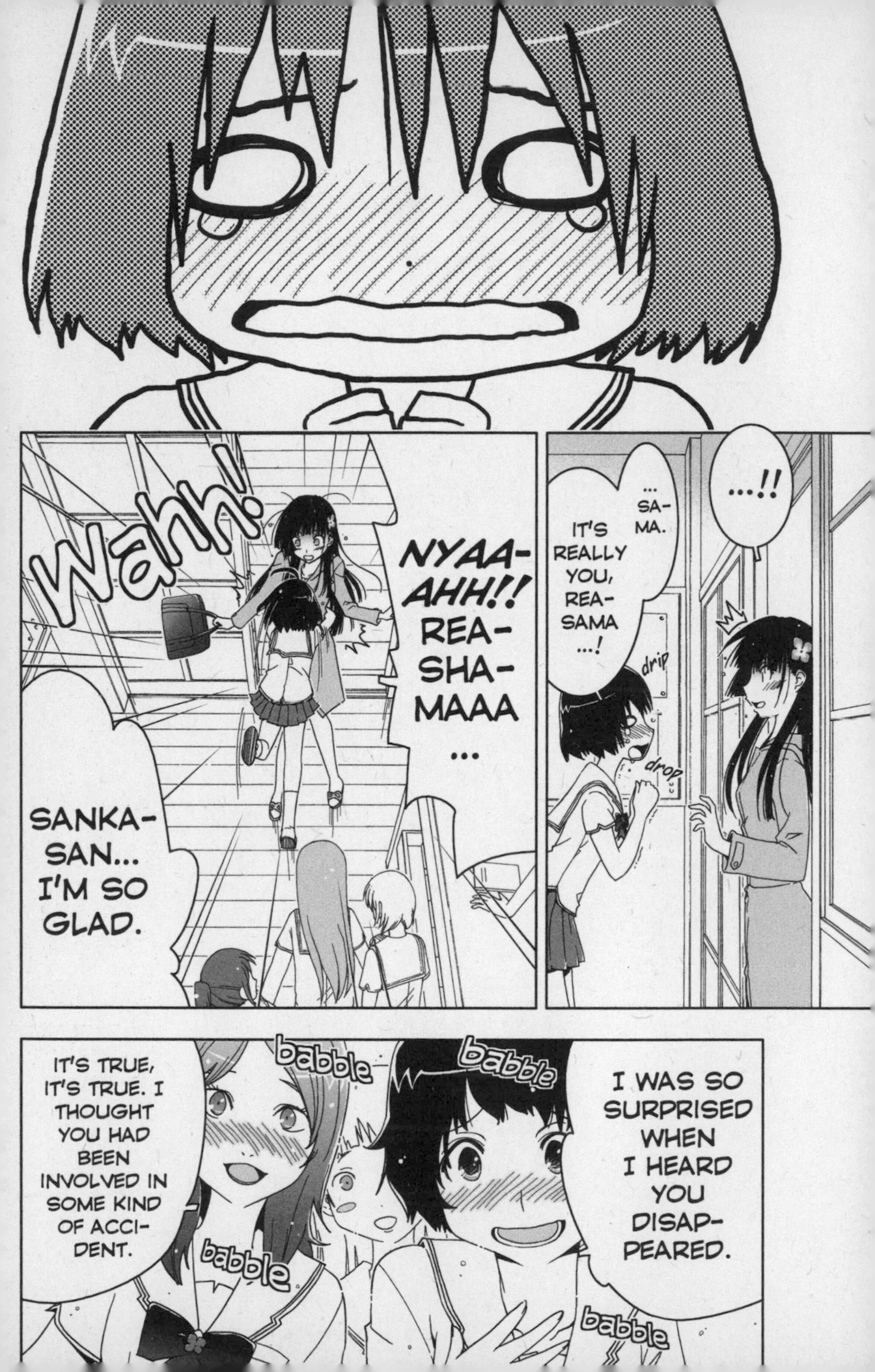
...!!
... SA-MA. IT'S REALLY YOU, REA-SAMA ...!
drip
drop
NYAA-AHH!! REA-SHA-MAAA ...
Wahh!
SANKA-SAN... I'M SO GLAD.
I WAS SO SURPRISED WHEN I HEARD YOU DISAP-PEARED.
babble
babble
IT'S TRUE, IT'S TRUE. I THOUGHT YOU HAD BEEN INVOLVED IN SOME KIND OF ACCI-DENT.
babble
babble

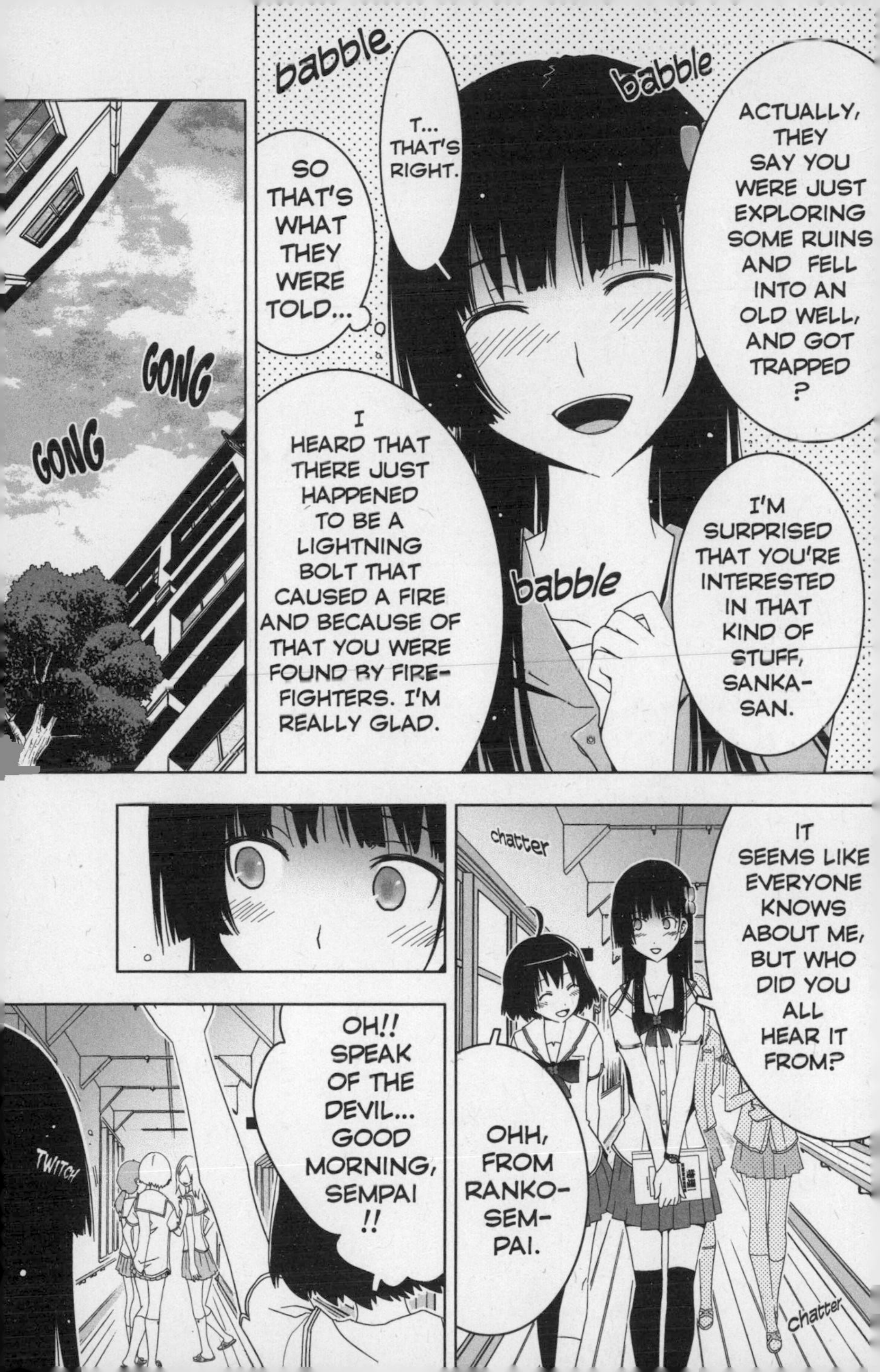
ACTUALLY, THEY SAY YOU WERE JUST EXPLORING SOME RUINS AND FELL INTO AN OLD WELL, AND GOT TRAPPED ?
babble
T... THAT'S RIGHT.
babble
SO THAT'S WHAT THEY WERE TOLD...
I'M SURPRISED THAT YOU'RE INTERESTED IN THAT KIND OF STUFF, SANKA-SAN.
babble
I HEARD THAT THERE JUST HAPPENED TO BE A LIGHTNING BOLT THAT CAUSED A FIRE AND BECAUSE OF THAT YOU WERE FOUND BY FIRE-FIGHTERS. I'M REALLY GLAD.
GONG
GONG
IT SEEMS LIKE EVERYONE KNOWS ABOUT ME, BUT WHO DID YOU ALL HEAR IT FROM?
chatter
OHH, FROM RANKO-SEMPAI.
chatter
OH!! SPEAK OF THE DEVIL... GOOD MORNING, SEMPAI !!
TWITCH

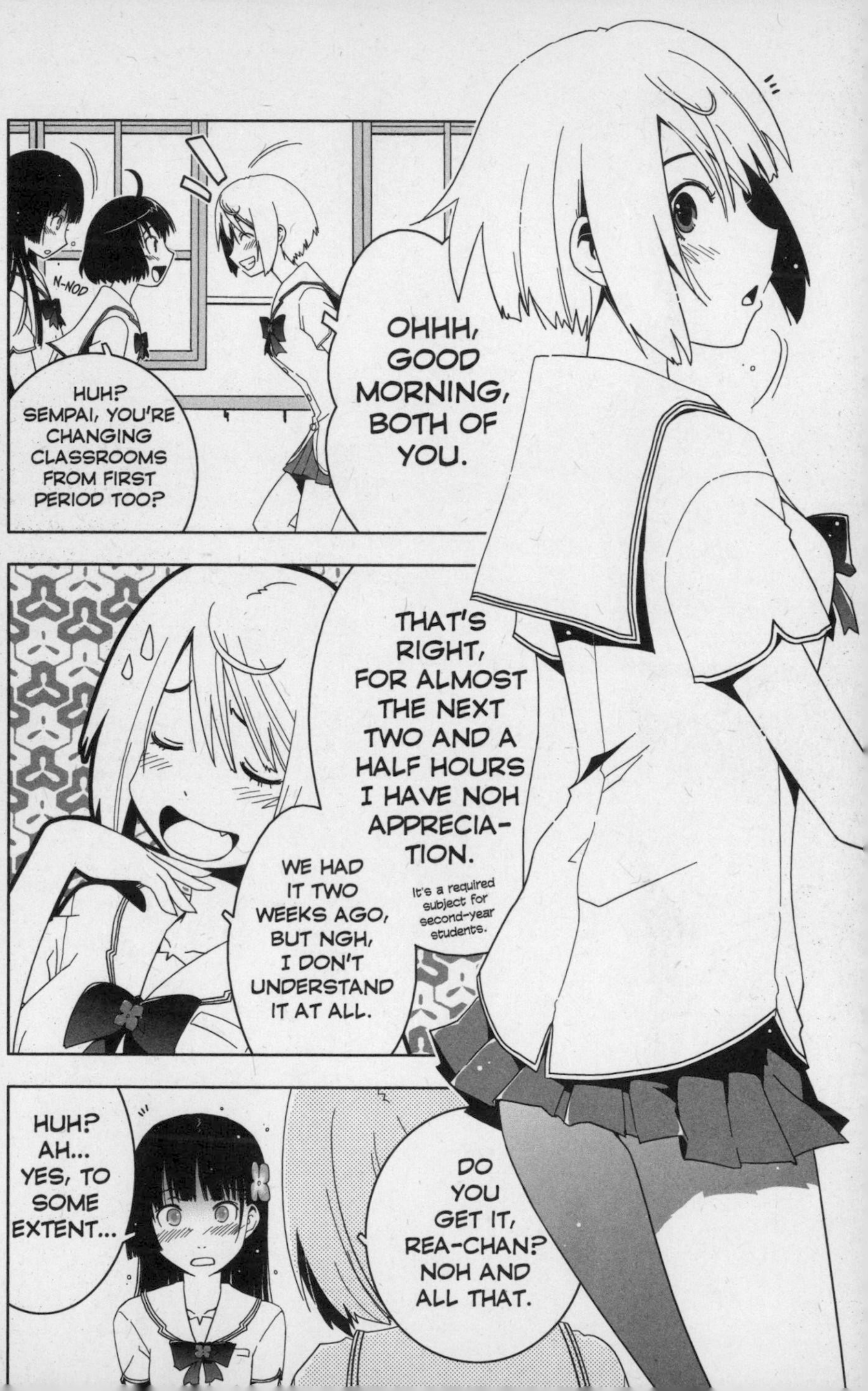
OHHH, GOOD MORNING, BOTH OF YOU.
N-NOD
HUH? SEMPAI, YOU'RE CHANGING CLASSROOMS FROM FIRST PERIOD TOO?
THAT'S RIGHT, FOR ALMOST THE NEXT TWO AND A HALF HOURS I HAVE NOH APPRECIA-TION.
It's a required subject for second-year students.
WE HAD IT TWO WEEKS AGO, BUT NGH, I DON'T UNDERSTAND IT AT ALL.
DO YOU GET IT, REA-CHAN? NOH AND ALL THAT.
HUH? AH... YES, TO SOME EXTENT...

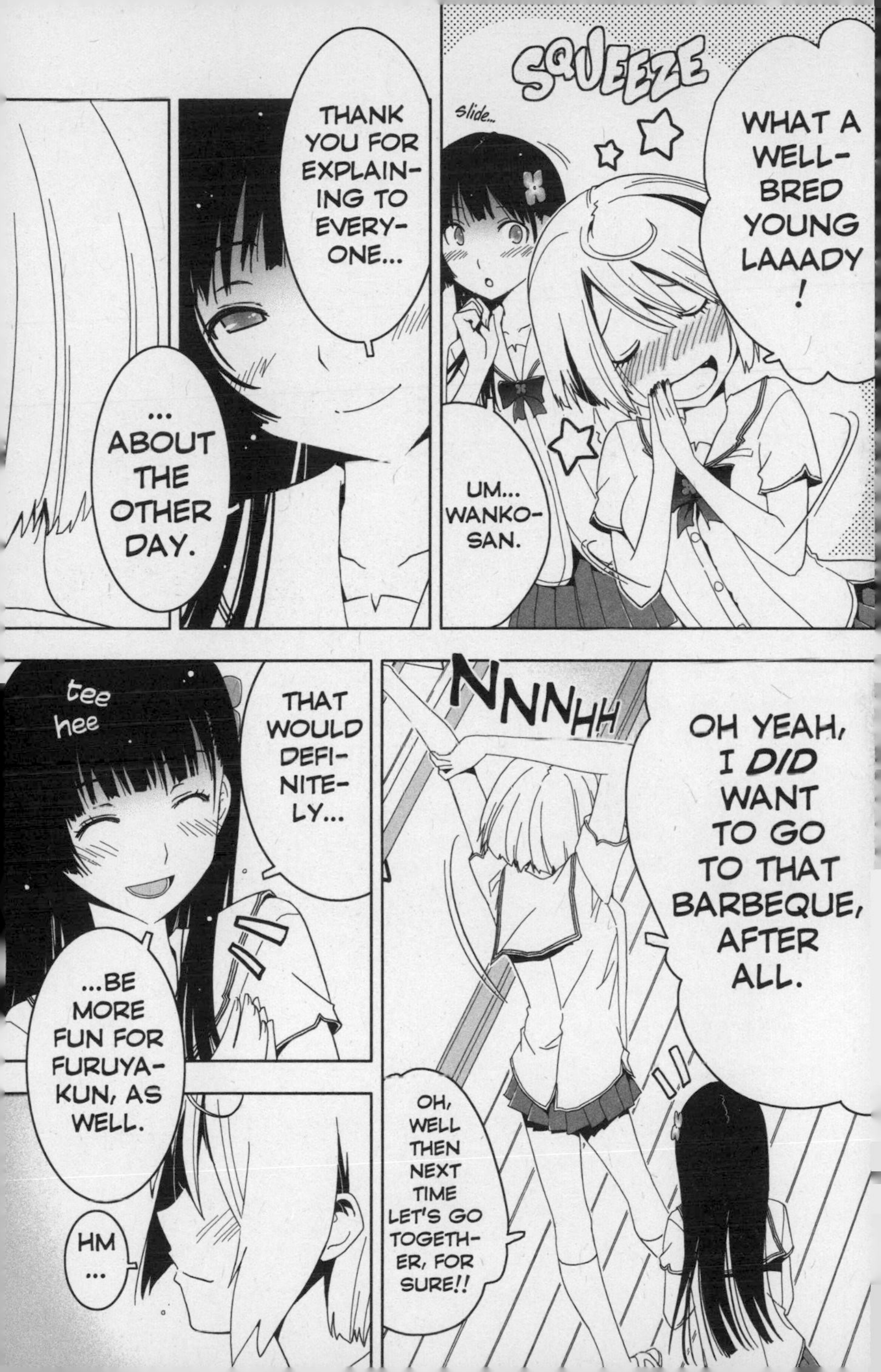
SQUEEZE
slide...
WHAT A WELL-BRED YOUNG LAAADY!
UM... WANKO-SAN.
THANK YOU FOR EXPLAINING TO EVERYONE...
...ABOUT THE OTHER DAY.
NNNHH
OH YEAH, I DID WANT TO GO TO THAT BARBEQUE, AFTER ALL.
OH, WELL THEN NEXT TIME LET'S GO TOGETHER, FOR SURE!!
tee hee
THAT WOULD DEFINITELY...
...BE MORE FUN FOR FURUYA-KUN, AS WELL.
HM...

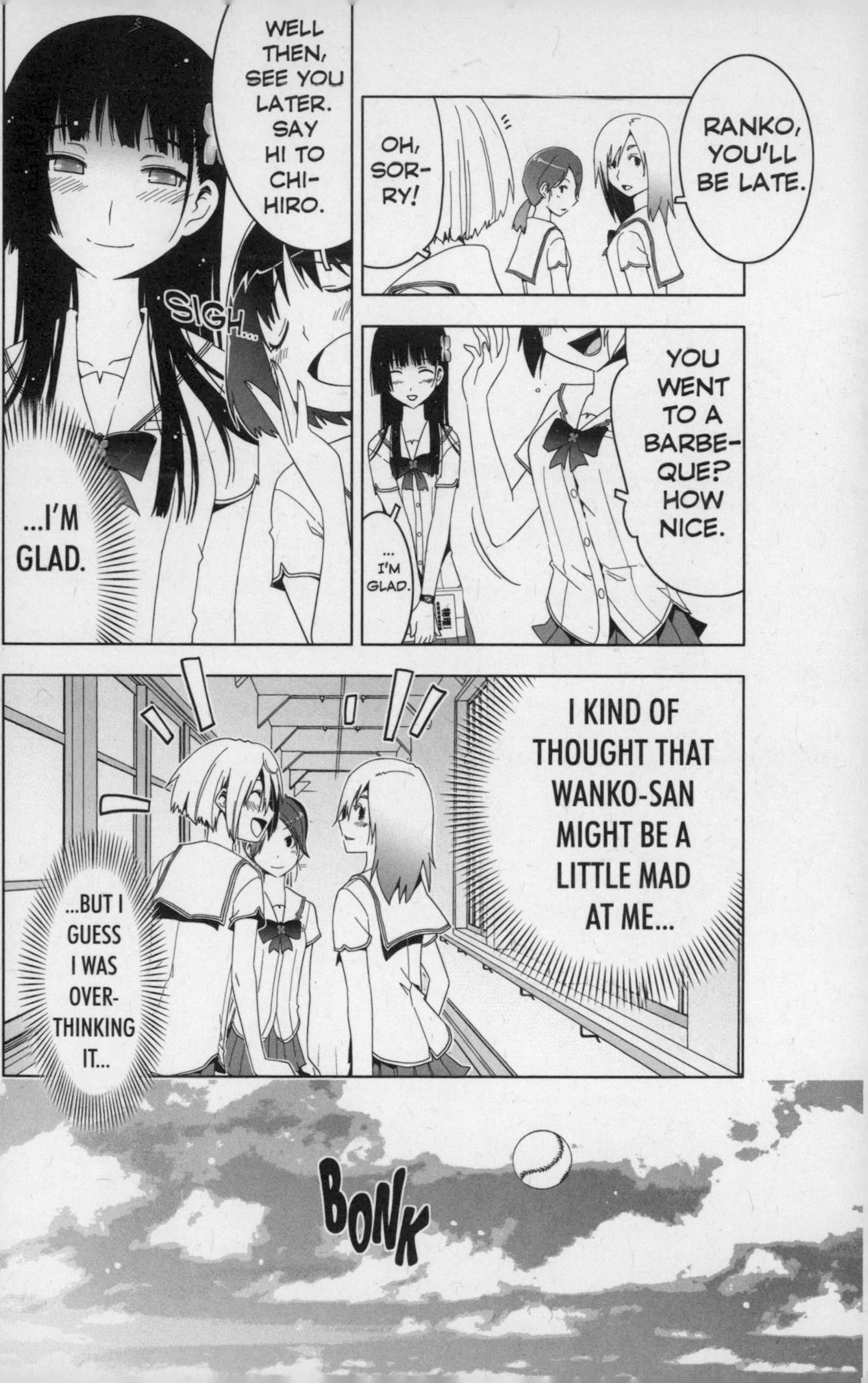
RANKO, YOU'LL BE LATE.
OH, SORRY!
YOU WENT TO A BARBEQUE? HOW NICE.
...I'M GLAD.
WELL THEN, SEE YOU LATER. SAY HI TO CHIHIRO.
SIGH...
...I'M GLAD.
I KIND OF THOUGHT THAT WANKO-SAN MIGHT BE A LITTLE MAD AT ME...
...BUT I GUESS I WAS OVERTHINKING IT...
BONK

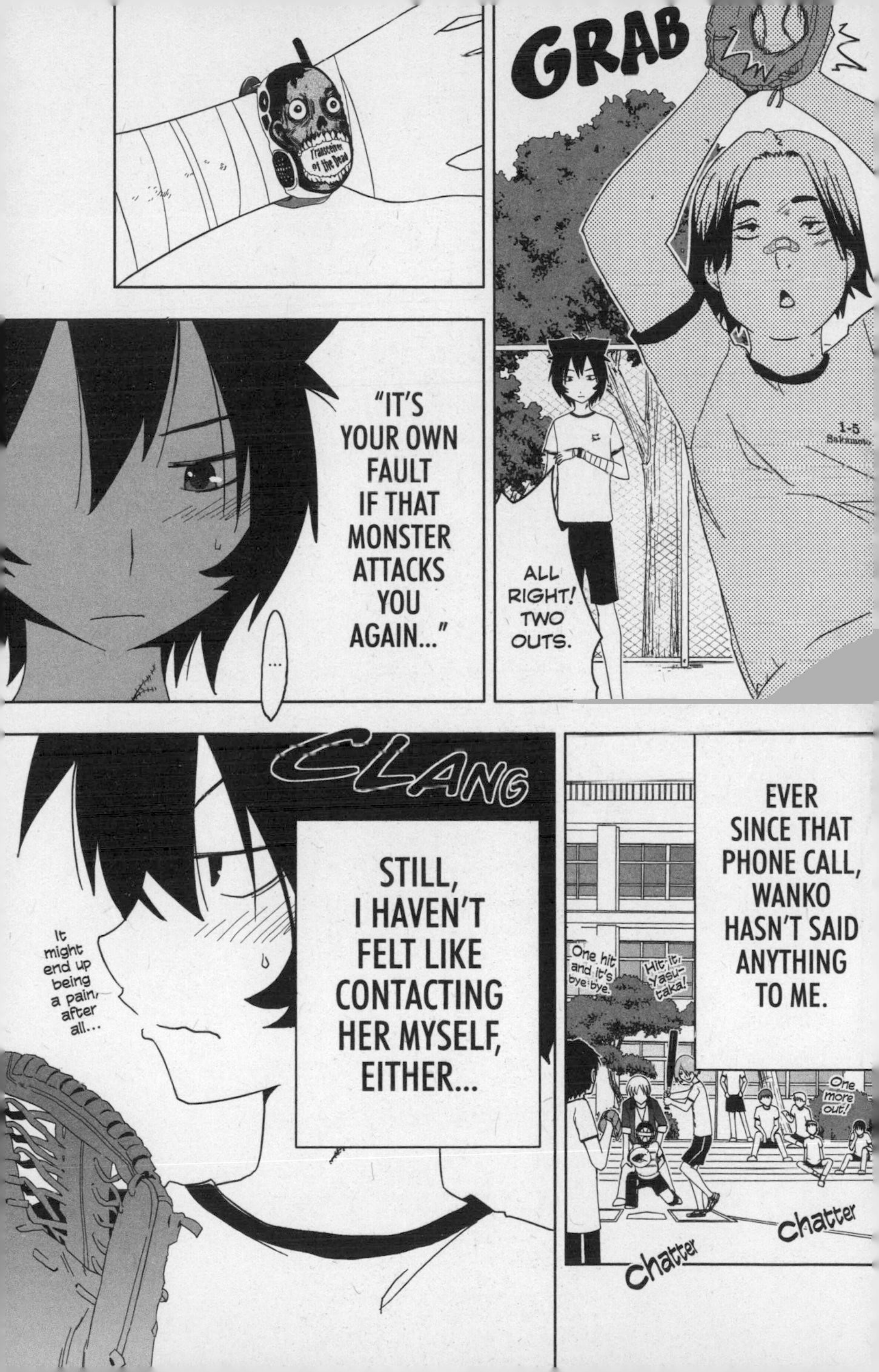

GRAB
1-5
Sakamoto
ALL RIGHT! TWO OUTS.
Transceiver of the Dead
"IT'S YOUR OWN FAULT IF THAT MONSTER ATTACKS YOU AGAIN..."
...
EVER SINCE THAT PHONE CALL, WANKO HASN'T SAID ANYTHING TO ME.
Hit it, Yasu-taka!
One hit and it's bye bye.
One more out!
Chatter
Chatter
CLANG
STILL, I HAVEN'T FELT LIKE CONTACTING HER MYSELF, EITHER...
It might end up being a pain, after all...

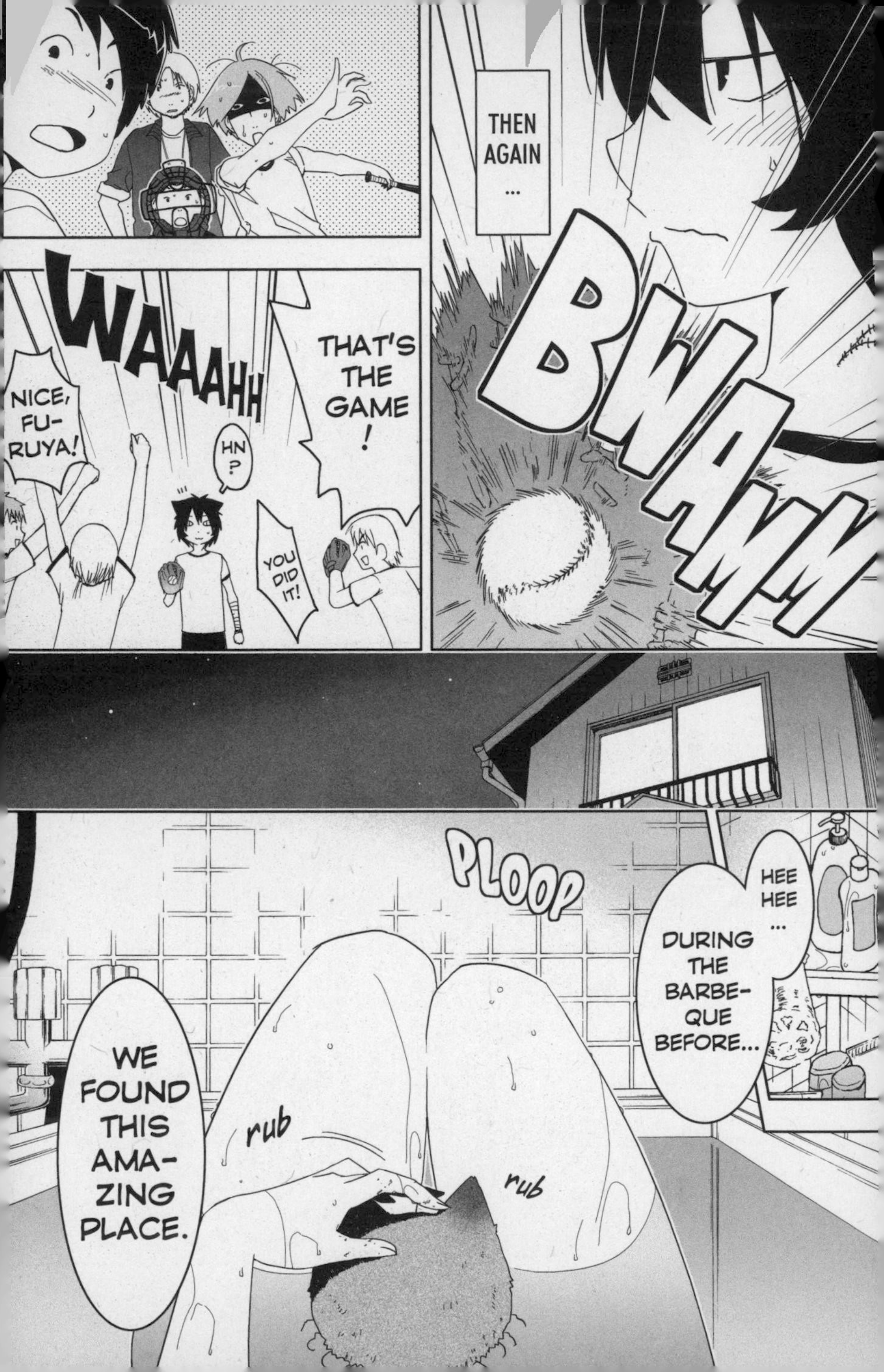
THEN AGAIN ...
BWA-AM-M
THAT'S THE GAME!
WAAAHH
NICE, FU-RUYA!
HN?
YOU DID IT!
PLOOP
HEE HEE ... DURING THE BARBE-QUE BEFORE...
rub
rub
WE FOUND THIS AMA-ZING PLACE.

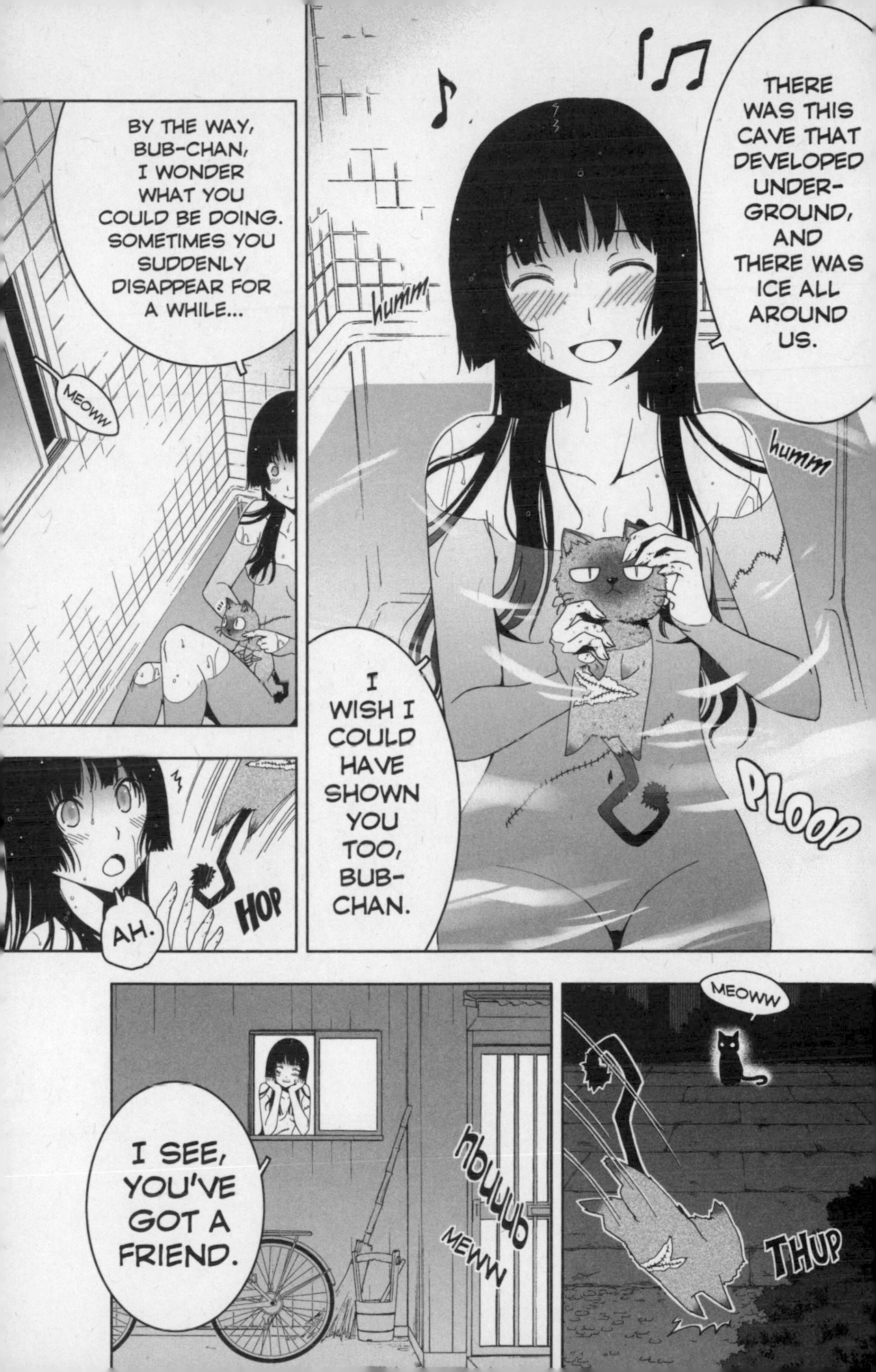

THERE WAS THIS CAVE THAT DEVELOPED UNDER-GROUND, AND THERE WAS ICE ALL AROUND US.
humm
humm
I WISH I COULD HAVE SHOWN YOU TOO, BUB-CHAN.
PLOOP
BY THE WAY, BUB-CHAN, I WONDER WHAT YOU COULD BE DOING. SOMETIMES YOU SUDDENLY DISAPPEAR FOR A WHILE...
MEOWW
AH.
HOP
MEOWW
MEWW
THUP
I SEE, YOU'VE GOT A FRIEND.

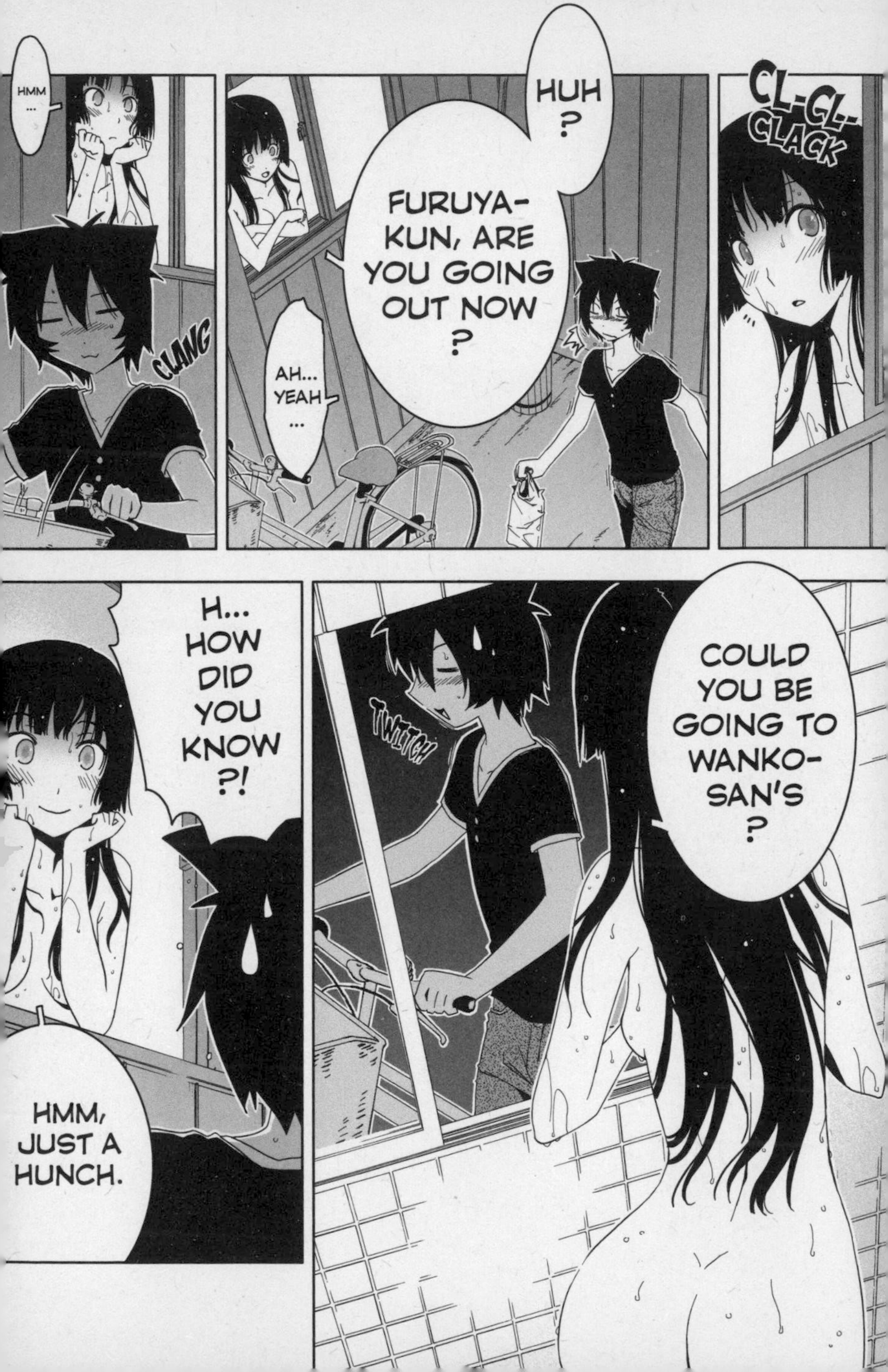
CL-CL-CLACK
HUH?
FURUYA-KUN, ARE YOU GOING OUT NOW?
AH... YEAH...
HMM...
CLANG
COULD YOU BE GOING TO WANKO-SAN'S?
TWITCH
H... HOW DID YOU KNOW?!
HMM, JUST A HUNCH.

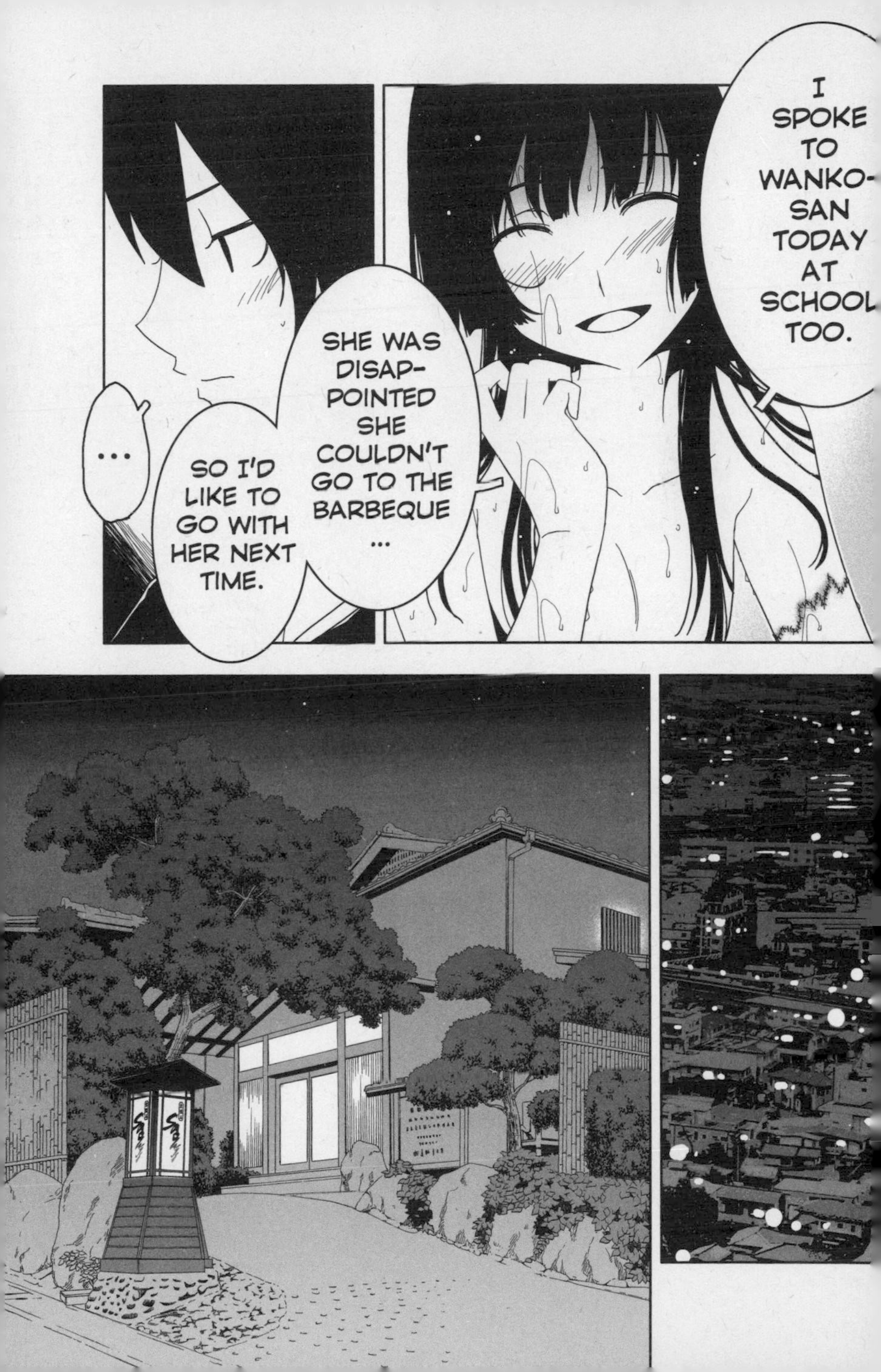
I SPOKE TO WANKO-SAN TODAY AT SCHOOL TOO.
SHE WAS DISAP-POINTED SHE COULDN'T GO TO THE BARBEQUE ...
SO I'D LIKE TO GO WITH HER NEXT TIME.
...

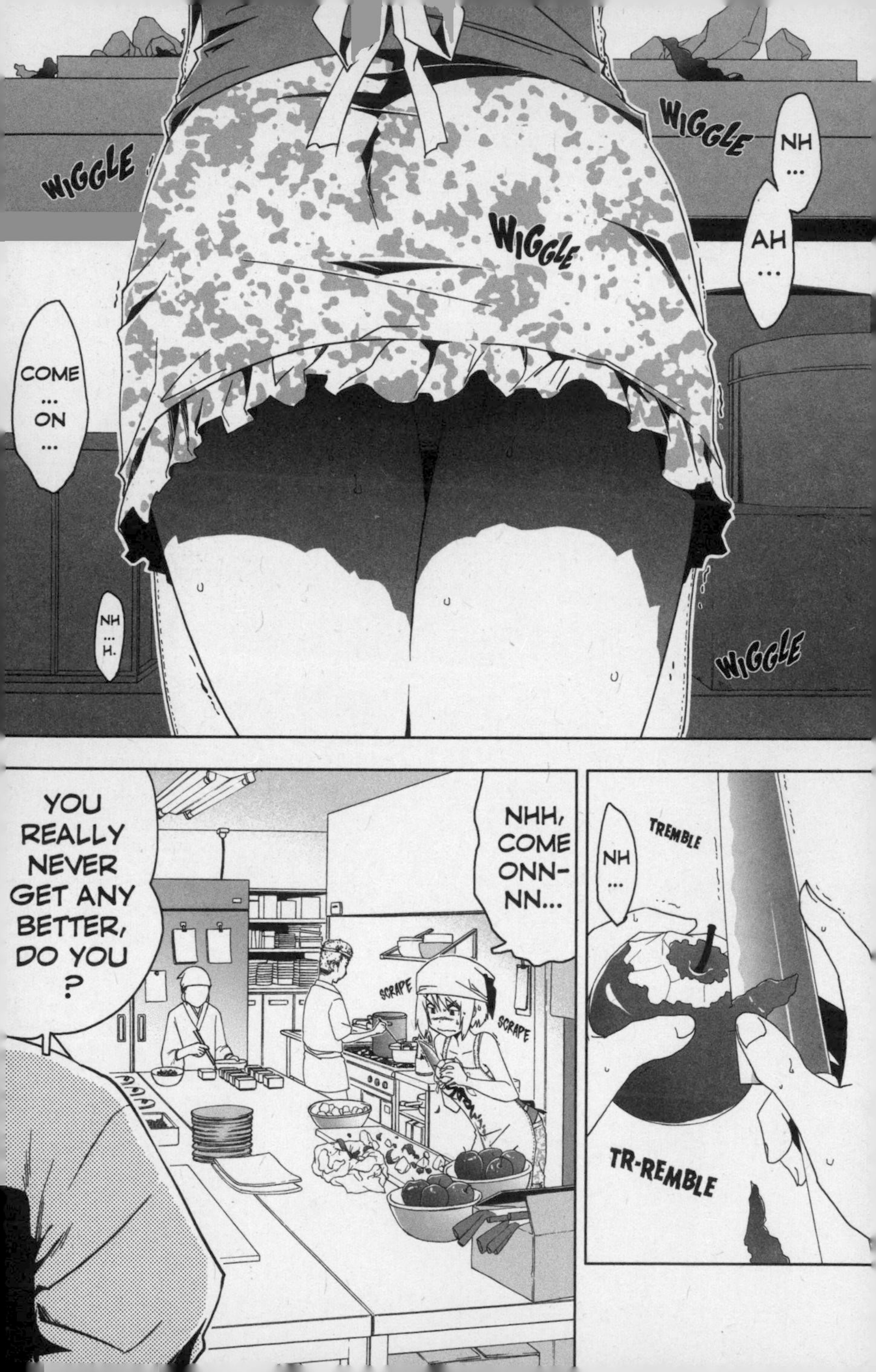
WIGGLE
NH...
AH...
WIGGLE
WIGGLE
COME... ON...
NH... H.
WIGGLE
NH...
TREMBLE
TR-REMBLE
NHH, COME ONN-NN...
SCRAPE
SCRAPE
YOU REALLY NEVER GET ANY BETTER, DO YOU?

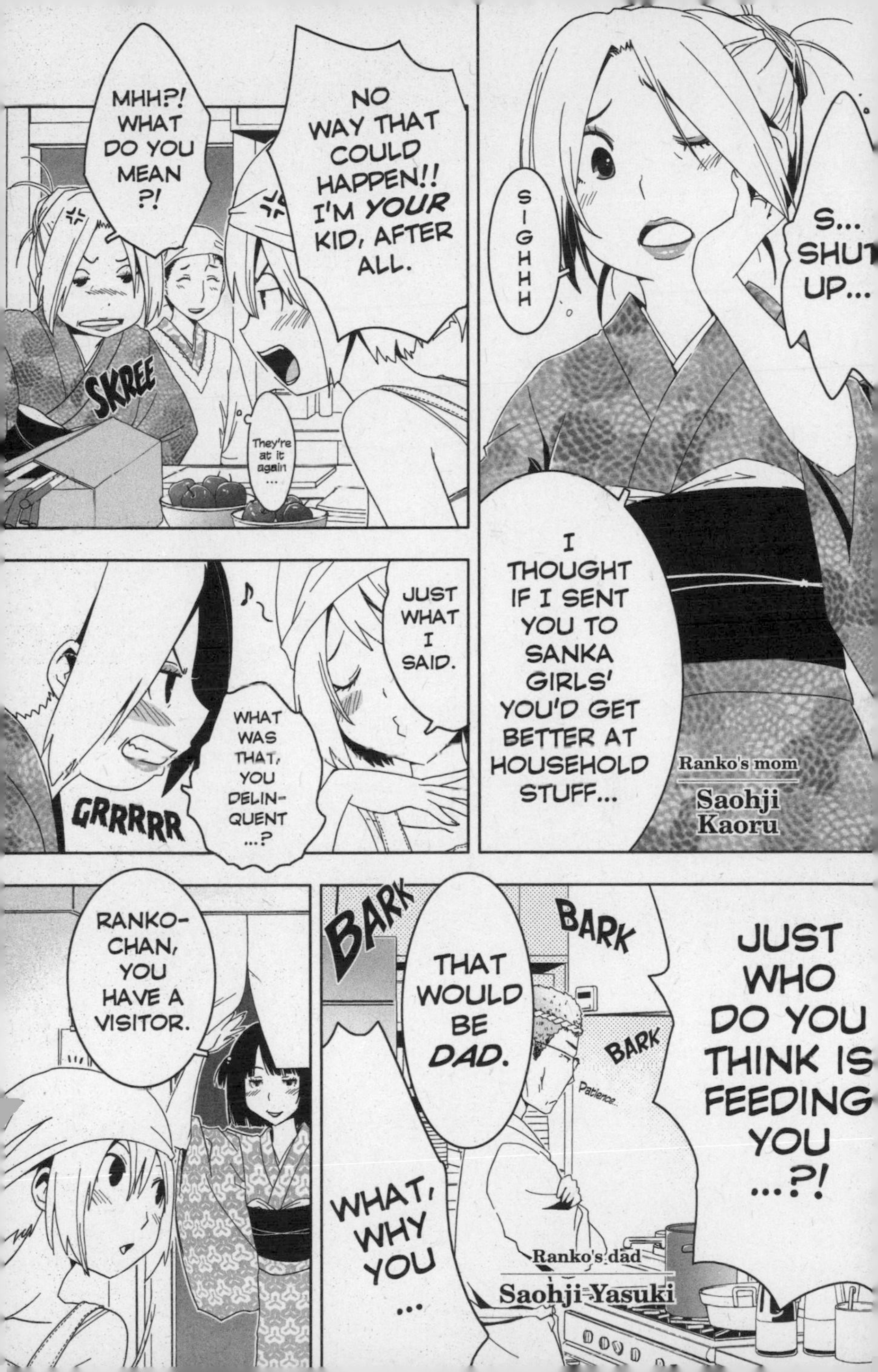
S... SHUT UP...
SIGHHH
I THOUGHT IF I SENT YOU TO SANKA GIRLS' YOU'D GET BETTER AT HOUSEHOLD STUFF...
Ranko's mom
Saohji Kaoru
NO WAY THAT COULD HAPPEN!! I'M *YOUR* KID, AFTER ALL.
MHH?! WHAT DO YOU MEAN?!
SKREE
They're at it again...
JUST WHAT I SAID.
WHAT WAS THAT, YOU DELINQUENT...?
GRRRRR
JUST WHO DO YOU THINK IS FEEDING YOU...?!
BARK
BARK
THAT WOULD BE *DAD*.
BARK
Patience...
WHAT, WHY YOU...
Ranko's dad
Saohji Yasuki
RANKO-CHAN, YOU HAVE A VISITOR.

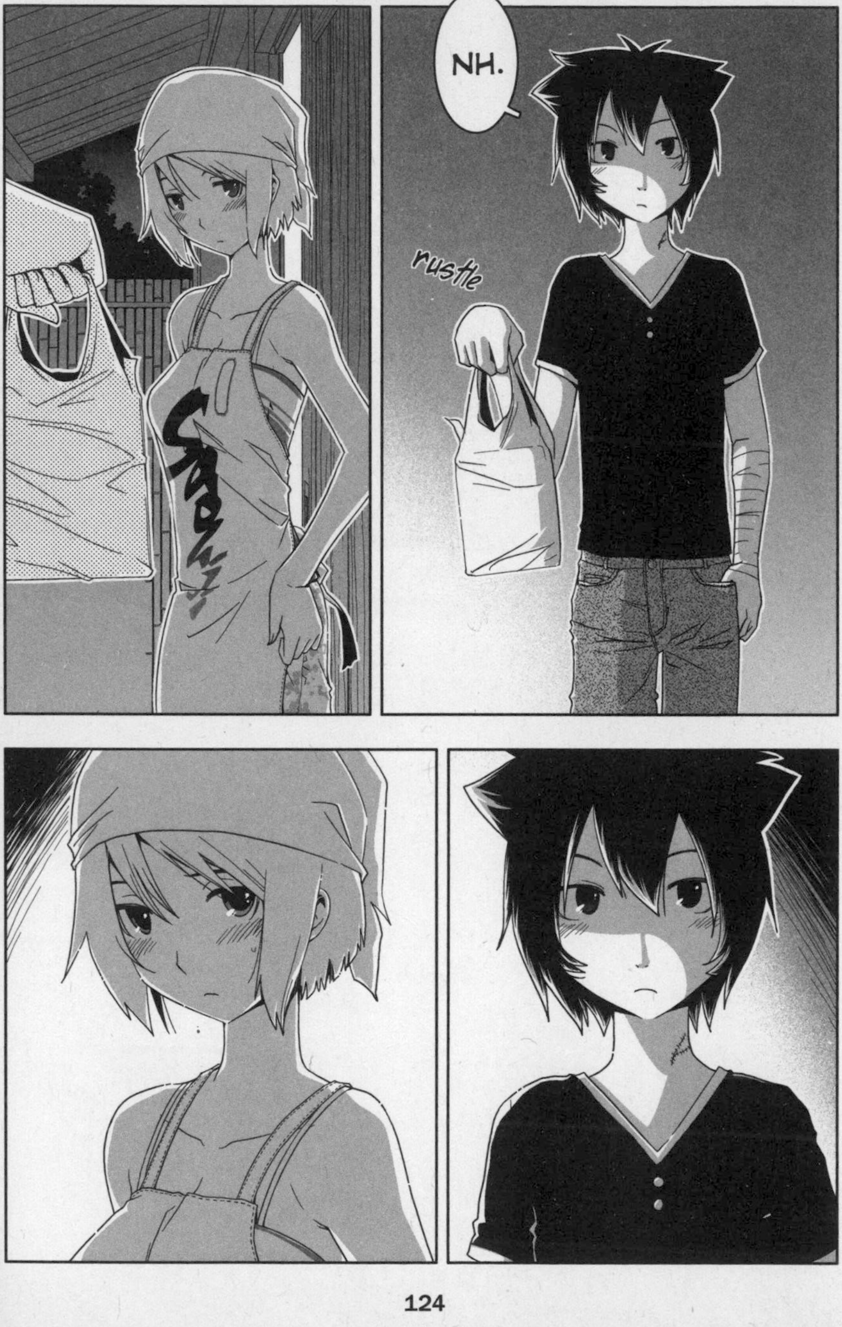
NH.
rustle

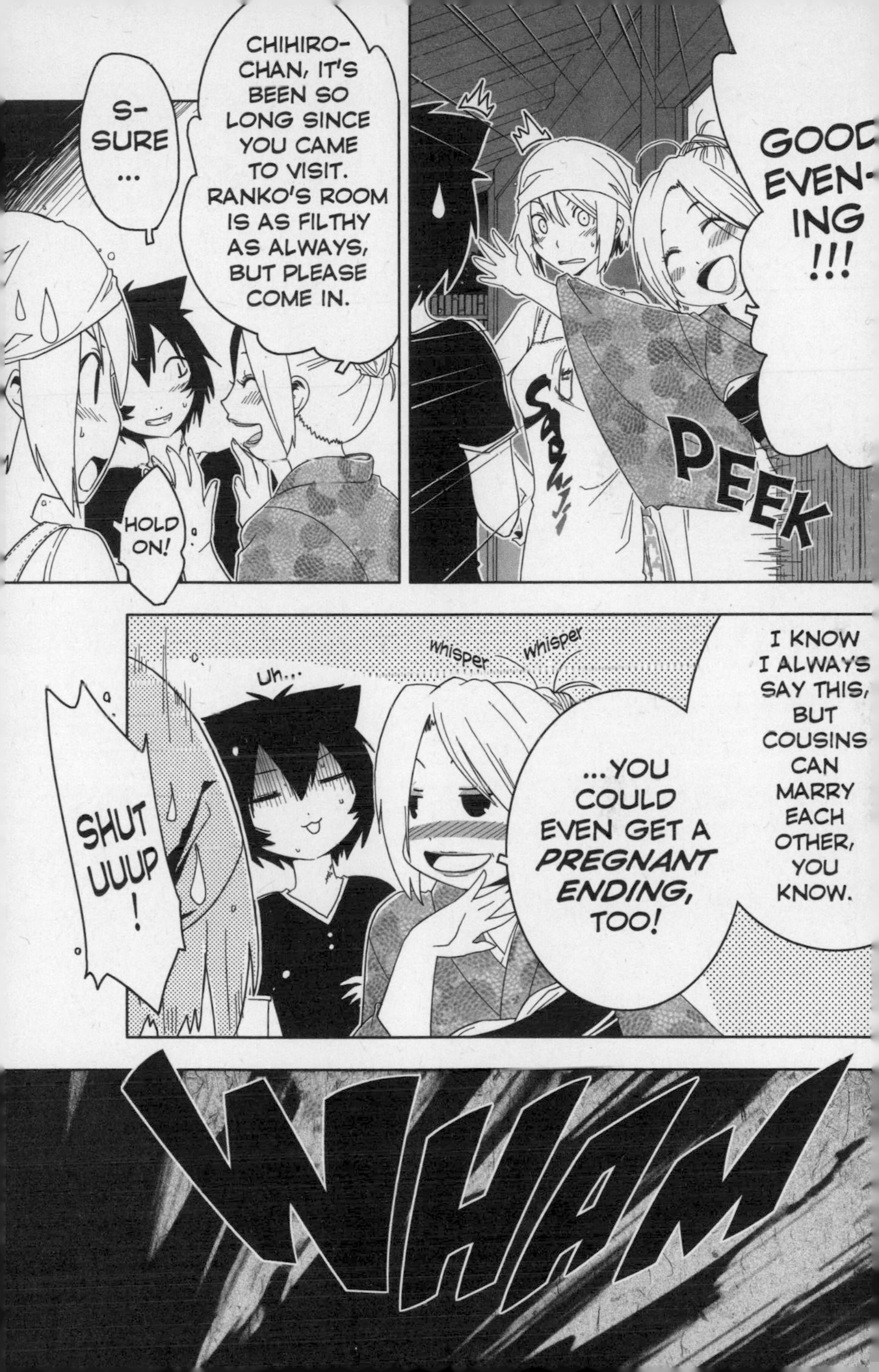
GOOD EVEN-ING !!!
PEEK
CHIHIRO-CHAN, IT'S BEEN SO LONG SINCE YOU CAME TO VISIT. RANKO'S ROOM IS AS FILTHY AS ALWAYS, BUT PLEASE COME IN.
S-SURE ...
HOLD ON!
I KNOW I ALWAYS SAY THIS, BUT COUSINS CAN MARRY EACH OTHER, YOU KNOW.
...YOU COULD EVEN GET A *PREGNANT ENDING*, TOO!
whisper whisper
Uh...
SHUT UUUP !
WHAM

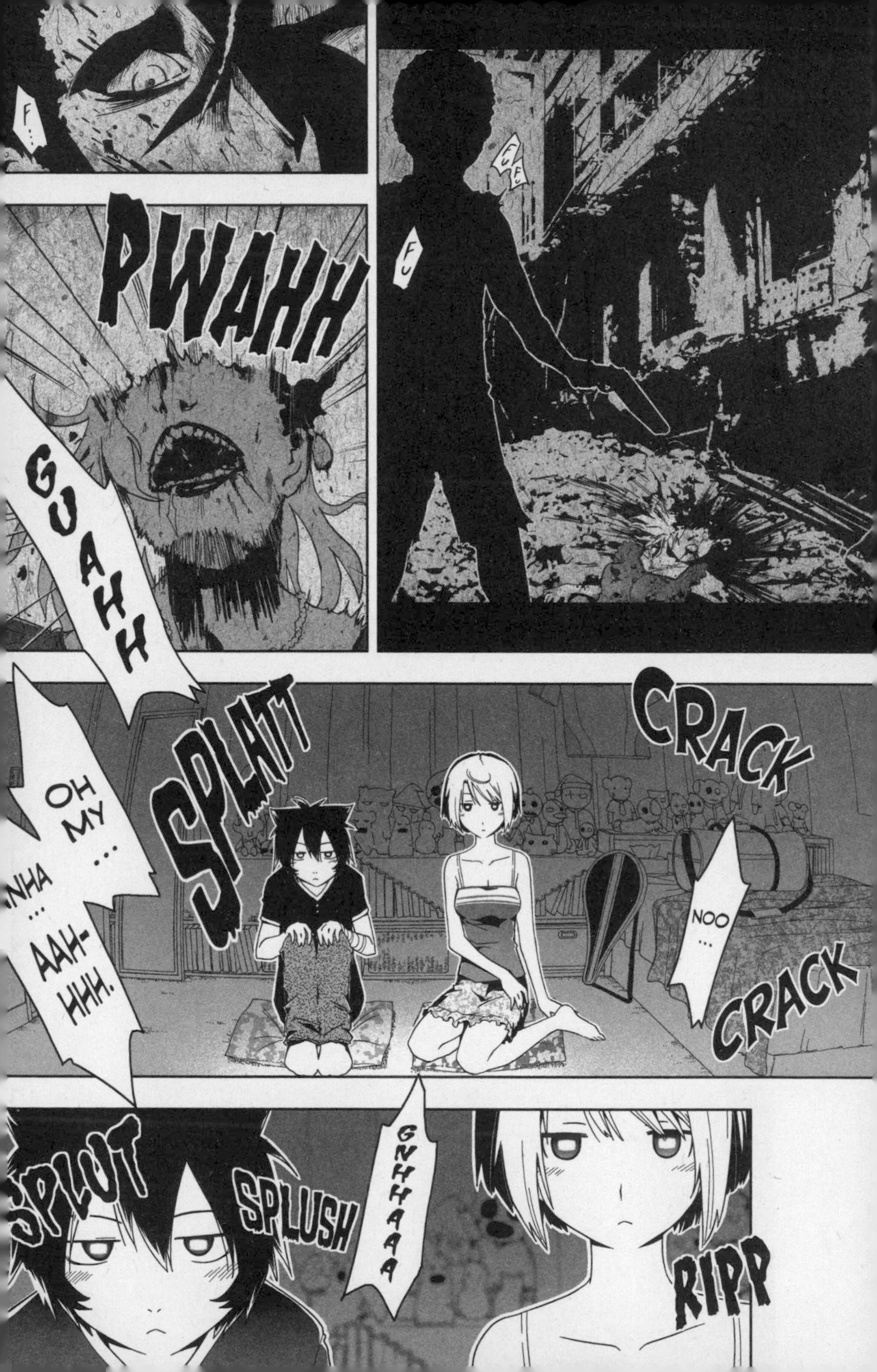
F... F... Fu
Fu
F...
PWAHH
GUAHH
CRACK
NOO...
CRACK
SPLATT
OH MY...
NHA... AAH-HHH.
RIPP
GNHHAAA
SPLUSH
SPLOT

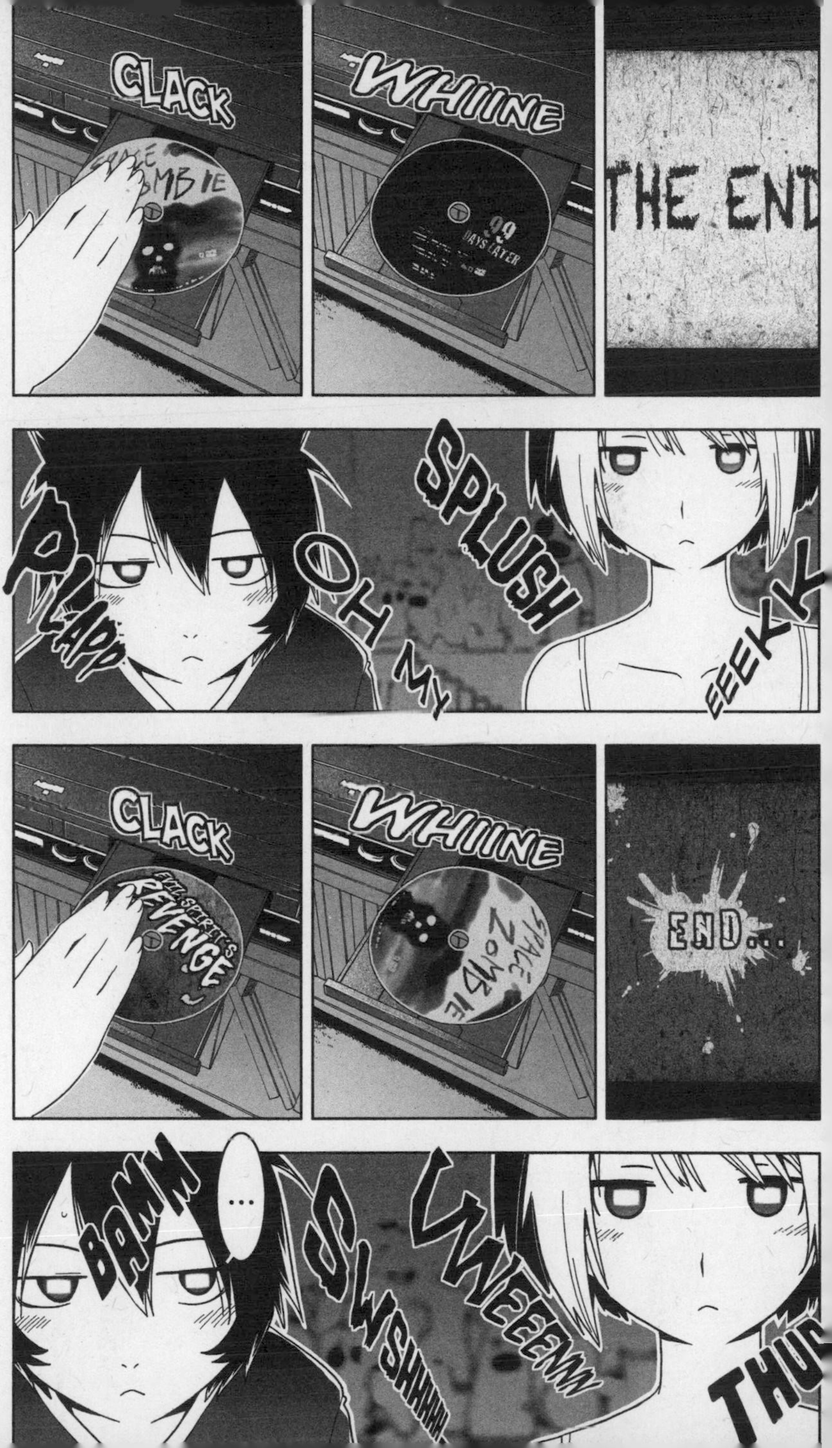
THE END
WHIINE
99 DAYS LATER
CLACK
EEEKK
SPLUSH
OH MY
PLAPP
END...
WHIINE
SPACE ZOMBIE
CLACK
EVIL SPIRIT'S REVENGE
THU
WEEENNN
SWSHHHH
...
BAMM

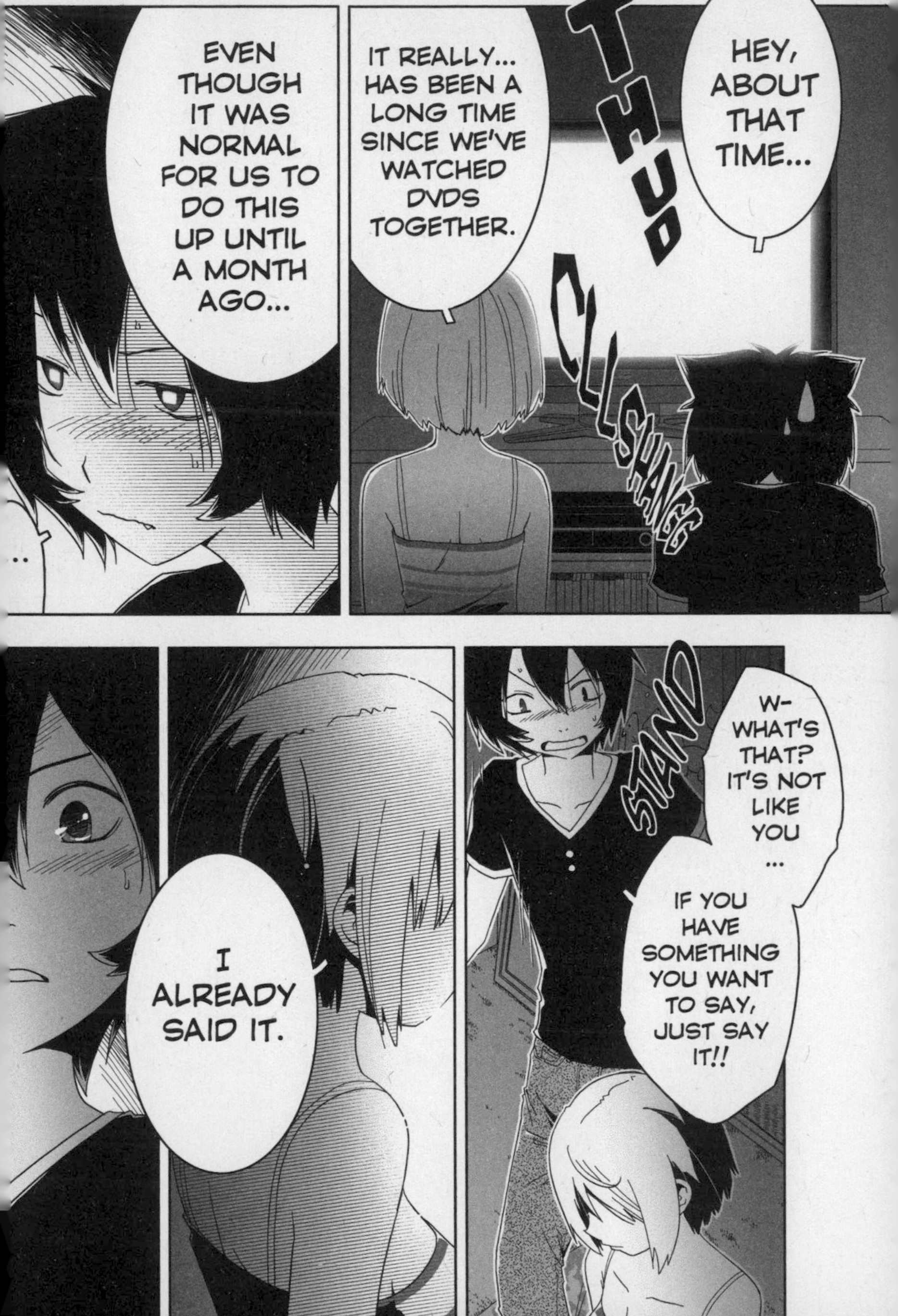
HEY, ABOUT THAT TIME...
THUD
CLLSHANG
IT REALLY... HAS BEEN A LONG TIME SINCE WE'VE WATCHED DVDS TOGETHER.
EVEN THOUGH IT WAS NORMAL FOR US TO DO THIS UP UNTIL A MONTH AGO...
...
STAND
W-WHAT'S THAT? IT'S NOT LIKE YOU ...
IF YOU HAVE SOMETHING YOU WANT TO SAY, JUST SAY IT!!
I ALREADY SAID IT.

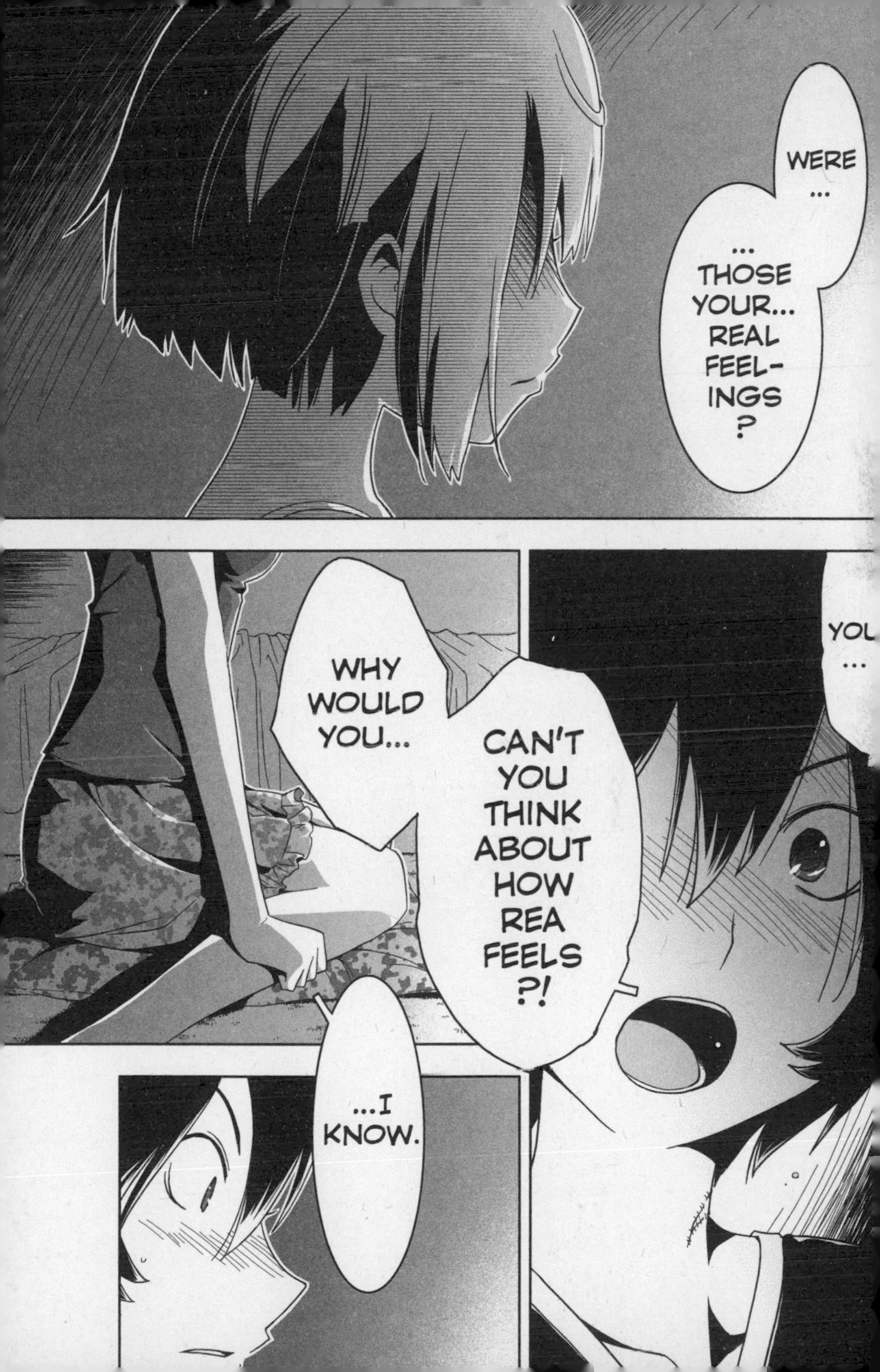
WERE ...
... THOSE YOUR... REAL FEEL-INGS?
YOU ...
WHY WOULD YOU...
CAN'T YOU THINK ABOUT HOW REA FEELS?!
...I KNOW.

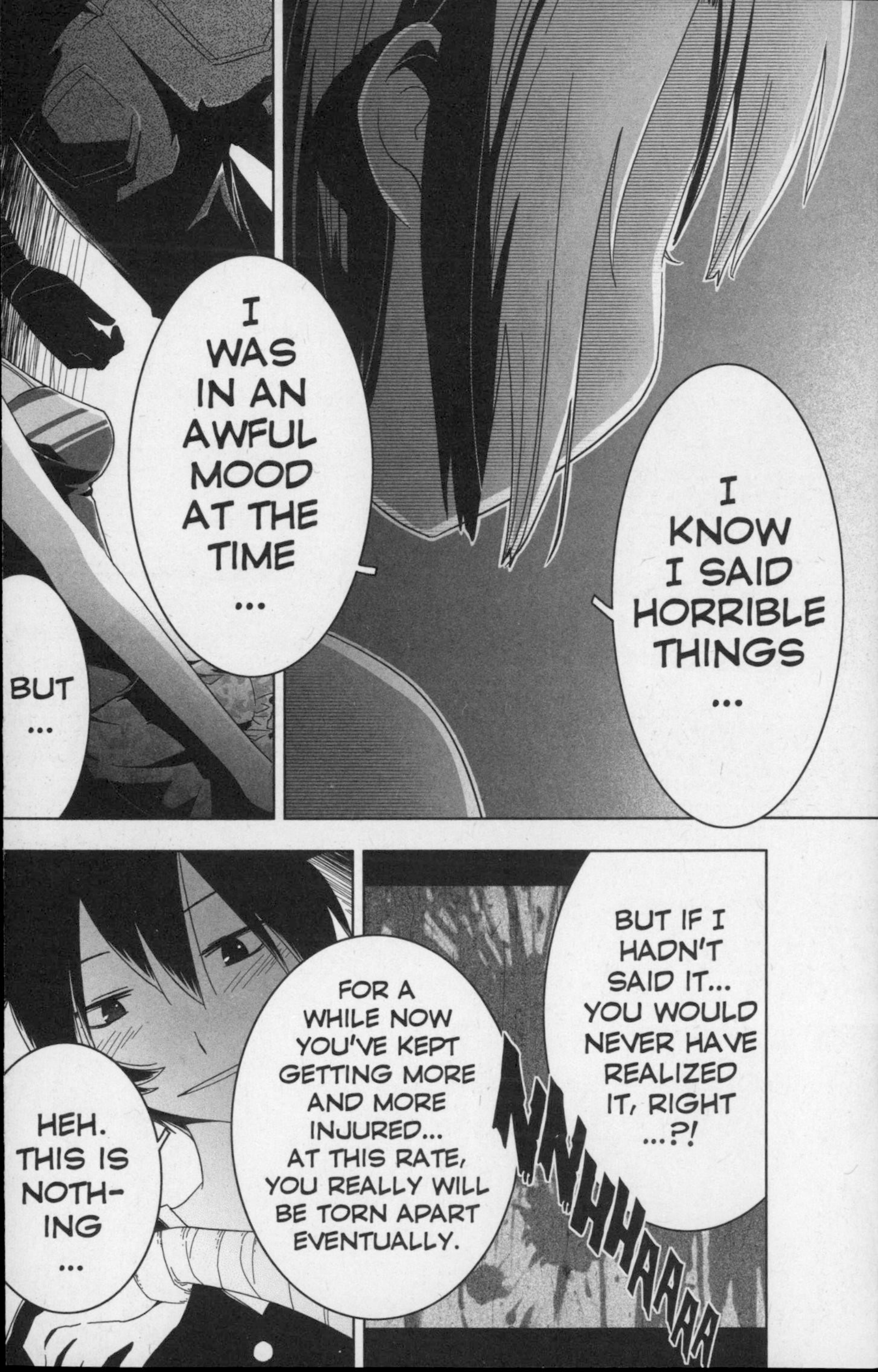
I KNOW I SAID HORRIBLE THINGS ...
I WAS IN AN AWFUL MOOD AT THE TIME ...
BUT ...
BUT IF I HADN'T SAID IT... YOU WOULD NEVER HAVE REALIZED IT, RIGHT ...?!
NNHHAAAA
FOR A WHILE NOW YOU'VE KEPT GETTING MORE AND MORE INJURED... AT THIS RATE, YOU REALLY WILL BE TORN APART EVENTUALLY.
HEH. THIS IS NOTH-ING ...

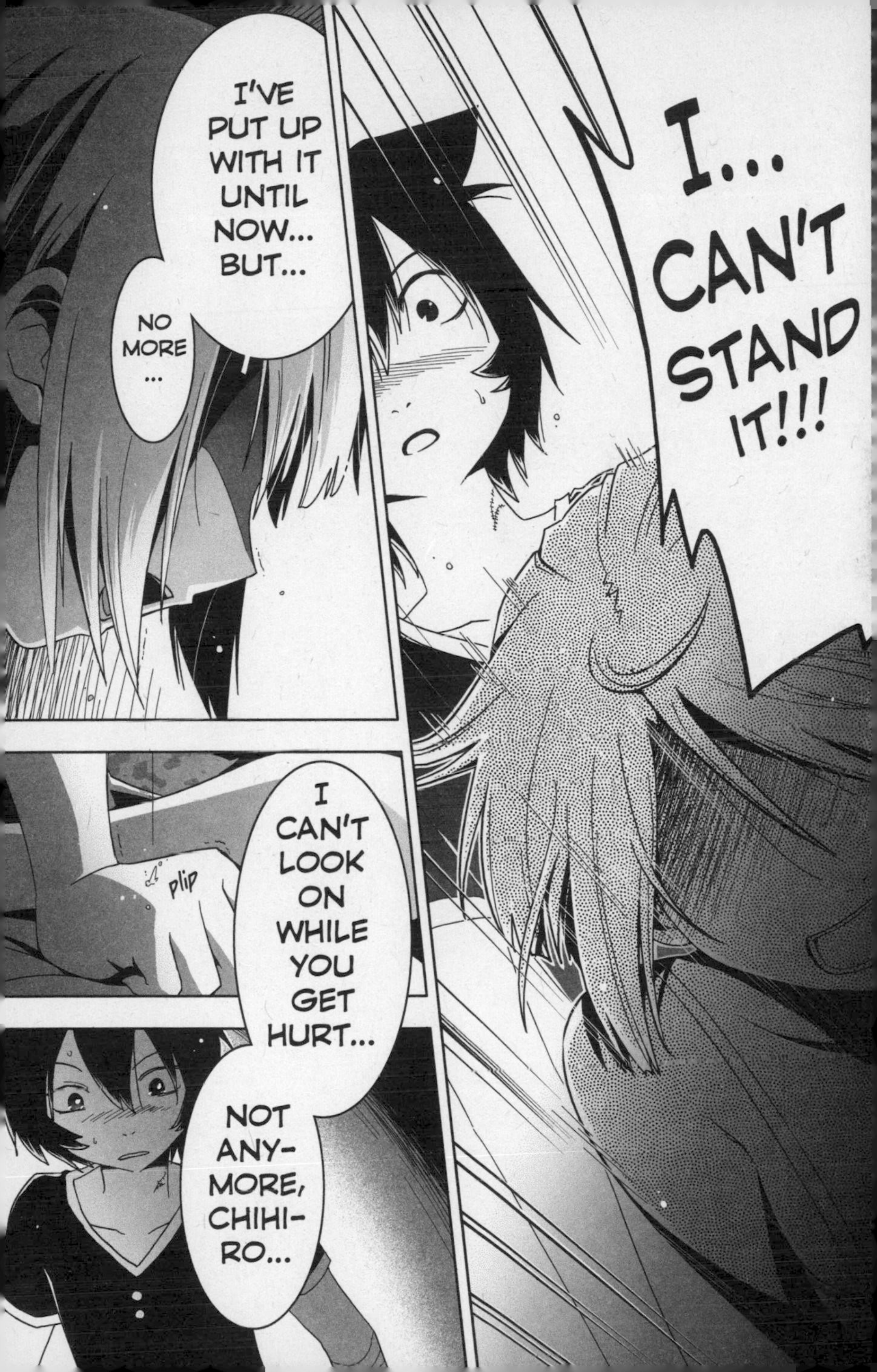
I... CAN'T STAND IT!!!
I'VE PUT UP WITH IT UNTIL NOW... BUT...
NO MORE ...
plip
I CAN'T LOOK ON WHILE YOU GET HURT...
NOT ANYMORE, CHIHIRO...

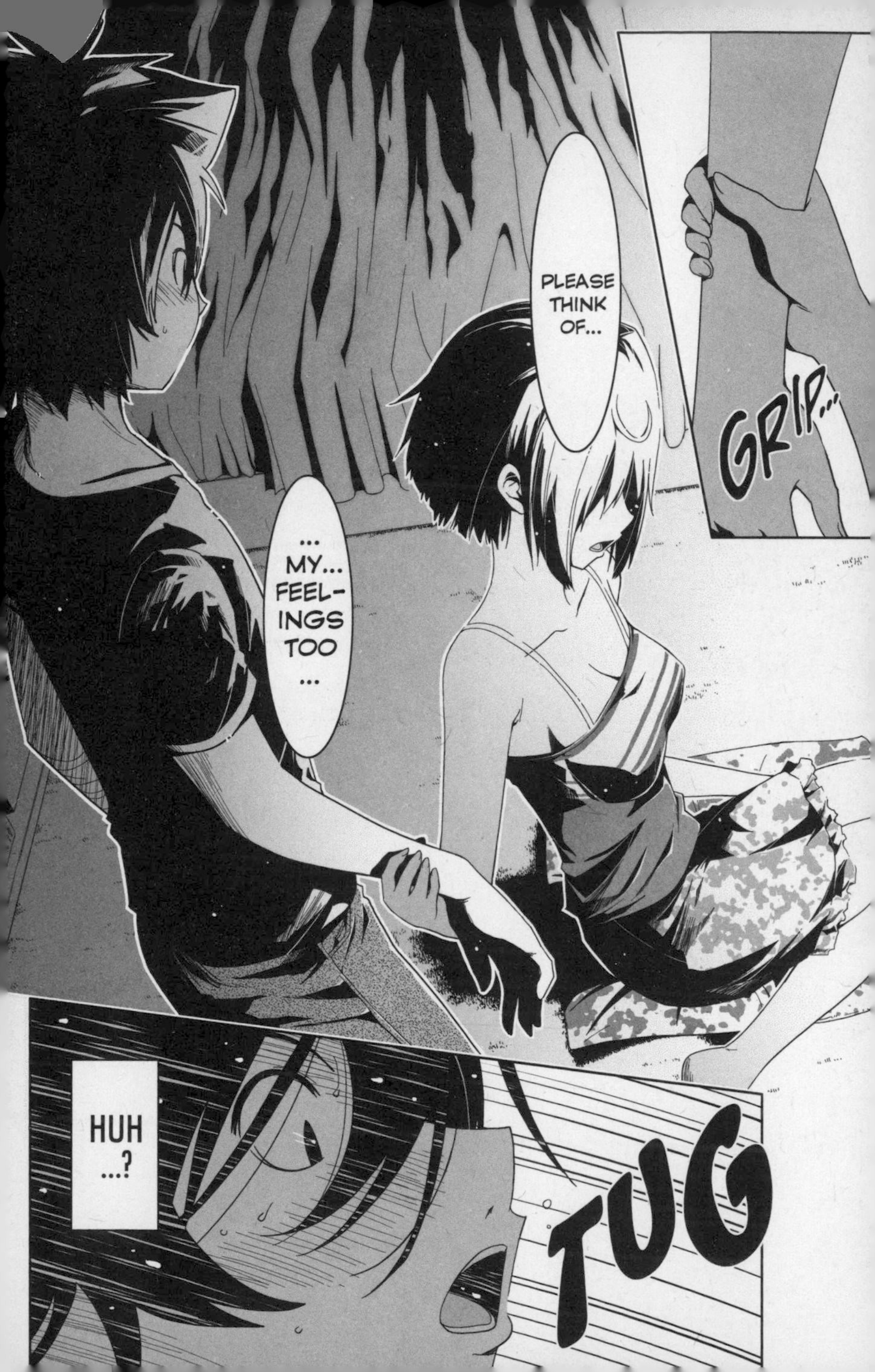
GRIP...
PLEASE THINK OF...
... MY... FEEL-INGS TOO ...
TUG
HUH ...?

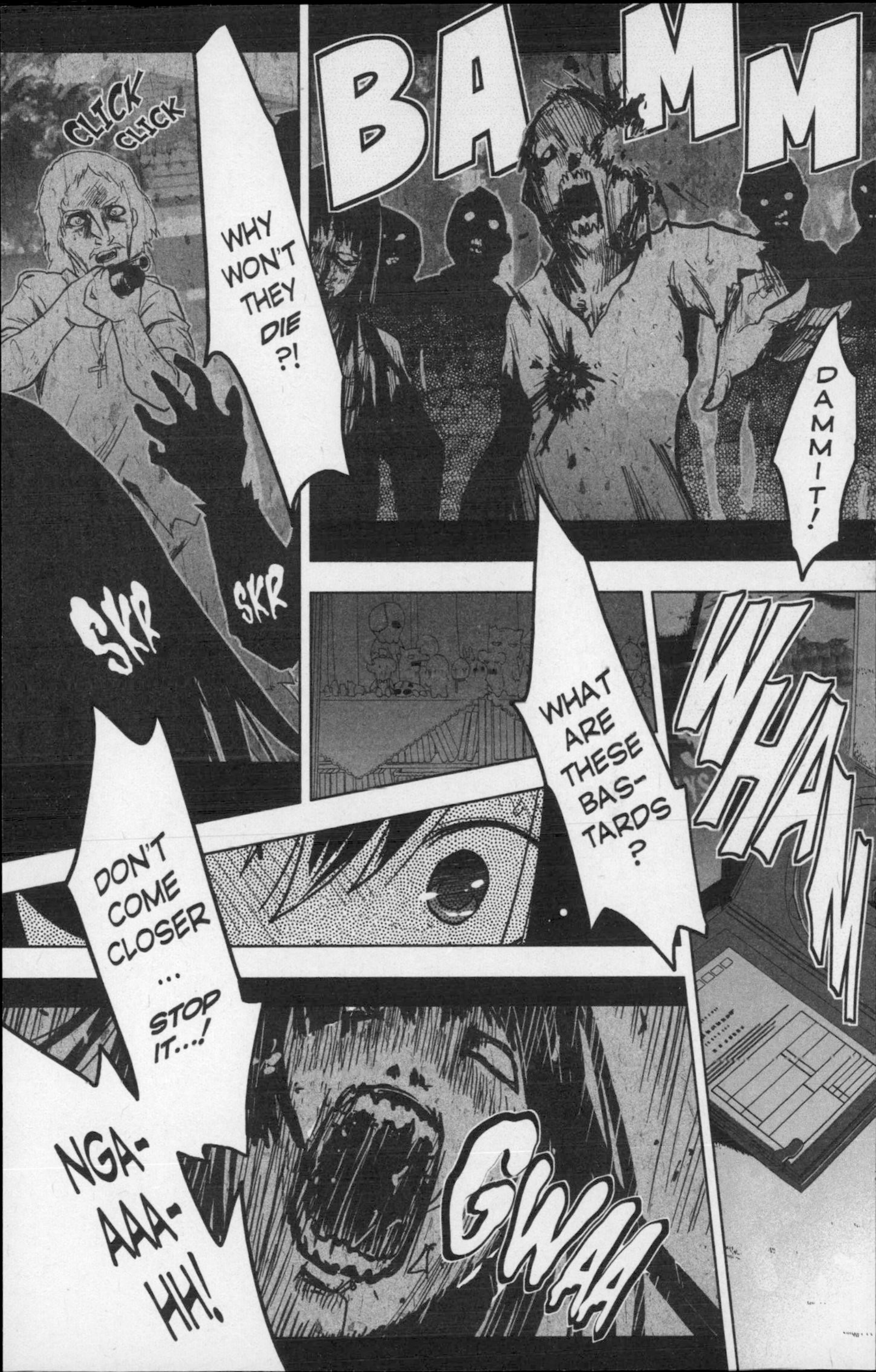
BAMM
DAMMIT!
CLICK CLICK
WHY WON'T THEY DIE?!
SKR SKR
WHAM
WHAT ARE THESE BASTARDS?
DON'T COME CLOSER ... STOP IT...!
GWAA
NGA-AAA-HH!

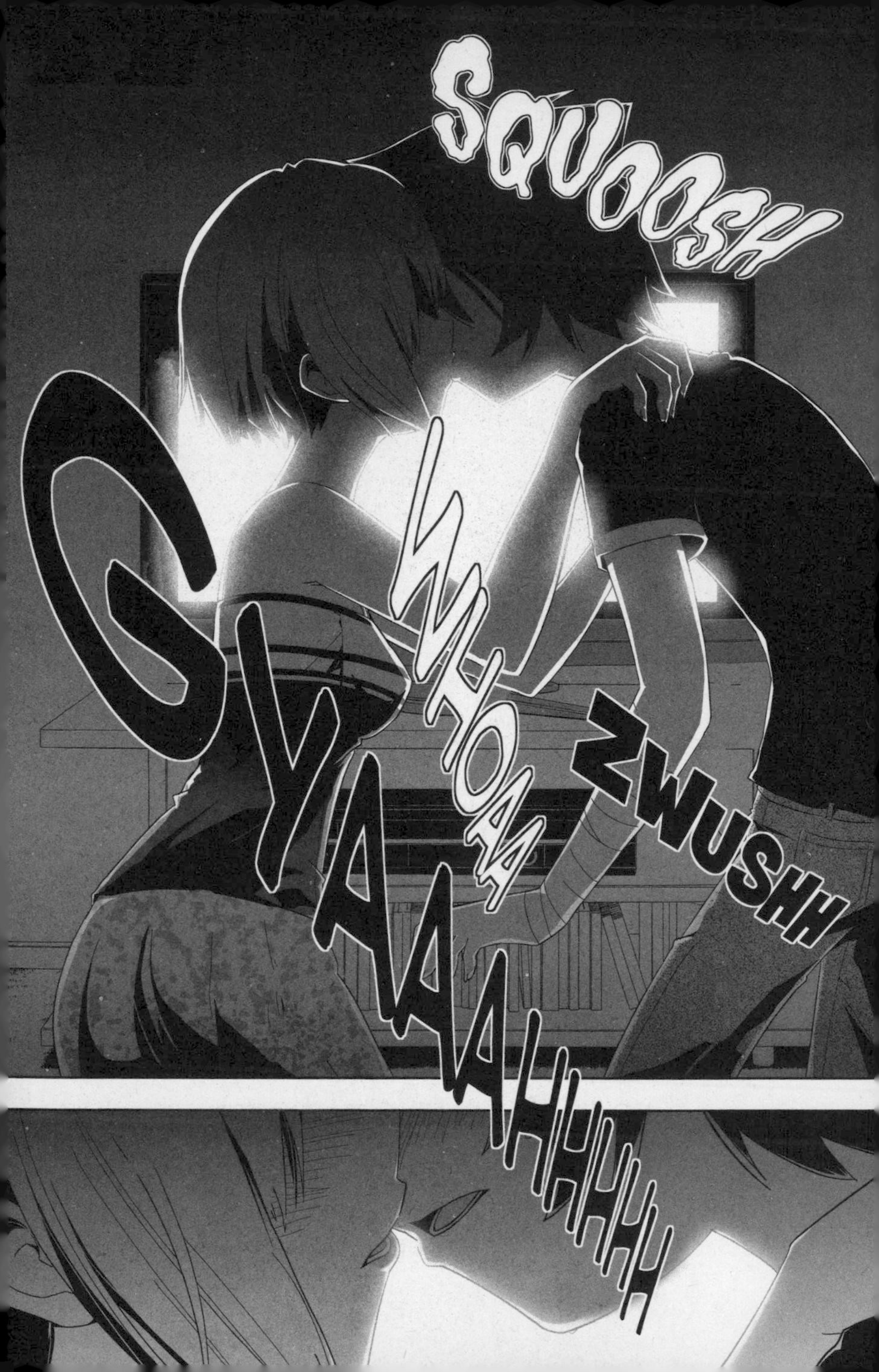
SQUOOSH
ZWUSHH
WHOAA
GYAAAAHHHHHHHHH

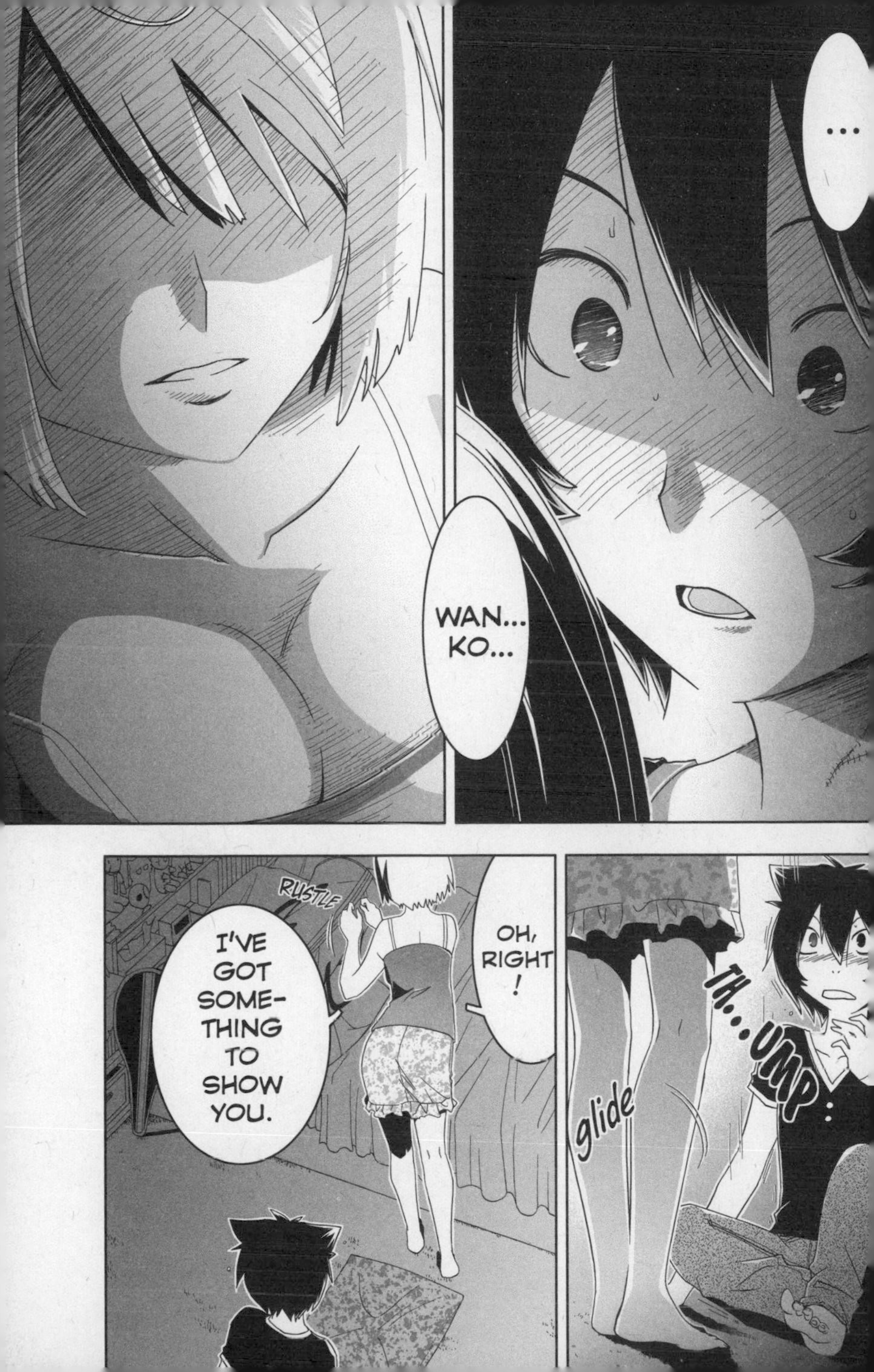
...
WAN... KO...
TH...UMP
glide
OH, RIGHT!
RUSTLE
I'VE GOT SOME-THING TO SHOW YOU.

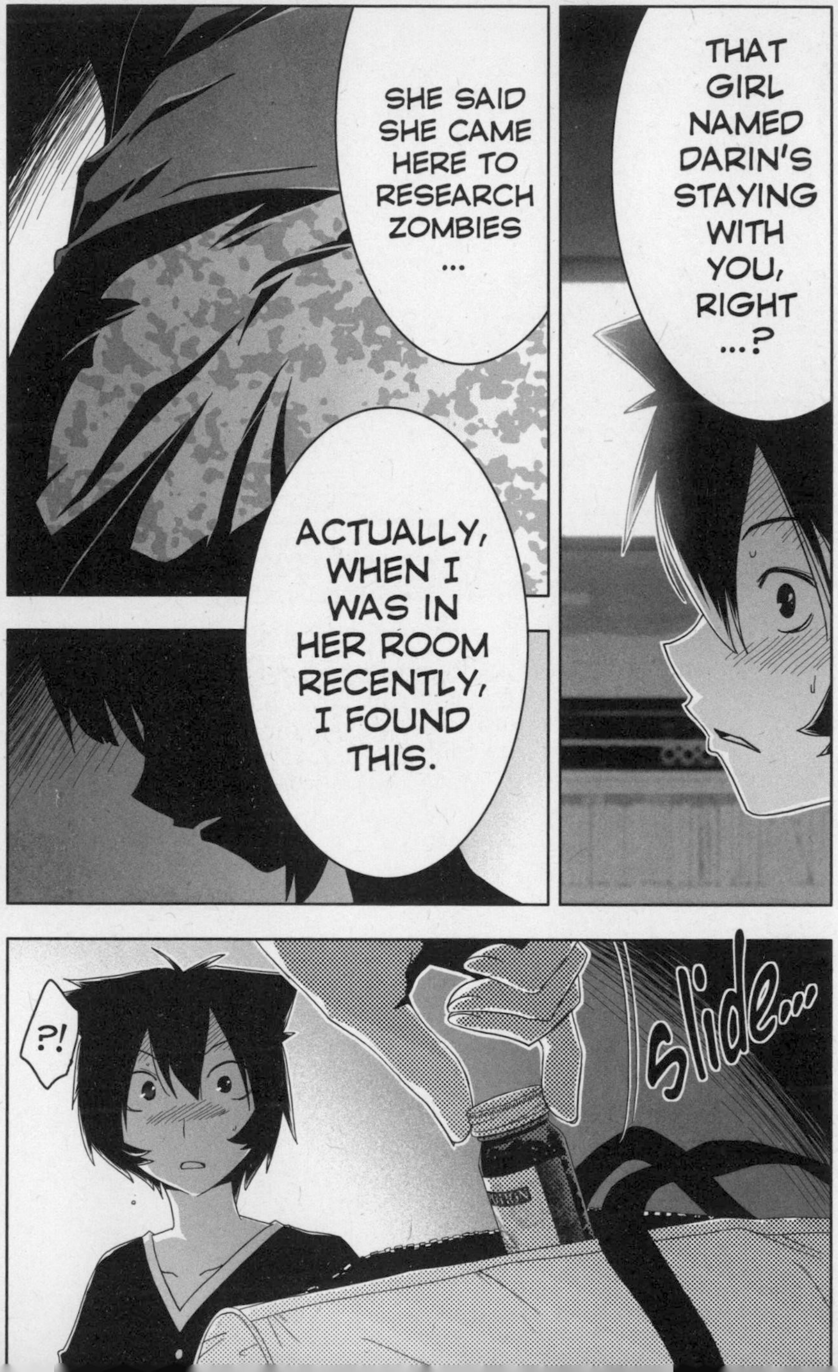
THAT GIRL NAMED DARIN'S STAYING WITH YOU, RIGHT ...?
SHE SAID SHE CAME HERE TO RESEARCH ZOMBIES ...
ACTUALLY, WHEN I WAS IN HER ROOM RECENTLY, I FOUND THIS.
slide...
?!

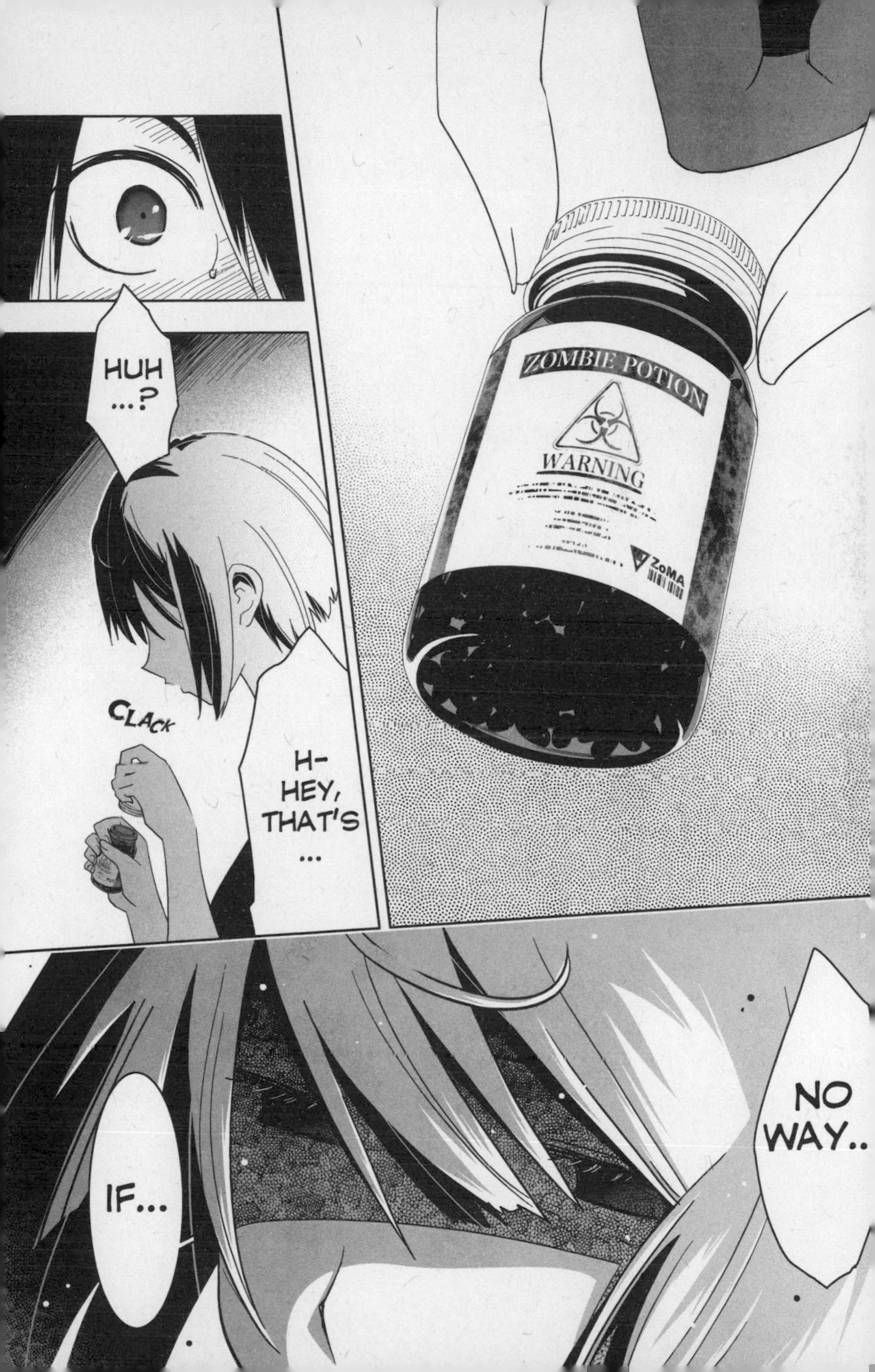
ZOMBIE POTION
WARNING
ZoMA
HUH ...?
H- HEY, THAT'S ...
CLACK
NO WAY..
IF...

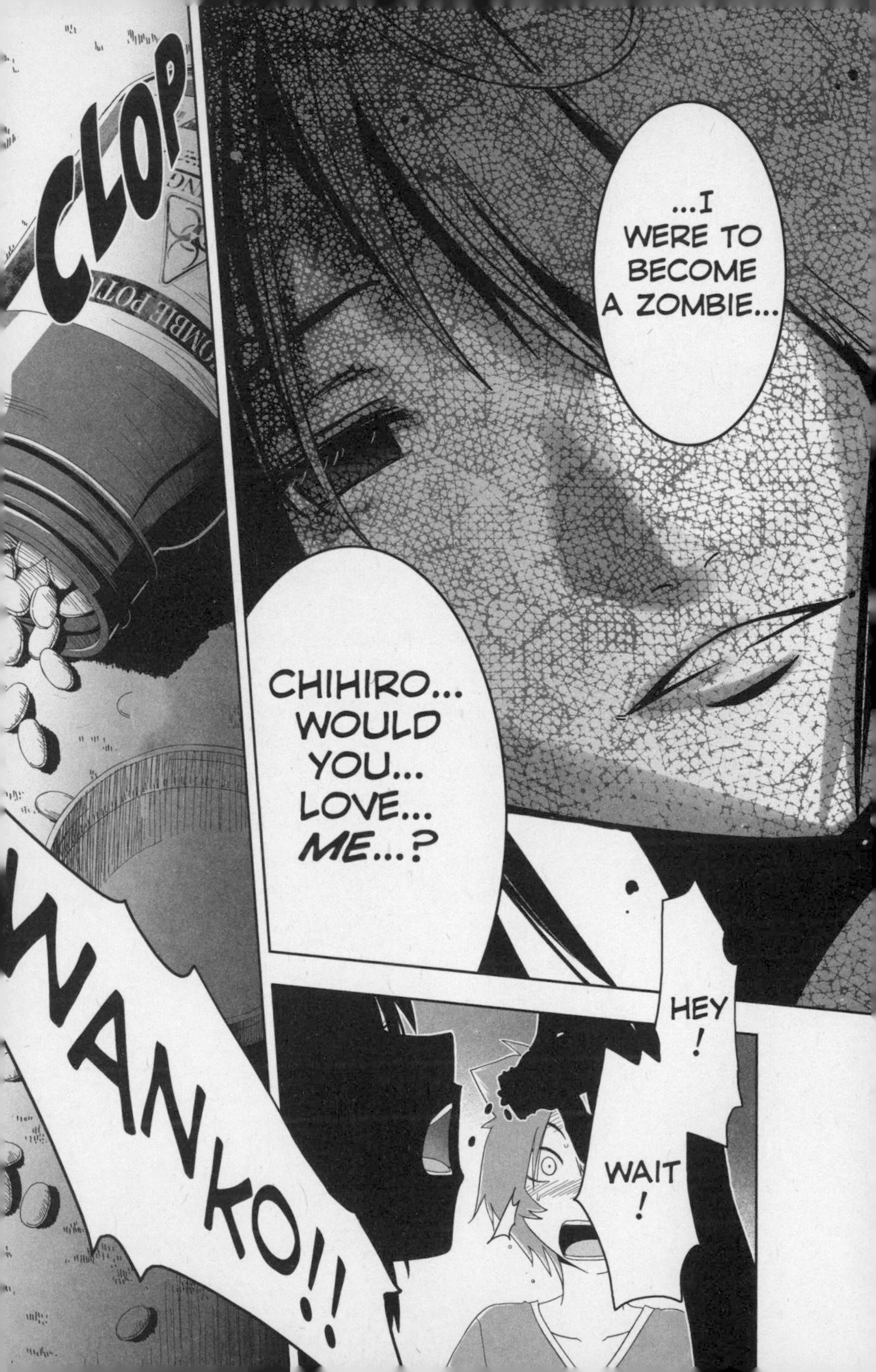
...I WERE TO BECOME A ZOMBIE...
CHIHIRO... WOULD YOU... LOVE... *ME*...?
CLOP
HEY!
WAIT!
WANKO!!

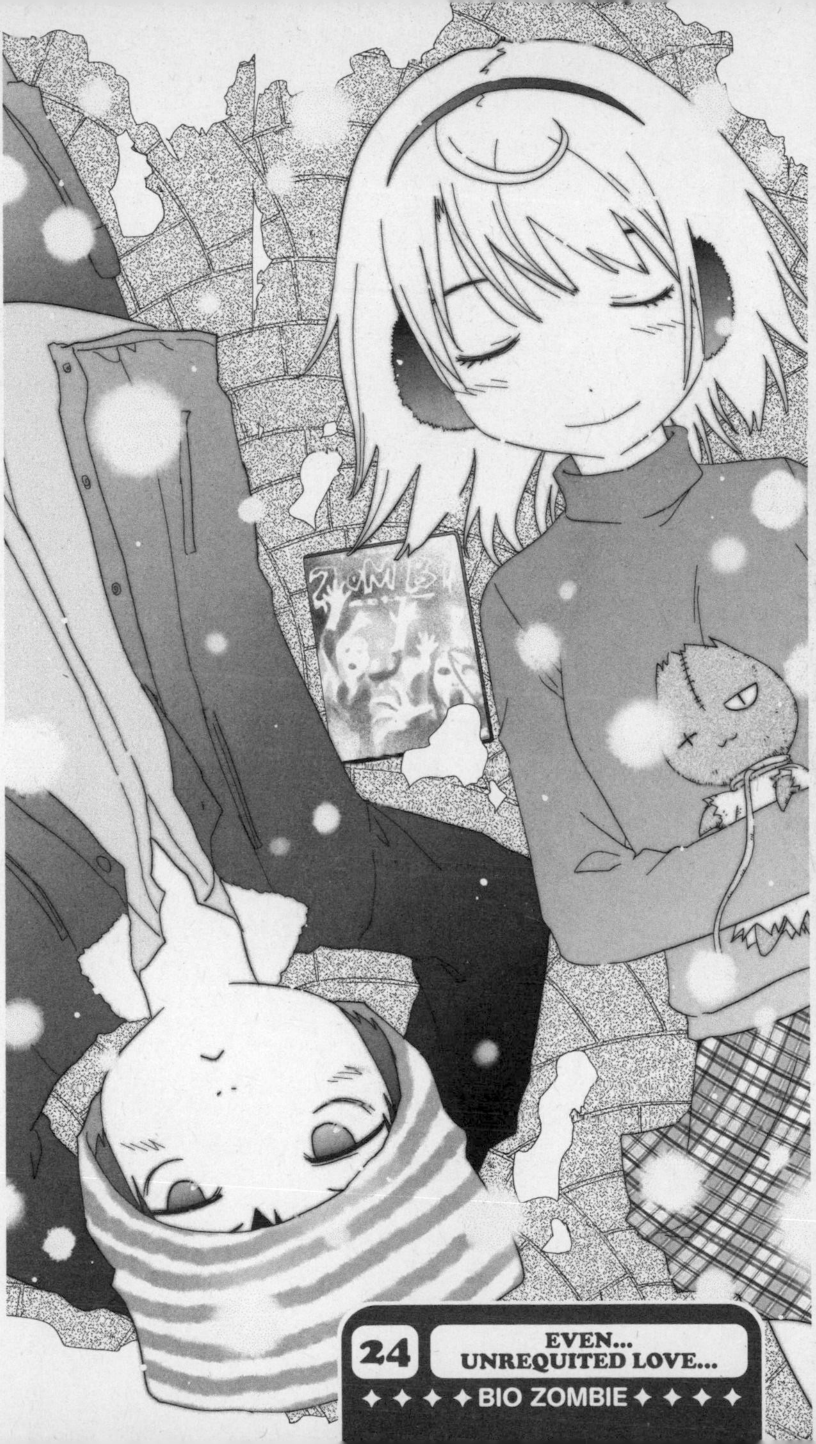
ZOMBIE
24
EVEN...
UNREQUITED LOVE...
BIO ZOMBIE

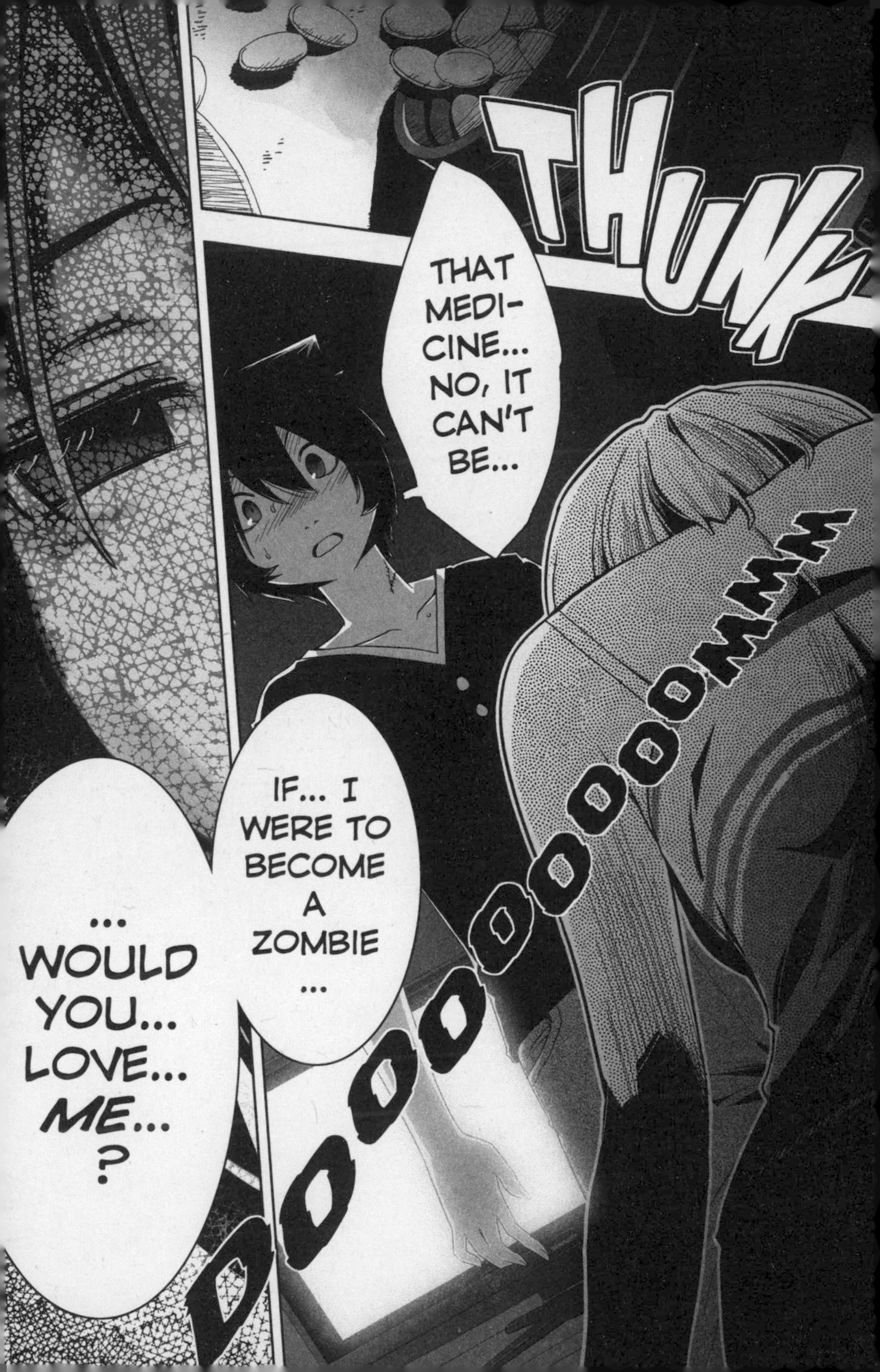
THUNK
THAT MEDICINE... NO, IT CAN'T BE...
DOOOOOOOOOOOOMMM
IF... I WERE TO BECOME A ZOMBIE ...
... WOULD YOU... LOVE... *ME*... ?

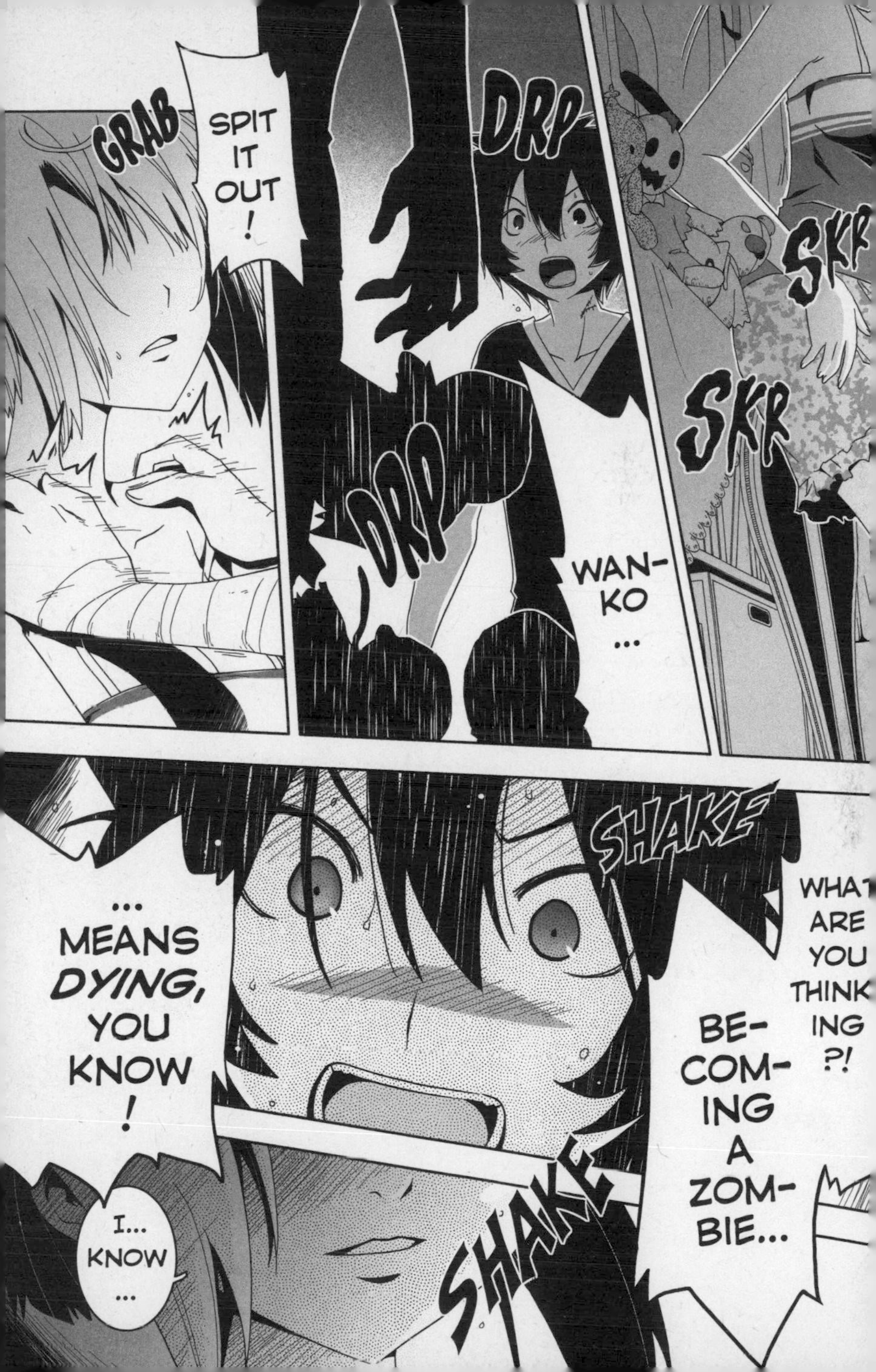
SKR
SKR
DRP
WAN-KO...
DRP
GRAB
SPIT IT OUT!
SHAKE
WHAT ARE YOU THINKING?!
BE-COMING A ZOM-BIE...
...MEANS DYING, YOU KNOW!
SHAKE
I... KNOW...

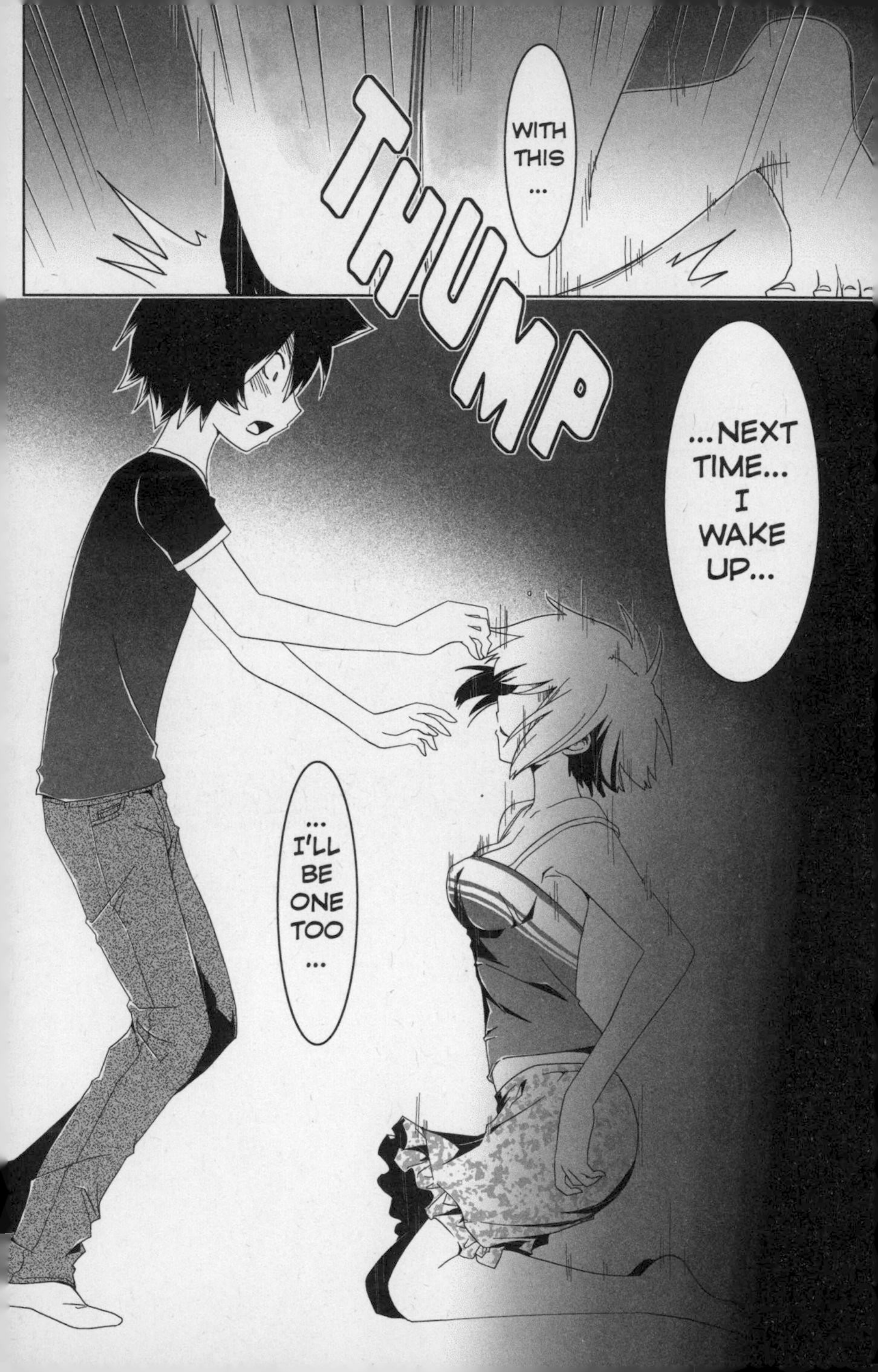
WITH THIS ...
THUMP
...NEXT TIME... I WAKE UP...
... I'LL BE ONE TOO ...

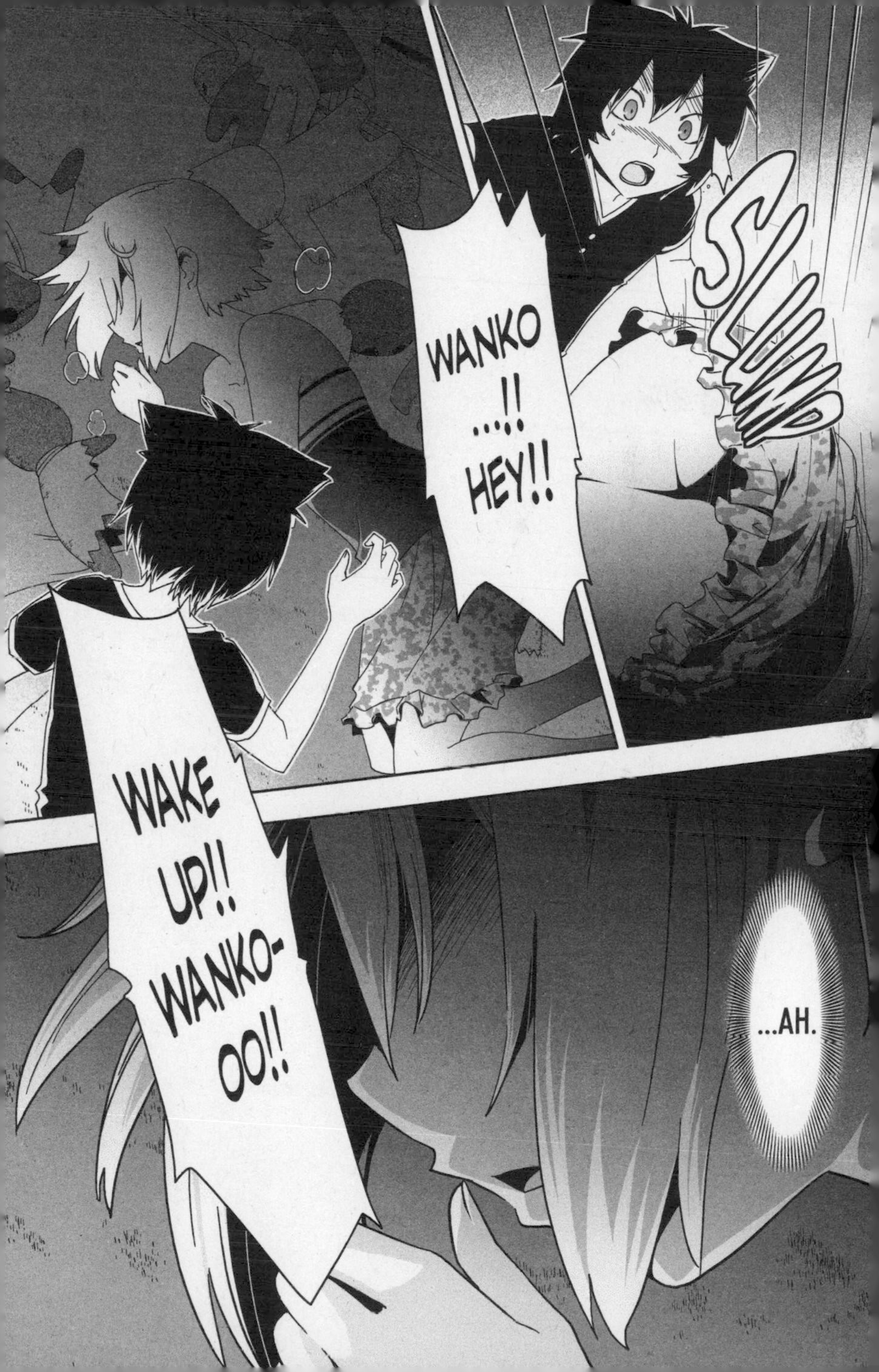
SLUMP
WANKO!! ...!! HEY!!
WAKE UP!! WANKO-OO!!
...AH.

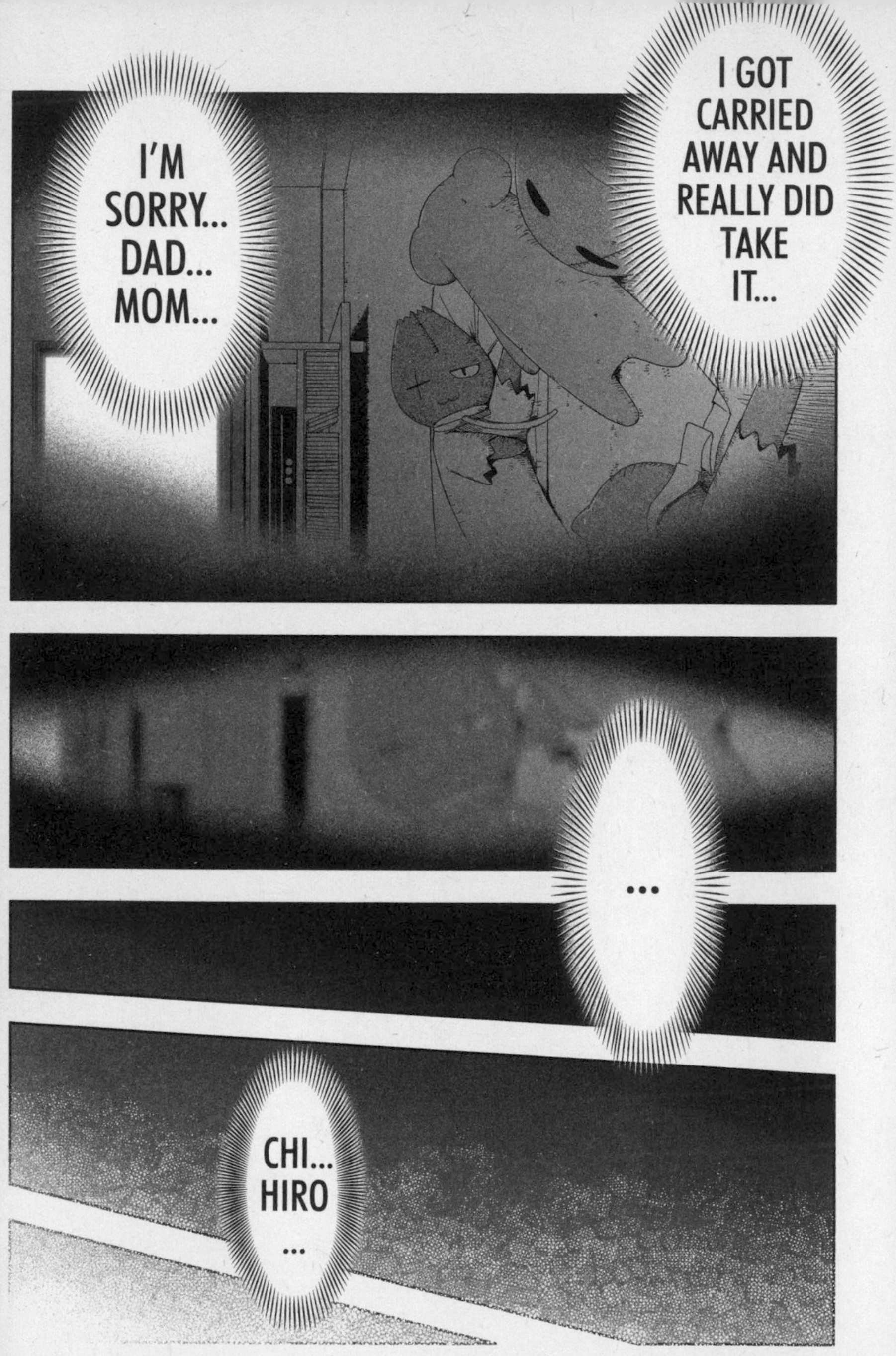
I GOT CARRIED AWAY AND REALLY DID TAKE IT...
I'M SORRY... DAD... MOM...
...
CHI... HIRO ...

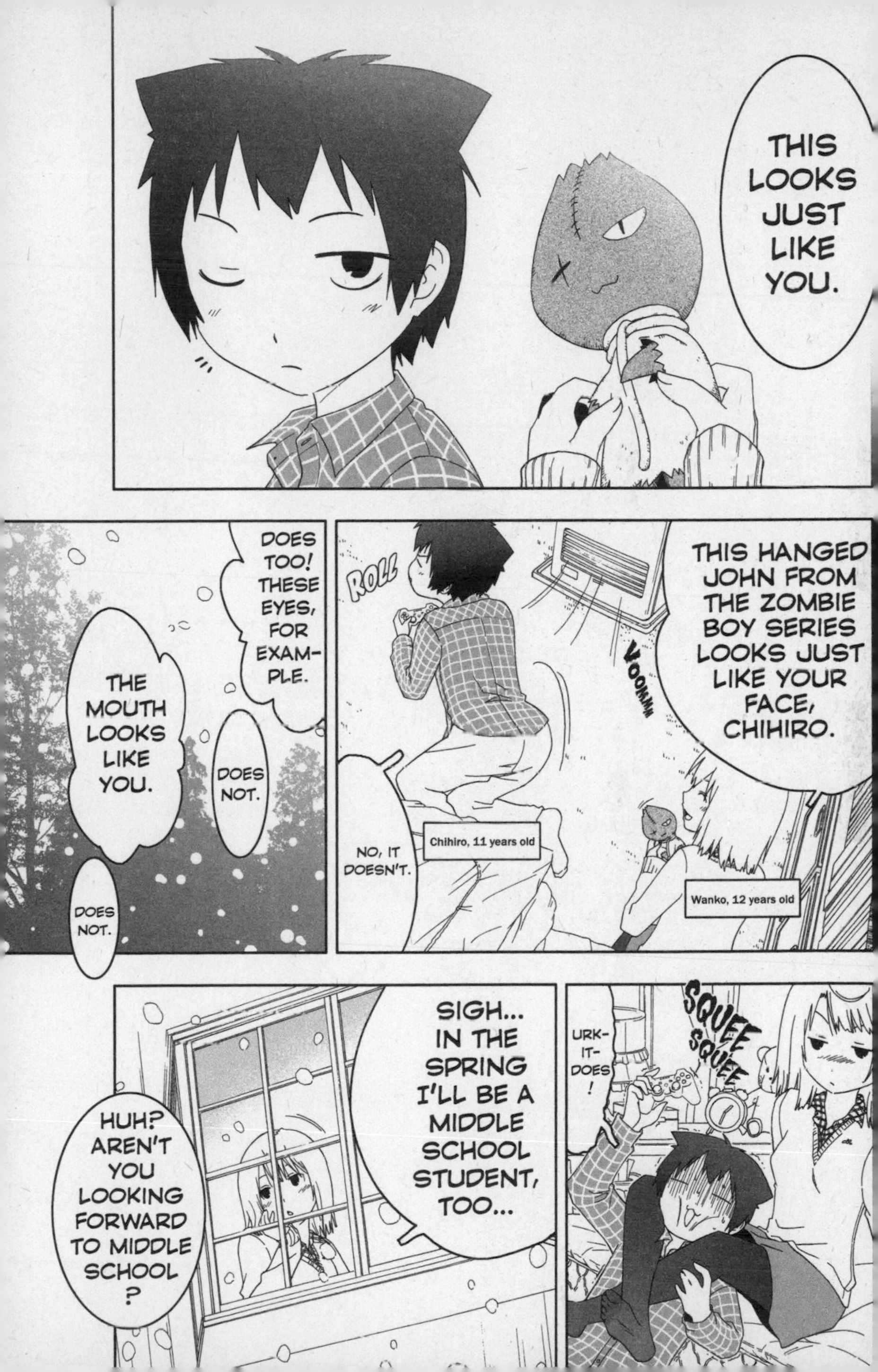

THIS LOOKS JUST LIKE YOU.
THIS HANGED JOHN FROM THE ZOMBIE BOY SERIES LOOKS JUST LIKE YOUR FACE, CHIHIRO.
ROLL
VOOMM
Chihiro, 11 years old
Wanko, 12 years old
NO, IT DOESN'T.
DOES TOO! THESE EYES, FOR EXAMPLE.
DOES NOT.
THE MOUTH LOOKS LIKE YOU.
DOES NOT.
SQUEE SQUEE
URK- IT- DOES!
SIGH... IN THE SPRING I'LL BE A MIDDLE SCHOOL STUDENT, TOO...
HUH? AREN'T YOU LOOKING FORWARD TO MIDDLE SCHOOL?

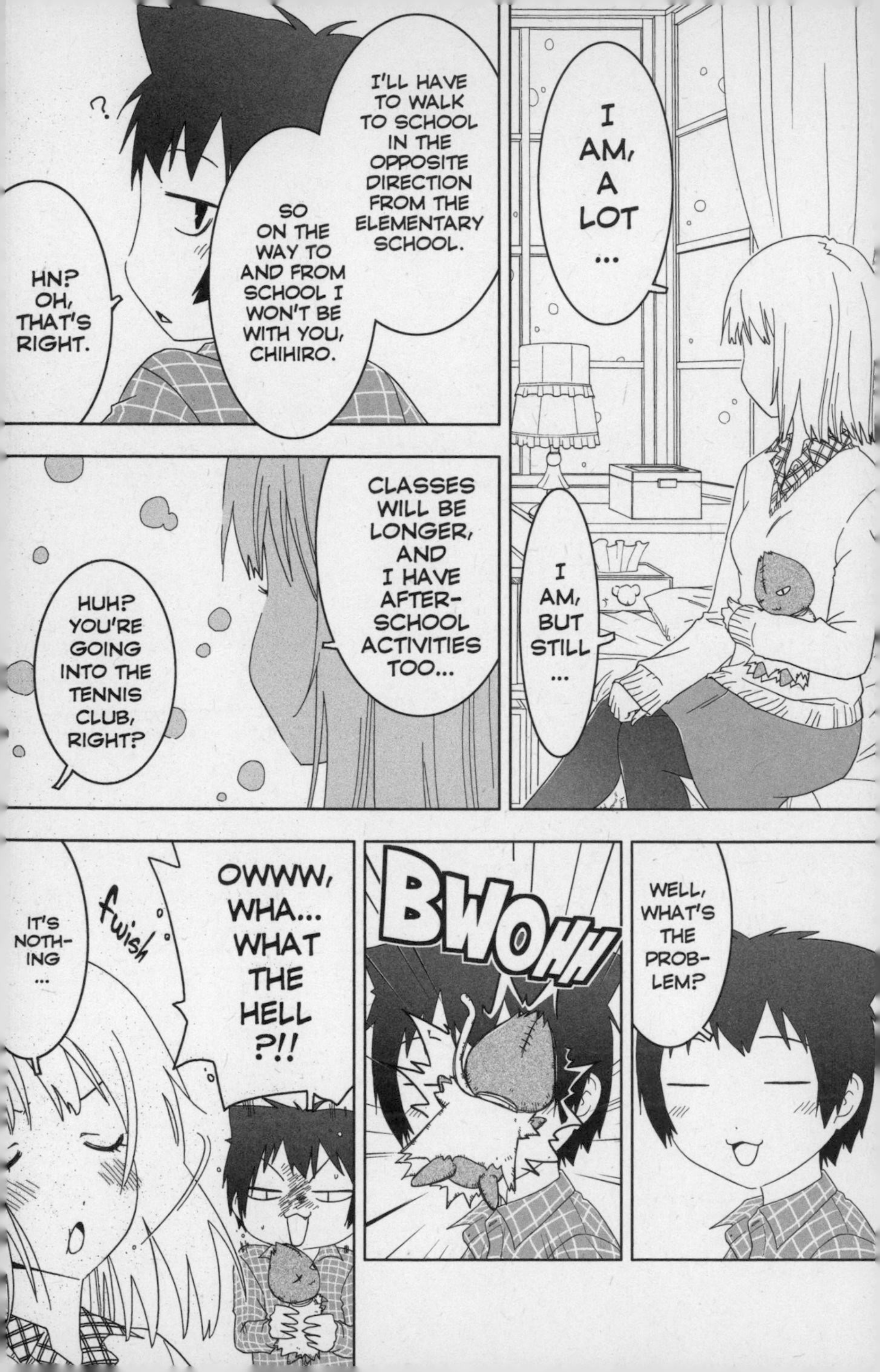
I AM, A LOT ...
I AM, BUT STILL ...
I'LL HAVE TO WALK TO SCHOOL IN THE OPPOSITE DIRECTION FROM THE ELEMENTARY SCHOOL.
SO ON THE WAY TO AND FROM SCHOOL I WON'T BE WITH YOU, CHIHIRO.
?
HN? OH, THAT'S RIGHT.
CLASSES WILL BE LONGER, AND I HAVE AFTER-SCHOOL ACTIVITIES TOO...
HUH? YOU'RE GOING INTO THE TENNIS CLUB, RIGHT?
WELL, WHAT'S THE PROB-LEM?
BWOHH
OWWW, WHA... WHAT THE HELL ?!!
fwish
IT'S NOTH-ING ...

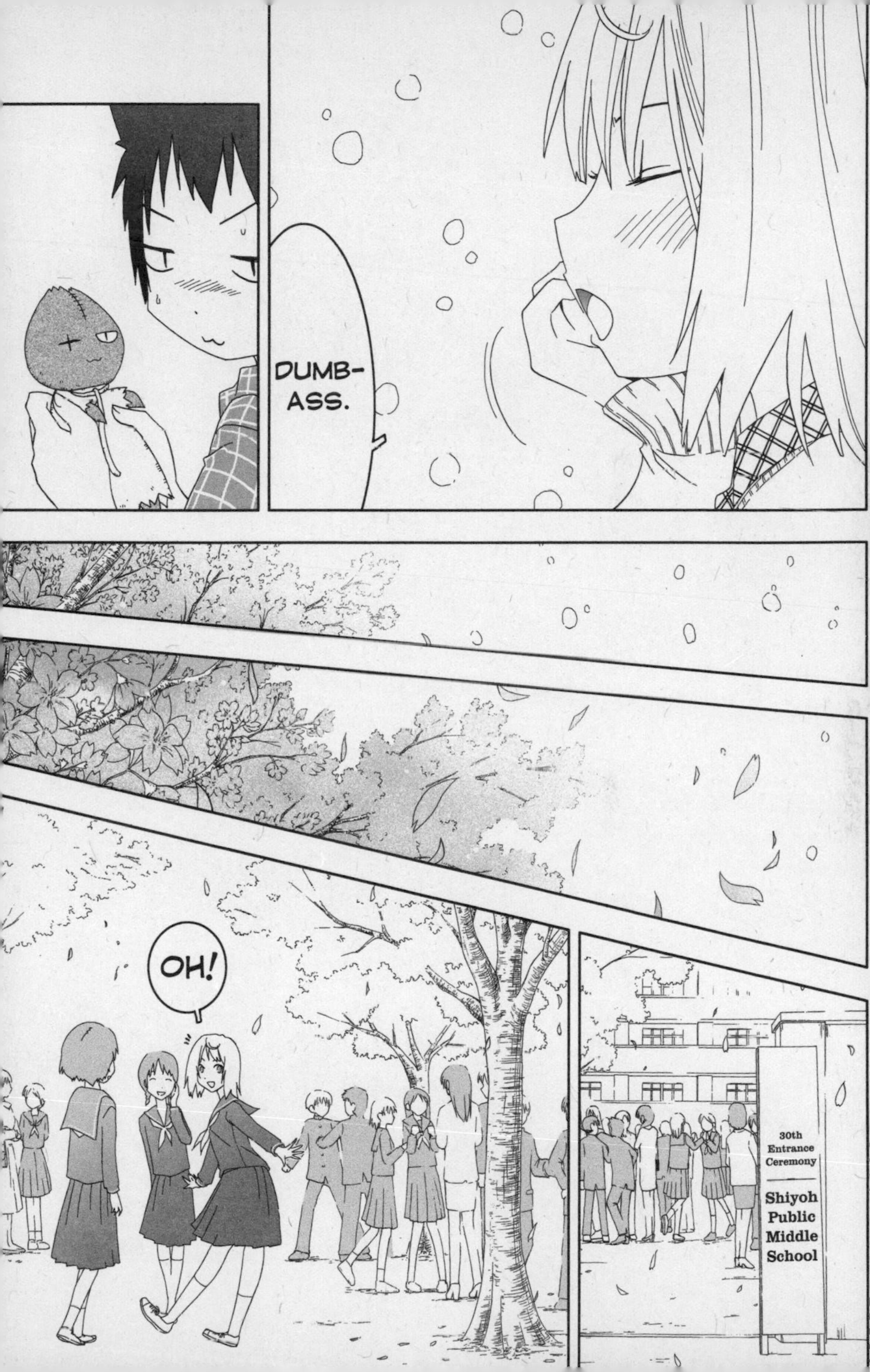
DUMB-ASS.
30th Entrance Ceremony
Shiyoh Public Middle School
OH!

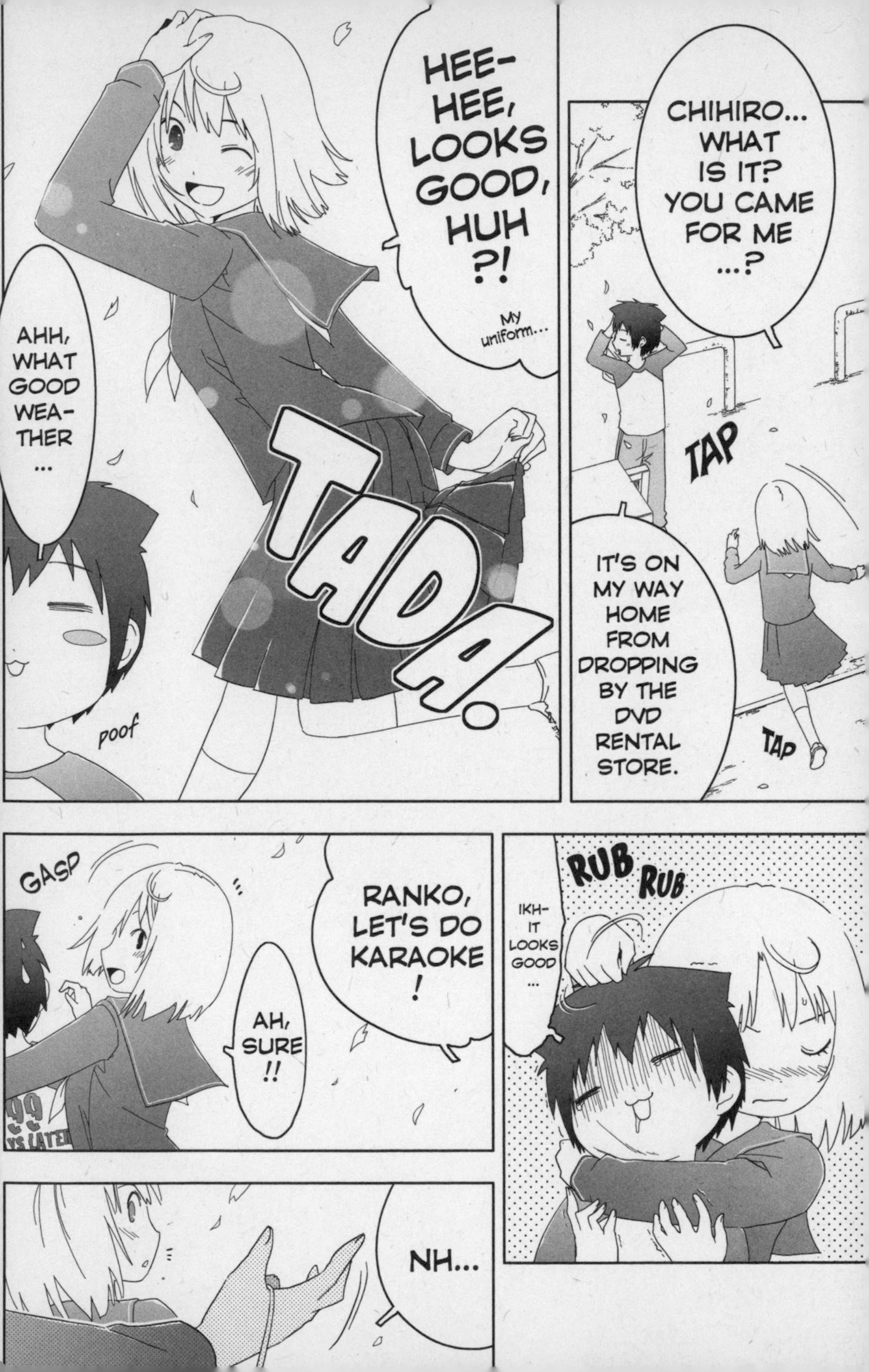
CHIHIRO... WHAT IS IT? YOU CAME FOR ME ...?
TAP
IT'S ON MY WAY HOME FROM DROPPING BY THE DVD RENTAL STORE.
TAP
HEE-HEE, LOOKS GOOD, HUH ?!
My uniform...
TADA.
AHH, WHAT GOOD WEA-THER ...
poof
RUB RUB
IKH- IT LOOKS GOOD ...
GASP
RANKO, LET'S DO KARAOKE !
AH, SURE !!
NH...

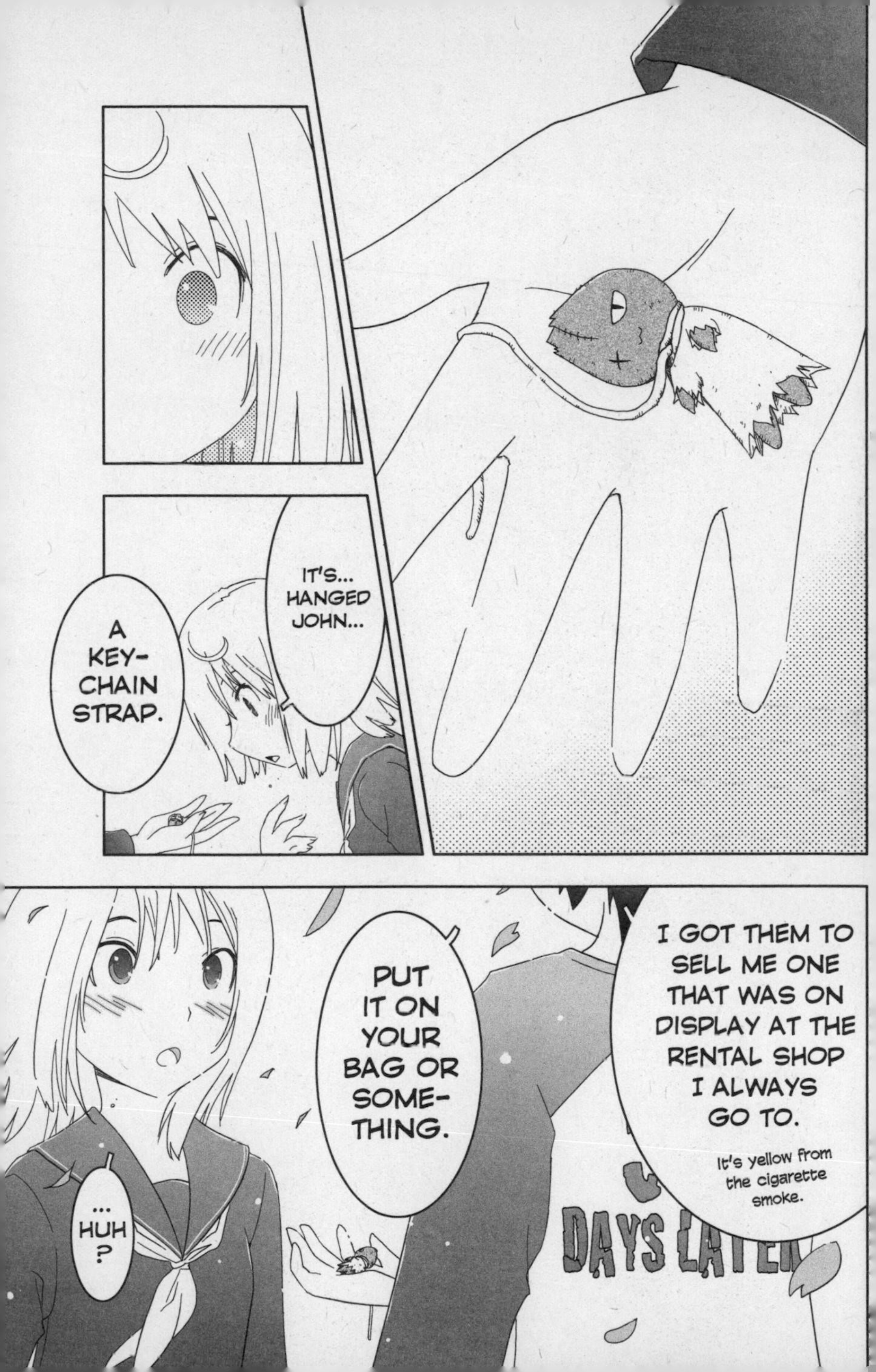
IT'S... HANGED JOHN...
A KEY-CHAIN STRAP.
I GOT THEM TO SELL ME ONE THAT WAS ON DISPLAY AT THE RENTAL SHOP I ALWAYS GO TO.
It's yellow from the cigarette smoke.
DAYS LATER
PUT IT ON YOUR BAG OR SOME-THING.
... HUH?

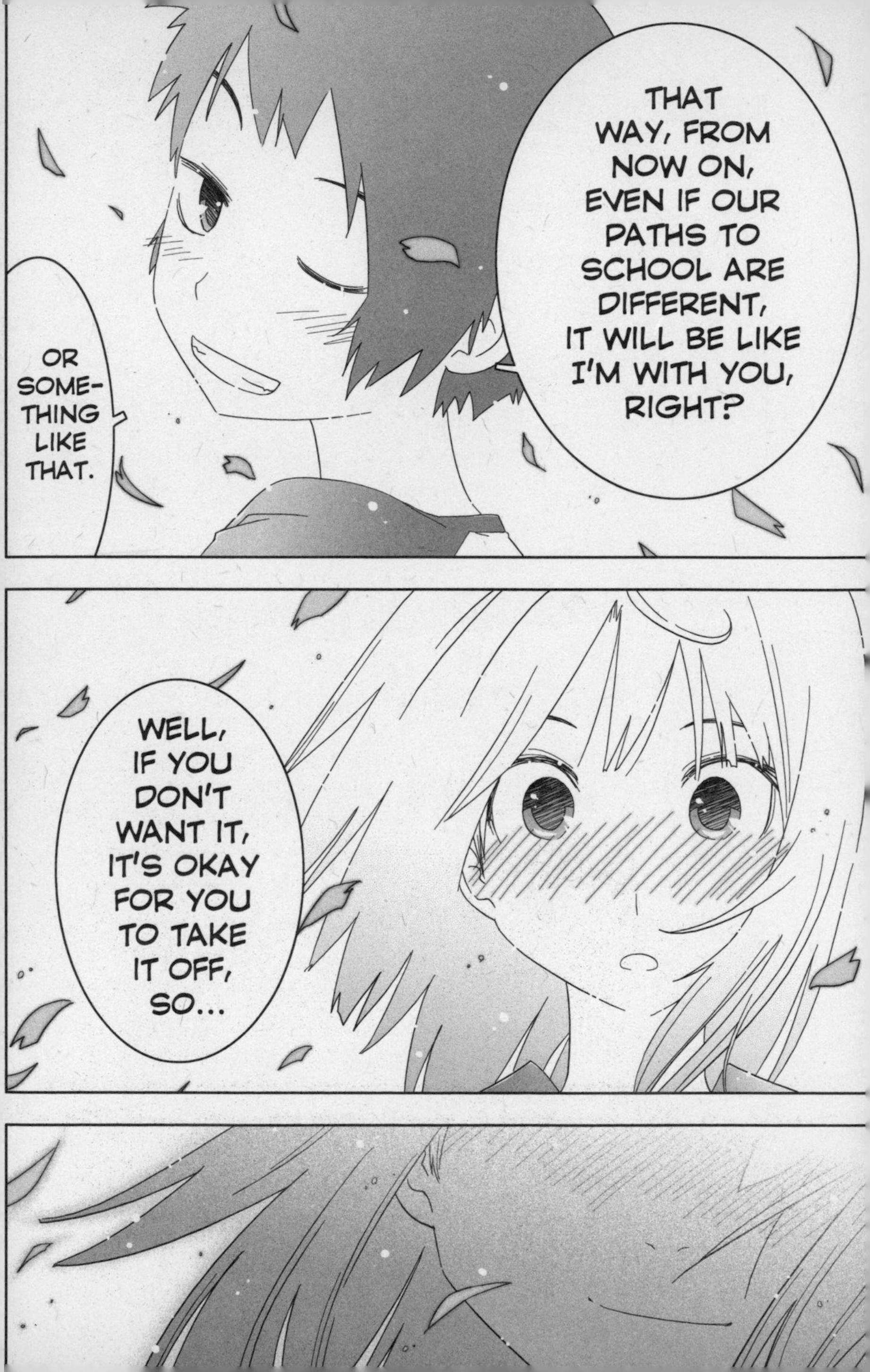
THAT WAY, FROM NOW ON, EVEN IF OUR PATHS TO SCHOOL ARE DIFFERENT, IT WILL BE LIKE I'M WITH YOU, RIGHT?
OR SOME-THING LIKE THAT.
WELL, IF YOU DON'T WANT IT, IT'S OKAY FOR YOU TO TAKE IT OFF, SO...

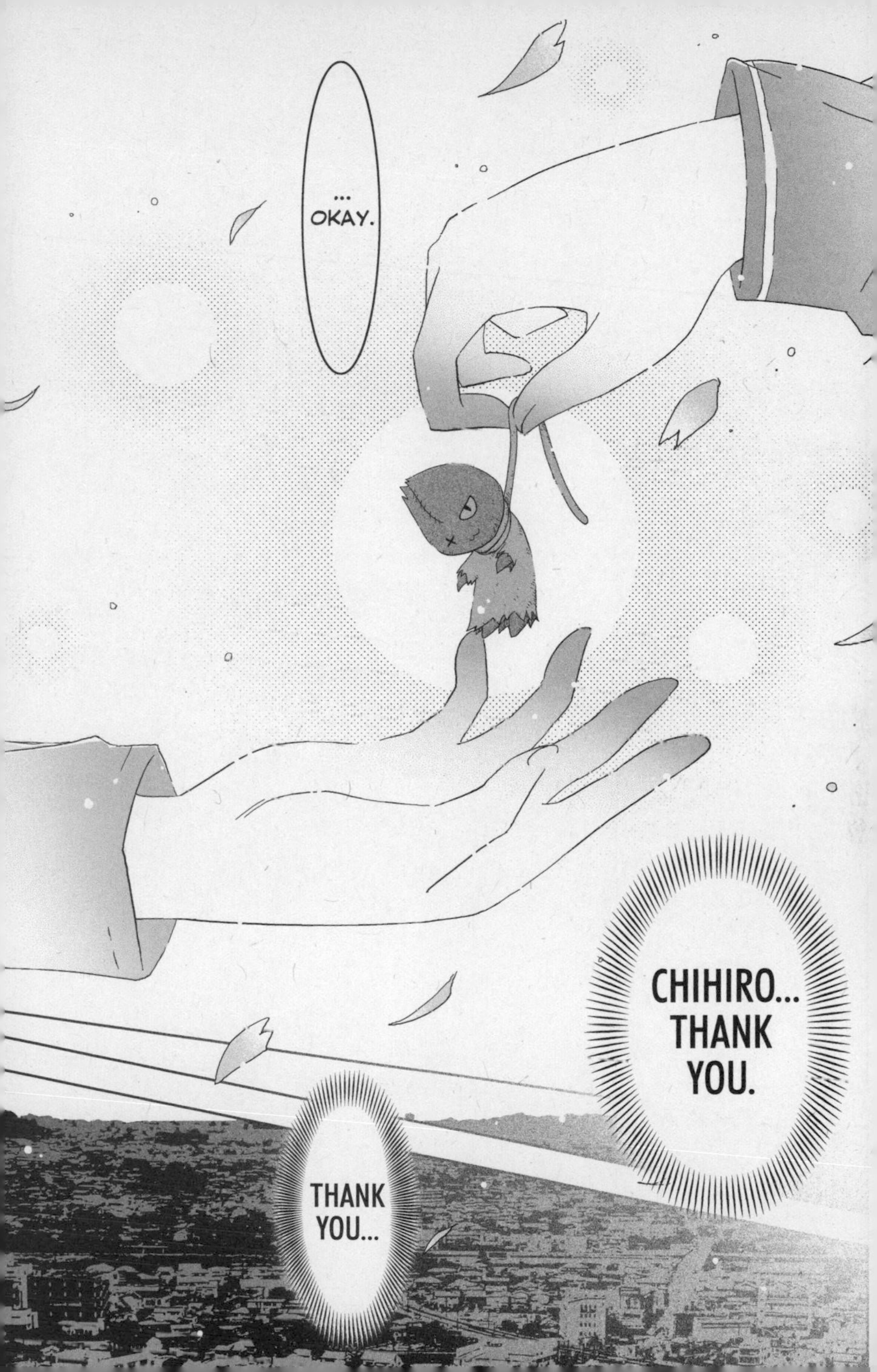
...OKAY.
CHIHIRO... THANK YOU.
THANK YOU...

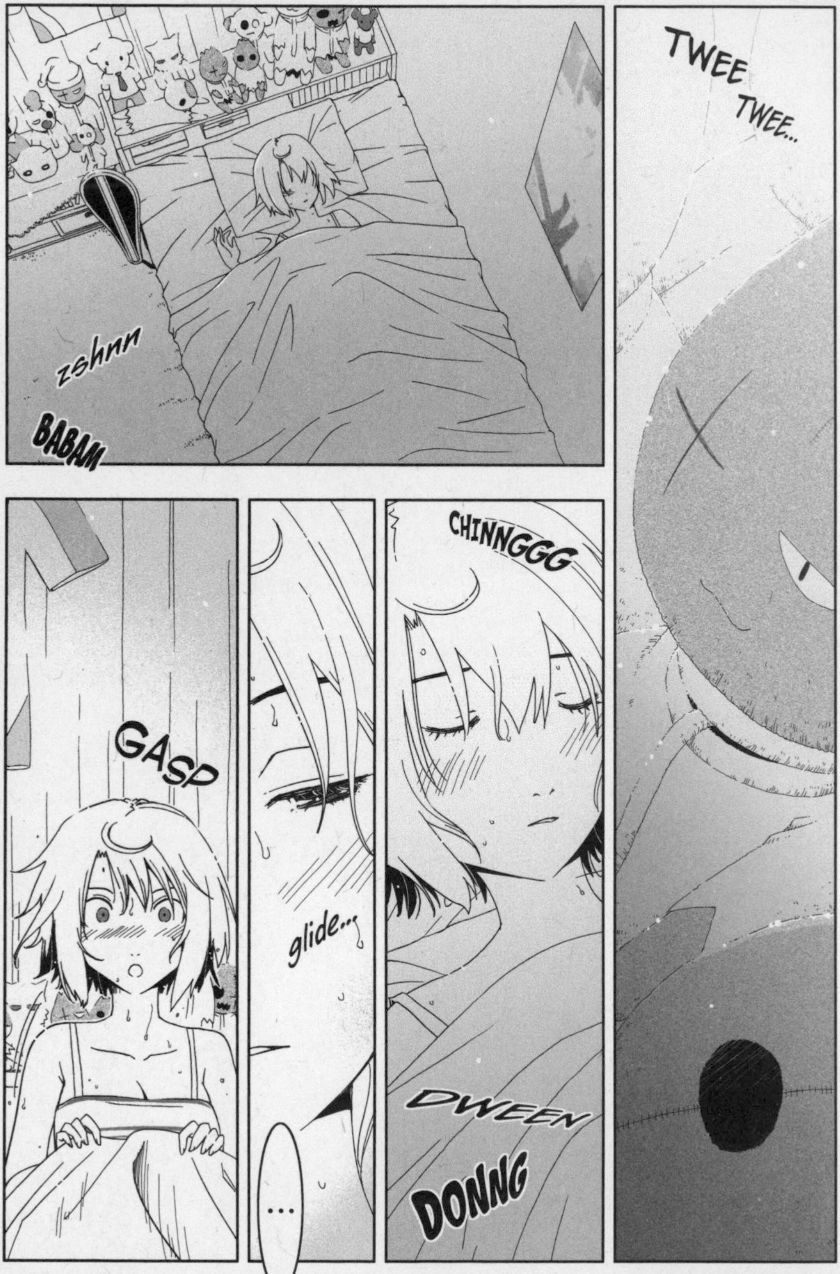
TWEE
TWEE...
zshnn
BABAM
CHINNGGG
DWEEN
DONNG
glide...
...
GASP

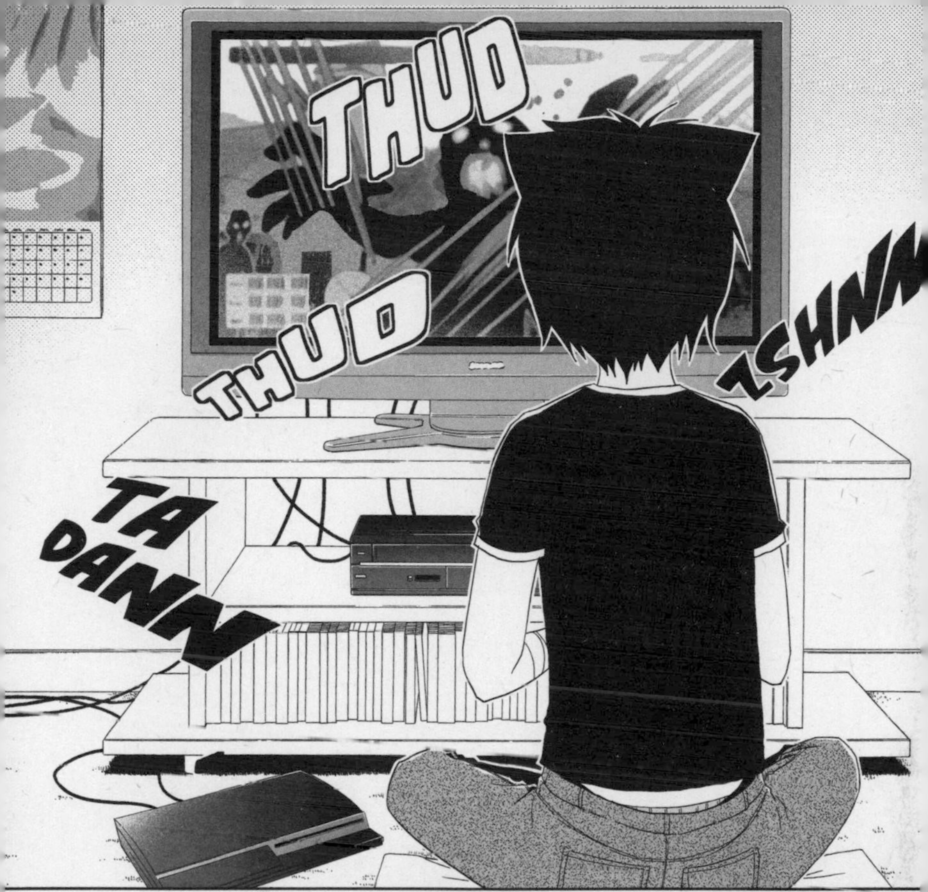
THUD
ZSHNN
THUD
TA DANN
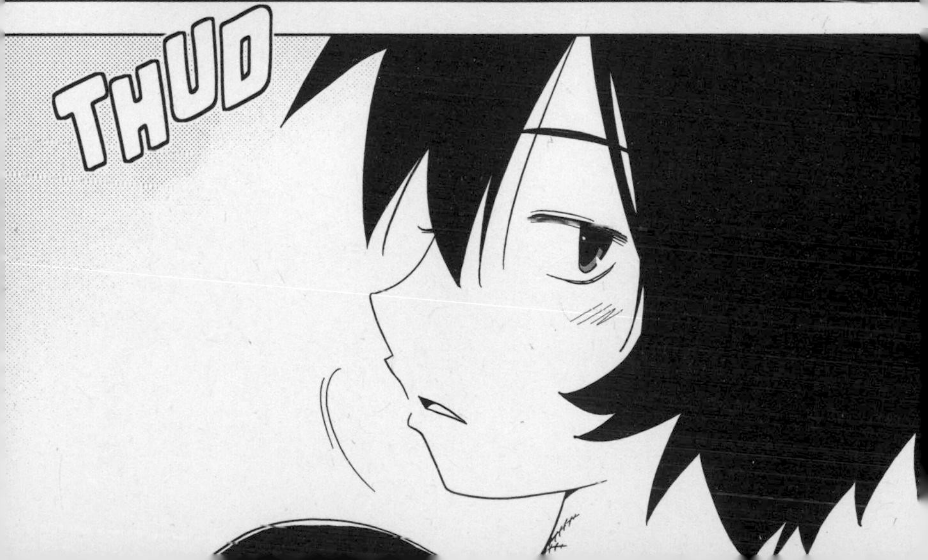
THUD

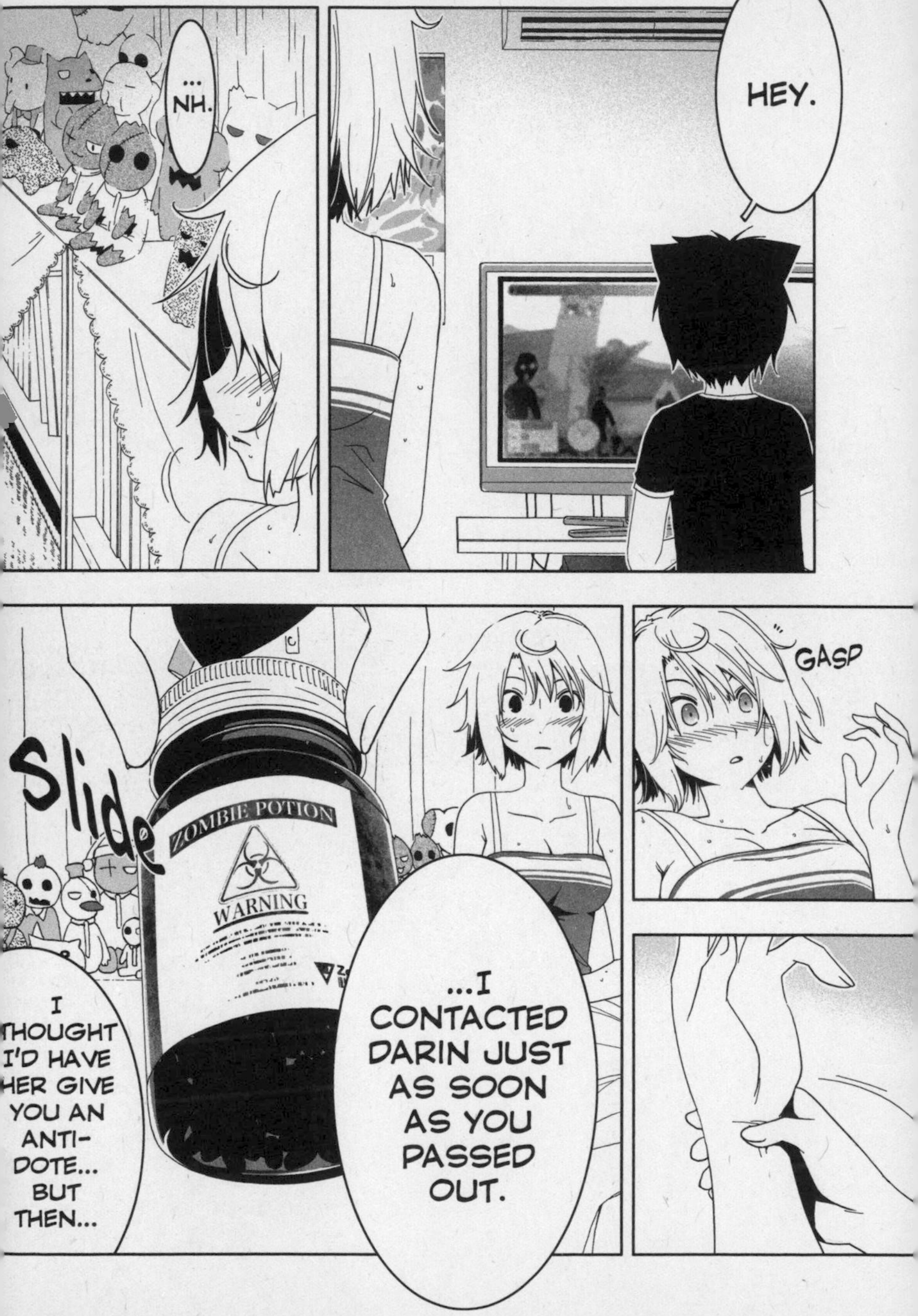
HEY.
...NH.
GASP
...I CONTACTED DARIN JUST AS SOON AS YOU PASSED OUT.
Slide
ZOMBIE POTION
WARNING
I THOUGHT I'D HAVE HER GIVE YOU AN ANTI-DOTE... BUT THEN...

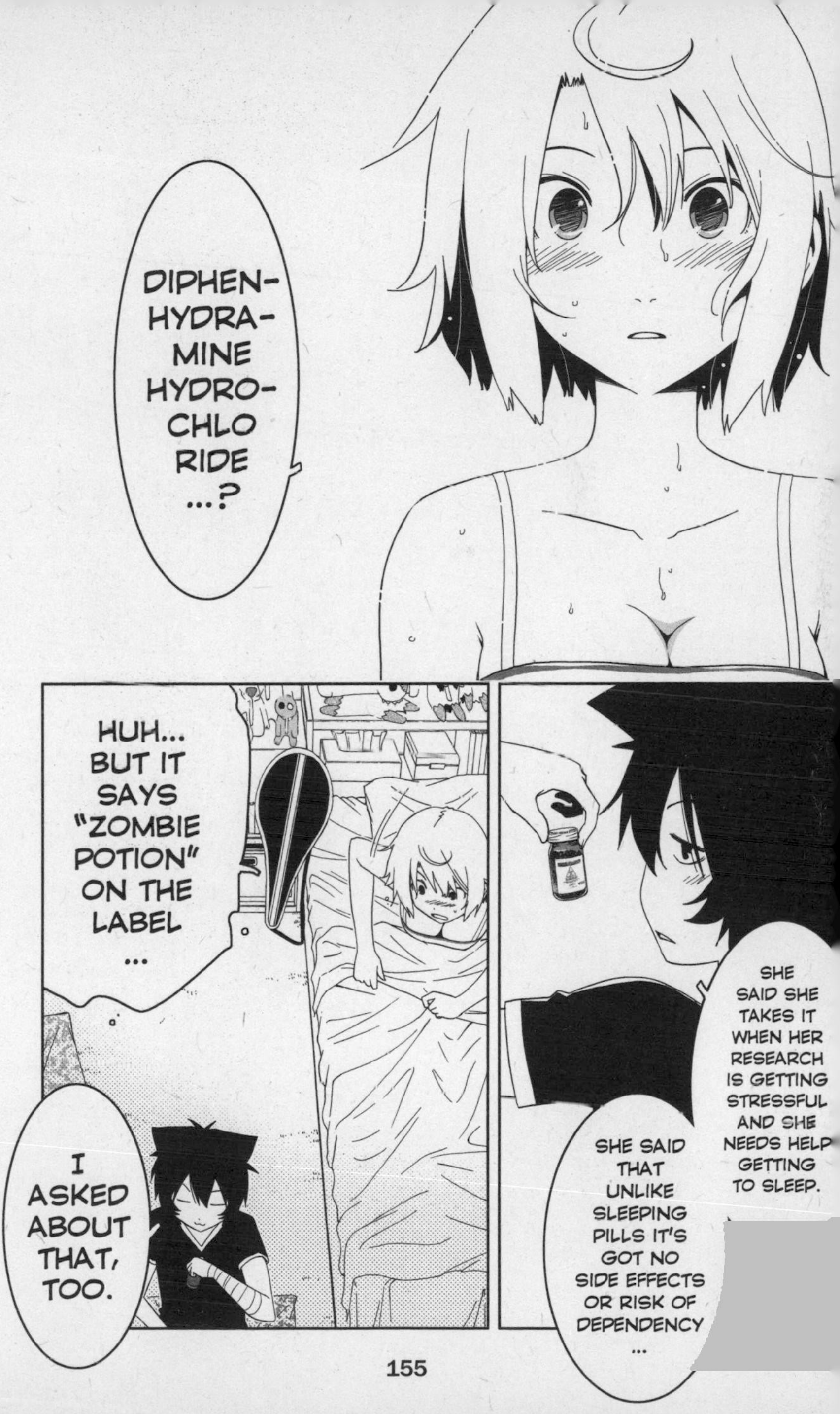
DIPHEN-HYDRA-MINE HYDRO-CHLO RIDE ...?
SHE SAID SHE TAKES IT WHEN HER RESEARCH IS GETTING STRESSFUL AND SHE NEEDS HELP GETTING TO SLEEP.
SHE SAID THAT UNLIKE SLEEPING PILLS IT'S GOT NO SIDE EFFECTS OR RISK OF DEPENDENCY ...
HUH... BUT IT SAYS "ZOMBIE POTION" ON THE LABEL ...
I ASKED ABOUT THAT, TOO.

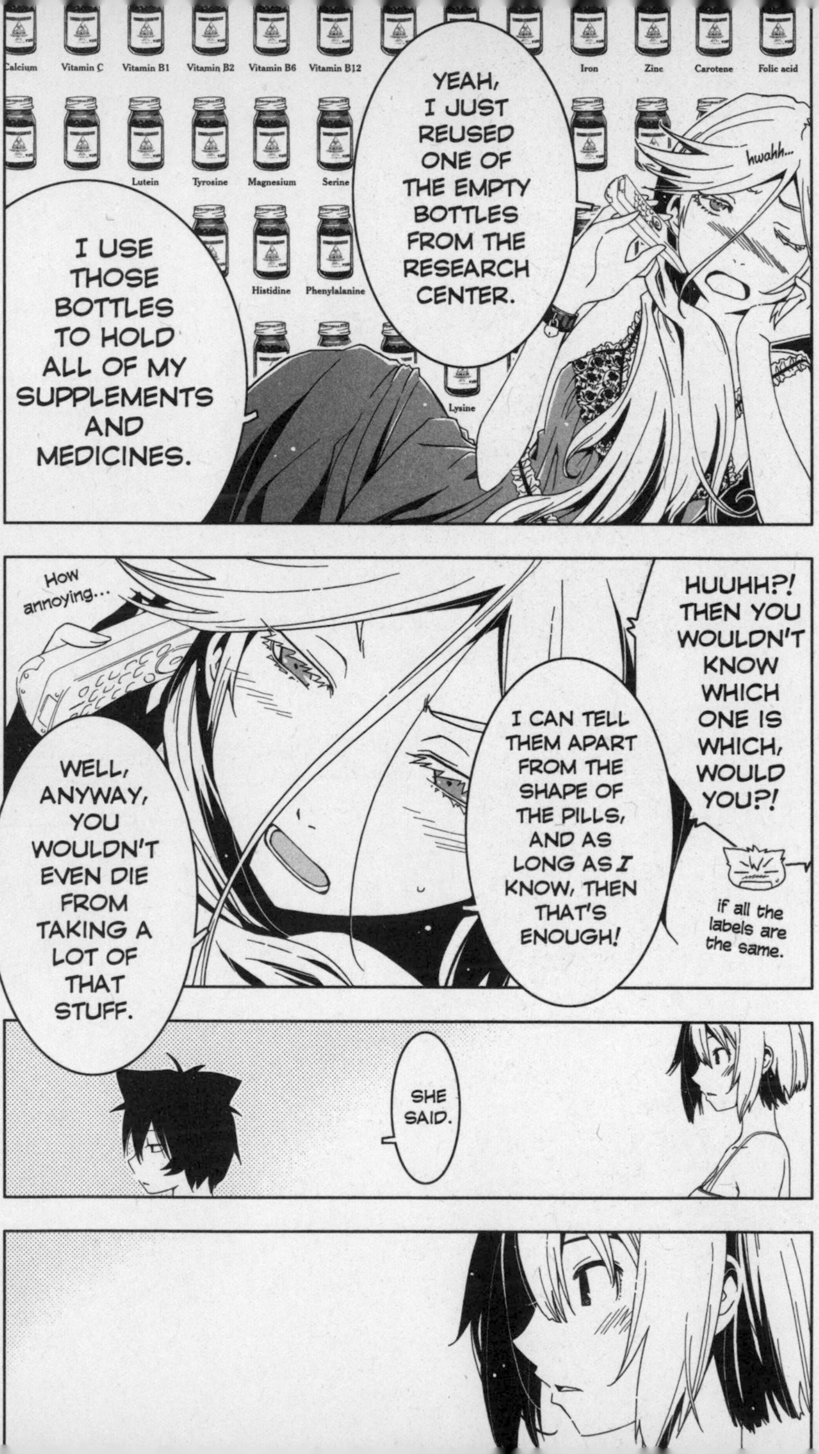
Calcium
Vitamin C
Vitamin B1
Vitamin B2
Vitamin B6
Vitamin B12
Iron
Zinc
Carotene
Folic acid
Lutein
Tyrosine
Magnesium
Serine
Histidine
Phenylalanine
Lysine
hwahh...
YEAH, I JUST REUSED ONE OF THE EMPTY BOTTLES FROM THE RESEARCH CENTER.
I USE THOSE BOTTLES TO HOLD ALL OF MY SUPPLEMENTS AND MEDICINES.
HUUHH?! THEN YOU WOULDN'T KNOW WHICH ONE IS WHICH, WOULD YOU?!
if all the labels are the same.
I CAN TELL THEM APART FROM THE SHAPE OF THE PILLS, AND AS LONG AS *I* KNOW, THEN THAT'S ENOUGH!
How annoying...
WELL, ANYWAY, YOU WOULDN'T EVEN DIE FROM TAKING A LOT OF THAT STUFF.
SHE SAID.

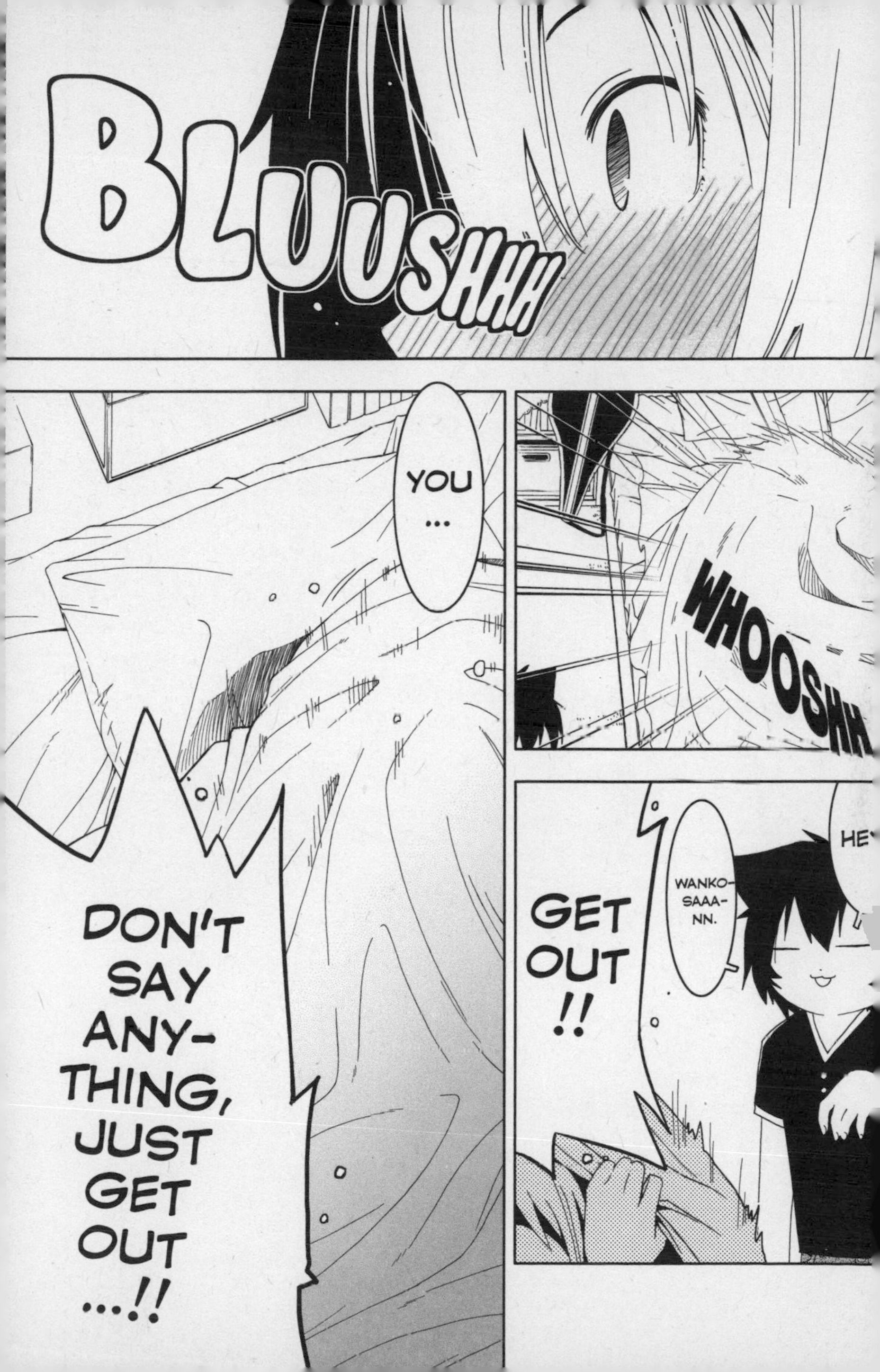
BLUUSHHH
WHOOSHH
HE
WANKO-SAAA-NN.
GET OUT!!
YOU...
DON'T SAY ANYTHING, JUST GET OUT...!!

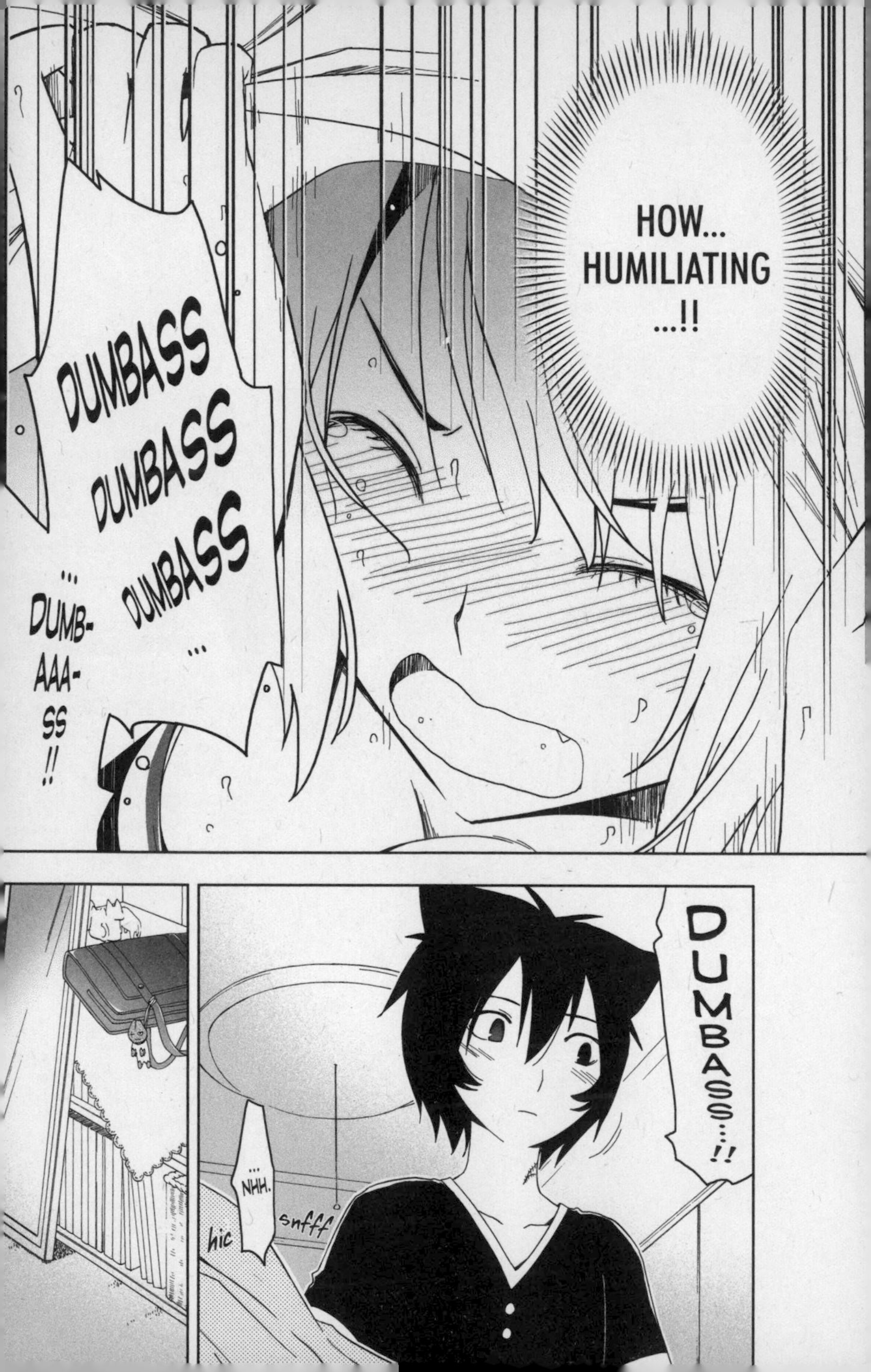
HOW... HUMILIATING ...!!
DUMBASS DUMBASS DUMBASS ...
...DUMB-AAA-SS!!
DUMBASS...!!
...NHH.
snfff
hic

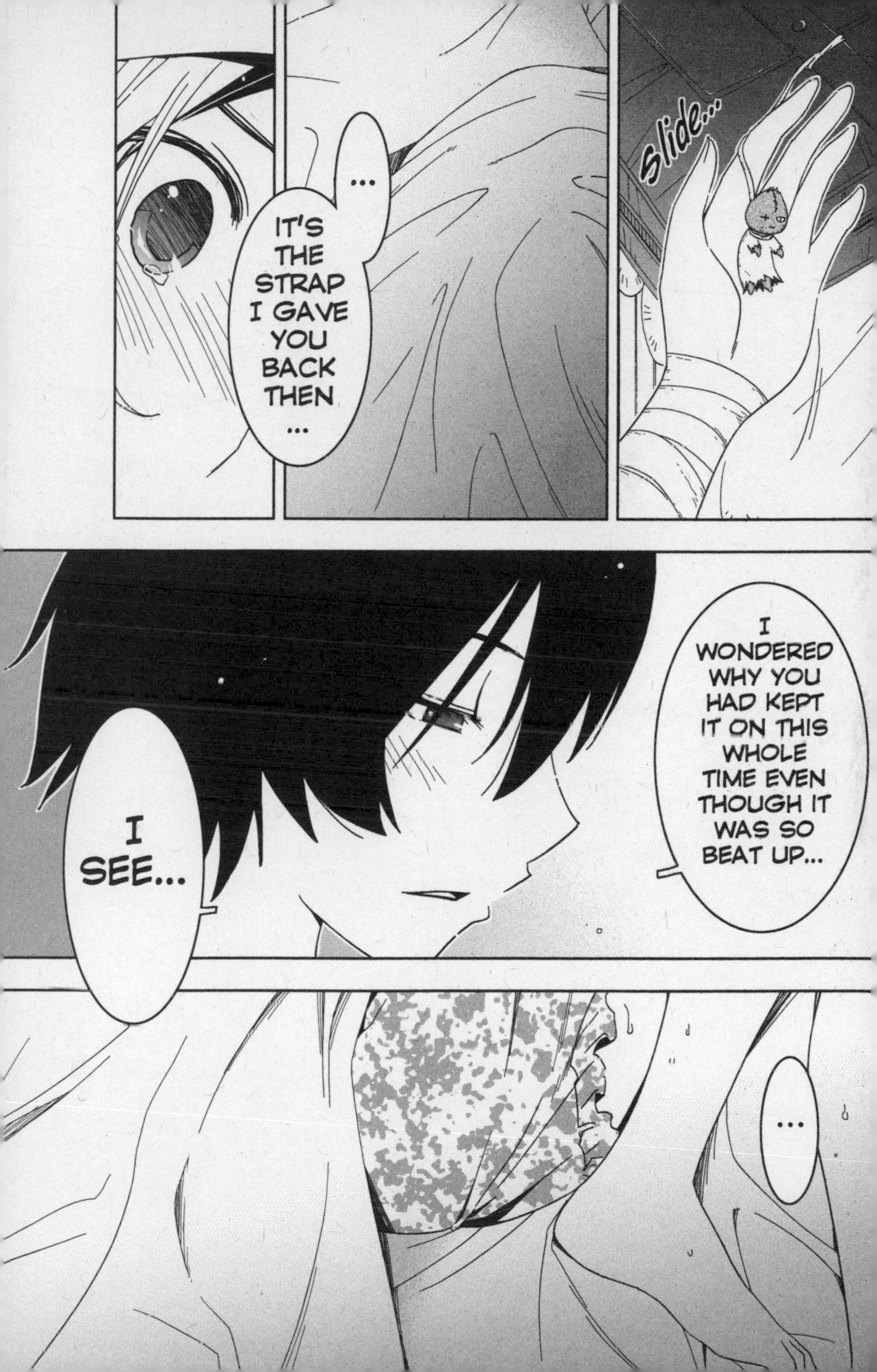
slide...
...
IT'S THE STRAP I GAVE YOU BACK THEN ...
I WONDERED WHY YOU HAD KEPT IT ON THIS WHOLE TIME EVEN THOUGH IT WAS SO BEAT UP...
I SEE...
...

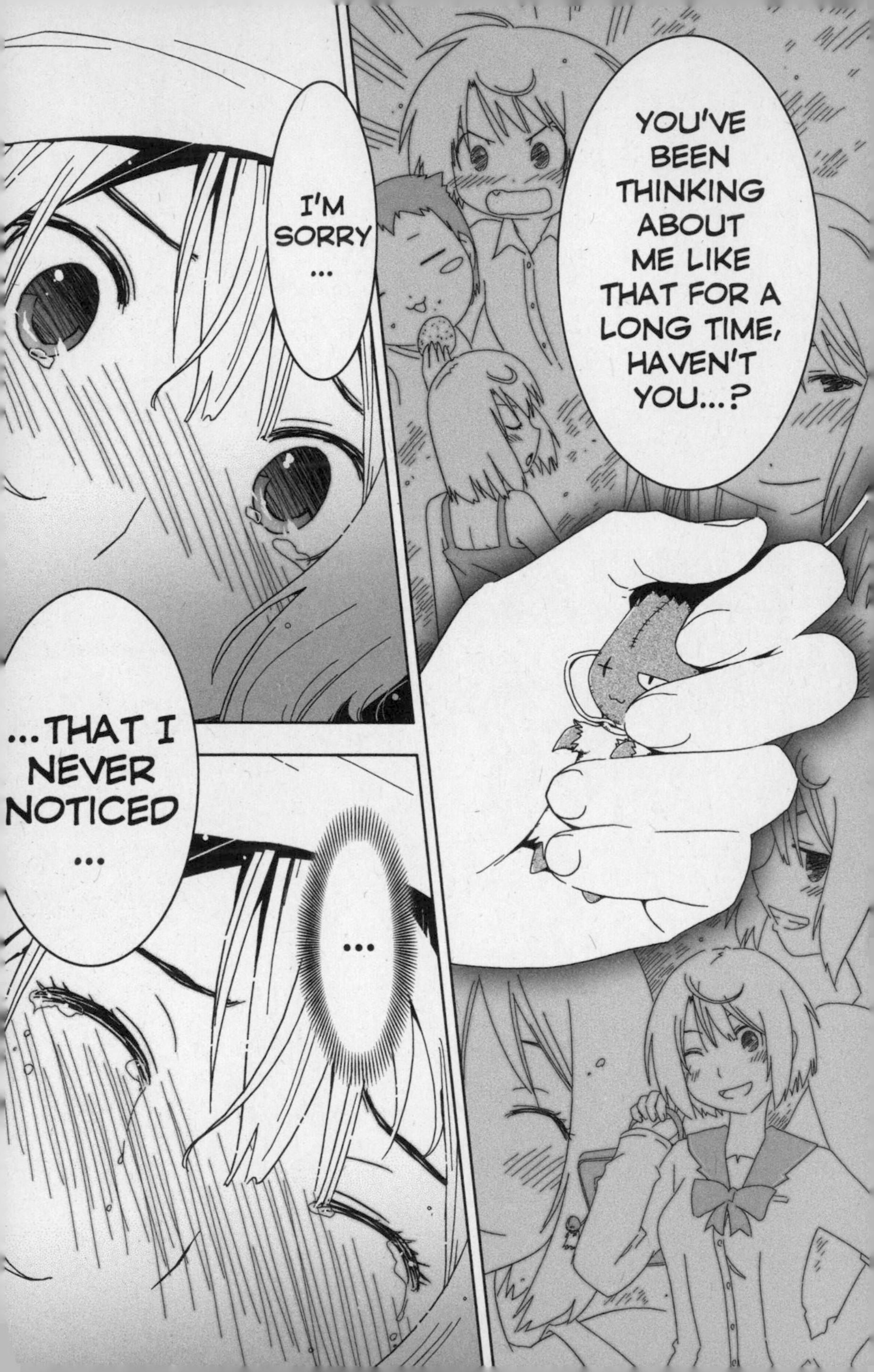
YOU'VE BEEN THINKING ABOUT ME LIKE THAT FOR A LONG TIME, HAVEN'T YOU...?
I'M SORRY ...
...THAT I NEVER NOTICED ...
...

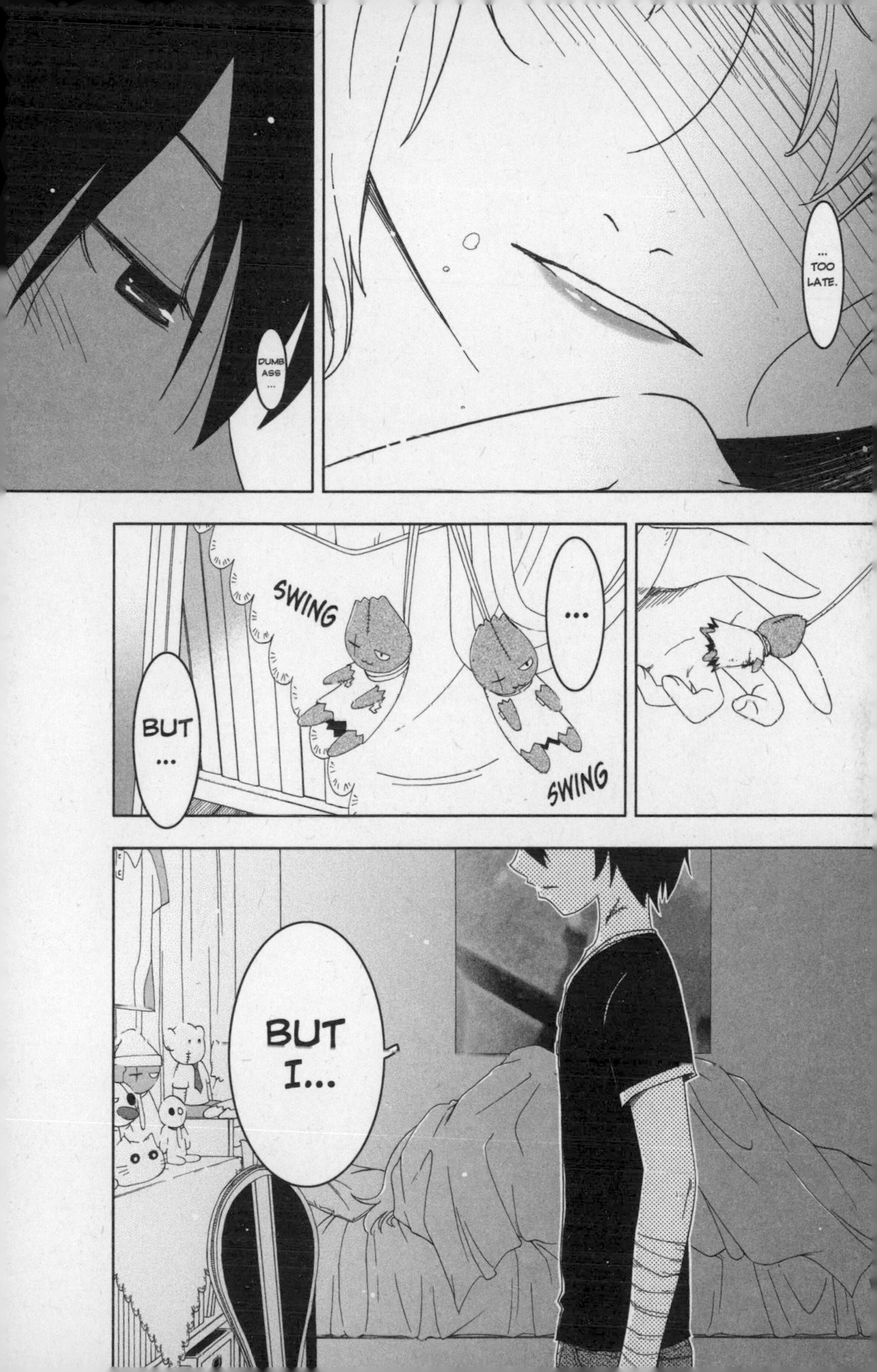
... TOO LATE.
DUMB ASS ...
...
SWING
BUT ...
SWING
BUT I...

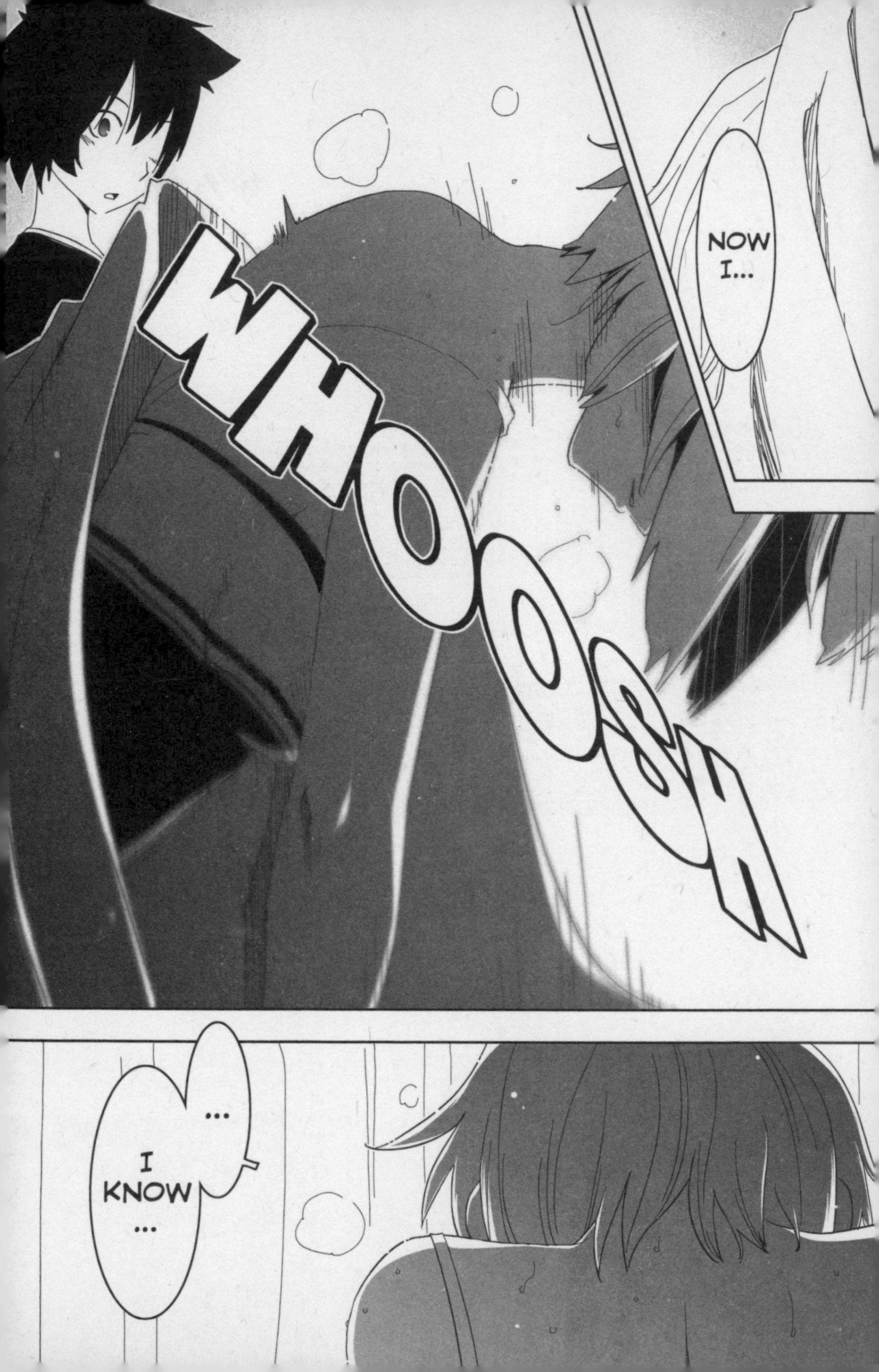
NOW I...
WHOOOSH
... I KNOW ...

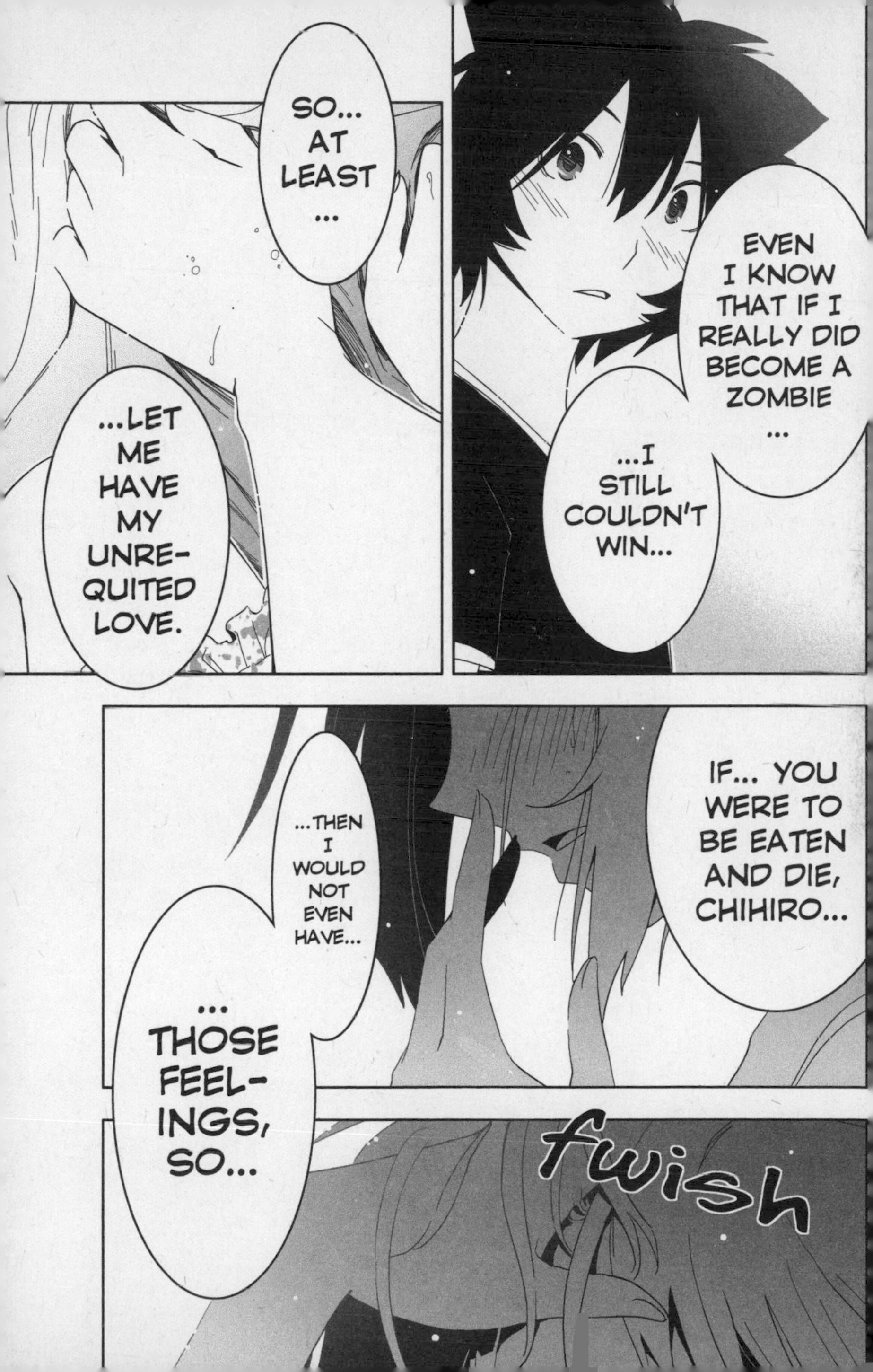
EVEN I KNOW THAT IF I REALLY DID BECOME A ZOMBIE ...
...I STILL COULDN'T WIN...
SO... AT LEAST ...
...LET ME HAVE MY UNRE-QUITED LOVE.
IF... YOU WERE TO BE EATEN AND DIE, CHIHIRO...
...THEN I WOULD NOT EVEN HAVE...
... THOSE FEEL-INGS, SO...
fwish

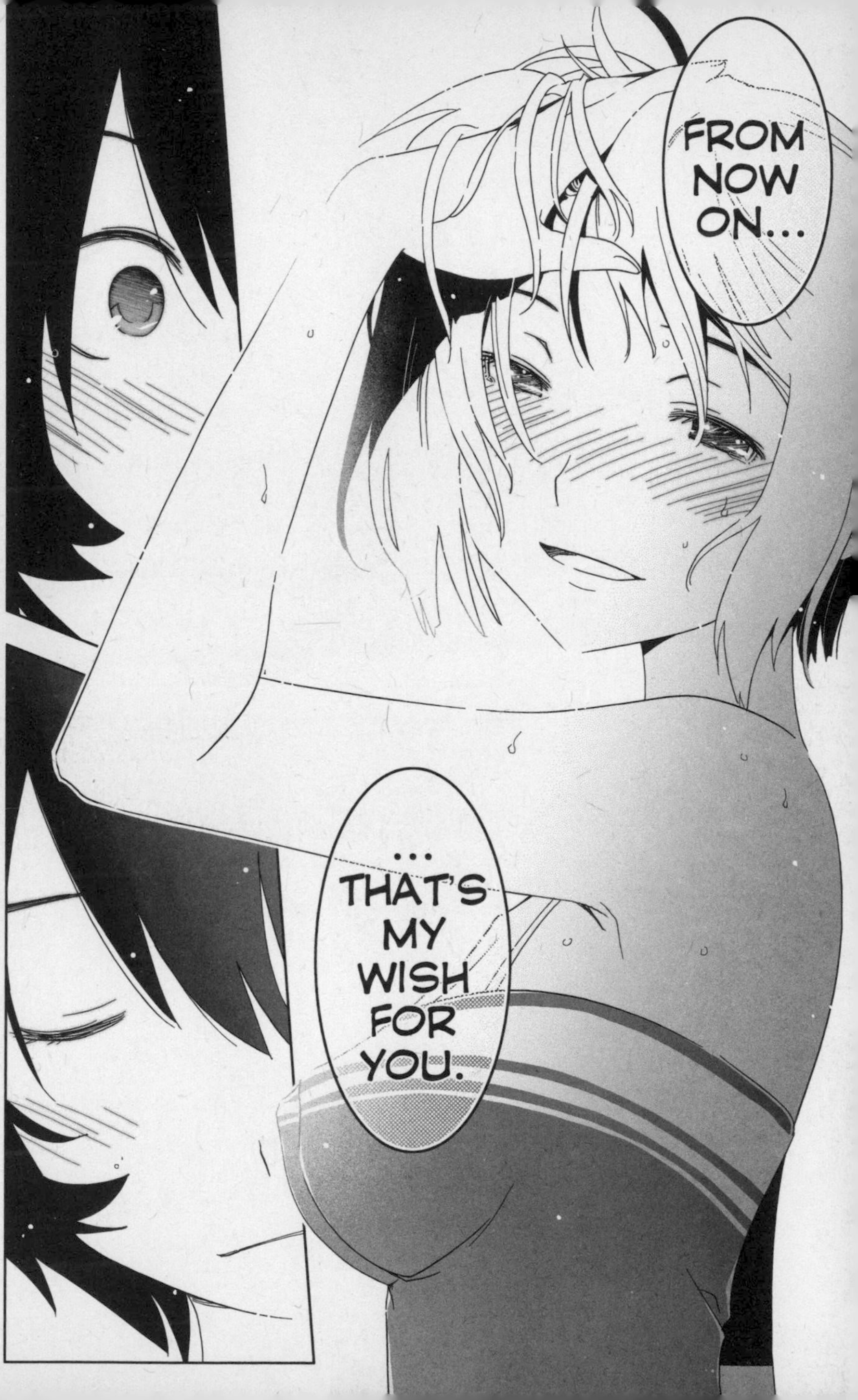
FROM NOW ON...
... THAT'S MY WISH FOR YOU.

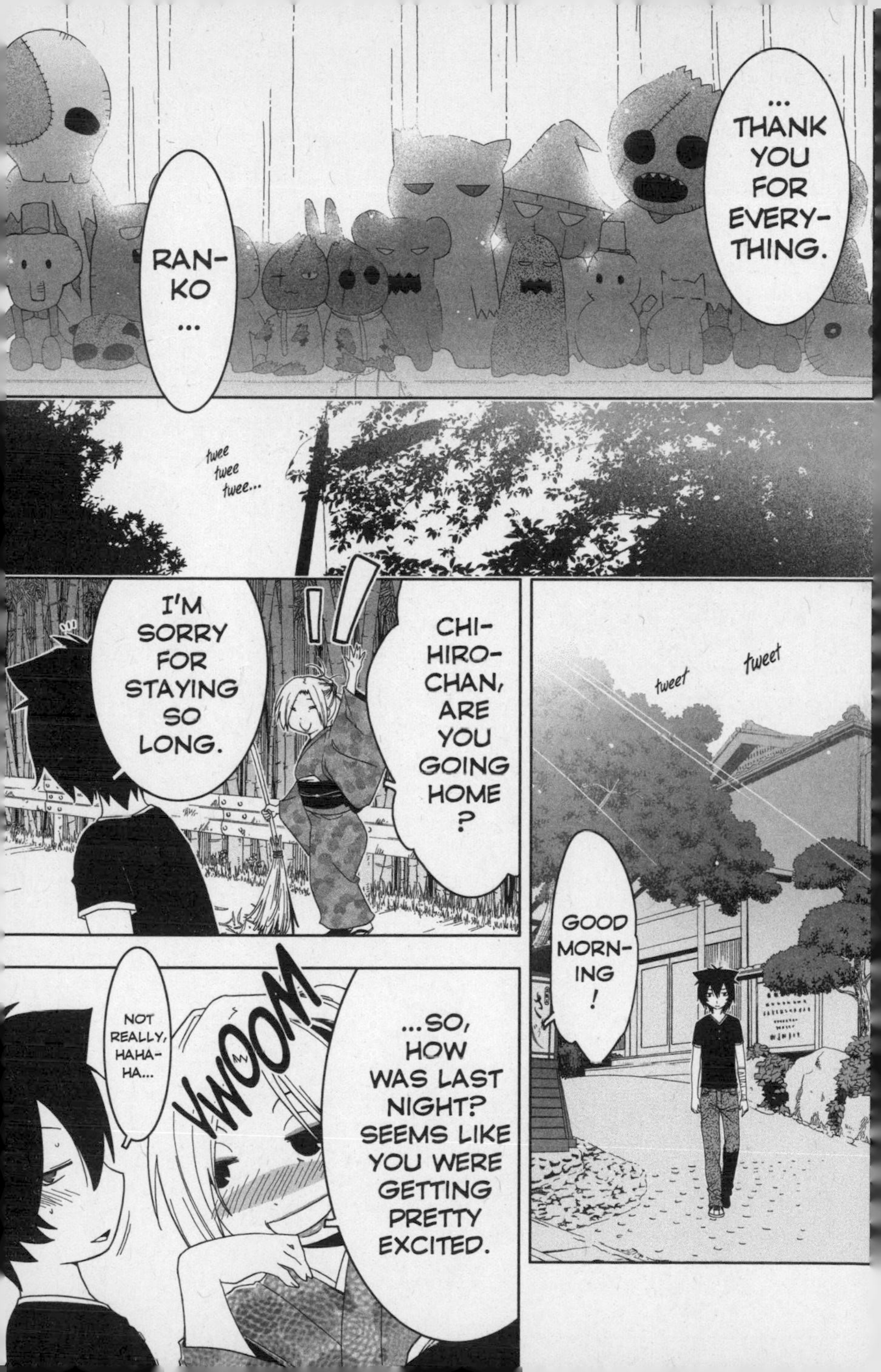

...THANK YOU FOR EVERYTHING.
RANKO...
twee twee twee...
tweet
tweet
GOOD MORNING!
!!
CHIHIRO-CHAN, ARE YOU GOING HOME?
I'M SORRY FOR STAYING SO LONG.
...SO, HOW WAS LAST NIGHT? SEEMS LIKE YOU WERE GETTING PRETTY EXCITED.
VWOOM
NOT REALLY, HAHAHA...

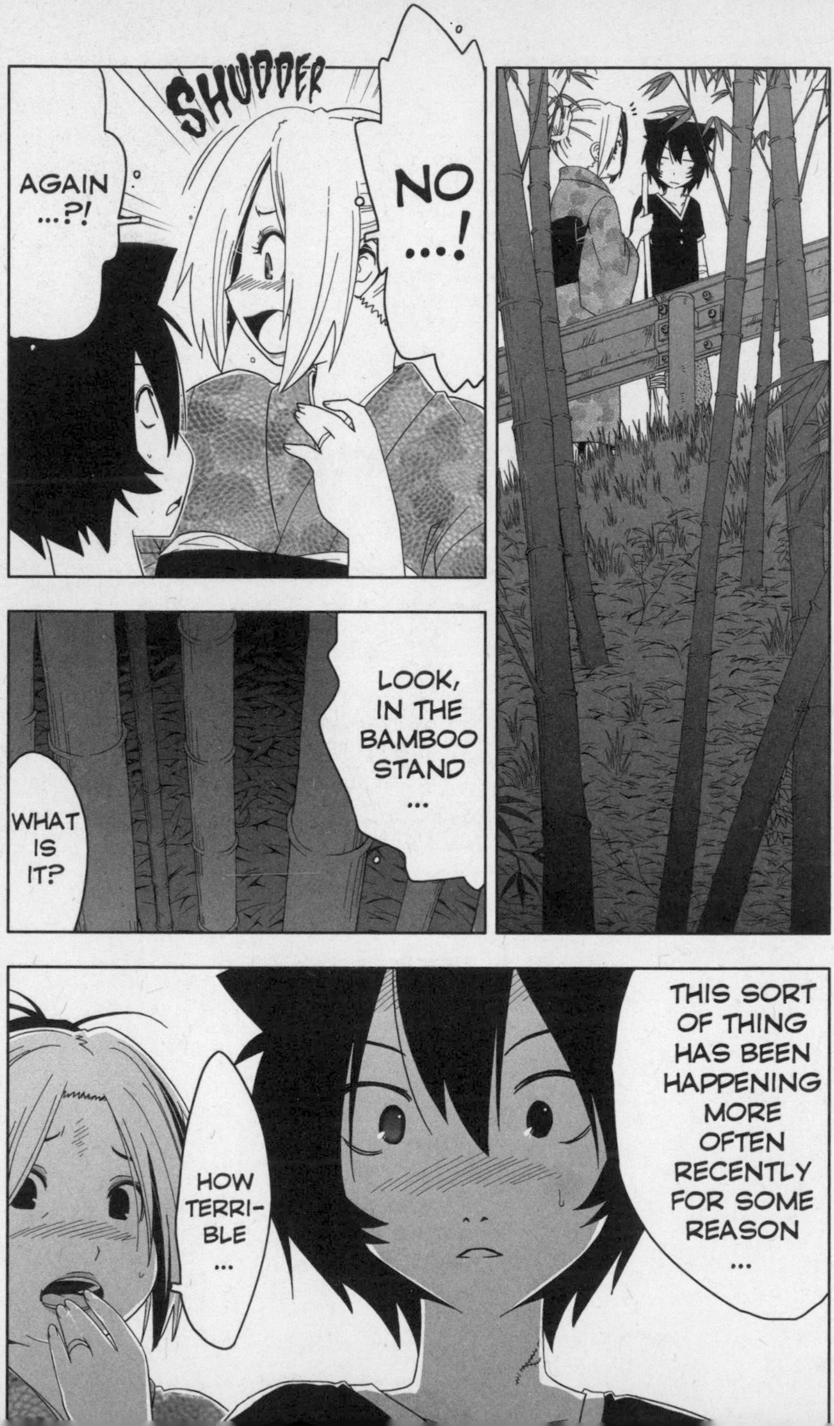
NO ...!
SHUDDER
AGAIN ...?!
LOOK, IN THE BAMBOO STAND ...
WHAT IS IT?
THIS SORT OF THING HAS BEEN HAPPENING MORE OFTEN RECENTLY FOR SOME REASON ...
HOW TERRI-BLE ...

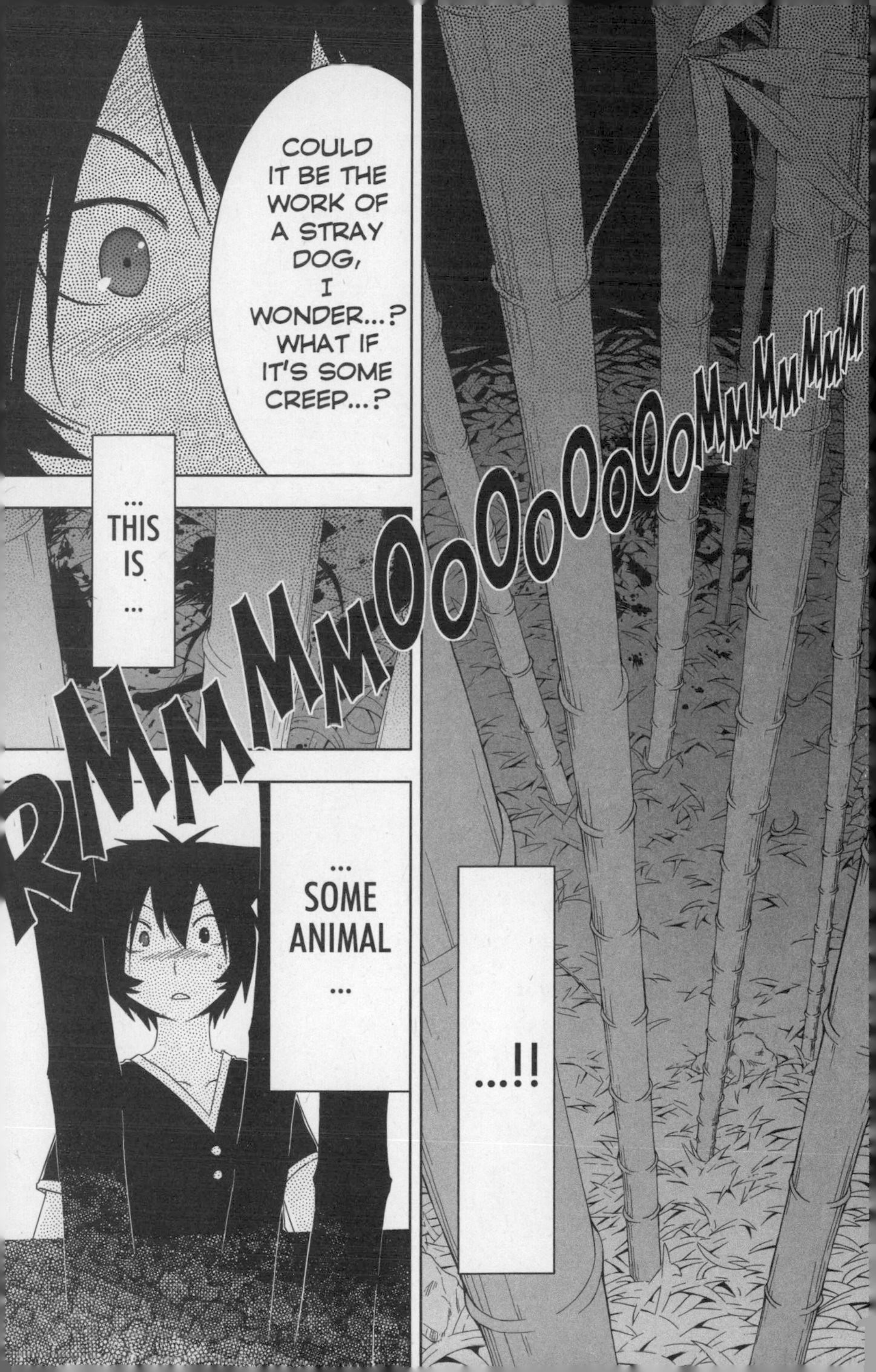
RMMMMMOOOOOOOOOOMMMMMMMM
...!!
COULD IT BE THE WORK OF A STRAY DOG, I WONDER...? WHAT IF IT'S SOME CREEP...?
... THIS IS ...
... SOME ANIMAL ...

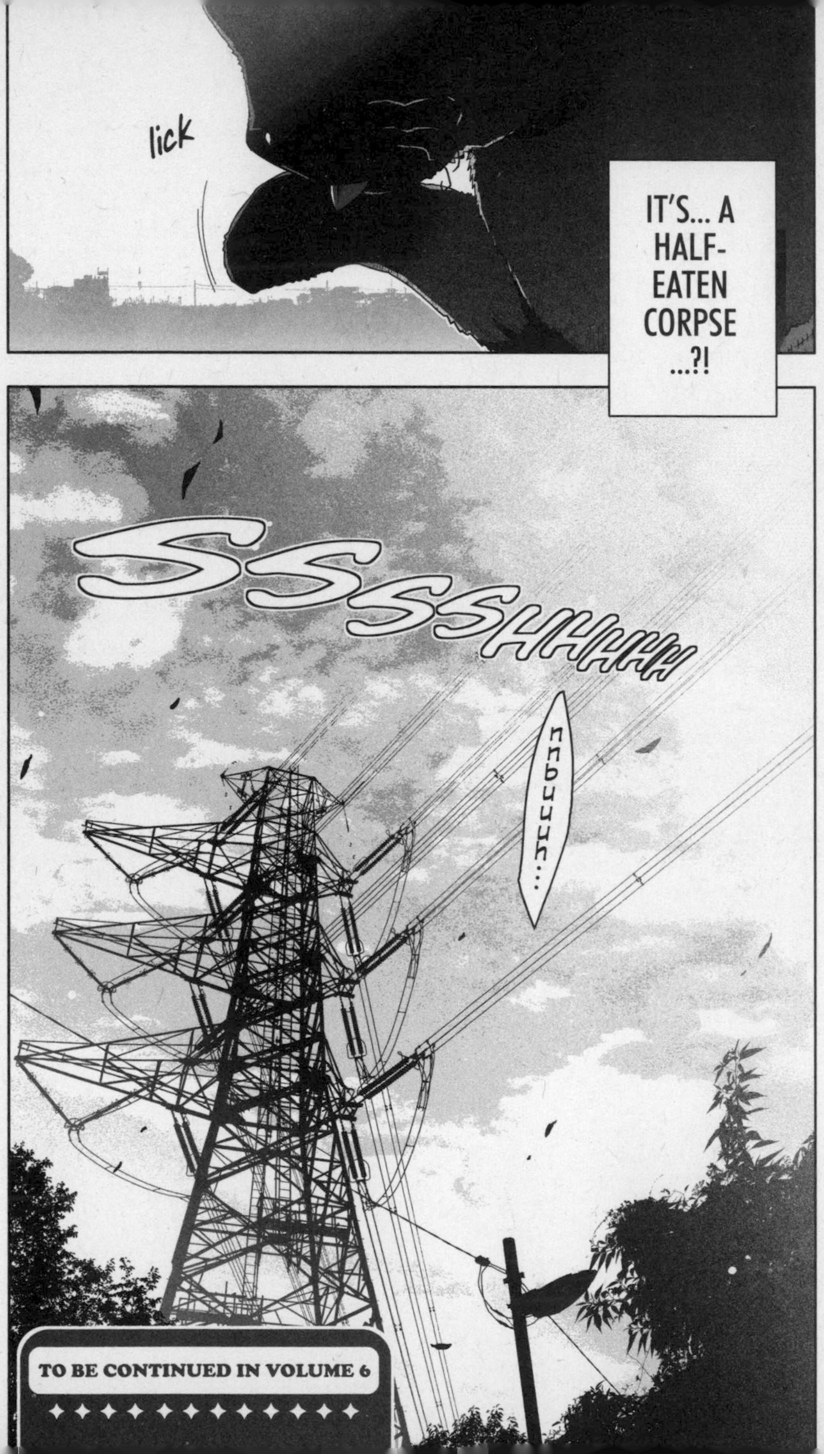
IT'S... A HALF-EATEN CORPSE...?!
lick
SSSSHHHHH
nnbuuuh...
TO BE CONTINUED IN VOLUME 6

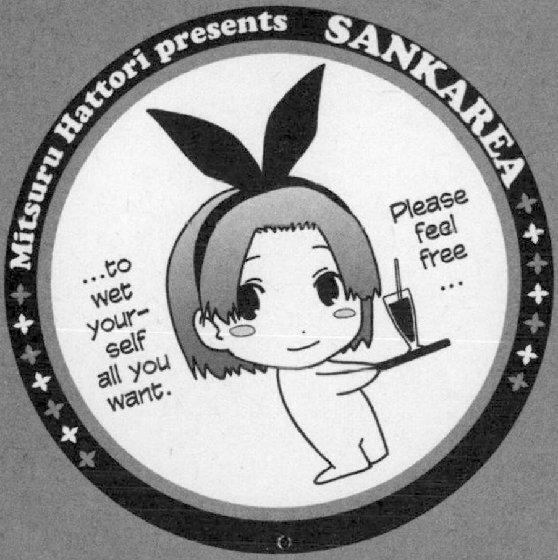
Mitsuru Hattori presents SANKAREA
Please feel free ...
...to wet your-self all you want.

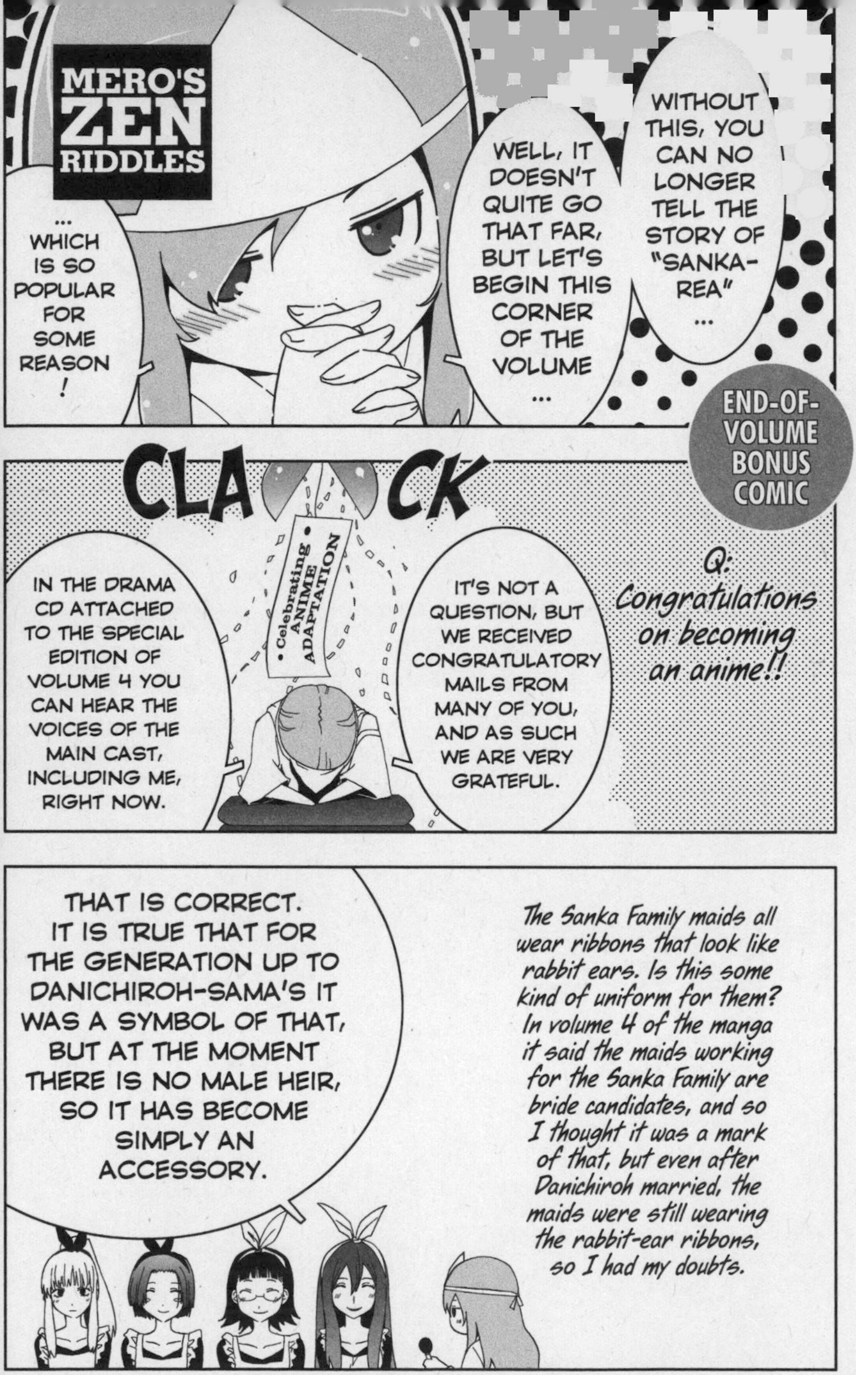
MERO'S ZEN RIDDLES
WITHOUT THIS, YOU CAN NO LONGER TELL THE STORY OF "SANKA-REA"...
WELL, IT DOESN'T QUITE GO THAT FAR, BUT LET'S BEGIN THIS CORNER OF THE VOLUME...
... WHICH IS SO POPULAR FOR SOME REASON!
END-OF-VOLUME BONUS COMIC
Q: Congratulations on becoming an anime!!
CLACK
• Celebrating • ANIME ADAPTATION
IT'S NOT A QUESTION, BUT WE RECEIVED CONGRATULATORY MAILS FROM MANY OF YOU, AND AS SUCH WE ARE VERY GRATEFUL.
IN THE DRAMA CD ATTACHED TO THE SPECIAL EDITION OF VOLUME 4 YOU CAN HEAR THE VOICES OF THE MAIN CAST, INCLUDING ME, RIGHT NOW.
The Sanka Family maids all wear ribbons that look like rabbit ears. Is this some kind of uniform for them? In volume 4 of the manga it said the maids working for the Sanka Family are bride candidates, and so I thought it was a mark of that, but even after Danichiroh married, the maids were still wearing the rabbit-ear ribbons, so I had my doubts.
THAT IS CORRECT. IT IS TRUE THAT FOR THE GENERATION UP TO DANICHIROH-SAMA'S IT WAS A SYMBOL OF THAT, BUT AT THE MOMENT THERE IS NO MALE HEIR, SO IT HAS BECOME SIMPLY AN ACCESSORY.

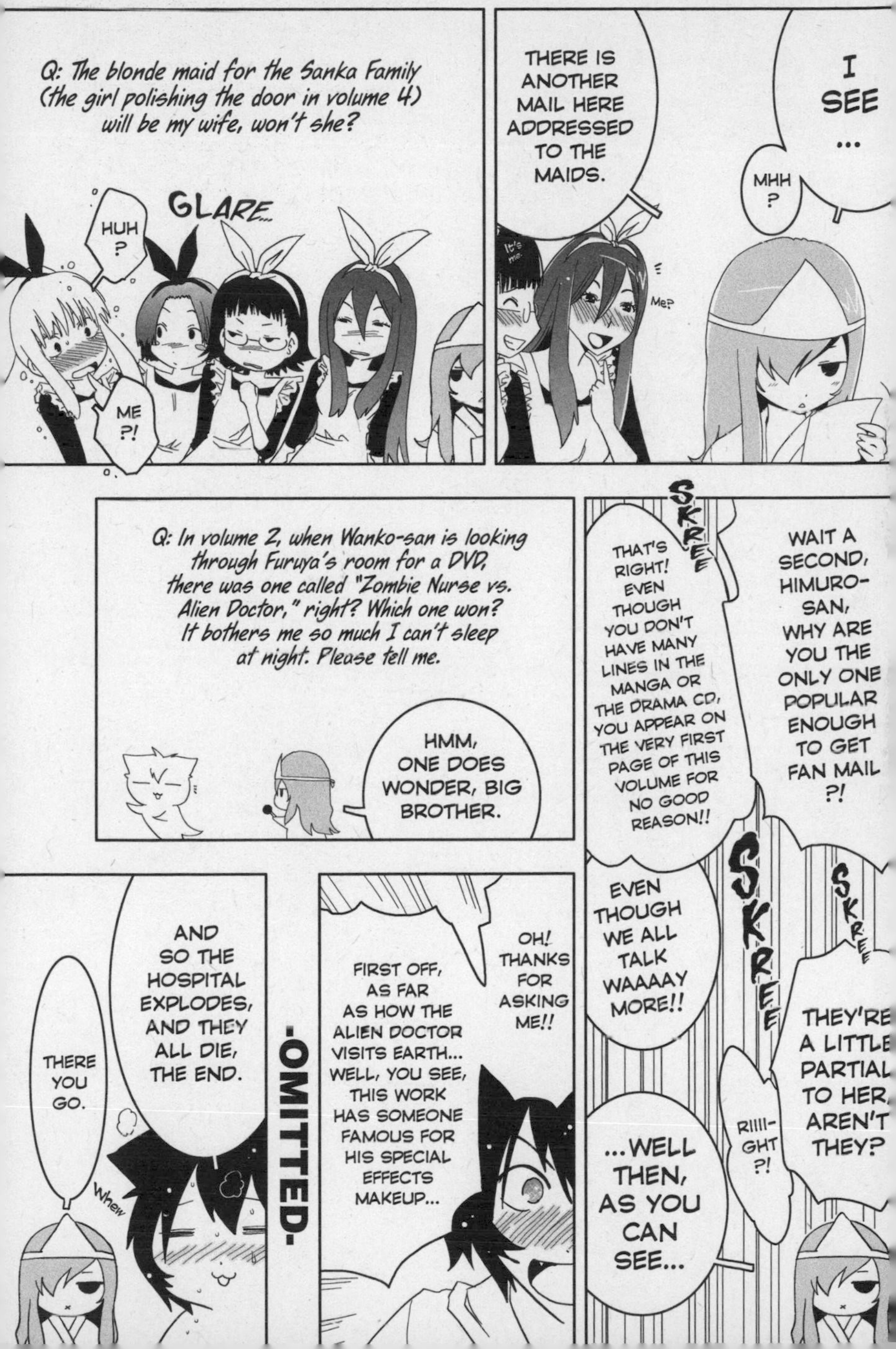
I SEE ...
MHH ?
THERE IS ANOTHER MAIL HERE ADDRESSED TO THE MAIDS.
It's me.
Me?
Q: The blonde maid for the Sanka Family (the girl polishing the door in volume 4) will be my wife, won't she?
GLARE...
HUH ?
ME ?!
WAIT A SECOND, HIMURO-SAN, WHY ARE YOU THE ONLY ONE POPULAR ENOUGH TO GET FAN MAIL ?!
SKREE
THAT'S RIGHT! EVEN THOUGH YOU DON'T HAVE MANY LINES IN THE MANGA OR THE DRAMA CD, YOU APPEAR ON THE VERY FIRST PAGE OF THIS VOLUME FOR NO GOOD REASON!!
SKREE
SKREE
EVEN THOUGH WE ALL TALK WAAAAY MORE!!
THEY'RE A LITTLE PARTIAL TO HER, AREN'T THEY?
RIIII-GHT ?!
...WELL THEN, AS YOU CAN SEE...
Q: In volume 2, when Wanko-san is looking through Furuya's room for a DVD, there was one called "Zombie Nurse vs. Alien Doctor," right? Which one won? It bothers me so much I can't sleep at night. Please tell me.
HMM, ONE DOES WONDER, BIG BROTHER.
OH! THANKS FOR ASKING ME!!
FIRST OFF, AS FAR AS HOW THE ALIEN DOCTOR VISITS EARTH... WELL, YOU SEE, THIS WORK HAS SOMEONE FAMOUS FOR HIS SPECIAL EFFECTS MAKEUP...
-OMITTED-
AND SO THE HOSPITAL EXPLODES, AND THEY ALL DIE, THE END.
THERE YOU GO.
Whew

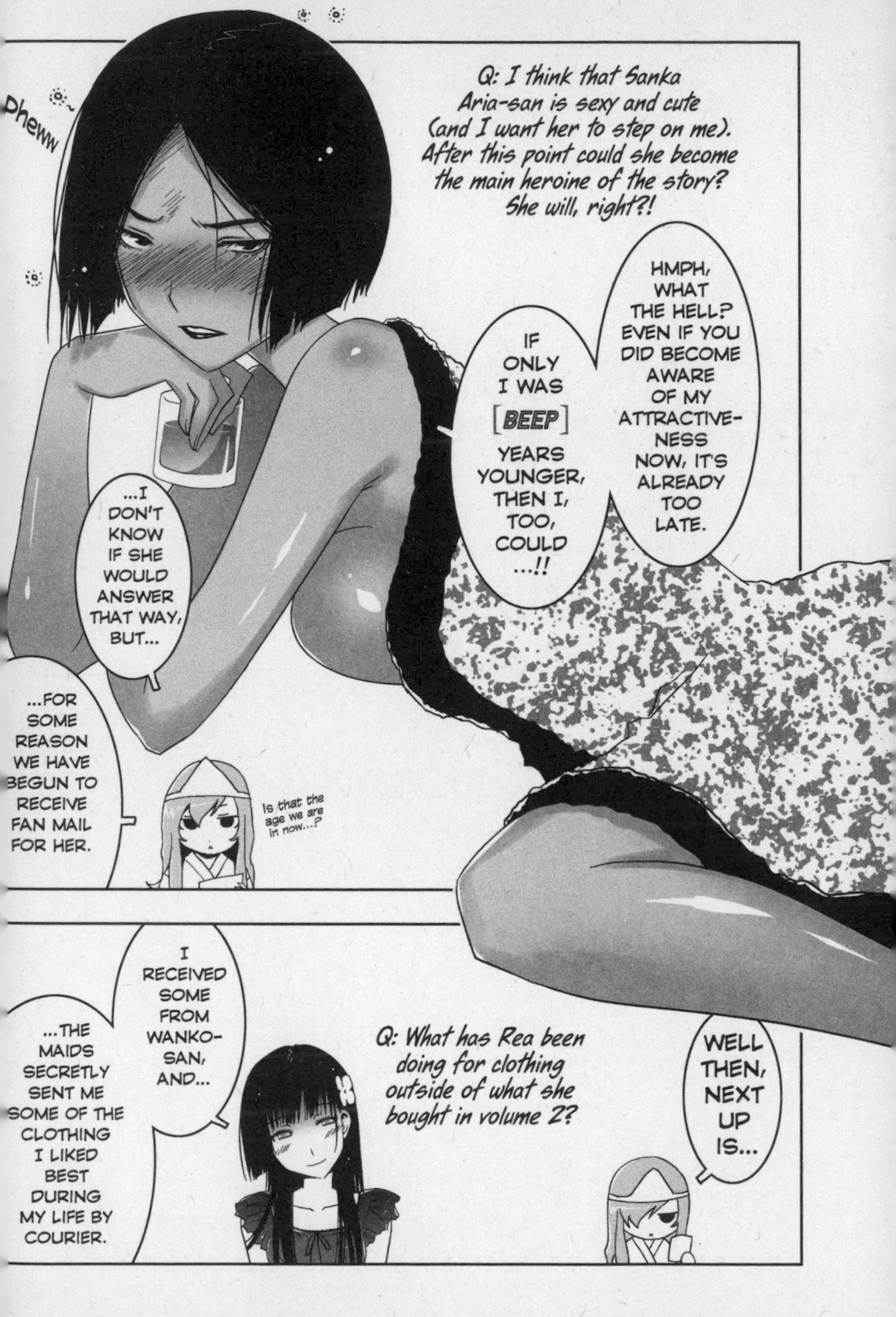
Q: I think that Sanka Aria-san is sexy and cute (and I want her to step on me). After this point could she become the main heroine of the story? She will, right?!
Phewww
HMPH, WHAT THE HELL? EVEN IF YOU DID BECOME AWARE OF MY ATTRACTIVENESS NOW, IT'S ALREADY TOO LATE.
IF ONLY I WAS [BEEP] YEARS YOUNGER, THEN I, TOO, COULD ...!!
...I DON'T KNOW IF SHE WOULD ANSWER THAT WAY, BUT...
Is that the age we are in now...?
...FOR SOME REASON WE HAVE BEGUN TO RECEIVE FAN MAIL FOR HER.
WELL THEN, NEXT UP IS...
Q: What has Rea been doing for clothing outside of what she bought in volume 2?
I RECEIVED SOME FROM WANKO-SAN, AND...
...THE MAIDS SECRETLY SENT ME SOME OF THE CLOTHING I LIKED BEST DURING MY LIFE BY COURIER.

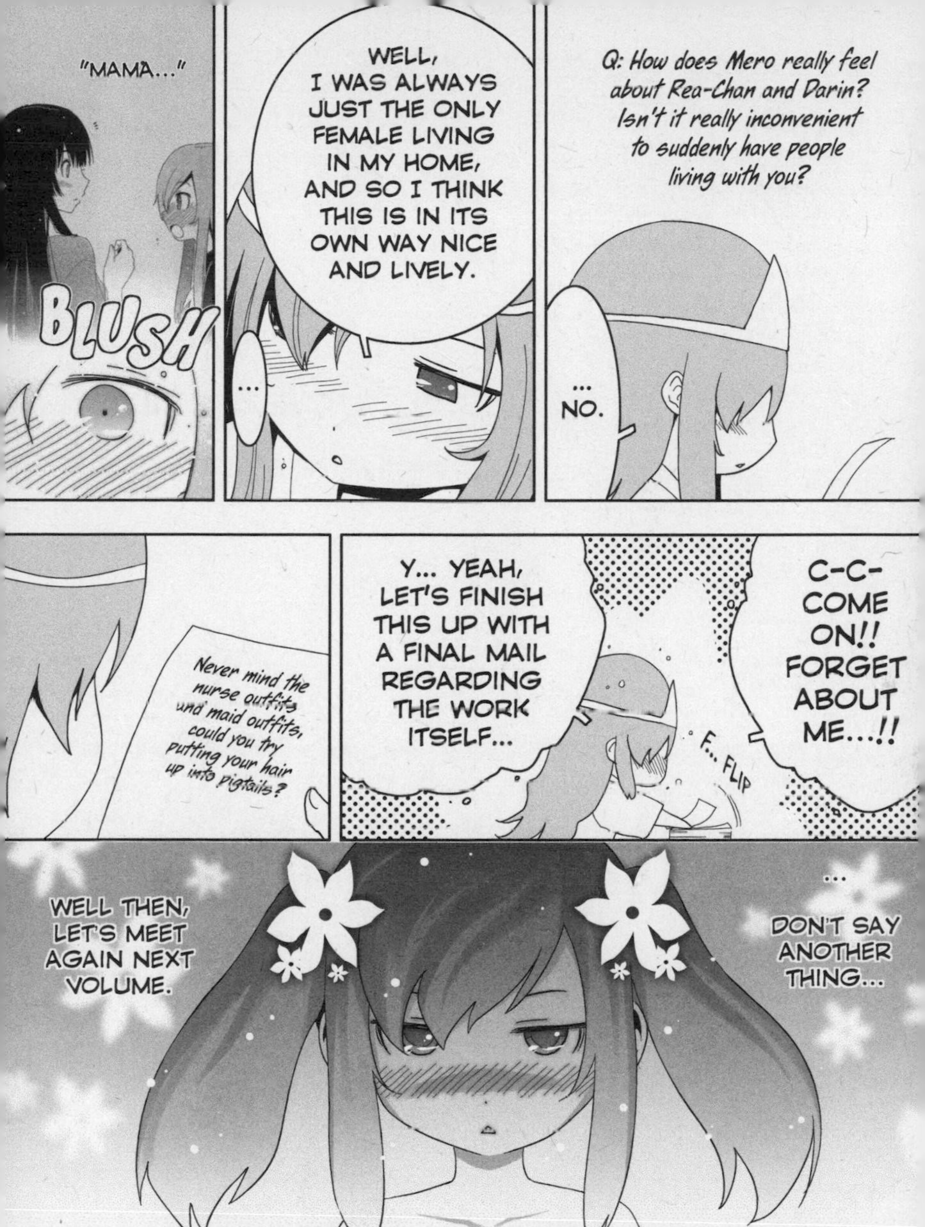
Q: How does Mero really feel about Rea-Chan and Darin? Isn't it really inconvenient to suddenly have people living with you?
... NO.
WELL, I WAS ALWAYS JUST THE ONLY FEMALE LIVING IN MY HOME, AND SO I THINK THIS IS IN ITS OWN WAY NICE AND LIVELY.
...
"MAMA..."
BLUSH
C-C-COME ON!! FORGET ABOUT ME...!!
Y... YEAH, LET'S FINISH THIS UP WITH A FINAL MAIL REGARDING THE WORK ITSELF...
F... FLIP
Never mind the nurse outfits and maid outfits, could you try putting your hair up into pigtails?
... DON'T SAY ANOTHER THING...
WELL THEN, LET'S MEET AGAIN NEXT VOLUME.

"Mero's Zen Riddles" e-mail address:

(Put something like "Zen Riddles" or "Questions for Mero" in the subject line.)

kodanshacomics@randomhouse.com

*Questions we couldn't answer this time may be picked up in the next volume or after, as well.

Shark vS. Rea

HSSSHHH...
ZOOM
Haumph
Guess he couldn't digest her.
No-no-no...

TRANSLATION NOTES

p. 3, Heart Sutra

Sutras are Buddhist sermons or prayers. The Heart Sutra is probably the best known and most popular of all the Buddhist Sutras. Though they were originally written in Sanskrit, the version known in Japan has been transcribed into Chinese characters.

p. 106, Moe

Many readers are probably familiar with this term, but just in case, moe is a hard-to-define characteristic used mainly for young, cute, and somehow loveable anime characters. Mero in her current form probably qualifies for this term, but in her original form, she definitely didn't!

p. 106, NEET

A young person who is "not in education, employment or training." Meaning Mero here probably isn't a student, and doesn't have any kind of steady job or plans to move out of the family home for now.

p. 114, Sempai

Sempai is a generic honorific used towards upperclassmen, or anyone who's more senior than you (but not your boss, of course!)

p. 114, Noh

Noh or nogaku is an extremely stylized form of Japanese drama that has been performed for centuries. Most of the titles are dramatic, although comedic pieces do exist. Appreciation for noh is considered proof of taste and refinement, and many Japanese feel about noh similarly to how a lot of Americans feel about opera.

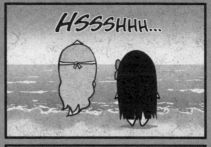

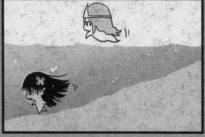

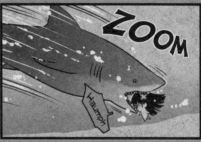

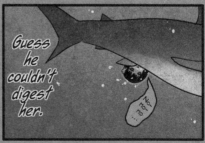

A Kodansha Comics Trade Paperback Original.

Sankarea volume 5 copyright © 2012 Mitsuru Hattori
English translation copyright © 2014 Mitsuru Hattori

Published in the United States by Kodansha Comics, an imprint of Kodansha USA Publishing, LLC, New York.

Publication rights for this English edition arranged through Kodansha Ltd., Tokyo.

First published in Japan in 2012 by Kodansha Ltd., Tokyo, as Sankarea, volume 5.

ISBN 978-1-61262-398-6

Printed in the United States of America.

www.kodanshacomics.com

9 8 7 6 5 4 3 2 1

Translation: Lindsey Akashi
Lettering: Evan Hayden
Editing: Ben Applegate

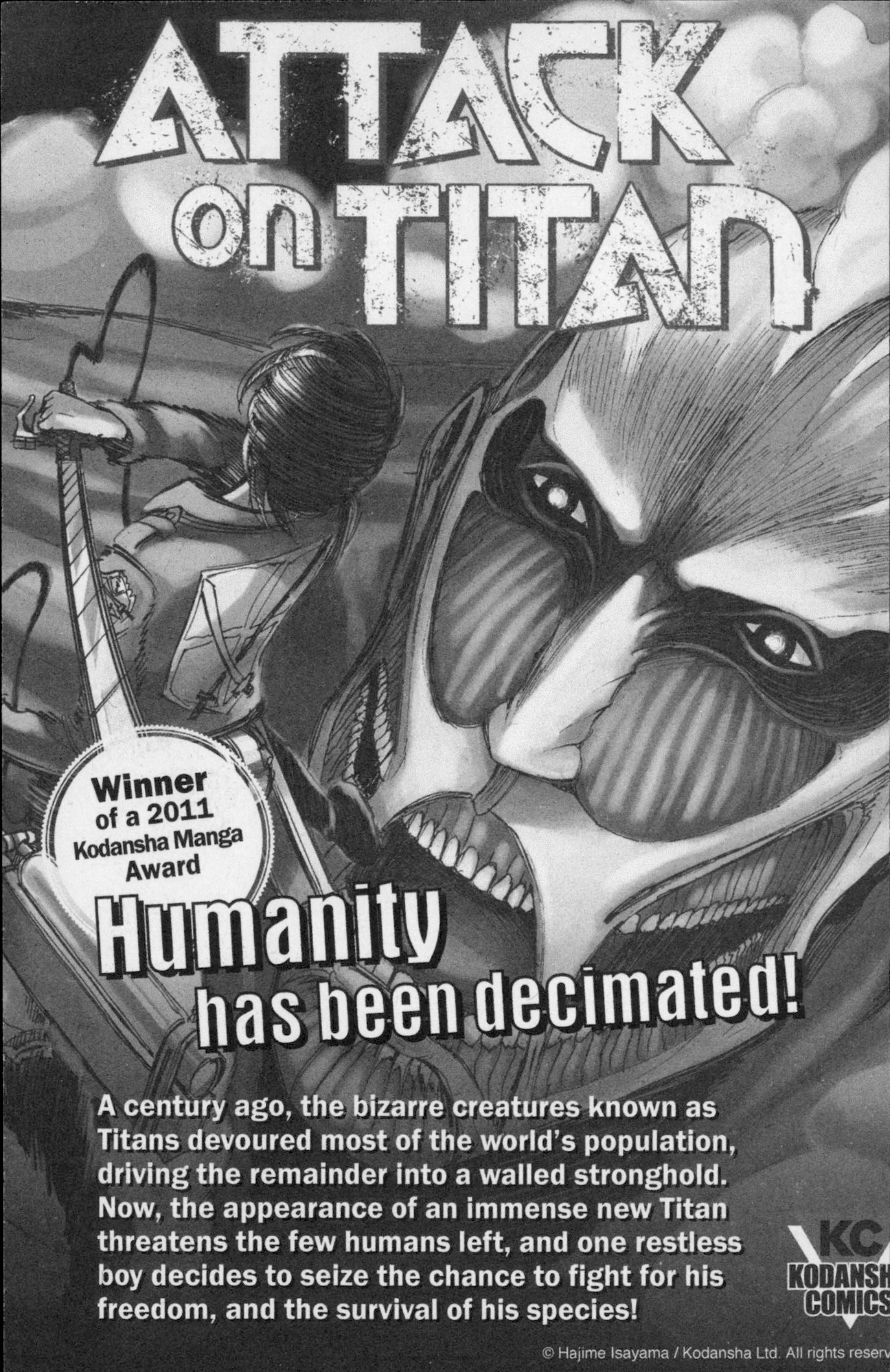
ATTACK on TITAN
Winner of a 2011 Kodansha Manga Award
Humanity has been decimated!
A century ago, the bizarre creatures known as Titans devoured most of the world's population, driving the remainder into a walled stronghold. Now, the appearance of an immense new Titan threatens the few humans left, and one restless boy decides to seize the chance to fight for his freedom, and the survival of his species!
KC KODANSHA COMICS
© Hajime Isayama / Kodansha Ltd. All rights reserv